CONTENTS

THE SELF AND THE LOTUS

A JUNGIAN VIEW OF INDIAN BUDDHISM

VOLUME II

GEORGE R. ELDER

Paperback ISBN: 978-1-958889-20-6

Published by BookLocker.com, Inc., Trenton, Georgia, U.S.A.

Printed on acid-free paper.

BookLocker.com, Inc.2023

Library of Congress Cataloguing in Publication Data
Elder, George R.
The Self and the Lotus: A Jungian View of Indian Buddhism by George R. Elder
Library of Congress Control Number: 2023903025

FIGURES AND CREDITS

"Prajnaparamita Java Front." Photograph by Gunawan Kartapranata. Creative Commons Attribution-Share Alike 3.0 Unported (https://creativecommons.org/licenses/by-sa/3.0/deed.en) license. Wikimedia Commons.

"Bodhisattva Padmapani, cave 1, Ajanta, India." Photograph by Yann Forget. In the Public Domain. Wikimedia Commons.

"La Déesse Khadiravaṇī-Tārā," Bihār, Pāla-Sena era, 9th century. Musée Guimet. Photograph by author.

"'Amitabha in Sukhavati Paradise,' Tibetan, circa 1700, San Antonio Museum of Art." In the Public Domain. Wikimedia Commons.

"Dynastie Wei du Nord. Shâkyamuni et Prabhûtaratna. Musée Guimet." Photograph by Ismoon. Creative Commons Attribution-Share Alike 4.0 International (https://creativecommons.org/licenses/by-sa/4.0/). Wikimedia Commons.

"Buddha e Vajrapani." Photograph by Antonio Amato. Creative Commons Attribution-Share Alike 4.0 International (https://creativecommons.org/licenses/by-sa/4.0/deed.en) license. Wikimedia Commons.

"Ghanta et Vajra (British Museum) (8697431158)." Photograph by Jean-Pierre Dalbéra. Creative Commons Attribution 2.0 Generic (https://creativecommons.org/licenses/by/2.0/deed.en) license. Wikimedia Commons.

Figure 16.2 Tantric Body 557
"Chakras and energy channels 2." Photograph by dockedship. Creative Commons Attribution 2.0 Generic (https://creativecommons.org/licenses/by/2.0/deed.en) license. Wikimedia Commons.

Figure 16.3 Saraha 584
"Saraha British Museum." Scroll painting of the Mahāsiddha Saraha. British Museum, No. 1956,0714,0.40. Photograph by Zippymarmalade. Creative Commons Attribution-Share Alike 3.0 Unported (https://creativecommons.org/licenses/by-sa/3.0/deed.en) license. Wikimedia Commons.

PRONUNCIATION GUIDE

The following list of terms is an informal guide to pronouncing Sanskrit. They have been selected to demonstrate the use of diacritical marks when transliterating into English.

ātman (OUGHT-muhn) self
āsrava (AAH-sruh-vuh) inflow, outflow

bhikṣu/nī (BICK-shoo/NEE) monk/nun
buddha (rhymes with COULD-uh) awake

cakra (CHUCK-ruh) wheel, tantric circle
citta (CHIT-uh) thought

deva (DAY-vuh) deity, god
devī (day-VEE) goddess
dhyāna (dih-YAWN-uh) trance
duḥkha (rhymes with hookah) suffering

jñāna (gin-YAWN-uh) knowledge

kāya (KYE-yuh) body
kleśa (CLAY-shuh) defilement

manas (muh-nuhs) mind

pāramitā (par-um-ee-TAAH) perfection
prajñā (pruh-gin-YAAH) wisdom
prapañca (pruh-PUNCH-uh) proliferation

ṛddhi (RID-ee) supernatural power

saṃgha (SUNG-uh) congregation
sukha (rhymes with hookah) happiness, bliss
śūnya/tā (SHOON-yuh/TAAH) empty/emptiness

tathāgata (tuh-TAAH-guh-tuh) thus come, thus gone
tṛṣṇā (trish-NAAH) craving

upāya (oo-PIE-uh) means, strategy

PART V

MAHĀYĀNA BUDDHISM

Chapter 11
"GREAT VEHICLE"

"The Perfection of Wisdom in 8,000 Lines"

If religion itself is like a *stūpa* or a statue, it is likely that over time it will become "plastered over" with too many complicated doctrines, too "gold-leafed" with habitual practices of mere piety—and cease radiating "Fiery Energy" from its core. This must have happened to Buddhism after its first five hundred years, since new forms of the religion emerged in the late first century BCE. Put more positively, the "Lotus" that is Buddhism simply blossomed more completely at that time. Whatever the cause, new scriptures began to appear and would continue to appear for many centuries. They called themselves, "Mahāyāna" ("Great Vehicle"), as distinct from what went before—that they sometimes called "Hīnayāna" ("Little or Inferior Vehicle"), what we have been calling Early Buddhism.

One of the earliest of these new scriptures was "The Perfection of Wisdom in Eight Thousand Lines," as Edward Conze translates, *Aṣṭa-sāhasrikā-prajñā-pāramitā* (*Aṣṭa*, for short, in this chapter).[1] It is one of a genre of "Perfection of Wisdom" texts of various lengths. Their length refers to the number of *ślokas* (usually units of thirty-two syllables) that comprise each *sūtra*—so the "Eight Thousand" is of much greater length than most sermons we encountered in the Nikāyas. And yet this scripture itself would grow into the "Perfection of Wisdom" in 10,000 lines, 25,000 lines, and finally the enormously long and repetitious 100,000 *Prajñāpāramitā*.

Like something protean, the contents of the *Aṣṭa* not only expanded but also contracted into the famous "Diamond Sūtra" of merely 300 lines, the "Heart Sūtra" of just 25 lines (popular because it can be easily memorized), and finally to this:

> Ānanda, do receive, for the sake of the weal and happiness of all beings, this perfection of wisdom in one letter, i.e., A.[2]

The Buddhist point is that—like the initial letter in the Sanskrit alphabet—all of these sacred materials are the "beginning" of Wisdom (*prajñā*). Of course, the letter "A" does not say very much. And it is probably inevitable that in Japanese Buddhism the Lord would say nothing at all but "preach" silently by holding up the stem of a lotus blossom.

Indeed, as we shall soon learn, the "Perfection of Wisdom" scriptures are elusive even when prolix. As the monk Subhūti puts it in the *Aṣṭa*: "There is nothing to understand, nothing at all to understand. For nothing in particular has been indicated, nothing in particular has been explained."

---

[1] Edward Conze, trans., *The Perfection of Wisdom in Eight Thousand Lines and its Verse Summary* (Bolinas: Four Seasons Foundation, 1973.

[2] Edward Conze, trans., *The Short Prajñāpāramitā Texts* (London: Luzac and Company, 1973), 201.

(2.3) Strange as this sounds, it is not really that different from Gautama Buddha's own words in the early *Majjhima Nikāya*: "This Dharma that I have attained is profound, hard to see and hard to understand, peaceful and sublime, unattainable by mere reasoning, subtle, to be experienced by the wise."[3] Let us note that the *Kena Upaniṣad* of Hinduism expresses the elusiveness of religious knowledge this way: "It is not understood by those who understand it; it is understood by those who do not understand it."[4]

Nevertheless, the title of the new genre of scriptures is somewhat understandable. We encountered *prajñā* in earlier chapters as one of several "knowledge" words (along with *jñāna, vidyā, buddhi*) associated with Gautama's Enlightenment. It was privileged in the teaching of the Three Trainings. The *Visuddhimagga* said it could be cultivated to "perfection;" while in the standard list of the Buddhist virtues called the "Six Perfections," the last and best was Prajñāpāramitā as the noetic goal. Thus, it can be said that the new "Perfection of Wisdom" scriptures merely perpetuate tradition.

It is also true that these new texts prefer to treat all the Perfections as a formulaic pair: 1) the first five (Generosity, Morality, Patience, Striving, Meditation) as a distinct group called *upāya* or "Means" leading up to 2) the sixth, "Wisdom." Thus, we read in the "Verse Summary" of the *Aṣṭa*:

> Without wisdom these [first] five perfections are eyeless:
> Those who are without the guide are unable to experience enlightenment.
> . . . .
> It is like a painting which is complete except for the eyes.
> Only after the eyes are painted in does one get one's fee. (7.1-2)[5]

We can appreciate this reference to art and the painting in of the "eyes." And we know that while "Means and Wisdom" can be said to belong together on the Path to Enlightenment, it is still the latter that enlivens the former.

Introductory Issues

Countless Buddhas

The *Aṣṭa* scripture has a fairly short versified form called *Prajñāpāramitā-ratnaguṇa-saṃcaya-gāthā* or "Verses Collecting the Jewel-like Qualities of the Perfection of Wisdom" (*Ratnaguṇa*, for short, in this chapter). We have just read some of its verses, and I will use it often in this discussion to avoid the "wordiness" of the *Aṣṭa*. Here, then, are the opening lines of the *Ratnaguṇa*:

> Call forth as much as you can of love, of respect, and of faith!
> Remove the obstructing defilements, and clear away all your taints!

---

3 Bodhi, *MN* 26.19, (p. 260).

4 For a discussion of the verse, see Elder, *Snake and the Rope*, 125.

5 Conze's translation of the "Verse Summary" appears on pages 9-70 of *The Eight Thousand.* I have not included his bracketed interpolations.

Listen to the Perfect Wisdom of the gentle Buddhas,
Taught for the weal of the world, for heroic spirits intended! (1.1)

At first glance, there is nothing new here. We have heard of "defilements" and "taints" and even of "faith." One might wonder, however, about the plurality of "gentle Buddhas." An early listener or reader could have taken this as a traditional reference to the twenty-four Buddhas who had existed in the universe prior to Gautama Buddha who, then, became the twenty-fifth—with Bodhisattva Maitreya now in Tuṣita heaven destined to become the twenty-sixth.

The Buddhist conception of the universe, however, had been gradually expanding over the centuries from a one-world system to a manifold one—albeit each with the same threefold structure of the Desire Realm, the Realm of Form, and the Formless Realm. This development occurred within Early Buddhism itself. But in these new Mahāyāna scriptures the universe fairly explodes into an infinity of worlds with the logical conclusion that many, many more Buddhas exist in many other "Buddha-fields" (what the Chinese Buddhists would call "Pure Lands"). This explosive feature is evidence of what Jung called the "dynamite" of the collective unconscious blasting through the encrusted surface of tradition.

Grace and Works

Reading on, we find another new religious idea:

The rivers all in this Roseapple Island,
Which cause the flowers to grow, the fruits, the herbs and trees,
They all derive from the might of the king of the Nāgas,
From the Dragon residing in Lake Anavatapta, his magical power.
Just so, whatever Dharmas the Jina's disciples establish,
Whatever they teach, whatever adroitly explain—
Concerning the work of the holy which leads to the fullness of bliss,
And also the fruit of this work—it is the Tathāgata's doing.
. . . .
Their teaching stems but from the might of the Buddhas,
and not their own power.(1.2-4)[6]

In Early Buddhism, we heard often that one's "own power" was all that mattered: "You alone are responsible for your karmic seeds and fruits;" "Work out your own salvation with diligence." We discussed this attitude as an emphasis upon will power—the energy available to the ego. We also criticized it as one-sided, a denial of actual experience, and an example of what Jung called the "proud claim" that "Where there's a will, there's a way." I have no doubt that this claim was necessary at the beginning of Buddhism. But now, five centuries after the death of Gautama Buddha, the religion is

[6] Regularized to standard Sanskrit.

correcting an imbalance and acknowledging that "own power" (of ego consciousness) must be met by divine "other power" (of the unconscious).

The scripture speaks of *nāgas*, those supernatural serpents residing at the base of trees (recall Mucilinda's cobra coils protecting Siddhārtha from storms under a Tree). They also reside in the depths of ponds and lakes and are the very source of those waters. By analogy, then, Buddhism is now prepared to acknowledge "Source" imagery. It is saying that becoming more Awake requires that one make every effort one can—while acknowledging that the very possibility relies upon the cooperation of Something greater than oneself. Indeed, the notion of *adhiṣṭhāna* ("blessing, grace") is often first and foremost now. Commenting on the *Laṅkāvatāra Sūtra*, D. T. Suzuki writes about the Mahāyāna Buddhist disciple (now called a Bodhisattva and not just a Śrāvaka):

> Can the Bodhisattva, however, reach his goal by his own effort and without any outside assistance? Is there really no "other power" that will come to his help? Here we have one of the special features of Mahayana Buddhism distinguishing itself from the Hinayana. . . . It is the power emanating from the will of the Buddha whose loving heart embraces the whole universe, and is added to that of a Bodhisattva to sustain him, to encourage him, and finally to carry him over to a state of self-realization.[7]

In the history of religions, we are looking here at the categories of "works" and "grace." They are explicit within Mahāyāna Buddhism and make their first joint appearance as another significant pair in the Perfection of Wisdom literature.

Yet is this Buddhist position really so new? The Jātakas' Sumedha was surely working hard on his own salvation as an ascetic. But without the unexpected (gracious) arrival of Dīpaṅkara Buddha on a muddy road, and without that Buddha's prediction that he would become another Buddha, nothing earth-shaking would have occurred. Again, Sumedha's vow to "attain Omniscience and become a Buddha for the sake of the multitude with its deities" was clearly an intentional act (a work). Nevertheless, this "Bodhicitta Vow"—once planted—acted like a powerful seed that would henceforth operate underground as a motivating force (graciously) over millions of lifetimes until manifesting its natural fruit as a Buddha. In his last lifetime, Gautama was not always on his own but had teachers, even though he surpassed them in Means and Wisdom. The early disciples of Gautama Buddha clearly relied upon the power of their Lord's presence and his teachings. There was, as well, that lingering sense that even after his death the Buddha was somehow Present at the *stūpa*—and that one could rely upon it.

These are structures of Grace, necessary to any great religion and perhaps the defining character of religion itself, as distinct from a self-reliant humanism. As for the relationship of ego works and unconscious grace, the analyst Marie-Louise von Franz has this to say: "Is it our good deeds which lead to salvation, or is it the grace of God? In my experience, you can only stay in the contradiction and stick to the paradox."[8]

---

[7] Suzuki, *Studies*, 202-203.

[8] Marie-Louise von Franz, *The Problem of the Puer Aeternus* (Toronto: Inner City Books, 2000), 37.

Authenticity

The "Perfection of Wisdom" literature had to justify itself, i.e., authenticate its teachings, since they did not appear until several centuries after Gautama Buddha's *parinirvāṇa*. At the First Council of Rājagṛha, each Early Buddhist *sūtra* had been authenticated by Ānanda's claim, "Thus have I heard . . . ." Yet, the *Aṣṭa* itself, composed much later, opens: "Thus have I heard at one time. The Lord dwelt at Rājagṛha, on the Vulture Peak, together with a great gathering of monks, all of them Arhats . . . ." (1.1)[9] When the Buddhist establishment heard this, they protested that it was a lie—"created by beings who were certainly demonic in order to deceive the obtuse and mislead those with evil minds!"[10] Otherwise, they argued, these sermons would have been recited early and included in the Nikāya collections.

The *Aṣṭa* anticipates the criticism. It claims that the Lord is actually preaching during his lifetime to a select group of followers (many of whom are recognizable, such as the beloved Ānanda, the highly-respected Śāriputra, and the less prominent monk Subhūti). The scripture also implies that detractors had already removed themselves from hearing it. The Teacher refers to persons who "revile this perfection of wisdom when it is being taught, and, having rejected it, they will walk out"—"As a matter of fact they should be regarded as defamers of Dharma, as mere rubbish, as blackguards, as mere vipers." (7.6)

The label is not used here, but we can sense the import of later texts' saying such defamers are traveling in a "Hīnayāna" or "Inferior Vehicle" of the religion—while those who stayed to listen to a higher Wisdom are riding in a "Mahāyāna" or "Great Vehicle" taking them more assuredly to Nirvāṇa.

That distinction between the Hīnayāna and the Mahāyāna was used in early Western scholarship somewhat naively until it was realized that *hīna* (that can also mean "little") was being used as a pejorative to berate Early Buddhists. Thus, today, one reads more neutrally of "Mainstream" Buddhism, or "Nikāya" Buddhism, or "Early Buddhism."

An explanatory myth arose. Not only did Gautama Buddha preach the *Aṣṭa* and its several versions to a select group, he also knew its content would have to wait until a more propitious time to be more generally accepted. So he placed the text (an anachronistic detail since Buddhist scriptures had yet to be written down) in a special container and entrusted it to pious *nāgas* who preserved it under water—until the time was right for its reading five centuries hence. Now the Early Buddhists knew for sure that the Mahāyānists were lying. But the religious fantasy had a life of its own and explained the name of Nāgārjuna—Buddhism's great philosopher of the second century CE—for it was he who discovered the "100,000 Perfection of Wisdom" hidden among the Nāgas. Tibetan Buddhists would later discover many of their texts this way as *gter ma*, "treasure" (i.e., hidden treasure)—under water or underground, inside crystals, but also within the mind of an important *guru*.

---

9 Diacritics added.

10 Donald S. Lopez, Jr., "Authority and Orality in the Mahāyāna," *Numen: International Review for the History of Religions* 42, no.1 (January 1995): 22-23.

Donald Lopez informs us that there was, also, a simpler Mahāyāna explanation for their new sermons. All wise statements in any age were equated with "Buddha word" (*buddha-vacana*): "All inspired speech should be known to be the word of the Buddha if it is meaningful and not meaningless" (with or without Ānanda's introductory formula).[11] This would include, of course, a *sūtra* like the *Aṣṭa* inspired in some mysterious way by the "other power" of the Tathāgata.

A Jungian thought Jung would say that we are observing here the operation of the creative unconscious ("under water") that is inspiring a new Buddhist revelation—and it is even the unconscious that is "inventing" the explanatory myths. As for its being fantasy, the Hīnayānists were not admitting that it was already a fantasy to believe Ānanda had recited the entire canon at the First Council and fantasy to believe that the Nikāyas were throughout the actual words of Gautama Buddha. Put differently, it is easy to see that other people are living inside a myth but nearly impossible to see one's own mythic container. Nevertheless, justified or not, religious change is inevitable and part of the general phenomenon of "continuing revelation" in the history of religion.

In Christianity, that is the function of a Holy Spirit (John 16:13, "he will lead you to the complete truth"). Continuing revelation explains Martin Luther's protest against Catholic abuses but also Nietzsche's protest against Christianity itself. It explains Jung's modern "Answer to Job" since Yahweh had not adequately answered Job's complaint in Hebrew scripture.

The inevitability of a "new word," however, does not mean that the established mainstream will not resist, believing their truth to be already complete. It can even be resisted, unwittingly, by scholars. At the turn of the twentieth century, T. W. Rhys Davids wrote in favor of what he called "real original Buddhism":

> It is only when the Mahā Yāna books, written many centuries after the time of Gotama [Skt., Gautama], wished to father on the Buddha opinions different from those which he actually promulgated, that we find the allegation, in Buddhist books, of an esoteric teaching. It was the only way in which the writers of those books could at the same time call themselves Buddhist followers of Gotama, and yet put forward the new ideas, contrary to those of Gotama, which they were anxious to propagate.[12]

The bias in these lines has actually influenced a great deal of subsequent writing on Buddhism. "Buddhism says . . ." is often followed by an Early Buddhist position and not a later one that is just as authentically Buddhist.

One is tempted to say that finding "hidden treasure" years after a Master has died is entirely religious fantasy. But, strangely, we in the West experienced something similar in 1945. Just as Christian orthodoxy was dying out, new heretical scriptures—dating perhaps from the first century CE—were found in a jar in the Egyptian desert by peasants digging for fertilizer. The discovered texts have been called the "Gnostic Gospels," proclaiming an alternative view of what it means to

[11] Lopez, "Authority," 27.

[12] T. W. Rhys Davids, *Buddhism: Its History and Literature* (1896; New York: Cosimo Classics, 2005), 211-212.

be a Christian. They speak more directly and positively of an inner life and are less patriarchal, even including a *Gospel of Mary*. The Gnostic *Gospel of Thomas* begins, "These are the secret words which the living Jesus spoke . . . "—even though, historically, that claim is highly unlikely.[13]

Friends of Jung purchased one of these long-lost books for his library; it is now called the Jung Codex and includes the *Gospel of Truth*. Perhaps the real gospel truth is synchronicity—the sitting side by side in some mysterious way of the psychological and the historical, of what is within and what appears to be only without.

Style and Content

Affirming that its teaching "stems from the might of the Buddhas," the *Aṣṭa*'s versified version continues in a perplexing way:

> No wisdom can we get hold of, no highest perfection
> No Bodhisattva, no thought of enlightenment either.
> When told of this, if not bewildered and in no way anxious,
> A Bodhisattva courses in the Well-Gone's wisdom. (1.5)

First of all, the text has yet to make it clear that when it refers to a "Bodhisattva," it is not just speaking of the rare occurrence of a Sumedha (who eventually became Gautama who became a Buddha) or of Maitreya who is waiting in Tuṣita to "come" next. Instead, everyone in the audience who stayed to listen to this sermon is a Bodhisattva, a "Bodhi-being," or—as the Tibetan glosses this term—a "being intent on Enlightenment." That immediately multiplies the number of Bodhisattvas in the world (and the number of future Buddhas!) and presumes that those listening have at some point in their karmic cycling made the twofold "Bodhicitta Vow" to seek Enlightenment not only for themselves but also for the sake of all sentient beings.

Ritually, they will have the opportunity to renew their vow daily in what came to be called the "seven-limbed worship" (*saptāṅga-pūjā*). One "limb" reads:

> As the ancient Buddhas seized the Thought of Enlightenment, and in like manner
> they followed regularly on the path of Bodhisattva instruction;
> Thus also do I cause the Thought of Enlightenment to arise for the welfare of the
> world, and thus shall I practice these instructions in proper order.[14]

Reciting this did not mean that the earlier "Triple Refuge" and the "Precepts" were discarded but that the focus has shifted toward "Perfecting" of Giving, Morality, Patience, etc.

Yet the verses say there is "no Bodhisattva," and "no thought of enlightenment" to vow, and "no wisdom" to perfect, and—if one is not bewildered by such statements—then one is, indeed, a Bodhisattva practicing or coursing in, of all things, that very same Wisdom the text says does not

---

[13] Elaine Pagels, *The Gnostic Gospels* (New York: Vintage Books, 1979), xi-xiii.

[14] Śāntideva, *Entering the Path*, 155.

exist. Some verses later, we learn, "No training is his training, and no one is trained in this training." (2.7) As we keep turning the pages, we come upon one contradiction after another.

Our translator, Edward Conze, explains that this is just a new version of apophatic expression, another way of "not saying":

> the *Prajñāpāramitā* had resorted to the enunciation of plain contradictions as a means of expressing the inexpressible. For if nothing can be said, one way of saying it is to make two contradictory pronouncements at the same time.[15]

Scholars suggest that this contradictory or "paradoxical" style led to the intellectually elusive *kung-an* sayings of the Ch'an school of Chinese Mahāyāna Buddhism. These became the compact *koans* of Japanese Zen, such as, "What is the sound of one hand clapping?"—an impossibility meant, at the least, to catch one's attention but also to jostle the mind out of thinking clearly about anything, opening it to what cannot be discursively "thought" (opening it to the unconscious).

Jung on paradox Jung says something similar about the Gnostic texts that were found:

> Paradox is a characteristic of the Gnostic writings. It does more justice to the *unknowable* than clarity can do, for uniformity of meaning robs the mystery of its darkness and sets it up as something that is *known*. That is a usurpation, and it leads the human intellect into hybris by pretending that it, the intellect, has got hold of the transcendent mystery by a cognitive act and has "grasped" it.[16]

He is saying that too much clarity of expression keeps one trapped at the personal level of consciousness.

Again, is this really so different from Early Buddhism? Granted, the style is new. Yet from the start of his ministry, Gautama Buddha said (even complained) that what he had to teach would be difficult, perhaps impossible, to understand. Then, there is that classic "problem of language" to which Nāgasena introduced us in his conversation with king Menander. They came to the conclusion that there was, of course, a monk standing there named Nāgasena and a chariot in which the king had just arrived for their debate—but also that there was no Nāgasena (no self, only a group of *skandhas*) and no chariot (only a combination of chariot parts or *dharmas* held together by a label). It follows that in Mahāyāna Buddhism there could be a Bodhisattva, a Bodhicitta vow, a practice, and the goal of Wisdom—but there could also be none of these. Early Buddhists called the first half of that sentence "conventional truth" and the second half "ultimate truth."

We saw that it is possible to consider this "ultimate truth" to be a Means toward becoming unattached from "repulsive" reality. In our Mahāyāna Wisdom text, however, this "repulsiveness" of reality is for the most part missing and has been replaced by "elusiveness"—created by contradictory statements. The former strategy is directed more at one's feeling response, the latter at one's common

---

[15] Edward Conze, *Buddhist Studies, 1934-1972*: *Thirty Years of Buddhist Studies and Further Buddhist Studies* (San Francisco: Wheelwright Press, n.d), 1.141.

[16] Jung, *CW* 11, par. 417. Jung's italics.

sense understanding. Nevertheless, the goal remains the same. After all, the *Ratnaguṇa* verses do not actually say "there is no wisdom," etc. They say, "No wisdom can we get hold of . . .," i.e., grasp and to which we can become attached. That is Jung's point about intellectual *hybris* imagining it has "grasped" nonrational truth—not that there is no truth of that kind.

We can now understand the next verse about the five *skandhas*:

> In form, in feeling, will, perception, and awareness
> Nowhere in them they find a place to rest on.
> Without a home they wander, *dharmas* never hold them,
> Nor do they grasp at them—the Jina's Bodhi they are bound to gain. (1.6)

The point is that when there is a whole "person" or "self," then there is something to grasp. When there are just the five *skandhas* (form, feeling, etc.), grasping is less likely—but still possible if one treats these *skandhas* themselves as substantially real.

The Sarvāstivāda sect of Early Buddhism appears to have done so in its Abhidharma section (*sarvāsti-*, after all, means "all exists"). And the Theravādins allowed Buddhaghosa to describe each individual *dharma* as having its "own nature" (*svabhāva*). True, this great commentator meant only for an extraordinarily short moment of time. But better not to have anything at all to grasp! And that includes ideas, even the idea that something is insubstantial or momentary.

Therefore:

> If he knows the five *skandhas* as like an illusion,
> But makes not illusion one thing, and the *skandhas* another;
> If, freed from the notion of multiple things, he courses in peace—
> Then that is his practice of wisdom, the highest perfection. (1.14)

That these scriptures feel obliged to make such statements indicates that there were Buddhist adepts in their day who had, indeed, let go of what we have called "Truth A" for the sake of seeing the "multiple things" of "Truth B"—but they held onto that second truth without allowing it to induce the detached state of "Truth C." The Mahāyāna, then, is criticizing the Abhidharma project—not in principle—but for allowing their *dharmas* as "building blocks" to become falsely reified, becoming "stumbling blocks" instead.

The Few

Apparently, there were many who were missing the point. That would explain a dialogue in the *Aṣṭa* between the Lord and Indra (here called Kauśika):

> What do you think, Kauśika, how many of those men of Jambudvīpa are endowed
> with perfect faith in the Buddha, the Dharma, and the Saṃgha?
> Only a few.

> So it is, Kauśika. Only a few men of Jambudvīpa are endowed with perfect faith in the Buddha, the Dharma, and the Saṃgha. Fewer than those few are those who attain the fruits of a Streamwinner, and, after that, the fruit of a Once-Returner, or of a Never-Returner. Fewer still are those who attain Arhatship. Fewer still realize Pratyekabuddha-enlightenment. Fewer still raise their thoughts to full enlightenment. Fewer still are those who, having raised their thoughts to full enlightenment, strengthen that thought. Fewer still . . . . (3.2)

And the text goes on at some length, distancing itself from the many, from whatever had become "Mainstream" Nikāya Buddhism and even, it appears, from many in the Mahāyāna.

This statement about the "few" and the "many" is a clue to the minority status of Mahāyāna Buddhism at the beginning and perhaps throughout its existence in India (despite becoming an obvious majority elsewhere, such as China). This assessment is recent and why Jan Nattier entitled her study of the *Ugraparipṛcchā*, an early Mahāyāna scripture, *A Few Good Men*.[17] This title actually accords with the select nature of the purported audience for these new texts.

Scholars had previously been misled by the grand name, "Great Vehicle," and by its character in East Asia—popular, devotional, even lay oriented—and thought it must have been a popular lay protest in India against stodgy monastics. To the contrary, Gregory Schopen writes:

> Ironically, then, if the Mahāyāna was reacting to monastic Buddhism at all, it was probably reacting to what it—or some of its proponents—took to be too great an accommodation to lay needs and values on the part of monastic Buddhism . . . acquiring and maintaining property, constructing institutions that would survive over time, and so on. The Mahāyāna criticism of monastic Hīnayāna Buddhisms may have been, in effect, that they had moved too far away from the radically individualistic and ascetic ideals that the proponents of the Mahāyāna favored.[18]

It is inevitable that any religious tradition will soften its original "breakthrough" positions in order to accommodate the social and political environment—i.e., in order to survive. And no doubt that happened to Buddhism (after Aśoka) as it happened to Christianity (after Constantine). But it is also inevitable that some serious persons will notice and react against the trend, initiating a return to basics.

Nirvāṇa

A *Ratnaguṇa* verse reads:

> "He goes to Nirvāṇa," but no one can say where he went to.
> A fire's extinguished, but where, do we ask, has it gone to?
> Likewise, how can we find him who has found the Rest of the Blessed? (1.22)

[17] Jan Nattier, *A Few Good Men: The Bodhisattva Path according to The Inquiry of Ugra* (Honolulu: University of Hawai'i Press, 2003), 8.

[18] Gregory Schopen, "Mahāyāna," *EB* 2:494.

Again, this is not new. In the *Majjhima Nikāya*, the Lord explains as best he can to a wandering ascetic that it is useless to speculate on whether a Tathāgata appears or does not appear after Nirvāṇa. For one thing, pondering the matter distracts the ascetic from what he should be pondering. For another, the saṃsāric terms "appear" and "not appear" do not apply to someone who has relinquished "all conceivings, all excogitations." But this explanation "bewilders" the ascetic—like someone hearing a "Perfection of Wisdom" text. So Gautama offers the image of a fire that has "blown out" (*nirvāṇa*): "When that fire before you was extinguished, to which direction did it go: to the east, the west, the north or the south?"[19] Of course, the answer is that it did not "go" anywhere—the term or the category does not apply. Perhaps the lesson got lost over the centuries and needed to be taught again.

Mahāyāna Buddhism, however, does seem to teach a new kind of Nirvāṇa—a "Nirvāṇa of no fixed abode" (*apratiṣṭhita-nirvāṇa*). It is meant to replace or go beyond the two Nirvāṇas already defined by Early Buddhism: "Nirvāṇa with remainder" of the karmic body while living, and "Nirvāṇa without remainder" at physical death. Properly understood, they were never actually "fixed" or pinned down by saṃsāric categories unless naming them at all was a cause for reification and grasping. Whatever the case, the image of the "bird" emerges now as what it means not to be pinned down to ordinary reality:

> This world is attached to the mud of name-and-form [i.e., the *skandhas*].
> The wheel of birth-and-death revolves, similar to a wind-wheel.
> Having cognized the revolving world as like a snare for wild beasts
> The wise roam about similar to the birds in space. (8.3)

The *Aṣṭa* puts it more discursively, as Subhūti teaches (inspired by the Buddhas):

> I will teach you how a Bodhisattva should stand in perfect wisdom. Through standing in emptiness, should he stand in perfect wisdom. Armed with the great armor, the Bodhisattva should so develop that he does not take his stand on any of these: not on form . . . not on the eye . . . not on forms. . . . not on eye consciousness . . . not on the elements. . . not on the pillars of mindfulness . . . limbs of the Path; not on the fruits of . . . Arhatship; not on Prayekabuddhahood, nor on Buddhahood. He should not take his stand on the *idea* [my italics] that "this is form . . . permanent or impermanent;" that "form is ease or ill;" that "form is self, or not the self;" that "form is lovely or repulsive;" that "form is empty, or apprehended as something" . . . . (2.2)

I have left out much of this passage which is really a catalog of terms we have already encountered—but with the added refinement that one should not even *think* about the catalog. Notice how the argument over "self or non-self" has been elided. Gautama had done that himself by remaining silent.

---

[19] Bodhi, *MN* 72.15-20 (pp. 592-593).

A *Ratnaguṇa* verse makes the same point: "A flying bird has no footing . . . . / So the Bodhisattva who courses in the doors to freedom / Neither experiences the Blessed Rest [Nirvāṇa], nor does he course in the sign [Saṃsāra with its "signs" or attributes]." (20.8) Many writers take this to mean that the Bodhisattva postpones entering Nirvāṇa in order to be helpful to persons in Saṃsāra out of compassion—and in that sense hovers between the two, perhaps forever, in "no fixed abode." But Nattier cautions against this interpretation:

> While the *Ugra* does state that the bodhisattva voluntarily remains in *saṃsāra* far longer than would be necessary if he were a candidate for the enlightenment of an Arhat, this is not a deliberate postponement of his own awakening; on the contrary, it is simply a result of the vast amount of time necessary to attain all the prerequisites of Buddhahood.[20]

Sumeda, who turned down the opportunity to become an Arhat in his lifetime, also told us that the time required for his Complete Enlightenment would be an inconceivable "three incalculable aeons."

Nevertheless, there is merit in considering the Enlightened One in Mahāyāna Buddhism as somehow between the opposites of Saṃsāra and Nirvāṇa. For here is another conceptual distinction that the religious style is loath to leave unchallenged. As we have seen already, nothing seems very "fixed" in the "Perfection of Wisdom." It is not even clear why the scripture is speaking here of Bodhisattvas as "birds" rather than Buddhas who are the ones who are "in or not in" Nirvāṇa. But, then, we will soon discover that the difference between a highly advanced Bodhisattva and a Buddha is ambiguous. We will learn, too, that there are Buddhas in Nirvāṇa who, nevertheless, show up in Saṃsāra in miraculous "Bodies" to save us; and the Bodhisattvas residing with these Buddhas can do the same, even showing up as "Buddhas" themselves!

Still, the *Aṣṭa* can proclaim with a certain traditional clarity: "As many such ideas as he has in the course of a day, for so many aeons a Bodhisattva spurns birth-and-death, turns his back on it, seeks to end it."[21]

Emptiness

Subhūti just said, "I will teach you how a Bodhisattva should stand in perfect wisdom. Through standing in emptiness, should he stand in perfect wisdom." This signals a new emphasis upon *śūnyatā*, "emptiness," an abstract noun derived from the Sanskrit adjective, *śūnya*, "empty." In Buddhism, these words always point to something specific that is not present. That is why Alex Wayman translated them as "voidness" and "void," complaining in lectures to us graduate students that, "Nobody says the refrigerator is empty of milk." We hesitated to counter that neither does anyone say, "The refrigerator is void of milk." But the reader can see that something must be missing for the terminology to make sense in Buddhism. This actually perpetuates the earlier apophatic style of the

---

[20] Nattier, *A Few Good Men*, 143.

[21] Nattier, *Few Good Men*, 210.

religion. In Early Buddhism, we found that a person is empty of self or substance, that a word like "self" is empty of any meaningful reference, that the Arhat who knows of this emptiness—having also emptied himself of defilements—achieves a state of mind that lacks or is empty of delusion.

In the *Majjhima Nikāya*, Gautama uses the term *śūnyatā* for a certain type of meditation that lacks distractions. Ānanda had asked him why he said, "I often abide in voidness" (Bhikkhu Bodhi also prefers that translation). And the Lord explains by referring to their present location, once a bustling palace but now a quiet monks' residence:

> Ānanda, just as this Palace of Migāra's Mother is void of elephants, cattle, horses, and mares, void of gold and silver, void of the assembly of men and women . . . so, too, a *bhikṣu*—not attending to the perception of village, not attending to the perception of people—attends to the singleness dependent on the perception of forest. His mind enters into that perception of forest and acquires confidence, steadiness, and resolution. He understands thus: "Whatever disturbances there might be dependent on the perception of village . . . of people, those are not present here."[22]

This is a kind of "mindfulness" exercise and also a reminder that the Buddha preferred the forest, and not the monastery, for meditation.

But, then, the forest that is "empty" of village distractions could still have "present" the distractions of wild animals, etc. So the meditator is encouraged to focus next only on the earth upon which he or she is sitting—especially, one "devoid" of ravines and rivers—leading on to increasingly refined objects of contemplation: to the four *dhyānas* (increasingly empty of thoughts and feelings); then, the four formless *samāpattis*, the highest of which is very empty, (containing "neither-perception-nor-non-perception"). Technically, the exercise is meant to produce a "calm" mind capable of "insight" into the Three Characteristics—giving rise, eventually, to the "presence" of a liberated mind. The Mahāyāna, we might say, merely isolates the term *śūnyatā* to point to all such circumstances in which something that had been present is now gone.

I find it helpful to understand Buddhist *śūnyatā* as functioning the way *māyā* ("illusion") functions for Hinduism. Scholars seldom equate them since *māyā* has meaning within a religious world view where Brahman is the only reality and all else is illusion. Yet both religions are saying that what we ordinarily perceive is dubious and, upon reflection, can be discovered to be not quite true or not true in the way we first thought. In a discussion of this topic, the Dalai Lama brings up the classic "snake-rope" story. He confides personally:

> Sometime during the early sixties when I was reflecting on a passage by Tsoṅ-kha-pa [the founder of his Tibetan Buddhist sect] about unfindability [of "self"] and the fact that phenomena are dependent on conceptuality, it was as if lightning coursed within my chest. Here is the passage: "A coiled rope's speckled color and coiling are similar to those of a snake, and when the rope is perceived in a dim

[22] Bodhi, *MN* 121.1-4 (p. 965).

> area, the thought arises, 'This is a snake.' As for the rope, at that time when it is seen to be a snake, the collection and parts of the rope are not even in the slightest way a snake. Therefore, that snake is merely set up by conceptuality. . . . " The impact lasted for a while, and for the next few weeks whenever I saw people, they seemed like a magician's illusions in that they appeared to inherently exist but I knew that they actually did not. . . . Nowadays, I always meditate on emptiness in the morning and bring that experience into the day's activities.[23]

The Tibetan for "conceptuality" in this passage is probably *rnam-par rtog-pa* that is the equivalent of Sanskrit *vikalpa*—commonly translated into English as "discursive thought." Thus, in Mahāyāna, "emptiness" often means not only the lack of self (*ātman* or *svabhāva*, "substance, solidity") but also the lack of discursive thinking or without concepts. Clearly, this Buddhist leader is saying that much of what we take to be objective is subjective and that it is possible to see that fact and to cultivate a more accurate experience.

Jungian thoughts This general truth can be called "emptiness"—and if used as an abstraction may, at some risk, be capitalized as "Emptiness." But that is not the same as the "life force that was covered with emptiness" at the opening of the Vedic "Creation Hymn" nor is it the "formless Void" at the beginning of the Hebrew Bible. There is a partial parallel with the German mystic Eckhart's advice: "Be like a desert as far as self and the things of this world are concerned"—because "God may not leave anything empty or void," and must pour Himself into that kind of person. On the other hand, the Dalai Lama is too rationalistic about why we see a "snake" when there is only a rope. It is not because we think we see a snake—it is not a "conceptual" error—but because we are projecting unconsciously our own psychological "snakiness" onto the rope and, thereby, distorting its reality.

Thus, Jung's explanation of "emptiness" in *The Secret of the Golden Flower* (a Chinese Taoist-Buddhist meditation manual) is more accurate:

> This description of fulfillment depicts a psychic state that can best be characterized as a detachment of consciousness from the world and a withdrawal to a point outside it, so to speak. Thus consciousness is at the same time empty and not empty. It is no longer preoccupied with the images of things but merely contains them. The fullness of the world which hitherto pressed upon it has lost none of its richness and beauty, but it no longer dominates. The magical claim of things has ceased because the interweaving of consciousness with world has come to an end. The unconscious is not projected any more, and so the primordial *participation mystique* with things is abolished.[24]

---

[23] Dalai Lama, *How to Practice: The Way to a Meaningful Life*, trans. Jeffrey Hopkins (New York: Simon and Schuster, 2002), 139-140.

[24] Jung, *CW* 13, par. 65.

This means that an increase in consciousness "empties" the world of unconscious projections—those "magician's illusions" of which the Dalai Lama spoke and that lure one into unrealistic attachments for better or worse. Positively, Jung is saying that when the "refrigerator" of the world is emptied of what is falsely imagined to be there, we can more fully enjoy what is actually present.

"Mother"

The *Ratnaguṇa* reads, as Conze translates:

> Change and no change, suffering and ease, the self and not-self,
> The lovely and repulsive—just one Suchness [*tathatā*] is this Emptiness they are.
> (2.2)

As usual, the Three Characteristics are paired with their opposite Distorted Views—with the addition of a fourth pair "lovely and repulsive." We discussed this last pair of opposites with regard to the dancing girls in Siddhārtha's palace. But here all the pairs are equated with something called *tathatā* that Conze has capitalized as "Suchness"—itself equated with "Emptiness." Although still committed to apophatic expression and even elusiveness, the "Perfection of Wisdom" scriptures can feel kataphatic if one chooses to capitalize its chief terms.

This is especially so with a new positive term, "Mother." It occurs throughout the *Aṣṭa* in both prose and verse, as in these examples:

> Those with good teachers as well as deep insight,
> Cannot be frightened on hearing the Mother's deep tenets. (1.15)
>
> Therefore, have faith in this Mother of all the Jinas [Victors]
> If you wish to experience the utmost Buddha-cognition. (7.7)

This affirms what we already know, that the Mahāyāna is willing to entertain "Source" imagery. We learned that Bodhisattvas have their Source in the grace of the Buddhas, and now we learn that the Buddhas themselves have their Source in a Wisdom that is their "Mother."

At first glance, this does not seem new. We know from our earlier study that the Perfections are treated as the pair, "Means and Wisdom," and that the "Means" half is often equated with Compassion. But, in Buddhism, the gender symbolism of this pair can be confusing. Many religions symbolize their compassionate or feeling side as feminine and their wisdom or cognitive side as masculine. In the Buddhist religion, however, the wise male Lord is traditionally associated with Compassionate Means while the Wisdom he has achieved—or that has graciously given "birth" to him—is associated with a feminine "Mother." That symbolism appears in Early Buddhism but is emphasized in the Mahāyāna. And Conze believes that signals an essential shift in Buddhism—"which perhaps divides the Mahāyāna from the Hīnayāna more than anything else." This scholar writes:

> If, as I believe, the *Prajñāpāramitā* originated in the South of India, it would represent an irruption into Buddhism of the devotion to the Mother-Goddess current in the more matriarchal Dravidian society in which it originated. This oldest religion of mankind was evolved in the caves of the Palaeolithic and by allying itself with it Buddhism became a truly Catholic religion, capable of spreading throughout Asia, far beyond the confines of India.[25]

In a different essay, Conze compares similarities in traits (and even chronology) with the feminine "Wisdom" of Yahweh in the Bible and "Sophia" of Hellenistic Gnosticism:

> In all this we may have to deal with parallel developments, under the influence of local conditions, from a general widely diffused culture pattern. Or it may, of course, be that there is some hidden rhythm in history which activates certain archetypes—as Jung would call them—at certain periods in widely distant places. All that I set out to do in this review was to remind readers that there is a problem here, which historians cannot ignore. . . .[26]

The acknowledgement of Jung is rare as is the acknowledgement of a problem in historical data that cannot be easily solved.

Along with most writers, Jacob Kinnard rather easily disagrees with Conze that the "Mother" in the *Aṣṭa* points to a Goddess, finding his conclusion to be "overdetermined":

> This is just a metaphor, used to assert the supremacy of the *Prajñāpāramitā* teachings, which, as the source of the wisdom of the past, present, and future Buddhas, is the ultimate expression of the *dharma*.[27]

Besides, as Kinnard accurately notes, there was never a cult of "Prajñāpāramitā" in India. He cannot deny, however, the eventual emergence of goddesses in Mahāyāna Buddhism (just not this early).

As we shall see, the female Celestial Bodhisattva Tārā is worshipped from about the sixth century CE, while sculpted images of the feminine "Perfection of Wisdom" appear in quantity in Indian art beginning in the ninth century during the Pāla period. They are small, not always of high quality, and may have been for the purpose of private devotions. Still, it is striking to find in thirteenth-century Java the "Perfection of Wisdom" sitting in meditative posture on a Lotus, hands in "Turning the Wheel of the Dharma" *mudrā*, with little deer upon her pedestal—looking just like a male Buddha teaching at Deer Park in Sārnāth but with the bared breasts of a woman. Kinnard writes that it was a "radical textual move" to displace Śākyamuni here and there with a "Mother" in

---

[25] Conze, *Buddhist Studies*, 1.80, 125.

[26] Conze, *Buddhist Studies*, 1.209.

[27] Jacob N. Kinnard, *Imaging Wisdom: Seeing and Knowing in the Art of Indian Buddhism* (Delhi: Motilal Banarsidass Publishers, 1999), 115, 130.

Prajñāpāramitā literature: but moreso when visually represented, "co-opting his iconography" (see Figure 11.1).[28]

Figure 11.1 Prajñāpāramitā

Jungian considerations It follows that "Mother" imagery in these materials is sometimes "just a metaphor" but sometimes not—and, instead, evidence that a Feminine side of the religion (i.e., of the psyche) is asserting itself more authoritatively in the Mahāyāna. It was never absent in Early Buddhism despite its appeal to doctrinal clarity and will power. We felt its presence in stories of Siddhārtha's own extraordinary mother, Māyā, and his extraordinary stepmother—sometimes just called Gautamī—the first nun and something of a "Buddha" for women. The Feminine was present when Gautama heard the word "Nirvāṇa" from the admiring Kisā, when he accepted special Food from Sujātā under a special Tree, and when he touched Mother Earth who saved him from Māra. She may have given him spiritual "birth" throughout the night by the light of the Moon.

But, then, the Sun rose at dawn as Gautama became Enlightened. In that symbolism, Moon and Sun unite—and so we know that the "union of opposites" are at the heart of Buddhism, whatever

[28] Kinnard, *Imaging Wisdom*, 139-140. For an analysis of the Figure, see Elder, *Body*, 222-225.

else resides there. That explains what Conze detects as the "hidden rhythm in history which activates certain archetypes"—to introduce for the first time or recover what is missing in the "whole." Indeed, we can say this is the general rhythm of culture, detected by the philosopher Hegel in his formula of a cultural thesis countered by its antithesis, moving toward a synthesis—as a new thesis, etc. In the individual, this is the rhythm of consciousness that encounters some new unconscious content—requiring integration at a higher level of consciousness—only to discover that the process must be repeated with something new.

Conze's reference to "the Mother-Goddess current in the more matriarchal Dravidian society" of India's south makes my point that Buddhism's task in part has been to recover for India the values first expressed in its Indus Valley past. Following Neumann, we referred to it in an early chapter as "matriarchal consciousness"—itself instigated by a "Sophia-Moon" archetype. Neumann told us: "Its wisdom is the wisdom of paradox that does not extricate and juxtapose opposites with the clear separation of patriarchal consciousness, but rather binds them together with a 'both-and.'"[29] And so the *Ratnaguṇa* repeats an old story:

> As a man, preoccupied with matters of greed, had made a date
> With a woman, and would, not having met her, indulge in many thoughts;
> As many preoccupations as he would have during a day,
> For so many aeons does a Bodhisattva strive to reach his goal. (18.3)

An Early Buddhist story about "delusion"—when the Buddha chided a man for being in love with a woman he had never met—has been transformed into a lesson about "longing." The woman is still unknown as is unperfected Wisdom, and yet just like a lustful man so does the Bodhisattva long for Her. Jung explains: "What is behind all this desirousness? A thirsting for the eternal. . . ."[30] A longing for the Mother, for the unconscious Source of psychic life.

Bodhisattvas

As already noted, any monastic or layperson becomes a Bodhisattva when he or she recites the twofold Bodhicitta Vow to become a Buddha—especially in a ritual setting in the presence of one's mentor and other Mahāyānists assembled for the ceremony. Then, one might do so daily—to cultivate the vow and help it to grow—by proclaiming one's karmic "intention" before all the Buddhas and Bodhisattvas of the expanded universe. Śāntideva advised just that in his eighth century *Bodhicaryāvatāra* ("Introduction to the Practice of Enlightenment") because: "The Buddhas and the Bodhisattvas are everywhere, unimpeded, and instantaneous. All is in their presence. I am standing before them."[31] This is a more imaginative religious attitude than we have heard, like prayer in other traditions that assumes communication is possible between the human and the Divine. We see

---

[29] Neumann, "Moon," 110.

[30] Jung, *CW* 14, par. 192.

[31] Śāntideva, *Entering the Path*, 165.

Śāntideva's attitude solving the problem of the continued Presence of the Buddha in a new way, and it must have clashed with the more sober attitude of the "Hināyānists."

For the most part, however, the texts do not emphasize this clash nor does the archaeological evidence. In the monasteries, Bhikṣus and Bodhisattvas apparently lived together in the early centuries CE; and they shared the same Vinaya rules. Even today, Tibetan Mahāyāna Buddhists keep the rules of the Early Buddhist Mūlasarvāstivāda sect. But the similarity of living conditions would have hidden a major difference in religious "intent." The mainstream monks sought to become Awake as Arhats. The Bodhisattva monks sought to become "Incomparably Perfectly Completely Awake" (*anuttara-samyak-saṃbuddha*) as Buddhas.

Thus, Alexander Wynne writes: "The Buddhist mainstream must have regarded such Bodhisattas [the Pāli spelling] with a mixture of amusement and suspicion, for what could be more ridiculous than trying to mimic the monumental career of the Buddha himself?"[32] The Bodhisattvas, however, must have thought that to do otherwise would be a religious mistake. It is true that Gautama Buddha called himself not only Tathāgata but also Arhat; and the words he used to describe Nirvāṇa for himself and for his Arhat disciples were exactly the same. But it is also true that since the Buddha's death, the Arhats ("Worthy Ones") seemed increasingly open to criticism for not being actually worthy of their title.

Questioning their attainments at the early council at Pāṭaliputra had produced the religion's first schism between the Sthavīravādins who insisted that Arhats were perfect and the more numerous Mahāsāṃghikas who thought otherwise. Now, there is a new group critical of the Early Buddhist ideal. It is tempting to see these "Mahā-yānists" ("belonging to the Great Vehicle") as an outgrowth from the earlier "Mahā-sāṃghikhas" ("belonging to the Great Community").

These more recent reforming Buddhists, however, are not at all in the majority and may have been relatively few. Still, they are also criticizing Early Buddhist Arhats for being "selfish," seeking a "private Nirvāṇa" as quickly as possible to end their own suffering—and having little thought for the suffering of others. The charge is no doubt overstated, but a deeper schism threatened. Schism was so serious a matter for Buddhists that Aśoka's pillar edicts warned against it, as we know. In the end, however, the Mahāyāna teaching would be accepted in the greater scheme of the Buddhist religion—if not embraced by all—as a new and different expression of Buddhism, indeed, as a "Second Turning" of the Wheel of Dharma with its followers called distinctively, not "Śrāvakas," but "Bodhisattvas."

This history is parallel to that of Christianity wherein an earlier Roman Catholic Church has had to accept—if not fully embrace—Protestantism as a different but genuine form of the religion. It may be of interest that writers often associate Early Buddhism with Christian Protestants for their more spare iconoclastic style, the Mahāyānists with Roman Catholics for their love of the Virgin Mother and Mother Church.

---

32 Wynne, *Buddhism*, 138.

Bodhisattva Path

A "being intent upon Bodhi" still had to achieve Complete Awakening. And the religious paradigm required much "good karma" or "merit" (*puṇya*) for aeons over millions of lifetimes—just as it had for Bodhisattva Śākyamuni. It meant, at the very least, fulfilling the demands of the Threefold Training already in place, then perfecting those virtues of Giving, Morality, Patience, etc. There were pilgrimages that one could undertake, to honor *stūpas* containing relics of the Lord; to the extent they were already available, images of the Buddha could be venerated since infused mysteriously with his holy Presence. Fortunately, there was yet another new way to advance along the Path. We read in the versified *Aṣṭa*:

> Someone may for the Sugata ["Well Gone One"] who went to rest build Stupas,
> Made of the seven precious things, and worship them;
> Until thousands of *kotis* of fields are filled with these Stupas
> Of the Sugata, countless as the sands of the Ganges;
> . . . .
> But if someone else had copied this book, the Mother of the Sugatas,
> From which come forth the Guides with the ten powers,
> Would bear it in mind, revere it with flowers and unguents,—
> An infinitesimal portion of his merit would have those who had given worship to the Stupas. (3.2-4)

Here is internal evidence for a bustling *stūpa* cult by the first century CE (another anachronism in a text claiming to be taught by Gautama Buddha before he died). But our scripture says there is a much more fruitful way to be virtuous. A pious Indra explains:

> It is not that I lack in respect for the relics,
> But they are worshipped because they are fostered by wisdom.
> Just as every man who is supported by the king gets worship,
> Just so the Buddha-relics, because they are supported by the perfection of wisdom. (4.2)

This *deva* is choosing to worship primarily not the *stūpas* that house the Lord's relics but—understandably—the sacred feminine power of Wisdom that lies behind them.

This adulation of "Wisdom" might be referring to the last of the six Perfections or, as Conze believes, to Her eventual cult. What is certain is that there is now a "cult of the book," something less likely to have emerged if scriptures had not been written down, beginning in the previous century. A sacred physical object containing Wisdom—a kind of "book"—is now available. This was a set of specially prepared palm leaves, upon which the Dharma has been written in ink, then held together top and bottom by rectangular wooden boards. Our passage even equates a copy of such a book with the "Mother" of the Buddhas. Indeed, one way that we identify an image of "Prajñāpāramitā" in art is by the presence of a "book"—either held in her hand or resting on a lotus, like the goddess is resting herself. And if the cult of images made Buddhism more portable, this new cult of the book is making it even more so.

We learn that copying the *Aṣṭasāhasrikā-prajñāpāramitā* and revering it with flowers, incense, a row of lamps, etc. is far superior to honoring the Lord with just another *stūpa*. It is not even entirely clear that one has to understand what the book contains! In addition, the practice of worshipping a book of Wisdom promises worldly advantages such as not being killed in battle (should one somehow be a Buddhist soldier) and protection from evil spirits. Devotees of the book who recite it, according to the *Aṣṭa*, "will not die an untimely death, nor from poison, or sword, or fire, or water, or staff, or violence." (3.3)

Although one might criticize this this new form of piety as idolatrous "book worship," it perpetuates the Buddha's claim that those who see his Dharma, his Teaching, see Him. It perpetuates, as well, the practice of substituting for a physical relic at the core of a *stūpa* a piece of scripture—especially the verse that converted Śāriputra and Maudgalyāyana so long ago, "For those things that have causes, he has set forth the causes. And he has also set forth their cessation."[33]

Finally, reverence for a book filled with words seems to compensate that other tendency of Buddhism to devalue words—because they can distort and reify or because they are incapable of saying what one really means. Yet all Buddhists knew that the Lord taught in words that transformed those fortunate enough to hear his Wisdom.

Bodhisattva Stages

Classically, there are ten Bodhisattva "Stages" (*bhūmi*) along the Path to Buddhahood. As listed in the *Daśabhūmika Sūtra* ("Sermon on the Ten Stages"), they are: 1) Joy; 2) Immaculate; 3) Illuminating; 4) Blazing; 5) Unconquerable; 6) Facing; 7) Far-reaching; 8) Motionless; 9) Perfect Wisdom; 10) Cloud of Doctrine.[34] These names themselves are not very helpful, but they are intended to replace Early Buddhist categories of "ascending" sainthood while coordinating with them. Also, the first, sixth, eighth, and tenth Stages are the most important or receive special attention.

Gethin informs us that the first stage of a Bodhisattva is equivalent to the Stream-winner status of Early Buddhism while the sixth stage is equivalent to Arhat status among Buddhists content with this "inferior" goal.[35] Then, the *Daśabhūmika Sūtra* tries to coordinate the Stages with the Perfections as tenfold: "Giving" is perfected on the first stage, "Morality" on the second, "Meditation" on the third, etc.—using the expanded expression of the Six Perfections that we already met in the "Introduction" to the *Jātakas*. The scheme is obviously artificial.

Since it is a "spiritual ladder" driven by the number "ten," it might be worth noting that in religion 10 is often considered a perfect number—as with Pythagoras—since it is the sum of the sacred numbers, 1, 2, 3, and 4. "Ten" symbolizes Perfection, the Buddhist goal. As well, there are ten lunar months required for gestation of a human being in the womb. It follows that Wisdom as the "Mother" of all Buddhas will need ten stages to "give birth" to a Completely Enlightened Buddha.

---

[33] Lopez, *Story of Buddhism*, 53.

[34] Wayman, "Buddhism," 440-441.

[35] Gethin, *Foundations*, 230.

Indeed, we saw in the last Life of Gautama that he needed ten "Acts" to become Awakened, with two more "Acts" as a consequence.

Har Dayal suggests a more mundane stimulus for this numerical symbolism, namely, the Indian discovery around the first century CE of the decimal place-value system in mathematics: "Many old formulae of Indian philosophy and religion were recast according to the decimal system on account of the enthusiasm evoked by this epoch-making invention."[36] It is one of India's gifts to the world.

Celestial Bodhisattvas

We now come upon an ambiguity that even Buddhists cannot resolve. Wayman writes: "A *bodhisattva* on the tenth stage can be referred to as a Buddha, but not a 'complete Buddha' (*saṃbuddha*), for whom a Buddha stage, sometimes called the eleventh, is reserved."[37] This means that a very advanced Bodhisattva is something of a Buddha. We learn that he has extraordinary powers:

> At will he displays the array of the realms of all the Buddhas at the end of a single hair; at will he displays unfold arrays of the realms of the Buddhas of all kinds; at will in the twinkling of an eye, he creates as many individuals as there are particles in untold world-systems. . . in his own body he controls countless manifestations of the qualities of the Buddha fields of innumerable Blessed Buddhas.[38]

What more could one ask of a tenth-stage Bodhisattva? Robert Thurman even refers to such a being as "more Buddha than all the Buddhas."[39] He may have in mind the Nirvāṇa of "no fixed abode" where, technically, neither Bodhisattvas nor Buddhas actually "abide."

For that matter, what more could one ask of an eighth-stage Bodhisattva? This is what the *Aṣṭa* calls the "irreversible stage" to which it devotes an entire chapter. The label means that Buddhahood is now inevitable (in the way that becoming a Stream-winner means that Arhathood is inevitable in Early Buddhism, although the "stream" is supposedly won at the first stage of a Bodhisattva). Scripture reads:

> Just so an irreversible Bodhisattva cannot be crushed by persons who belong to the vehicle of the Disciples and Pratyekabuddhas, he cannot, by his very nature, backslide into the level of Disciple or Pratyekabuddha, he is fixed on all-knowledge, and ends up in perfect enlightenment.[40]

---

[36] Dayal, *Bodhisattva Doctrine*, 167.

[37] Alex Wayman, "Soteriology: Buddhist Soteriology," *ER* 13:425.

[38] Gethin, *Foundations*, 231.

[39] Robert A. F. Thurman, "The Buddhist Messiahs: The Magnificent Deeds of the Bodhisattvas," in Donald S. Lopez, Jr. and Steven C. Rockefeller, eds., *The Christ and the Bodhisattva* (Albany: State University of New York Press, 1987), 93.

[40] Conze, *Eight Thousand*, 18.2.

Or not, depending on what one reads; and it is surprising to find the word "fixed" here when everything seems so "unfixed."

Other materials inform us that a Bodhisattva on the eighth, ninth, or tenth Stage is a "Mahāsattva," an extraordinary or "Great Being" whose body exhibits the Thirty-two Characteristics. It follows that Maitreya is at least an eighth-stage Bodhisattva residing in Tuṣita heaven but probably a tenth-stage Bodhisattva. But, then, all of these very advanced Buddhist beings seem to be residing in heavens of some kind. Scholars simply call them, "Celestial Bodhisattvas." Nattier notes, "celestial bodhisattvas seem to hover at an approachable distance within our own world-system, ever ready to assist devotees in distress"—reminding her of helpful Christian Catholic saints who are in a far off heaven with God and yet somehow nearby.[41]

The reader can now see why I argued against the common claim that, "There are no gods in Buddhism." Here, one scarcely needs to argue—merely point out that the human Indian Bodhisattva Śāntideva takes Refuge in the heavenly "hosts of Bodhisattvas" who function just as the gods (and the ancestors, saints, and angels) do in other religions:

> Trembling with fear, I give myself to Samantabhadra, and again I give myself,
> by my own action, to Mañjughoṣa;
> and to the Lord Avalokita, who is entirely occupied with the practice of compassion,
> I, who am terrified, cry aloud a cry of suffering, "May he protect me, a sinner!"
> To the noble Akāśagarbha and to Kṣitigarbha, and indeed to all the great
> Compassionate Beings, I cry aloud, looking for protection.
> And I worship the Lord of the Thunderbolt [Vajrapāṇi].[42]

The earlier *Aṣṭa* had named only Bodhisattvas Ratnaketu, Śikhin, and Gandhahastin among "countless" such helpful beings. They will eventually be called, *devatās* ("divinities"), sure in the knowledge that ancient Buddhists knew the difference between them and ordinary transmigrating *devas* who may or may not be pious protectors of the Dharma.

A list of eight "Great Bodhisattvas," as these Celestial Bodhisattvas are also called, became standard: Avalokiteśvara, Mañjuśrī, Vajrapāṇi, Maitreya, Kṣitigarbha, Sarvanīvaraṇaviṣkambhin, Ākāśagarbha, and Samantabhadra.[43] These are all male, but in longer lists female Bodhisattvas like Tārā also appear. Of course, the historical Gautama may not have approved of this development in the religion. And he might have wanted to scold Śāntideva for his heartfelt "cry aloud" as he had Ānanda at the Parinirvāṇa, "Enough, do not weep and wail!" But, then, the Lotus of the Buddha's teaching is still unfolding.

A Jungian thought Jung understands why modern persons, including modern Buddhists, want to deny the existence of "Buddhist" gods. Indeed, Nietzsche announced over a century ago that "God is dead"—and Buddhists want to seem *au courant* for missionary reasons. Psychologically,

---

41 Nattier, *Few Good Men*, 189.

42 Śāntideva, *Entering the Path of Enlightenment*, 151.

43 See "eight great bodhisattvas," *PDB*, 1079-1080.

they are also part of a general process of withdrawing Divinity from projection onto metaphysical realms where it does not belong—in anticipation of rediscovering Divinity where it does belong, within the depths of the psyche. Jung encourages this process, as he explains:

> My admiration for the great philosophers of the East is as genuine as my attitude towards their metaphysics is irreverent. I suspect them of being symbolical psychologists to whom no greater wrong could be done than to take them literally. If it were really metaphysics that they mean, it would be useless to try to understand them.[44]

But, then, it was too early for Buddhists (or Christians, etc.) to be aware of themselves as "symbolical psychologists." They could know that the Great Bodhisattvas and the Buddhas were "empty" of naïve physicality and did not conform to everyday concepts; they could not know that they were divine personifications of archetypal forces lying within the collective unconscious. This is a radically new religious perception whose day is only now dawning.

Avalokiteśvara

As an example of "Bodhisattva" reality, let us consider the very popular Avalokiteśvara. His name means the "Lord" (*īśvara*) who "looks" (*lokita*) "down upon" (*ava*) the world with compassion. This is reminiscent of Gautama Buddha's surveying the world with a compassionate "divine eye" shortly after his Enlightenment. Although ostensibly not yet a Buddha, Avalokiteśvara's eye is very powerful. We read in the twenty-fifth chapter of the *Lotus Sūtra*:

> O you of the true gaze, of the pure gaze,
> Of the gaze of broad and great wisdom,
> Of the compassionate gaze and the gaze of good will!
> We constantly desire, constantly look up to,
> The spotlessly pure ray of light,
> The sun of wisdom that banishes all darkness,
> . . . .
> His benevolent eye beholding the beings,
> He is happiness accumulated, a sea incalculable,
> For this reason one must bow one's head to him.[45]

This association of eye, light, and sun is more generally reminiscent of the "Eye of God" motif in other world religions, while the devotee's response here—"looking up to" that Eye yet also "bowing one's head"—is entirely appropriate in the presence of the numinous.[46]

---

[44] Jung, *CW* 13, par. 74.

[45] Hurvitz, *Lotus Blossom,* 318-319.

[46] See my essays in the "Eye" chapter of *Body*. They include an interpretation of Avalokiteśvara as the "Thousand-armed, Thousand-eyed Kuan-Yin."

Figure 11.2 Avalokiteśvara

His Image A painting of Avalokiteśvara on a cave wall at Ajaṇṭā expresses this visually (see Figure 11.2). We saw earlier in this book that Buddhists had carved out monastic residences and shrine halls at this site as early as the first century BCE. Then, in a rush of artistic activity during the Gupta "Golden Age," new caves with decoration were created in the fifth century. Our image dates from this second period and, while damaged by moisture and bats (as well as people, when the caves were rediscovered in the nineteenth century), it has survived with some restoration as a major expression of Indian high art. The painting is actually contemporary with the Gupta sculpture of the "Seated Buddha" at Sārnāth that we analyzed in the previous chapter.

Technically, this is "Padmapāṇi" (Holder of the Lotus), an epithet of Avalokiteśvara. The lotus blossom in his elegantly drawn right hand alludes to the goal of Awakening as a fully opened flower—less directly, it alludes to its watery Source. The Bodhisattva is depicted as a "royal" person with a high crown encrusted with jewels over long black hair, with heavy earrings, a necklace and armbands—the regalia that Gautama renounced upon his Departure from home. But this is no human ascetic and instead a Celestial Bodhisattva in some heaven dressed like a god. That helps to explain the unstructured fluid background of worshipping attendants, animals and birds, palms. From that Paradise, he is looking down with compassion—at us.

Avalokiteśvara's powers are very great. The *Lotus* tells us that his preaching of the Dharma removes the Three Poisons—just as does the preaching of a Buddha. But he helps in more practical ways, as well:

> If there is one who keeps the name of this bodhisattva He Who Observes the Sounds of the World [*avalokitasvara*], even if he should fall into a great fire, the fire would be unable to burn him, thanks to the imposing supernatural power of this bodhisattva. If he should be carried off by a great river and call upon this bodhisattva's name, then straightway he would find a shallow place. . . . If, again, a man who is about to be murdered calls upon the name of the bodhisattva He Who Observes the Sounds of the World, then the knives and staves borne by the other fellow shall be broken in pieces, and the man shall gain deliverance . . . Even if there is a man, whether guilty or guiltless, whose body is fettered with stocks, pillory, or chains, if he calls upon the name of the bodhisattva He Who Observes the Sounds of the World, they shall be severed and broken, and he shall straightway gain deliverance.[47]

Freed even if guilty of a crime? What grace, what mercy!

This Great Bodhisattva even moves in our midst disguised in whatever manner is likely to aid our being "delivered"—manifesting himself as a Śrāvaka, a Pratyekabuddha, even a Buddha, not to mention as a god, a king, a householder, and even a householder's wife. There is no *kṣetra* ["field"] where he does not display his body:

> The various evil destinies,
> Those of hell, ghosts, and beasts,
> As well as the pains of birth, old age, sickness, and death,
> All little by little are extinguished.[48]

That is why in many renderings of the Bhavacakra or "Wheel of Life" there stands an image of Avakokiteśvara in each of the six Destinies.

His Holy Name All of this blessing is available, we are told, by just calling upon his holy name. But what name? We have been assuming that when one prayed in Sanskrit *namo bodhisattvaya* . . . ("Homage to the Bodhisattva . . . ") that the invocation would end with "Avalokiteśvara." There is manuscript evidence, however, of an alternative spelling. In fact, early Chinese translations reflect "Avalokitasvara"—whereby the ending is not *īśvara* ("lord') but *svara* ("sound"). That is why we have just read in Hurvitz's translation from the Chinese that the Bodhisattva's name is "He Who Observes the Sounds of the World." His saving activity is not altered by the differences in spelling,

---

[47] Hurvitz, *Lotus Blossom*, 313-314.

[48] Hurvitz, *Lotus Blossom*, 318.

but one emphasizes the Lord's ability to "see" our suffering while the other his ability to "hear" our cries of distress.

His Mantra Over time, the issue could be avoided by calling upon Avalokiteśvara (or Avalokitasvara) by way of his *mantra.* This term is often translated as "spell" or "incantation" but is best left untranslated. It refers to a short formula of syllables that may or may not have dictionary meanings but definitely have sacred power—because they evoke a divine Presence. These *mantras* become prominent in the late unorthodox form of Mahāyāna Buddhism called Tantra. But, as we see here, non-tantric orthodox Buddhism already included them in its practice. They are actually deeply imbedded in Indian religions generally.

Avalokiteśvara's special *mantra* is the six-syllable phrase, "Oṃ Maṇi-Padme Hūṃ" (pronounced, OHM-muh-nee-pud-may-HOOM). The opening and closing syllables are called "seed" (*bīja*) syllables and have no dictionary significance. But "Oṃ" had been, since at least the time of the Upaniṣads, the sacred sound of the "Oneness" of Brahman or Ātman—thus, something of an anomaly in a Buddhist context. Buddhists would say that it signified, instead, the "One" unique Awakening. "Hūṃ" often closes a Buddhist "male" *mantra*, i.e., one intended to evoke a male divinity, as here.[49] The two words within the phrase, however, do have dictionary meanings: *maṇi* ("jewel") and *padme* ("lotus"). But their relationship has not always been clear. Lopez tells us that for over a century scholars have taken it to mean "Jewel in the Lotus"—even suggesting tantric sex.[50] But this meaning is based on taking *padme* as a locative construction ("in") when, in fact, it is a vocative ("O") as it should be when calling upon a god.

At the risk of being too technical, "*maṇi-padme*" is a Sanskrit Bahuvrīhi compound in the vocative case wherein *maṇi* is uninflected. In addition, the grammar reflects Buddhist Hybrid Sanskrit and not classical Sanskrit. This means that *padme* is the vocative not of a feminine noun but of a masculine noun—again, as it should be when calling upon the male Bodhisattva Avalokiteśvara.[51] Thus, "Maṇi-Padma" is a name or epithet; and *oṃ maṇi-padme hūṃ* can be rendered, "Oṃ, O Jewel-Lotus, Hūṃ."

The very sound evokes this Being who holds not only a precious "Jewel" granting all one's wishes but also a "Lotus" blossoming as Enlightenment. Tibetan Buddhists say the *mantra* is so effective that it need not be recited aloud but merely written on a piece of paper and inserted into a prayer wheel. With every turn of the wheel, bad *karma* is erased, future good births are guaranteed, and the Bodhisattva is praised! That helps everyone in Tibet, even the whole world. In fact, these Buddhists believe that Avalokiteśvara (Maṇipadma) has blessedly incarnated in our midst as the current Dalai Lama. It is like saying Christ is still with us.

---

[49] Elder, *Snake and the Rope*, 166-167. See Wayman, "The Significance of Mantras, from the Veda down to Buddhist Tantric Practice," in *Buddhist Insight*, chapter 22. See also Richard D. McBride II, "Mantra," *EB* 2:512.

[50] Lopez, "The Spell," in *Prisoners of Shangri-La*, chapter 4.

[51] For the grammar, see Peter Alan Roberts with Tulku Yeshi, trans., *The Basket's Display: Kāraṇḍavyūha*. Published by 84000, Translating the Words of the Buddha (2013), xii. http://www.84000.co.

Tārā

In our cave painting of Avalokiteśvara, we see that he is not very masculine. Part of this is due to the Gupta canon of beauty and a preference for the *tribhaṅga* or "triple bend" pose—a gentle S-curve in a standing body. It is an aesthetic device expressing Indian culture's increasing acceptance of the values of grace and softness that we associate with femininity. Besides, the Bodhisattva is not carrying a "sword" of Wisdom like Bodhisattva Mañjuśrī or a symbolic "thunderbolt" of Power as does Bodhisattva Vajrapāṇi. He is holding a flower. When his image reached China, Avalokiteśvara even ceased being a "feminine male"—and transformed entirely into a female Bodhisattva. By the 10th century, we find Kuan-Yin (Chinese for *avalokitasvara*) fully clothed with softly defined breasts. She will have a special regard for children and be labeled in European sources, the "Buddhist Madonna." Chün-fang Yü comments:

> Monastic Buddhism and Neo-Confucianism were masculine and patriarchal. Despite its rhetoric of nonduality, Ch'an Buddhism did not provide the same opportunities for women practitioners as it did for men. Buddhist doctrine, after all, always interpreted being female as a consequence of bad karma. . . . There was thus an imbalance and a deprivation. There was too much yang and not enough yin.[52]

That explains the Western fascination with Kuan-Yin's transgender since our own culture has been for centuries too "yang" and insufficiently "yin."

Avalokiteśvara, however, did not have to leave India for this transformation. We already learned that he could "manifest" in the body of a woman. In fact, like a goddess, he was solicitous of women's prayers for a child. Susan Huntington traces an interesting history of this Bodhisattva's art.[53] She notes, first of all, that triads are very frequent in Indian art; and from an early date Avalokiteśva stood to the right of a seated Buddha with another attendant Bodhisattva, usually Vajrapāṇi, to the left. Then, at the sixth-century caves of Kānheri, one finds a different kind of triad: the central standing figure is the Bodhisattva Avalokiteśvara—flanked by two standing females. These female figures have been identified as the goddesses Tārā ("savior," "star") to his right and Bhṛkutī ("wrinkled brows") to his left.[54] Finally, in a relief on a cave wall at Ellora, we find Tārā—as a highly advanced "Great Bodhisattva"—standing in the center of her own triad, flanked by diminutive female companions.

In this art history, we witness Avalokiteśvara moving from a secondary role in his relationship to the Buddha to a primary role in the religion. And we witness Tārā moving from a secondary role in her relationship to Avalokiteśvara to a primary one—standing where he would stand and worthy of her own distinct worship. In other words, these two Celestial Bodhisattvas were closely related. But there is little written in Sanskrit accompanying this visual development.

---

[52] Chü-fang Yü, *Kuan-yin: The Chinese Transformation of Avalokiteśvara* (New York: Columbia University Press, 2001), 20.

[53] Huntington, *Art of Ancient India*, 263-268.

[54] Alex Wayman and R. Tajima, *The Enlightenment of Vairocana* (Delhi: Motilal Banarsidass, 1992), 11, 123.

Tibetan Buddhists, however, preserve stories that may have had their beginnings in India. We learn:

> Avalokiteśvara was overwhelmed by the feeling that his extraordinary efforts had not significantly diminished the seemingly endless miseries of living beings. His tears of mercy gathered into a pool on which a lotus blossomed. From the lotus arose Tārā, exquisite in beauty, lovelier than a million lotuses. She consoled the bodhisattva, assuring him that she would join him in his mission to liberate the world from suffering.[55]

Here, Tārā is a female companion of a great male Bodhisattva, joining him as a miraculous female manifestation of himself—as his tears. Obviously, the emotional response of tears is now permitted in Buddhism, at least by the imagery. The tears of Gautamī, despairing of her stepson's acceptance as a *bhikṣuṇī*, have been redeemed.

In a different story, Tārā is more independent. Having worshipped a Buddha in a far distant past, she became so advanced as a Bodhisattva in a female body that monks encouraged her to change gender to speed the process. She answered:

> There is neither man nor woman nor self nor person-hood nor notion of such. Attachment to "male and female" is meaningless and deludes worldly people with poor understanding. She then vowed: Many desire enlightenment in a man's body, while not even a single [person] strives for the benefit of sentient beings in a woman's body. Therefore, I shall work for the benefit of sentient beings in a woman's form as long as samsara has not been emptied.[56]

Tārā is teaching with words—and her own unconventional behavior—that the distinction between male and female is real enough (indeed, she will remain a female Celestial Bodhisattva and not join the plethora of male Celestial Bodhisattvas). At the same time, she is teaching a "non-dual" Wisdom: that the conceptual pair, "male and female," is an occasion for "attachment" to certain ideas or fixed attitudes about men and women. This pair is just one of many such discursive distinctions that she as a Bodhisattva is obliged to challenge since they lead to suffering.

Thus, Tārā teaches a non-grasping Wisdom, a "Prajñāparamitā" with which (or with Whom) she is often identified. In this way, Tārā's identity becomes ambiguous: Is she an advanced Celestial Bodhisattva on the Path or is she actually an accomplished female Buddha, perhaps even the Mother of all Buddhas? Of course, the ambiguity lies within the Mahāyāna Path itself since a highly-advanced Bodhisattva at the tenth Stage is indistinguishable from a Buddha. Nor do the distinctions made by language matter very much. Tibetan Buddhists have no doubt, however, that Tārā is somehow at

---

[55] Miranda Shaw, *Buddhist Goddesses of India* (Princeton: Princeton University Press, 2006), 307-309.

[56] Susan S. Landesman, "Goddess Tārā: Silence and Secrecy on the Path to Enlightenment," *Journal of Feminist Studies in Religion* 24, no. 1 (Spring, 2008): 47.

once a Great Bodhisattva and a Complete Buddha in her own right, and not only the Mother of all Buddhas but also the Mother of the Tibetan people themselves.

Figure 11.3 Tārā

Her Image Consider a deeply carved relief in sandstone from ninth century Bihar (see Figure 11.3). Like the painted Avalokiteśvara, she stands in a graceful *tribaṅga* pose dressed in the finery and jewelry befitting royalty and divinity. She wears a crown and is standing in front of a large throne whose crossbar is topped by *stūpa* forms and whose sides are decorated with standing lions. Below, on either side of the main figure, stand diminutive female attendants: a portly one to our left holding a sword and a skullbowl and a more lively one to our right with her feet in the pose of a *yakṣiṇī* and carrying an *aśoka* tree branch. They are here identified respectively as Ekajaṭā and Mārīcī, "fierce and benign" manifestations of Tārā herself (a pair of attributes important in Tantra).

Yet this figure could have been Avalokiteśvara—if it did not display large breasts (barely covered by a diaphanous blouse) and ample exposed flesh at her belly. For he carries a lotus flower as does Tārā's left hand (now broken). He, too, stands on a lotus pedestal and offers all blessings, as does she, with a lowered open palm in *varada* ("rewarding") *mudrā*.

The sculpture is lush, perhaps too busy, but specifically identified as, "Khadiravaṇī Tārā." She is goddess of the "Acacia Forest," described in one poem as: "A grove of glomerous figs, acacias, jujube trees, / Banyans, sandal, three thousand fruits, nutmeg, and cloves, / A pleasant leafy place of flowers budding and blossoming."[57] Accordingly, the artist has rendered Tārā's halo not as a sun circle but as an oval of bound branches and leaves. She redeems not only tears but also nature.

Her Holy Name and Mantra To evoke this bountiful Presence, one had only to call upon Tārā's holy name. It is contained within her ten-syllable *mantra* in Sanskrit: "*Oṃ Tāre tut-tāre ture svāhā*" (pronounced, OHM-TAAH-ray-TOOT-taah-ray-TOO-ray-SVAAH-HAAH). It is not as grammatically difficult as Avaloketeśvara's *mantra* and can be readily translated as: "Oṃ, O Tārā, O rescuer from pain, O quick one, Svāhā."

We have already discussed "Oṃ," the opening *bīja* or "seed" syllable. At its close, *svāhā*—that has no dictionary meaning—often designates a *mantra* addressed to a female deity.[58] Tārā's own name (here in the vocative case) is derived from the Sanskrit root *tṛī* which means "to cross, to ford"—alluding to very ancient Indian rituals of crossing sacred waters (rivers, pools) and eventually extended to all sacred places, even those without water. In Buddhism, as we know, the meaning was extended to "crossing over" from Saṃsāra to Nirvāṇa, from the unenlightened state to an enlightened one. In early scripture, Gautama Buddha was called *trāyin, tāraka*—"Crosser, Savior."[59] And now a Great Bodhisattva who is female is being called *tārā*—"Crosser, Savior, Rescuer."

The word *tārā* can also mean "star"—perhaps because stars "cross" the night sky. This meaning was not lost on the merchant sailors who set out from Mumbai (near the Buddhist caves where Tārā's image could be worshipped). They would need her as a guiding "Star" as they embarked upon a perilous journey toward the Mediterranean coast.

In the *mantra*, "rescuer from pain" (*tud* plus *tāre* = *tuttāre*) refers specifically to the Eight Perils from which Avalokiteśvara could spare his own devotees: lions, wild elephants, fire, venomous snakes, thieves, violent waters that cause shipwreck and drowning, captivity, and evil spirits.[60] Sometimes, Buddhists psychologize these Perils: the "lion" of pride, the "wild elephant" of delusion, etc.

Tārā, too, protects against these external and internal dangers. And she does so "quickly" (*ture*), as quick as an echo follows sound. Shaw informs us that traditionally Tibetans intoned the *mantra* of Tārā just as often as they did that of Avalokiteśvara, her male counterpart—and may still do so despite Chinese Communist hostility. Children memorized a long hymn to her, printed on prayer flags to waft Tārā's blessings on the wind over the landscape.[61]

A Sociological Note

Unfortunately, the ascent of this female Celestial Bodhisattva—along with the feminine figures of Prajñāpāramitā, Cundī, etc.—was not reflected socially to the benefit of women. This is largely due to the restrictions placed upon women in India generally, even in Gupta times But, as Nattier observes, there is a specifically unexpected Buddhist component: "we can discern a substantial body of corroborating evidence indicating that the emergence of the goal of Buddhahood (as opposed

[57] Shaw, *Buddhist Goddesses*, 328-330.
[58] Wayman, *Buddhist Insight*, chapter 22.
[59] Wayman, "Buddha as Savior," *Buddhist Insight*, chapter 1.
[60] Shaw, *Buddhist Goddesses*, 318.
[61] Shaw, *Buddhist Goddesses*, 346.

to Arhatship) brought with it a perceptible drop in women's status."[62] Her point is that in Early Buddhism, women could become Arhats; while in Mahāyāna Buddhism, only males could become Buddhas. Tārā herself says she is the exception.

Indeed, the archaeological evidence shows a marked decline of women's names, lay or religious, as donors at Buddhist sites. Ronald Davidson writes, "from the seventh century forward we see an erosion of women's involvement, most particularly in the virtually total eclipse of the office of the nun (*bhikṣuṇī*) in North India."[63] Perhaps, we should not be surprised since Buddhism had long been wary of women for their "desirousness," wary even of mothers for being "attached" to their children—both natural symbols of Saṃsāra that monks were struggling to escape. The feelingful Śāntideva thought it compassionate to pray: "Whoever are women in the world, may they achieve manhood."[64]

Another component, psychologically, is a lack of consciousness among the ancients that "Tārā" was not only a revelation but a requirement to be integrated in some way. Even today, a scholar can say: "It must be kept in mind, however, that these images were, for the most part, constructed by and for men. . . . . designed" for male practitioners.[65] To the contrary, living religious images are not "constructed" or "designed" by anyone. They are, instead, spontaneous manifestations of the collective unconscious—demanding "worship" in the modern sense of bringing them into the everyday in some new way. Obviously, that is very difficult to achieve socially and must be left to individuals who sense this moral obligation.

The Problem of Opposites

We heard Tārā criticize the distinction between "male and female," saying it was much like the dangerous notion of "self." This is an instance of Indian Buddhism's usual distrust of "discursive thought"—expressed by Sanskrit words derived from *kalpa* ("to form;" but not in the sense of a formed "aeon") such as *kalpita, vikalpa*. They are very close to the notion of *prapañca* as "conceptual elaboration." What seems particularly troublesome about *kalpita*, etc. is that they not only make false distinctions but do so as "pairs of opposites": male-female, right-left, high-low, cool-warm, good-bad, etc. Tārā explains that they are—like some "substantial" *ātman*—an occasion for clinging, to one side of the pair as opposed to the other side. In her case, it means being attached to the idea that only a "male" can become a Buddha.

Buddhism, in fact, has had a "problem of opposites" throughout its history: the problem of indulgence and mortification, eternalism and annihilationism, ignorance and knowledge, Saṃsāra and Nirvāṇa, absence and presence of the Lord, Means and Wisdom, etc.—as if opposites are unavoidable. But the religion says they are avoidable by ridding oneself of "discursive thought."

---

[62] Nattier, *Few Good Men*, 98-100.

[63] Ronald M. Davidson, *Indian Esoteric Buddhism: A Social History of the Tantric Movement* (New York: Columbia University Press, 2002), 91.

[64] Śāntideva, *Entering the Path*, 230.

[65] Natalie D. Gummer, "Women," *EB* 2:899, 901.

Hence, Buddhism is in principle opposed to paired "duality" (*dvaya*) and in favor of "nonduality" (*advaya, nirdvandva*)—expressed in the *Aṣṭa* as a kind of "unfixed" or undetermined Nirvāṇa that goes beyond the major paired distinction, "Saṃsāra and Nirvāṇa."

The "opposites" in psychology Jung was so impressed by the problem of "opposites" that this entry in the "Index" to his *Collected Works* runs for five pages. Edinger explains why in a lecture:

> The opposites constitute the most basic anatomy of the psyche. The flow of libido, or psychic energy, is generated by the polarization of opposites in the same way as electricity flows between the positive and negative poles of an electrical circuit. . . . The opposites are truly the dynamo of the psyche. They are the motor, they're what keep the psyche alive.[66]

This means—as "opposed" to the *Aṣṭa*—that the opposites are not only unavoidable in psychic life (the basic pair being "consciousness and the unconscious") but also desirable. They are understood in Jungian psychology as forces and not as errors. Should the dynamic of opposites cease, we are dead or, at least, "lifelessly" depressed.

Jung put this bluntly in a letter to an Indian man:

> Take, for instance, the concept of *nirdvandva*. Nobody has ever been entirely liberated from the opposites, because no living being could possibly attain to such a state, as nobody escapes [the opposites of] pain and pleasure as long as he functions physiologically.[67]

Besides, consciousness—so highly valued by the Buddha and by Jung—makes distinctions. By definition, it "discriminates, judges, analyzes, and emphasizes the contradictions" for our benefit.[68] It may even be that a clash of the moral opposites, "good and evil," is what we need to instigate a new step in psychological development. Individuation often begins under the goad of a painful "conflict of duties"—when a decision either way would be wrong and right (abortion is an example; divorce may be another).

Nevertheless, Tārā is surely correct that the opposites are an occasion for unwarranted attachment. This occurs when a person "identifies" with one side of a pair of opposites either due to denial of the other side or due to ignorance that the pair even exists. Jung writes:

> A *conscious* capacity for one-sidedness is a sign of the highest culture, but involuntary one-sidedness, i.e., the inability to be anything but one-sided, is a sign of barbarism. . . . losing sight of his total personality is a great and constant danger.[69]

---

[66] Edinger, *Mysterium*, 11-12.
[67] Jung, *Letters* 2:303.
[68] Jung, *Jung Speaking*, 420.
[69] Jung, *CW* 6, par. 346. Jung's italics.

It follows that "nonduality" is a powerful symbol for psychological "wholeness" even if impossible to achieve as the Buddhists imagine. This means that instead of identifying with being male or female, being right or wrong, a Democrat or a Republican, a Jungian or a Freudian, and on and on, we can take the position that fits who we are authentically—while knowing that its opposite has some kind of merit in some form for someone else. In fact, we can probably find it in our own unconscious.

In this way the "problem of opposites" becomes a "play of opposites." It would be the symbolic meaning of Avalokiteśvara's transgender and his manifestation as Tārā. This "male-female" pair of Bodhisattvas, then, is archetypal imagery encouraging us to be all that we actually are—consciously.

Celestial Buddhas and Pure Lands

Akṣobhya

Deep into the *Aṣṭa*, we witness a miracle:

> Thereupon the Lord on that occasion exercised His wonderworking power. The entire assembly—monks, nuns, laymen and laywomen, Gods, Nagas, Yakshas, Gandharvas, Asuras, Garudas, Kinnaras, Mahoragas, men and ghosts—they all, through the Buddha's might, saw the Tathagata Akshobhya surrounded by the congregation of monks, accompanied by a retinue of Bodhisattvas demonstrating dharma, in an assembly which was vast like the ocean . . . . Thereupon the Lord again withdrew his wonderworking power. The Lord Akshobhya, the Tathagata, then no longer appeared . . . .[70]

Using his "wonderworking" *ṛddhi*, Śākyamuni Buddha induced a vision for his devotees—who were gathered on Vulture Peak outside the city of Rājagṛha—of another world-system millions of world-systems away. There, an Enlightened Buddha named Akṣobhya was teaching his own retinue of Bodhisattva devotees. Everyone already knew that the universe was extremely vast, with "galaxies" in all directions; and all had heard of Buddhas in the past and of many more to come in the future. But no one knew until now that some of these other worlds were "Buddha-fields" (*buddha-kṣetra*) with their own living Buddhas teaching in the present. It was a great and consequential revelation.

Gautama's congregation was actually looking toward a region in the "east." Had they looked "west," they would have seen yet another Buddha, Amitābha; toward the "north," Amoghasiddhi; toward the south, Ratnasambhava. But then, according to Mahāyāna Buddhism, there are living Buddhas in all ten directions—these four cardinal directions, the four intermediate ones, and the zenith and nadir. Moreover, these four named Buddhas merely stand in for the plethora of other Buddhas, as many as there are "sands in the Ganges."

Scholars call them "Celestial Buddhas"—surrounded by worshipful "Celestial Bodhisattvas"—since they are far off somewhere, as vaguely far off as our "Heaven." But they are not in heavens,

---

[70] Conze, *Eight Thousand*, 28.4.

technically, since their Buddha-fields contain heavens in a typically tripartite world, while these Buddhas themselves teach on their earths. Nevertheless, these other "earths" have something divine about them and are no doubt modeled on the heavens we have already seen in Buddhist cosmology.

In the *Akṣobhya-vyūha Sūtra* ("Sermon on the Display of Akṣobya"), composed perhaps as early as the first century CE, we find this Lord Akṣobhya ("imperturbable") sitting under a Tree of great height:

> Around the bodhi-tree are rows of palm trees and jasmine trees, which in the gentle breeze, gave forth a harmonious and elegant sound surpassing all worldly music. . . . The ground is as flat as a palm and the color of gold, with no gullies, brambles, or gravel; it is as soft as cotton, sinking as soon as one's foot steps on it and returning to its original state as soon as the foot is lifted.[71]

It is not clear why "flatness" should be emphasized, not to mention the memory-foam feature of the ground. Nattier thinks it may be an Iranian religious influence—contradicting India's usual positive associations to mountains, like Meru and Vulture's Peak.[72] But the point is clear: this Buddha-world is ideal, worthy of its name, Abhirati ("delightful"). Accordingly, there are only two Destinies in Abhirati, that of gods and humans. Nor is there any suffering, any ugliness, while everyone tends to perform good deeds.

It follows that this Buddha-field is an ideal location for treading the Buddhist Path. Paul Williams writes: "In fact, the principal purpose of being reborn in Abhirati is to follow the Buddhist path in the presence of Akṣobhya, under optimum facilities for spiritual growth."[73]

Amitābha

Chinese Buddhists call these other world-systems, with their resident Buddhas, "Pure Lands"—although the term does not appear in Indian materials. Still, it is true that these "Buddha-fields" are purer, freer from defilements and other obstacles to spiritual growth, than our own world of woe. Scholars, therefore, have adopted the term when writing about this style of Buddhism. But there are degrees of purity—and the world called Sukhāvatī ("blissful") toward the "west" is the purest of all. In one of two *Sukhāvatīvyūha Sūtras* ("Sermons on the Display of the Land of Bliss"), both composed in the third century CE, Śākyamuni speaks to Ānanda of the Buddha present there:

> Ānanda, this tathagata has not passed away, nor is he yet to come; rather, this tathagata, having awakened to unsurpassable, perfect, full awakening, at this very moment lives to the west of us, in a buddha-field that is one hundred thousand million trillion buddha-fields away from where we are, in the world system called the Land of Bliss; and his name is Amitabha, that is, Measureless Light. He remains

[71] Paul Williams, *Mahāyāna Buddhism* (London: Routledge, 1989), 244.

[72] Jan Nattier, "The Realm of Akṣobhya: A Missing Piece in the History of Pure Land Buddhism," *Journal of the International Association of Buddhist Studies* 23, no. 1 (2000): 81n.

[73] Williams, *Mahāyāna*, 245.

> there, and even now continues to teach the Dharma in that field. This tathagata, arhat, full buddha is surrounded and honored by innumerable bodhisattvas and by an endless retinue of disciples, and presides over a Buddha-field adorned with the most perfect qualities.[74]

These perfect qualities include "jewel trees" made of gold, silver, emerald, etc. The ground is "carpeted in every direction with lotus flowers" that are leagues in diameter and also made of jewels. The boundless Indian imagination itself is on display:

> And from each jewel lotus issue in every direction thirty-six thousand million rays of light. And from the tip of each of these rays of light emerge thirty-six hundred thousand million buddhas, with bodies of golden color, possessed of the thirty-two marks of the superior human being. Each one of them goes to measureless, countless world systems in the eastern region of the universe[75]

—in order to teach. In Pure Land Buddhism, the entire universe is crackling with divinity (see Figure 11.4).

Figure 11.4 Amitābha in Sukhāvatī

[74] Luis O. Gómez, trans., *The Land of Bliss: The Paradise of the Buddha of Measureless Light* (Honolulu: University of Hawai'i Press, 1996), 80.

[75] Gómez, *Land of Bliss*, 85.

Rebirth in a Pure Land

But why go on in this way to a congregation residing in Magadha? The answer is that our Buddha, Gautama, is encouraging—out of his compassion—those gathered to make a special vow to be reborn in their next lifetime in some pure Buddha-field to reach their ultimate religious goal of Buddhahood more easily, more quickly. The *Akṣobhyavyūha* says this is entirely possible provided one practices traditional Buddhism, cultivates the Perfections—and, then, "dedicates" or intentionally directs the merit gained thereby to rebirth in Abhirati.

The *Sukāvatīvyūha* says it is actually easier than that. As the Bodhisattva (who became Amitābha Buddha) put it a very long time ago:

> may I not awaken to unsurpassable, perfect, full awakening if, after I attain awakening, living beings in unlimited, countless numbers of buddha-fields will hear my name, will set their minds on being reborn in my buddha-field and dedicate their roots of merit to rebirth in it, and yet not be reborn in my buddha-field. And this will be true even if they have made the resolution only ten times—except in the case of those who have committed the five offenses entailing immediate retribution and of those who are hindered by their own opposition to the Good Dharma.[76]

In other words, if one merely hears the holy name "Amitābha" and, inspired thereby, resolves just ten times mentally or in recitation to be reborn in Sukhāvatī—and has not committed any of the five "Great Sins" (patricide, matricide, etc.)—then a Pure Land rebirth is assured.

Elsewhere in this scripture, we learn of persons "bringing to mind the Tathagata, envisioning him again and again" and "vowing to be reborn" in Amitābha's Buddha-field:

> When the time of their death approaches, the Tathagata, Arhat, the perfectly and fully awakened Amitabha will stand before these living beings, and he will appear surrounded and honored by a host of countless monks. Thereupon, having seen the Blessed One, their thoughts will only be thoughts of serene trust, and forthwith they will be reborn in the Land of Bliss.[77]

How extraordinary! The Lord of a Buddha-field trillions of worlds away from here will show up at the deathbed of a pious person to escort him or her to Paradise. Indeed, at the very least, if that devotee has managed to "bring to mind this tathagata in only one moment of thought," that merciful Celestial Buddha will appear at the time of death in a dream. Luis Gómez, the translator of these materials, says that at some point the "core of the practice" became calling on the name of the Lord—probably, in Sanskrit, *namo amitābhāya buddhāya* ("Homage to Amitābha Buddha").[78] What could be easier than that?

---

[76] Gómez, *Land of Bliss*, 71

[77] Gómez, *Land of Bliss*, 92.

[78] Gómez, *Land of Bliss*, 138.

It is often said that "Pure Land" Mahāyāna Buddhism is radically different from the Buddhism that went before. Gómez himself remarks that these scriptures are "moving away from traditional notions":

> First, most obviously, and supported by a large body of Mahayana literature, it is moving away from the goal of liberation attained in this world towards the hope of salvation in a blissful paradise. Second, it is moving away from a tradition of self-cultivation in the path of the bodhisattva to a tradition of hope in the saving grace of buddhas and bodhisattvas.[79]

In fact, the *Kāraṇḍavyūha* scripture makes an unexpected promise:

> You will no longer continue in saṃsāra. You will never again see birth, aging, sickness, and death. You will not be separated from that which is beloved and pleasant, and you will not encounter that which is disliked. You will go, noble son, to the realm of Sukhāvatī. You will hear the Dharma from Tathāgata Amitābha.[80]

This text is equating leaving this Buddha-field for a purer one with freedom from Saṃsāra—even though, technically, one would still be within the universe of numberless world-systems. The claim is illogical yet not in the least pessimistic—as Buddhism is sometimes considered to be—but so hopeful! As optimistic as the promise of Paradise to a Christian or a Muslim after death.

Face-to-Face with the Lord

Even greater "accessibility" to a Celestial Buddha appears in the Mahāyāna as early as the first century CE—as announced by the *Pratyutpanna-buddha-saṃmukhāvasthita-samādhi Sūtra* ("Sermon on the Samādhi of One Who Stands Face-to-Face With the Present Buddhas"). Translating from the Tibetan, Paul Harrison demonstrates that the featured *samādhi* derives from the Early Buddhist meditation called, "Recollection of the Buddha." We read:

> a bodhisattva, whether he is a householder or one who has gone forth, when he has gone alone to a secluded place and seated himself, after concentrating on the Tathāgata, Arhat, Samyaksaṃbuddha Amitāyus [another name for Amitābha] in accordance with what he has heard, then faultless in the mass of the precepts and undistracted in mindfulness should he concentrate for one day and night, for two, three, four, five, six, or seven days and nights. If he concentrates on the Tathāgata Amitāyus with undistracted thought for seven days and nights, then when seven days and nights have elapsed he shall see the Lord, the Tathāgata Amitāyus. If he

[79] Gómez, *Land of Bliss*, 37-38.
[80] Roberts, *The Basket's Display*, 69-70.

> does not see that Lord by day, then in a dream while sleeping the face of the Lord, the Tathāgata Amitāyus will appear.[81]

This scripture explains that the practitioner not only "sees" the Lord within seven days of intense concentration but "hears" the Dharma: "Having heard their exposition he accepts, masters, and retains those Dharmas. . . . After he has emerged from that *samādhi*, that bodhisattva also expounds widely to others those Dharmas as he has heard, retained and mastered them."

Harrison comments:

> What we have here is in all probability a justification in advance (if not also retrospectively) for the sudden appearance of Mahāyāna sūtras . . . It involves rather the proposition that meditation is a legitimate means whereby the eternal Buddha-principle may continue to reveal religious truths to those fit to receive them, and thus it throws an interesting light on the composition of Mahāyāna sūtras in general."[82]

The "interesting light" is that continuing revelation comes from visions induced by *samādhi*, wherein one not only sees Buddhas but hears new teaching. The scripture adds that the visionary even has the opportunity to ask questions: "Having seen them he asks them questions, and is gladdened by the elucidation of those questions."[83]

Let us note that these materials are softening the Buddhist attitude toward dreams. They are no longer just a metaphor for illusion (although the metaphor persists), nor are they merely premonitory as an augury, but instead a means to come "face-to-face" with the Divine. This ancient text anticipates active imagination in Jungian psychology; it justifies, from a religious perspective, paying attention to one's dreams to stay in touch with the Sacred.

Trikāya

Mahāyānist thinkers—especially those in the Yogācāra school of philosophy that we will discuss in another chapter—felt the need to systematize some of the new teaching. That would lead to a classic Buddhist doctrine of the "Three Bodies" (*tri-kāya*) of the Buddha or, more abstractly, of Buddhahood. It begins with the fact that the historical Gautama Buddha had a physical or "form" body (a *rūpa-kāya*) but one that was generally viewed unfavorably, as a disgusting reality from which one needed to become detached. Nevertheless, the Lord's body also possessed Thirty-two Marks of marvelous quality along with the ability to produce out of this physical body a mental body "made of mind" (a *mano-maya-kāya*) for travel to the heavens, in order to teach gods.

---

[81] Paul M. Harrison, "Buddhānusmṛti in the *Pratyutpannabuddhasaṃmukkhāvasthitasamādhi-sūtra*," in Paul Williams, ed., *Buddhism: Critical Concepts in Religious Studies*, vol. 3 (London: Routledge, 2005), 91-92.

[82] Harrison, "Buddhānusmṛti," 104.

[83] Harrison, "Buddhānusmṛti," 95.

There is in this distinction a nascent "two-body" theory of the Buddha that the early schismatic Mahāsāṃghikas began to exploit. Among them were *lokottaravādins* ("followers of the supramundane view") who said that beings like Gautama Buddha were not quite real:

> They wash their feet, but no dust ever adheres to them, and their feet are like lotus-leaves: this is mere conformity. . . . they take nourishment, but hunger does not distress them. . . . Even though the body of the Sugata is not the result of sexual union, the Buddhas mention their mothers and fathers: this is mere conformity . . . . the very odor of their excrement surpasses all perfumes. . . . they have never resided in the world of men.[84]

The Buddha was here, they said, but not really here—he was merely a *nirmāṇa* ("creation, magical creation; emanation"). In the history of religions, this is a "docetic" development (from the Greek, *dokesis*, "appearance"). We see it among early Christian Gnostics who said Jesus the Christ ate food but did not need to defecate; his body was crucified, but he never actually suffered. The Early Church declared that line of thinking heresy.

Buddhists also held the notion of a "Teaching body" (*dharma-kāya*). Gautama had consoled his grieving disciples in the *Dīgha Nikāya* that there would always be his Dharma as the "Teacher" among them. This seems originally to be a metaphor for the collection or "corpus" of what he taught. But rather quickly—especially under the influence of the "Recollection of the Buddha" meditation—this "Body of his Teaching" became known as the "Body of his virtuous *dharmas*," i.e., the Lord's real extraordinary qualities. Har Dayal writes of the consequence for Mahāyāna thought:

> If the fragile and limited *rūpa-kāya* is not the real Buddha, what and who is the Buddha? In contradistinction to the *rūpa-kāya*, the Mahāyānists speak of a Buddha's *dharma-kāya*, which is his real Body. . . . This Body, which is also called *sad-dharma-kāya*, *bodhi-kāya*, *buddha-kāya*, *prajñā-kāya*, *svābhāvika-kāya* . . . is invisible and universal. It is imperishable and perfectly pure. All beings "live and move and have their being in it."[85]

This sounds like God. Jan Nattier comments that the Dharma-kāya is a "transcendent, almost Brahman-like force"—of the kind we find in the Upaniṣads that is also called "Ātman."[86] Here, then, is a dramatically new kind of "two-body" theory: 1) an incomprehensible, ineffable Dharma-kāya capable of "emanating" 2) Nirmāṇa-kāya magical creations into our midst for our salvation. The *Pratyutpanna* could say this was continuing revelation heard in *samādhi*.

But what are we to make of those Celestial Buddhas who are more numerous than the sands of the Ganges and teaching in their respective Buddha-fields? They, too, are considered "emanations" (*nirmāṇa*) of the Dharma-kāya but of a distinct kind called 3) "Enjoyment Bodies" (*saṃbhoga-*

---

[84] Lamotte, *History*, 624-625.

[85] Dayal, *Bodhisattva Doctrine*, 27.

[86] Nattier, *Few Good Men*, 177.

kāyas). Their primary purpose is to instruct irreversible Celestial Bodhisattvas "enjoying" their Presence in ideal worlds. And, in a refinement of doctrine, it is really they who possess the "Thirty-two Marks" and not the bodies of so-called historical Buddhas engaged in teaching ordinary human beings and transmigrating gods.

That Akṣobhya, Amitābha, and the others in far-off Buddha-fields are not really "Real" is necessarily the case since—despite what some scriptures imply—their fields of influence remain inside Saṃsāra; and they have yet to experience complete *pari-nirvāṇa*. True, Amitābha ("Measureless Light") is called Amitāyus ("Measureless Life") and seems to be capable of living forever. Even Śākyamuni hinted to Ānanda that he could live an enormously long time if only asked. But countless aeons of time is not eternity. So each Celestial Buddha must die one more time in order to become an "Incomparably Perfect Complete Buddha"—equivalent to the Dharma-kāya that emanates from itself both Saṃbhoga-kāyas and Nirmāṇa-kāyas for the sake of the suffering and unenlightened world. In this way, Mahāyāna Buddhism arrived at its classic theory of the "Three Bodies" (*trikāya*) of the Buddha.

Incidentally, the Celestial Bodhisattva Avalokiteśvara is currently serving the Celestial Buddha Amitābha in Sukhāvatī, and it is he who will succeed Amitābha when he enters Parinirvāṇa as a Dharma-kāya.

Closing Jungian thoughts When Jung wrote his essay, "A Psychological Approach to the Dogma of the Trinity," he began by reviewing "threefold" symbols of divinity elsewhere—triads in Babylon and ancient Egypt, even the symbolism of the number "three" that Pythagoras considered sacred.[87] Had he wished, he could have added commentary on Hinduism's Brahman as a three-formed "Trimūrti" and, of course, Buddhism's "Trikāya."[88] They are all, in Jung's view, particular manifestations of a universal archetype of "Threeness" having an unconscious influence on matters of profound significance.

Even Freud could not avoid structuring his psychology in this way: as ego, superego, and Id. Jung's psychology is similarly threefold: consciousness, personal unconscious, collective unconscious. Jung writes:

> The archetype *an sich*, as I have explained elsewhere, is an "irrepresentable" factor, a "disposition" which starts functioning at a given moment in the development of the human mind and arranges the material of consciousness into definite patterns. That is to say, man's concepts of God are organized into triads and trinities, and a whole host of ritualistic and magical practices take on a triple or trichotomous character, as in the case of thrice-repeated apotropaic spells . . . . Wherever we find it, the archetype has a compelling force which it derives from the unconscious, and whenever its effect becomes conscious it has a distinctly numinous quality.

[87] Jung, *CW* 11, pars. 169f.

[88] See Elder, *Snake and the Rope*, 195.

It is this numinous, sacred quality that causes a doctrine like the Christian Trinity to "stick" for centuries even though irrational. It is why Buddhists felt compelled to articulate a Three-body theory with which the mind can scarcely keep pace or that one may feel is merely contrived. An archetype insisted upon this theological formulation.

Jung made an effort to understand the Trikāya when encountering it in a Tibetan Buddhist text. Its translator had provided him with the sentence: "Therefore the *Trikāya* is the All-Enlightened Mind itself." And Jung comments:

> Put into psychological language, the above sentence could be paraphrased thus: The unconscious is the root of all experience of oneness (*dharmakāya*), the matrix of all archetypes or structural patterns (*sambhogkāya*), and the *conditio sine qua non* of the phenomenal world (*nirmāṇakāya*).[89]

This means that:

1) the "Dharma-kāya," symbolizes, in Jungian terms, the collective unconscious or archetypal psyche *an sich*—the "thing in itself," as Kant put it, that we cannot know directly. Indeed, Buddhists speak of a sacred Something that is incomprehensible and ineffable. We can, however, surmise its existence from its own manifestations or "emanations."

2) They are the archetypal symbols—"archetypes or structural patterns"—that we can know directly or, at least, see in our profounder dreams and visions. We see them in the many religions. And it is that level of psychic reality we find expressed in Buddhism as the "Sambhoga-kāya in a Pure Land."

3) Jung, then, associates the "Nirmāṇa-kāya" with the "phenomenal world." That sounds like the external world of phenomena. Let us take it instead as the phenomenal ego—that is also a manifestation of the unconscious. Indeed, egoity does have something docetic or "illusory" about it, especially when it pretends to be more than it really is.

As mentioned, however, the Roman Catholic Church denounced Docetism as heresy and insisted upon Jesus' having a "real body." Edinger takes that to mean "real ego" and comments:

> The whole Western tradition then has built into it, in its mythology, an importance to the ego that the Eastern tradition does not grant.[90]

By "Eastern tradition," he means the Eastern Orthodox Church as opposed to the Roman Church. But he could have meant Eastern religions in general that are not as careful about granting the ego the "importance" of incarnating or humanizing the Self in everyday life. Still, both mythologies—East and West, the Trikāya and the Trinity—inform us that the psyche is sacred throughout, that it is so in degrees, and that the ego is included in the divine drama.

---

[89] Jung, *CW* 11, par. 790.

[90] Ediinger, *New God-Image*, 99.

Chapter 12
"GREAT VEHICLE" (CONTINUED)

"Lotus Sūtra"

Studying Buddhism, even just Indian Buddhism, is quite different from studying a major Western religion because the canon of scriptures is so large. The Early Buddhist canon requires several large volumes, while the Mahāyāna collection of scriptures is actually vast. A standard Chinese Buddhist canon, for example, runs to a hundred volumes of a thousand pages each. Thus, Paul Harrison writes:

> Even when it was fully extant, it is unlikely that many Buddhists ever knew their canon in its entirety, as a Muslim might know the Qur'an or a Christian the Bible. The Buddhist scriptures are simply too extensive, so that most members of the order would have been familiar with and used only a small number of them, a functional partial canon as opposed to an ideal complete one.[1]

As a consequence, modern scholarship itself has focused on a "functional partial canon" of Buddhist materials—distorting the total picture, whatever that may be.

This is not just because the Buddhists did so but because doing otherwise has been technically difficult. Much of what is included as Mahāyāna has yet to be edited accurately, then translated accurately. A Sanskrit text may no longer exist and be available only in an early Chinese or Tibetan translation—raising questions of fidelity to the original. It is also true that the "cult of the book"—with its focus on a particular text—made it not quite necessary to know many other scriptures than what one worshipped, recited, copied. With all that in mind, let us now look at three scriptures that have received a great deal of attention by Buddhists and modern writers.

From a very early date, the *Saddharma-puṇḍarīka Sūtra* ("*Lotus Sūtra*," for short) became a focus for the study of Mahāyāna Buddhism. In 1837, a Sanskrit manuscript of this text arrived in Paris—sent by an enterprising official of the British East India Company in Nepal—and was examined by a brilliant young scholar named Eugène Burnouf. Burnouf would write back to his benefactor:

> I have without reserve devoted every moment that I could steal from my occupations as professor of Sanskrit and academician to this work, of which I have already read rather considerable portions. You will not be astonished that I did not understand everything; the material is very new for me, the style as well

[1] Paul Harrison, "Canon," *EB* 1:113.

> as the content. . . . Without being impious (but you are not a clergyman), I know of nothing so Christian in all of Asia. Brahmanism now seems to me a rigid and merciless Judaism; you have found moral Christianity, full of compassion for all creatures. . . . Finally, I confess to you that I am passionate about this reading, and that I would like to have more time and health to attend to it day and night.[2]

A child of the French Enlightenment and no friend of organized religion, Burnouf was yet gripped by the *Lotus* and would complete a translation in French in two years' time.

Eventually, several translations in English would appear. I will use that of Leon Hurvitz for its readability and, by all accounts, its accuracy.[3] Although rendered from a fifth century Chinese translation—of which there were several, due to its popularity in China—this *Lotus* takes account of an extant Sanskrit original, the core of which may have been composed in India as early as 100 BCE. It grew over time until reaching its final form in the third century CE.

The title may be translated as follows: *sad-* ("true, real") *dharma-* ("teaching, law") *puṇḍarīka-* ("lotus, white lotus") *sūtra* ("sermon"): "Sermon on the Lotus of the True Dharma." Or, as Hurvitz prefers: "Scripture of the Lotus Blossom of the Fine Dharma." As with the *Aṣṭasāhasrikā-prajñāpāramitā*, this scripture claims it was taught by Gautama Buddha himself in the fifth century BCE. Further, it claims to be a "true teaching"—as distinct from that of other religions and, also, from other forms of Buddhism. The pejorative term "Hīnayāna" and self-congratulating term "Mahāyāna" now appear in the text itself. As in the Pure Land materials we have just seen, there are a multitude of Bodhisattvas—both earthly and Celestial—and not only an earthly Śākyamuni as Teacher of the text but also countless Celestial Buddhas teaching, always and everywhere, in their countless Buddha-fields.

Like the "Perfection of Wisdom" genre, this scripture praises itself for all the benefits its devotees will reap and damns those who would question its authenticity. And, yes, we hear of the perfect Wisdom that "all *dharmas* are empty," a special knowledge that must be united with Compassion (reminding Burnouf of Christian Love).Yet, as Hurvitz puts it: "All the same, the *Lotus*'s references to 'emptiness,' if laid end to end, would not amount to much."[4] Likewise, paradoxical language is present but not emphasized.

Instead, the *Lotus Sūtra* is a very early example of Buddhist literature willing to speak positively of the religious life, of what one is reaching—and not just negatively of what one is letting go. The scholar Carolyn Rhys Davids (unlike her husband, T. W. Rhys Davids), criticized that apophatic feature of Early Buddhism, saying that: "there is an amazingly small number of positive terms, but there is an abundance of negative terms"—as if the good life can be entirely "resolved in birth and dying, and the thing to make cease was the being reborn and the being redead."[5] She was reminded of those Greek soldiers in the ancient classics who had wandered bereft through hostile Anatolia to reach the sea—and a way home—exclaiming famously at the shoreline, "The sea! The sea!" They did not shout, she points out, "No more land!" As we shall soon discover, the Buddhas and the Bodhisattvas will now preach the "Sea."

---

[2] Donald S. Lopez, Jr., *The "Lotus Sūtra": A Biography* (Princeton: Princeton University Press, 2016), 126-127.

[3] Hurvitz, *Lotus Blossom*.

[4] Hurvitz, *Lotus Blossom*, xxiii.

[5] C. A. F. Rhys Davids, "Buddhism and the Negative," *Journal of the Pali Text Society* 8 (1924-1927): 239, 248.

They will often do that by using religious fantasy—someone has called it "phantasmagoria"—that continues to play havoc with discursive thinking yet also captures one's feeling, touches the soul. There are even passages in the *Lotus* that suggest we have souls, something that Early Buddhism tried to avoid. A new kataphatic strategy in this scripture is to tell "stories," with all their suggestive allusions—relying upon the listener or reader to catch the meaning.

This is actually what captivated Burnouf. He had skimmed the *Aṣṭa* and wondered, "But what is this *prajñā* itself?"[6] In the *Lotus*, however, he found parables; and that reminded him of the parables of Jesus. This helps explain why the *Saddharmapuṇḍarīka Sūtra* became the most influential Buddhist scripture in East Asia, why there would be movements in China and Japan claiming it was the only true scripture in all of Buddhism, why even today millions chant its title (in Japanese, *Namu myōhō renge kyō*) to find worldly success, long life, Enlightenment. There are copies in Chinese in which "each of the *Lotus Sūtra*'s 69,384 characters has been drawn seated on a lotus or within a *stūpa*, thereby expressing the conviction that 'each character of the *Lotus* is a living buddha.'"[7]

We do not know this scripture's actual fate in ancient India—a history that remains obscure—but it calls itself, "White Lotus Blossom," a floral symbol that had long served Buddhism. It was an epithet of Gautama's Mother and the "Mother" of all Buddhas, a symbol for the religion itself.

Introduction

The scripture opens:

> Thus have I heard. At one time, the Buddha was dwelling in the city of Rājagṛha, on Vulture Peak, together with twelve thousand great *bhikṣus*. All were *arhants*, their outflows already exhausted . . . . Their names were . . . [twenty-two are listed, many of them familiar such as Mahākāśyapa, Śāriputra, Ānanda, etc.]. There were also another two thousand persons, including those who had more to learn and those who had not. There was Mahāprajāpati, the *bhikṣuṇī*, together with six thousand followers. Rāhula's mother Yaśodharā, the *bhikṣuṇī*, was also there together with her followers. There were eighty thousand *bodhisattva-mahāsattvas*, all nonbacksliders [at least, Eighth Stage on the Bodhisattva Path] in *anuttarasamyaksaṃbodhi* ["Incomparable Perfect Complete Enlightenment"] . . . . Their names were. . . [eighteen great Bodhisattvas are named, many of them familiar such as Mañjuśrī, Avalokiteśvara, Maitreya, etc.].[8] (1-2)

It is already crowded on the top of a medium-sized mountain outside the capital city of Magadha. Yet the assembled multitude is soon joined by tens of thousands of gods along with supernatural beings such as *nāgas*, *yakṣas*, *garuḍas*—themselves joined by "several hundreds of thousands" of

---

6 Lopez, *Lotus*, 125.

7 Jacqueline I. Stone, "Lotus Sūtra," *EB* 1:474.

8 To avoid cumbersome citation, I will use page numbers of Hurvitz, *Lotus Blossom*, in the body of my text. I have also altered this passage slightly to fit my book's style—and will take that liberty elsewhere.

human beings, including king Ajātaśatru and his retinue. They all make obeisance to the Buddha's feet, we are told, and somehow all sit to one side.

Little wonder that some Chinese Buddhist exegetes considered the possibility that "Vulture Peak" was only apparently a mountain and, instead, a miraculous Pure Land where anything can happen. Nichiren preached in thirteenth-century Japan that anyone who chanted the title of the *Lotus Sūtra* was, in fact, on "Vulture Peak" with the Buddha.

We then learn that the "World-Honored One" preached a sermon—appropriately named, "Immeasurable Doctrine"—whereupon he crossed his legs and entered into *samādhi*, "where his body and mind were motionless." Flowers fell from heaven, the world trembled in six different ways, and the impossibly large audience "felt that this had never happened before, and, joyously joining palms, single-mindedly they beheld the Buddha." In other words, they, too, entered *samādhi*—and experienced the following:

> At that time the Buddha emitted a glow from the tuft of white hair between his brows that illuminated eighteen thousand worlds to the east, omitting none of them, reaching downward as far as the Avīci hell and upward as far as the Akaniṣṭha gods. In these worlds there could be fully seen the six kinds of living beings in those lands. There could also be seen the Buddhas present in those lands, and the *sūtradharmas* preached by those Buddhas could be heard. (4)

The entire universe (at least, "to the east") has been made visible by a light ray emanating from one of the Thirty-two Marks on the Lord's body. Technically, according to Trikāya doctrine, a Nirmāṇa-kāya cannot perform that feat—only a Saṃbhoga-kāya—but this is early Mahāyāna, and there is no consistency even later.

The Bodhisattva Maitreya, who had come from Tuṣita, asked the wise Bodhisattva Mañjuśrī the meaning of the miracle. Mañjuśrī answered that he had seen it all before—"incalculable, numberless kalpas ago"—when a previous Buddha, just before his death, had preached his final and most important sermon, the *Saddharmapuṇḍarīka*. And so he concluded that would happen again. He also recalled that the disciples of that Lord were grieved at their master's impending Parinirvāṇa. This is that same religious crisis we saw in Early Buddhist *Digha Nikāya* at the death of Gautama Buddha.

The *Lotus Sūtra* proceeds to offer new solutions to the crisis. One is to announce a saving succession of Buddhas. A former Buddha promises in verse:

> "When I cross to extinction,
> Have neither care nor fear,
> For this bodhisattva, Womb of Excellence,
> . . . .
> He shall next become a Buddha
> Named Pure Body;
> He, too, shall save an incalculable multitude." (19)

That solution would make sense even to assembled disciples since past Buddhas were succeeded eventually by other Buddhas.

Much later in the text, however, we hear a different solution. Śākyamuni Buddha says that after preaching this last sermon and dying: "After my extinction . . . I will become a Buddha in another realm, having again a different name"—continuing to teach in that other Buddha-field so that sentient beings will have the opportunity to hear marvelous truth (147). In other words, he will succeed *himself* elsewhere and remain available, at least distantly.

Deeper still into the text, the Lord confesses a final new truth, namely, that is he not going to be succeeded by another nor is he going to succeed himself but he is actually "enduring, never perishing"—eternally teaching at all times and everywhere for the sake of the salvation of everyone. The scripture reads:

> For a hundred thousand myriads of millions of *nayutas* of *asaṃkhyeya-kalpas* ["incalculable *kalpas*" of time] I have been constantly dwelling in this Sahā ["enduring," i.e, here] world-sphere, preaching the Dharma, teaching and converting; also elsewhere, in a hundred thousand myriads of millions of *nayutas* of *asaṃkhyeyas* of realms I have been guiding and benefitting the beings. . . . My life-span is incalculable *asaṃkhyeyakalpas*, ever enduring, never perishing . . . . Yet even now, though in reality I am not to pass into extinction, yet I proclaim that I am about to accept extinction. (238-239)

While that final thought sounds like a paradox—drawing us into the world of the *Aṣṭa*—we can interpret it in light of the developed Trikāya doctrine. This Teacher who calls himself "Śākyamuni" is actually a Nirmāṇa-kāya pretending to be a "human being" in order to teach humans (a compassionate strategy). In this illusory but effective form he says that he will soon be "gone," in order to instill a religious urgency in his audience. As a Dharma-kāya, however, he will in reality never pass into extinction—since eternal.

Miracle of the Stūpa

The Indian mind has a great capacity for hyperbole. And so the religious drama continues in chapter eleven with the "Apparition of the Jeweled Stūpa":

> At that time, there appeared before the Buddha a seven-jeweled *stūpa*, five hundred *yojanas* in height and two hundred and fifty *yojanas* in breadth, welling up out of the earth and resting in mid-air, set about with sundry precious objects. (183)

Lopez tells us that, judging from the unit of distance called a *yojana*, this "massive *stūpa* is four thousand miles high and two thousand miles wide"—lest we think we can imagine its size as it hovers there.[9] The text does not say why this bejeweled structure arrives from under the earth, but

---

9 Donald S. Lopez, Jr., and Jacqueline I. Stone, *Two Buddhas: Seated Side by Side* (Princeton: Princeton University Press, 2019), 138.

things past are often "down" in Indian symbolism, while things in the future are "up."[10] And that fits what happens next:

> At that time, from the midst of the jeweled *stūpa* issued forth the sound of a mighty voice, praising and saying, "How excellent! How excellent, O Śākyamuni, O World-Honored One, that with great undifferentiating wisdom you can teach the Bodhisattva-dharma, that you can preach to the great multitude the *Scripture of the Blossom of the Fine Dharma*, which Buddhas keep protectively in mind!

We learn that the voice belongs to a long-deceased Buddha named Prabhūtaratna ("Many Jewels"). He had vowed even as a Bodhisattva that, whenever the *Lotus Sūtra* was preached, he would appear to "bear witness to it by praising it, saying, 'Excellent.'" But that meant—so the audience of the text suddenly realizes—that Prabhūtaratna was not really dead!

It meant what we already know, that a Buddha who has passed into Nirvāṇa has not really passed into Nirvāṇa—giving new meaning to the notion of a Nirvāṇa of "no fixed abode" that we found in the *Aṣṭa.* It meant what we concluded about *stūpa* worship: that the relic remains of a deceased Buddha housed in a funerary mound—however beautifully designed with gateways and sculpted reliefs—were not what they seemed to be. Instead, as the Lord of the *Lotus Sūtra* explains: "Within this jeweled *stūpa* is the whole body [and not just the cremated remains] of a Thus Come One." Now every Buddhist could know why circumambulating the monuments at Sāñcī and at Bhārhut felt like the right thing to do despite being told, by more conservative teachers, that the Buddha was beyond worship or communication.

Richard Gombrich discovered this same tension in his anthropological study of current conservative Theravāda Buddhism in Sri Lanka, as summarized by Harvey: "while, *cognitively*, the Buddha is acknowledged as beyond worldly contact, *affectively*, at the level of feelings, he is often looked on as a living source of benefit."[11]

Eager to confirm what they now know and always felt, the Buddha's devotees request that the Teacher open the Jeweled Stūpa. So the Lord rises into the air:

> Thereupon with his right finger Śākyamunibuddha opened the door of the seven-jeweled *stūpa*, which made a great sound as of a bar being pushed aside to open the gate of a walled city. At that very moment all the assembled multitude saw the Thus Come One Many Jewels in the jeweled *stūpa*, seated on a lion throne, his body whole and undecayed, as if entered into Dhyāna-concentration. (187)

Then, in one of the great moments of Mahāyāna Buddhism, Śākyamuni Buddha joined Prabhūtaratna Buddha to share the same seat.

---

[10] John S. Strong, *Relics of the Buddha* (Delhi: Motilal Banarsidass Publishers, 2004), 36.

[11] Peter Harvey, "Portrayals of Ultimate Reality and of Holy and Divine Beings," in *Buddhism*, ed. Peter Harvey (London: Continuum, 2001), 104.

Figure 12.1 Two Buddhas on One Diamond Seat

But this was not supposed to happen! The Early Buddhist *Majjhima Nikāya* had been explicit: "It is impossible, it cannot happen that two Accomplished Ones, Fully Enlightened Ones, could arise contemporaneously in one world-system—there is no such possibility."[12] And that is because this Sahā world would be "shattered" by the numinous impact. It is why Pure Land Buddhism had to keep the Buddha-fields at great distances from each other. Yet Asian art would faithfully record this unexpected and surprisingly benign event in sculpture and painting.

See Figure 12.1 for a sixth century Chinese gilded bronze of the two Lords surrounded by mandorlas of Wisdom "Fire," with bodies elongated to indicate their transcendence, yet sitting in *lalita-āsana* ("relaxed posture") with one leg raised and the other pendant as if to say that their presence together is only natural. It is even wonderfully disconcerting to realize they are sitting inside a *stūpa*—one of them "extinct" but not and the other "not yet extinct" while sitting inside a tomb as if he were. The image seems to say that we should not trust what we have heard or can understand but only what we "see" in our own "stories."

[12] Bodhi, *MN* 115.14 (p. 929).

Parable of the Burning House

The Mahāyāna of the *Lotus* is still young and must justify itself. How can it be that the Buddha taught a Path to become an Arhat, and presumably a Path to become a Pratyekabuddha, but is now teaching a Bodhisattva Path to become a Buddha? The answer is found in the following story told by the Lord to his wisest early disciple who was already an Arhat:

> Śāriputra, imagine that a country, or a city-state, or a municipality has a man of great power, advanced in years and of incalculable wealth, owning many fields and houses, as well as servants. His house is broad and great; it has only one doorway, but great multitudes of human beings, a hundred, or two hundred, or even five hundred, are dwelling in it. The halls are rotting, the walls crumbling, the pillars decayed at their base, the beams and ridgepoles precariously tipped. Throughout the house and all at the same time, quite suddenly a fire breaks out, burning down all the apartments. The great man's sons, ten, or twenty, or thirty of them are still in the house. (58)

The story is somewhat contrived since it is unlikely that a very wealthy man would own a rotting house—its disrepair being one of the reasons it caught fire. Actually, the Buddha will explain everything later, turning what begins as parable or indirect teaching into an allegory whereby each element can be identified as something else. We will eventually hear that the powerful "man" is the Buddha, the "multitude" is the human Destiny, the "sons" are the Buddha's disciples, and the "house" signifies the Three Realms of existence—that are "rotten" with birth, old age, and sickness—and always "on fire" with lust, hatred, and ignorance.

The story continues:

> The great man, directly he sees this great fire breaking out from four directions is alarmed and terrified. He then has this thought: "Though I was able to get out safely through this burning doorway, yet my sons within the burning house, attached as they are to their games, are unaware, ignorant, unperturbed, unafraid. The fire is coming to press in upon them, the pain will cut them to the quick. Yet at heart they are not horrified, nor have they any wish to leave."

This is interesting. It tells us that the First Noble Truth must be learned, that Buddhism is no longer addressing an India in social turmoil from its second urbanization but is now socially more stable. It is not "suffering" so much. The Lord says, "they do not even know what a 'fire' is."

But rather than preach another "Fire Sermon" as he had in the *Saṃyutta Nikāya*, he devises an "expedient" to take advantage of his sons' addiction to play and their predilection for certain toys. That makes its own biting critique: that ignorance of the human predicament is accompanied by childishly playing around with life in a dangerous way. I am reminded of something Jung said about the difficulty of psychotherapy: "It is as if somebody said: 'Hurry up, the house is on fire!' and one replied, 'Do you really think that houses in Zurich can catch fire?' Perfectly unable to hear what is said."[13]

Accordingly, the father proclaims to his preoccupied sons:

> "The things you so love to play with are rare and hard to get. If you do not get them, you are certain to regret it later. Things like these, a variety of goat-drawn carriages, deer-drawn carriages, and ox-drawn carriages, are now outside the door for you to play with. Come out of this burning house quickly, all of you! I will give all of you what you desire." (59)

Of course, the children rush out of the burning house, even pushing each other aside to see who can get out (of Saṃsāra) first!

And what do they find?

> Śāriputra, at that time, the great man gives to each child one great carriage. The carriage is high and wide, adorned with a multitude of jewels . . . it is yoked to a white ox, whose skin is pure white, whose bodily form is lovely, whose muscular strength is great, whose tread is even and fleet like the wind. . . . What is the reason? Because this great man, of wealth incalculable, his various storehouses all full to overflowing, has this thought: "My wealth being limitless, I may not give small, inferior carriages to my children. Now these little boys are all my sons, I love them without distinction." (60)

The Teacher explains the story in Buddhist terms:

> Have no lust for coarse and broken-down visible matter, sounds, smells, tastes, and tangibles! If, clinging to them greedily, you display lust for them, then you shall be burnt. Quick, get out of the three worlds! You shall get three vehicles, those of voice-hearers [*śrāvakas*], *pratyekabuddha*, and Buddha. I now guarantee it, and I am never false. All you need do is strive earnestly with effort . . . . Then he gives the Great Vehicle equally to all, not allowing any of them to gain passage into extinction for himself alone, but conveying them all to the extinction of the Thus Come One. (62-63)

This is another great moment in the Mahāyāna because it attempts to reconcile the variety of Buddhist Paths coexisting in the early centuries CE or, at least, the different religious goals of the ordained who are living together in the same monastery under the same Vinaya rules.

Does the attempt actually work? Judging from debates in later Buddhism, the "Parable of the Burning House" contains too many ambiguities to be definitive. Yes, it proclaims the good news that the goal is, unambiguously, Buddhahood. In response, "Śāriputra danced for joy"—or, lest that

---

[13] Jung, *Dream Analysis*, 652.

appear unseemly for a monk, we also read, "I have in my heart the thought of dancing for joy. I have gained something I never had before." (49)

But what did the Arhat actually hear? He could have heard that whether one seeks Arhathood (with a "goat cart") or Pratyekabuddhahood (with a "deer cart") or Buddhahood (with an "ox cart") one will always gain at the end of one's efforts the "ox cart" of Buddhahood But Śāriputra could have heard that first one needs to practice the Path in a "goat cart" toward Arhathood, then practice in a "deer cart" toward Pratyekabuddhahood, and then be ready to take the Bodhisattva Vow and ride in an "ox cart" for three incalculable aeons to reach the Incomparable Complete Awakening of Buddhahood. Those are two quite different interpretations of the parable—the difference between inclusive and exclusive that has exercised Buddhist thinkers for centuries.[14]

And the reader may have already noticed an oddity: if a "cart" signifies a particular "Vehicle" or Path for reaching Nirvāṇa (however defined), it is odd that one would receive a "Vehicle" outside the "house" of Saṃsāra. Another problem concerns the Buddha's description of the third cart. As a lure, it is just an "ox cart" preferred by some of his sons. As a surprise gift to all, however, it is "one great carriage" that is "adorned with a multitude of jewels" and "yoked to a white ox, whose skin is pure white," etc. Is the promised ox cart the same or different from the one that is given? Lopez tells us: "Passages in the *Lotus Sūtra* can be found to support either interpretation, and the issue was debated by East Asian exegetes, among whom it became known as the 'three carts or four carts' controversy."[15] This is yet another example of the archetypal symbolism of the "Three and the (problematic) Fourth."

Did the Buddha Lie?

Curiously, the Lord is not very interested in clearing up these problems but wants to know if Śāriputra thinks the "father" in the story lied to his sons about his gift. After all, he had shouted a promise of three different toys, "I now guarantee it, and I am never false." The wisest Arhat answers dutifully: "No, World-Honored One! This great man has but enabled his children to escape the calamity of fire, thus preserving their bodily lives. He is guilty of no falsehood"—it was just an "expedient device" (*upāya*). (60) But we are free to decide otherwise, that the "father" (who is Buddha) has violated the fourth of the Five Precepts.

It is not the first time. In the *Khuddhaka Nikāya* of Early Buddhism, a monk named Nanda realized he could not "keep up the holy life" and was determined to return to householder status. This was Gautama's half-brother, so he was particularly concerned and asked the reason why. He learned that prior to his renunciation Nanda had been engaged to a most lovely Śākyan girl—"the envy of the countryside"—and she had looked up at her betrothed as he left, her hair half-combed, and pleaded, "Hurry back master." Nanda could not get that last look out of his mind. Taking matters into his own hand, the Lord flew off with this vacillating monk to the heaven of the Thirty-Three gods. He showed him the divine nymphs there and asked how they compared to his earthly intended:

---

[14] Stephen F. Teiser and Jacqueline I. Stone, "Interpreting the *Lotus Sūtra*," in Stephen F. Teiser and Jacqueline I. Stone, eds., *Readings of the "Lotus Sūtra"* (New York: Columbia University Press, 2009), 20.

[15] Lopez, *Two Buddhas*,79.

> "There's no comparison. The 500 dove-footed nymphs are lovelier, better looking, more charming."
>
> Then take joy, Nanda. Take Joy! I am your guarantor for getting 500 dove-footed nymphs.
>
> "If the Blessed One is my guarantor for getting 500 dove-footed nymphs, I will enjoy leading the holy life under the Blessed One."

It all works out well. First of all, Nanda's fellow monks criticize him for practicing in order to get nymphs. But he practices really hard—and becomes Enlightened, discovering thereby the folly of his intention. Dutifully, this Arhat "releases" the lying Lord from his "guarantee."[16]

"Darker" themes In these stories, Buddhism is allowing some "darkness" into its religion—for the sake of the greater good. It is what Kierkegaard called the "teleological suspension of the ethical" for the greater good of obeying God. What we have just seen in Buddhism could be called harmless "white lies" and not nearly that serious. But darker shades appear increasingly in the religion—probably inevitably since the "opposites" are unavoidable.

The Mahāyāna will even find room for something called "compassionate violence." Peter Harvey explains:

> an (advanced) *Bodhisattva* may kill a person about to kill many people—so that he saves them and the assailant avoids the evil karma of killing—provided that this is done out of genuine compassion, and with a willingness to suffer the karmic consequences of killing; however, if this is sincere, such consequences will be lighter than normal. He may also lie to save others, and steal the booty of thieves and unjust rulers, so that they are hindered in their evil ways.[17]

The Buddhist emphasis on karmic "intention," "skillful means," and "compassion" come together here; but it is somewhat disconcerting to discover this argument in a religion founded on "nonviolence" (*ahiṃsā*). Not surprisingly, it is an occasion for perversion, as when Buddhist masters during WWII preached the doctrine of compassionate violence to justify "soldier-Zen" and even encourage Japanese aggression and torture "for the greater good."[18]

It is similarly disconcerting to find violence toward the body in these more "feminine" Mahāyāna scriptures. Although enacted with an attitude of devotion and for the sake of great merit, this extreme practice is hardly in accord with Siddhārtha Gautama's own "Middle Way." In the *Aṣṭa*, we can read of an earthly Bodhisattva named, "Ever Weeping," who wished to offer a gift to a more advanced Bodhisattva—by selling his own body, piece by bloody piece, the price to be used as a

---

16 Ṭhānissaro Bhikkhu, trans., "Nanda Sutta," *Khuddaka Nikāya*, Udāna 3.2. *Access to Insight (BCBS Edition)*, 30 August 2012, http://www.accesstoinsight.org/tipitaka/kn/ud/ud.3.02/than.html.

17 Harvey, *Introduction to Buddhism*, 271.

18 See Brian Daizen Victoria, "A Buddhological Critique of 'Soldier-Zen' in Wartime Japan," in Michael K. Jerryson and Mark Juergensmeyer, eds., *Buddhist Warfare* (Oxford: Oxford University Press, 2010), 105-130.

pious donation. Fortunately, the grisly scene is interrupted by the daughter of a merchant who gives him the money he needs.[19]

Even in the otherwise lovely *Lotus*, we hear of a Celestial Bodhisattva named, "Medicine King" (Bhaiṣajyarāja), who wished to offer his own body to the Buddha and, accordingly: "wrapped his body in a garment adorned with divine jewels, anointed himself with fragrant oils, with the force of supernatural penetration took a vow, and then burnt his own body." (295) The scripture declares this suicide to be the "prime gift"—the "most honorable, the supreme." Since the body burned for over a thousand years, the self-sacrifice is clearly symbolic of religious commitment—and need not be taken literally.

Nevertheless, the scripture advises worshippers to "burn a finger or even a toe as an offering" to gain much merit. How this advice was taken in India is unknown. But many Chinese Buddhists would, in fact, perform such acts out of piety. James Benn writes:

> Although the practice of burning the body was criticized on occasion, by both secular authorities and Buddhist monks, it has been an accepted feature of Buddhist devotionalism in East Asia until recent times. The offering of fingers and burning of incense on the skin (another symbolic act of self-immolation) still occur in China, Taiwan, and Korea. The tradition of making small burn marks on the crown of the head as part of the ordination ceremony for Chinese monks and nuns ultimately derives from the example of Medicine King.[20]

Although Jungian psychology values ritual as symbolic action to express and activate the archetypal psyche—and knows that "suffering" is required for greater consciousness—there is something wrong with these accounts. They perpetuate too easily Buddhism's disgust for the human body.

Parable of the Prodigal Son

Four Arhats who learn that they are actually on their way to becoming Buddhas somehow tell the following story together:

> Suppose there were a man who was young in years and who also, forsaking his father and running off, dwelt long in another country, whether ten, or twenty, or as much as fifty years. Not only did he grow old, but he was also reduced to destitution, running about in all four directions in quest of food and clothing. At length, in his wanderings, he accidentally headed toward his native land. His father, who had preceded him, and who had sought his son without finding him, had stopped midway in a certain city. The father's house was great and rich, with treasure and jewels immeasurable. . . . The profits that flowed in and out would

[19] Conze, *Eight Thousand*, 285.

[20] See James A. Benn, "The *Lotus Sūtra* and Self-Immolation," in Teiser and Stone, *Readings,* 107-108.

> fill the whole realm, and also merchants and itinerant traders were very numerous. (85)

Thus begins what Burnouf called the "Parable of the Prodigal Son," referring to Jesus' parable in Luke 15. It is a label that has stuck despite significant differences. The Buddhist story is that of a single unfaithful son while the much shorter biblical story is that of two sons, one of them loyal and one not. The former story speaks of an accidental return of the son while the Bible says the disloyal son "came to his senses" and deliberately went home to confess his "sinfulness." Both tales, however, record a loving reconciliation between a wayward son and a forgiving father. Without having to be told this time, we know that we are the "son" who has lost his way and that the rich and welcoming "father" is the Buddha—whose "house" this time is not rotten but grand.

The *Lotus* continues:

> At that time, the poor son, having visited various settlements and passed through kingdoms and metropolises, at length reached the city where his father was staying. The father and mother were thinking of their son, for it had already been more than fifty years since they parted with him. . . . "Old and decrepit, we have much gold and silver and many precious gems, with which our treasure houses are filled to overflowing, but we have no son." . . . At that time, the poor son, hiring himself out as a laborer in his wanderings, by chance reached his father's house, where, stopping by the side of the gate, he saw in the distance his father seated on a lion throne. . . .

Let us note that the "time periods" of this Buddhist story are much too long if taken literally but symbolically express a long, slow process of "gradual" realization—as distinct from notions of "sudden" Enlightenment that we will discuss. We note, too, that "accident" or "chance" plays an important part in the desired outcome (although that is not a feature in the biblical account). But, surely, this is "meaningful chance" given the Law of *karma*, not to mention the hidden workings of the Bodhicitta ("Thought of Enlightenment") within all Bodhisattvas.

Jungian thoughts First of all, psychologically, there does not seem to be such a thing as "accident" when one gets to know the inner meaning of events. This fact led Jung to value the Chinese *I Ching* and its oracles based on "chance." It led to his hypothesis of synchronicity between inner and outer events. In the Buddhist parable of the "Prodigal Son," then, we are observing what we already witnessed at the "Great Departure" when Gautama left home for the sake of his authentic vocation. His disobedience was described positively, for the sake of Enlightenment, the father's resistance a religious error. Here, that conflict is reversed, and the son is in error (as in the biblical parable).

We can understand both versions as psychologically correct, however, from different angles: it is necessary that the ego leave its embeddedness in the "family psyche" in order to discover its own identity. Yet that is, by definition, an act of "disloyalty"—albeit a necessary one, and even the first lesson in discovering there must be room for "sin" against the collective if one is to develop as a psychological adult. Usually, the lesson does not require an actual break in family ties, but it may.

In any case, this pictures only the "first half" of life, one that often enough gets one into trouble by too much "self-reliance" and overrating of one's will. It pictures a person having left not only identification with the family psyche but also any sense of relying upon the larger Forces of the unconscious for survival. Thus, the Buddhist "son" is "reduced to destitution" (the biblical son sinking to the indignity, especially for a Jew, of tending pigs).

Yet it is precisely here that the "second half" of life can begin. It is also only then that anyone is willing to enter into psychotherapy to discover what is "wrong"—although that is not always necessary. Either way, there must be an experience of failure—and, more important, an admission of one's part in it (something that is often easier in a therapy setting of trust). But confessing one's "sinfulness" is emphasized by the biblical story and not the Buddhist one. What is emphasized by the *Lotus* is that the "father" (we would call this the Self archetype) is actively searching for his lost "son"! He longs for reconciliation, even as this son is aimlessly "running about in all four directions." He wants him to share in his "gold and silver and many precious gems" now and inherit all of it upon his death.

The Buddhist scripture is psychologically astute, informing us that the "son" panicked upon seeing all that "wealth"—and "quickly ran off." Edinger noticed in his practice that the archetypal psyche can be so overwhelming—even when "affirming"—that "wounded" patients often "cling obstinately to their original experience" of rejecting parents, for example. They "find it very difficult to accept and endure a positive parent experience"—now mediated by a sympathetic analyst, or an affirming superior at work, a loving spouse at home.[21] Our scripture informs us that it can take a long time to overcome one's fear of "Good News."

The *Lotus* reports that the father—"who instantly recognized" his son at the gate—resorted to ruses, compassionate strategies (*upāya*) to lure his reluctant offspring "home." First, he sent servants to hire him to "sweep away dung" at the house (psychologically, to work first on the personal shadow). But, then, the father devised a way to meet his son who was "grimy and soiled with dung" at his own level of understanding:

> Straightway he removed his necklaces, his fine outer garments, and his ornaments, and put on instead a rough, torn, dirty, tar-stained garment and, smearing dust over his body, took in his right hand a dung-shovel.

In that guise, the wealthy man approached his long-lost son personally and praised him for his work, increasing his wage: "I am like your father: have no more cares!"

We hear the *double entendre*. But it is an image of extraordinary divine Grace—the Buddhist version of the Christian Incarnation of God in Jesus, a lowly carpenter, sent to save tax collectors and prostitutes, and bring us all closer to the Self. The guise serves, also, to redeem the role of Gautama Buddha who was being demoted as a mere *nirmāṇa*-kāya—that we now know is entirely necessary, albeit "demeaning," for enlightening the human Destiny.

---

[21] Edinger, *Melville's "Moby-Dick,"* 84.

After another "twenty years," the "prodigal" son is promoted to manage the father's accounts—until on his deathbed the great and wealthy owner of the house summoned all the "kings, great ministers, Kṣatriyas, and householders" to proclaim:

> "Sirs! Know that this is my son, begotten by me. Having forsaken me in such-and-such a city and run off, he suffered loneliness and hardship for more than fifty years. . . . Formerly, in my native city, affected by grief, I sought him. Some time ago, I suddenly encountered him by accident and got him back. He is really my son. I am really his father. Now all the treasure I have belongs to my son. (88)

We hear in this passage the same Voice that Jesus heard at his baptism, after a troubled youth of illegitimacy: "Thou art *my* beloved Son, in whom I am well pleased." (KJV, Mark 1:11; italics added). The Arhats who recounted this parable of the "Prodigal Son" proclaimed: "we did not know we are truly the Buddha's children. Now, at last, we know." (89)

Parable of the Hidden Jewel

The "Parable of the Hidden Jewel" is not very different from what we have just heard—which is to say that these stories are not primarily conveying religious information but a feeling for it. Now, five hundred Arhats convey the following (somehow in unison):

> There is a man who arrives at the house of a close friend, where he gets drunk on wine, then lies down. At that time, his friend, having official business, is on the point of going away, when he sews a priceless jewel into the interior of the first man's garment and departs, leaving it with him. The first man. . . . [eventually] suffers such hardship that he is content with however little he may get. Then his friend, encountering him by chance, speaks these words to him: "Alas, Sir! How can you have come to this for the sake of mere food and clothing? Once I, wishing to afford you comfort and joy. . . sewed a priceless jewel into the inside of your garment. Surely it is still there. . . . How foolish you have been!" (164-165)

It would have been good if the friend had written a note explaining his generosity before leaving town, but that is clearly not the point of the story.

The psychology The story's point is that we have a Jewel "hidden" in our "garment" (our body? our materialism? our personalistic psychology?) of which we cannot take advantage due to our "drunken" ignorance. That is reminiscent of the Tibetan notion of scripture as *gter ma* or "treasure" hidden under water or underground waiting for the right time to be discovered. Jung wrote frequently of this motif of the "Treasure hard to attain"—hidden in a field, in the depths of the sea, or surrounded by a serpent—found in myth and fairy tale. He says it refers to the precious Self at the core of our being of which we are unaware. We live our lives in psychological "squalor" while seeking riches that never satisfy, not knowing that we are already "rich."

These are just some of the many stories found in the *Lotus Sūtra,* all meant to keep its readers—its reciters, copiers, worshippers—in touch with great Buddhist truths by way of its symbols. Thus, the scripture can rightly refer to itself as a "great benefit" to all living beings, "fulfilling their desires":

> Like a clear, cool pond, it can slake the thirst of all. As a chilled person finds fire, as a naked person finds clothing, a merchant finds a chief, as a child finds its mother, as a passenger finds a ship, as a sick person finds a physician, as darkness finds a torch, as a poor person finds a jewel, as the people find a king, as a commercial traveler finds the sea, as a candle dispels darkness, this scripture of the "Dharma Blossom" . . . . (299)

We might even hear in our own background a favorite Christian hymn: "Amazing grace! (how sweet the sound) / That sav'd a wretch like me! / I once was lost, but now am found, / Was blind, but now I see."

"Vimalakīrti Sūtra"

Like the *Lotus*, the *Vimalakīrti-nirdeśa-sūtra* ("Sermon on the Instructions of Vimalakīrti") belongs to that small "canon" of Buddhist works to which modern scholars have paid close attention, translating it into English several times. The scripture was so popular in East Asia that the Chinese translated it at least seven times (the first in 188 CE) and the Tibetans did so twice. In part, that is because the text is short and accessible yet also because it purports to be a *sūtra* or "sermon" taught primarily not by Śākyamuni Buddha but by a householder named Vimalakīrti. The Buddha is still present in the narrative—performing miracles and teaching in a monastic setting—but this layman gives the main *nirdeśa* or "instruction" to the Buddha's disciples at his house.

That was very appealing to the Chinese who had difficulty integrating a renunciant Indian religion, that they otherwise found attractive, into their own culture with its Confucian emphasis upon the family. Indeed, they translated the Sanskrit word for "householder" (incorrectly) as "retired scholar," a person of recognizable respect in their own culture, certainly moreso than a monk.[22]

The text is early, perhaps early second century CE, and seems to be aware of even earlier scriptures like the *Aṣṭa* and the *Lotus*. Like them, it is self-referent, belonging to that "cult of the book" and valuing itself as superior to *stūpas* for making merit. Like all early Mahāyāna scripture, it feels the need to justify itself in the face of established tradition— thus, giving the Śrāvakas a hard time, but then giving its own Bodhisattvas a hard time, often with sarcasm and humor. That appealed to the Taoist side of Chinese culture that was at odds with the Confucian side. It is why Burton Watson noted in his translation of the *Vimalakīrti* that "in philosophical depth and brilliance of language it rivals the *Chuang Tzu*," a Taoist classic known as much for its wit as for its profundity.[23]

---

[22] Jonathan A. Silk, "Taking the *Vimalakīrtinirdeśa* Seriously," *Annual Report of The International Research Institute for Advanced Buddhology at Soka University for the Academic Year 2013*, vol. 17 (2014), 160.

[23] Burton Watson, trans., *The Vimalakirti Sutra* (New York: Columbia University Press, 1997), ix.

But the scripture is much valued on its own terms. Edward Hamlin calls it "*sui generis*": "Because it so admirably merges the visionary with the conceptual, the aesthetic with the scholastic, the VNS stands as perhaps the purest example of philosophical drama the surviving Mahāyāna materials provide."[24] In his own French translation, Étienne Lamotte calls the *Vimalakīrti-nirdeśa-sūtra* the "crowning jewel" of Mahāyāna literature.[25]

That is to say more of this scripture's reception outside India, however, than inside the home of its composition. As with the *Lotus*, we do not know much of the Indian history of the *Vimalakīrti*, nor was it quoted very often by other Mahāyāna texts. In fact, there was no Sanskrit manuscript available for modern translation and study until a copy (from the twelfth century) was discovered in the Potala palace of Lhasa in 1999. Gérard Fussman assures us, however, that there are no real surprises in the recovered manuscript: "*des passages beaucoup plus brilliants, beaucoup plus vivaces, en sanskrit plus élégant*."[26] Therefore, I will use an English translation by Robert Thurman from a ninth-century Tibetan translation of the Sanskrit.[27]

Introduction

The scripture opens:

> Reverence to all Buddhas, Bodhiattvas, Āryaśrāvakas ["noble hearers," Arhats], and Pratyekabuddhas, in the past, the present, and the future.
> Thus have I heard at one time. The Lord Buddha was in residence in the garden of Āmrapāli, in the city of Vaiśālī, attended by a great gathering. (10)

There is nothing new here, except for a change in punctuation in the opening phrase of the so-called *nidāna*. The Tibetans prefer a period break after "time": so instead of, "Thus have I heard. At one time . . .," we read, "Thus have I heard at one time." Wayman says this places the reporter at the scene—perhaps hinting at Ānanda's sudden mystical understanding, "all at once."[28] The location is that park donated by the courtesan Āmrapālī, the "mango woman" who beat out the Licchavi princes who were trying to invite the Buddha to lunch. These men resided in the nearby city of Vaiśālī (capital of the Vṛji Republic). Vimalakīrti himself is from that same clan and lives "downtown," as Thurman puts it.[29]

That introduces at the outset a geographical and community distinction between the lay *saṃgha* in the city and the ordained *saṃgha* in the countryside, closer to the forest where the religion began.

---

[24] Edward Hamlin, "Magical *Upāya* in the *Vimalakīrtinirdeśa-sūtra*," *The Journal of the International Association of Buddhist Studies* 11, no. 1 (1988), 89.

[25] Cited by Silk, "Taking the *Vimalakīrtinirdeśa* Seriously," 157.

[26] Gérard Fussman, "Histoire du monde indien: Lecture du texte sanskrit du *Vimalakīrtinirdeśa*," *Cours et travaux du Collège de France*. Résumés 2007-2008. Annuaire 108è année (Paris: Collège de Framce): 646.

[27] Robert A. F. Thurman, *The Holy Teaching of Vimalakīrti: A Mahāyāna Scripture* (University Park: Pennsylvania State University Press, 1976). To avoid cumbersome citation, I will use page numbers to refer to this text.

[28] See Wayman, "Buddhism," *Historia Religionum*, 419.

[29] Robert A. F. Thurman, "The Teaching of Vimalakīrti," in *Approaches to the Asian Classics*, eds. William Theodore de Bary and Irene Bloom (New York: Columbia University Press, 1990), 234.

We sense already that there is a "problem of opposites" in this text—indeed, it will be at the heart of the layman's "sermon." The scripture even mentions at its close an alternative title, "Reconciliation of Dichotomies." (102) In fact, two miracles introduce profound "pairs of opposites" at the outset.

The Buddha's Miracles

"One and the Many" The Buddha's own "great gathering" is, of course, impossibly great. This we have come to expect, but among the "thirty-two thousand Bodhisattvas" in attendance, fifty-six are named. This means that the Tibetan version has incorporated, at some point, a fully developed Bodhisattva cult that would have only begun when the Sanskrit was composed. With the Buddha seated upon his "lion throne," five hundred youths step forward with five hundred "precious parasols made of seven different kinds of jewels": "Each approached the Buddha, bowed at his feet, circumambulated him clockwise seven times, laid down his precious parasol in offering, and withdrew to one side." We have seen parasols or umbrellas as a symbol of royal "protection," appearing even in stone at the top of the *stūpa* at Sāñcī. Then, a great miracle:

> As soon as these precious parasols had been laid down, suddenly, by the miraculous power of the Lord, they were transformed into a single precious canopy so great that it formed a covering for this entire billion-world galaxy. The surface of the entire billion-world galaxy was reflected in the interior of the great precious canopy, where the total content of this galaxy could be seen . . . . And the voices of all the Buddhas of the ten directions could be heard proclaiming their teachings of the Dharma in all the worlds, the sounds reverberating in the space beneath the great precious canopy. (12)

Thurman aptly calls this canopy a "magical planetarium."[30]

It is reminiscent of the cosmic vision in the *Aṣṭa* and the beginning of the *Lotus* when a ray from the Buddha's forehead "illuminated" the universe—revealing its vastness, its Buddha-fields, its Buddhas. As before, the congregation is "ecstatic, enraptured, astonished, delighted, satisfied, and filled with awe and pleasure." For now they see that Buddhas are forever present somewhere, that it is possible to seek rebirth among them, while their saving "emanations" are even now in our midst.

A new element, however, may have emerged. While the vision repeats the basic Buddhist theme of "appearance as opposed to reality," it adds the specific lesson that what appears to be "many" is really "one"—i.e., hundreds of parasols give way to one great cosmic canopy. Alan Cole writes that the congregation is being treated here to a "total overview of the Real . . . [a] view of the Real that radically exceeds the boundaries of the participants' expectations."[31] Our translator adds that this vision of "total Reality" is the Buddha's way of correcting our deluded view that we are all separate from each other (like so many different parasols), when in fact we are all "interconnected"

[30] Thurman, "Teaching," 234.

[31] Alan Cole, *Text as Father: Paternal Seductions in Early Mahāyāna Buddhist Literature* (Berkeley: Universtiy of California Press, 2005), 244.

(under one great umbrella). That is reminiscent of the modern Buddhist interpretation of Dependent Origination as "interdependent" origination—that we discussed earlier as not what the Buddha actually taught.

Nevertheless, Thurman—who is a Buddhist—says that if one meditates on this opening image long enough:

> We lose all sense of boundary, all tension of struggle, and experience a vast, sky-like feeling of endless, all-inclusive realness, a realness that gently and unobtrusively seems to be connected to all other beings and things. This is the real self . . . . the essence of what the Buddha saw during his own meditation.[32]

If this is correct, it would mean we have come a long way from the Early Buddhist teaching that we are deluded when we see "whole entities" but wise when we perceive only the "non-self" of different *skandhas* and many *dharmas*. It would mean that the Mahāyāna is teaching the reverse: that we are deluded when we see separate persons and things but wise when we perceive the interconnected whole, that Thurman calls the "real self." The *Vimilakīrti* text, however, does not say this explicitly and does not mention a "real self." But modern Buddhists often report a similar "feeling" of Oneness—that apparently is induced by their meditations.

"Purity and Impurity" Śāriputra thought he saw a problem in the Buddha's miracle—so the Lord performed a second one to solve it. What bothered this Arhat when observing so many Pure Lands of the other Buddhas is that Śākyamuni's own Buddha-field—the one in which he was now preaching to those assembled—was so obviously impure: with its "highs and lows, its thorns, its precipices, its peaks and its abysses, as if it were entirely filled with ordure." (18) It was not a very nice thing to notice. Śākyamuni Buddha had just taught that a Bodhisattva "purifies" a "field" in which he becomes a Buddha by the purity of his own mind produced by his incalculable merits. But this meant, as this Buddhist "doubting Thomas" concluded: "when Gautama was engaged in his career as a bodhisattva, his mind must have been impure."

A curiously Enlightened god steps in and explains: "The fact that you see such a Buddha-field as this as if it were so impure, reverend Śāriputra, is a sure sign that there are highs and lows in your mind and that your positive thought in regard to the Buddha-gnosis is not pure either." In other words, purity is in the mind of the beholder. This is a subjective, even a psychological world view—namely, that the world one "sees" or experiences is the world one gets.

Yet it sits right alongside an objective supernatural cosmology of Buddha-fields and a well-informed god. We saw that ambiguity first in the *Saṃyutta Nikāya* when the Lord taught a shining young *deva* that the "beginning and end of the world" is within "this fathom-high carcass"—without denying that god's existence.

That the Buddha is "doubted" reflects the difficulty that the religion is having with Gautama's demotion from the one and only Buddha to just the closest one of innumerable Buddhas in the universe and his demotion—according to Trikāya doctrine—to just a Nirmāṇa-kāya emanation of

[32] Thurman, *Inner Revolution*, 81.

the Dharma-kāya. Commentators made several attempts to restore their Lord's reputation. One was to suggest that the traditional teaching site of "Vulture Peak" was itself not what it seemed but something of a "mini-Pure Land," as Harvey puts it.[33] That allowed Śākyamuni the more exalted status of a Saṃbhoga-kāya with his "Thirty-two Marks" retained. Another solution was to say he actually resided as a Saṃbhoga-kāya in Akaniṣṭha heaven—the highest of the Pure Abodes in the Realm of Form—pressed into service as a "Pure Land" within the Mahāyāna. It is there that his name is Vairocana ("resplendent") who has sent a compassionate "emanation" named Siddhārtha Gautama to India in the sixth century BCE to teach on Vulture Peak. But others argued that Gautama Buddha was himself superior to all other Buddhist Beings by being willing and able to teach in our own "impure" world. What compassion!

In the *Vimalakīrti*, however, the Lord settles the matter this way:

> Thereupon the Lord touched the ground of this billion-world-galactic universe with his big toe [ostensibly, the least pure part of his body], and suddenly it was transformed into a huge mass of precious jewels, a magnificent array of many hundreds of thousands of clusters of precious gems, until it resembled the [undoubtedly pure] universe of the Tathāgata Ratnavyūya . . . . Everyone in the entire assembly was filled with wonder, each perceiving himself seated on a throne of jeweled lotuses. (18-19)

Chastened, Śāriputra exclaims: "I see it Lord!" We learn that the opposition of "impurity and purity" has been resolved in favor of one side of the pair—the revelation that impurity is an illusion and Purity is real. One has the impression that the same is true with the opposition of "many and one," the many only apparent and in reality united by a single overarching principle.

This is not, however, the main or most important way that the *Vimilakīrti* "reconciles dichotomies." To anticipate, our text is closer to the *Aṣṭa* and other "Perfection of Wisdom" literature: namely, when faced with a pair of opposites or *dvaya* ("twoness") occasioned by discursive thinking, one should realize that "neither one nor the other" is true. One should realize *nir-dvandva* ("not two-ness") beyond either side.

Jungian thoughts The problem of the "One and the Many" belongs to what is often called "perennial philosophy" and a theme that keeps coming up in Western thought. The early Greeks wrestled with it and became convinced that the "many" objects of the world are held together by "one" principle—that the pre-Socratic philosophers called variously, Water, Fire, Mind, etc. In the third century CE, Plotinus would say that there is a divine "One" emanating itself into the "many" in an increasing multiplicity that eventually reaches us. It is an idea or attitude that influences even modern-day science. Physicists are not content with observing the many particles and forces of the natural world but seek a "grand unifying theory" that holds them all together. There was much excitement recently upon the discovery of a fundamental particle called the Higgs boson that some scientists dubbed the "God particle." But, then, the Mahāyāna Buddhists appear to be saying that the Dharma-kāya is that One primordial "Particle" responsible for all else.

---

33 Harvey, *Introduction*, 166-167.

Jung would say there is a hidden psychology in all of this. We cannot live in meaningless *chaos* and are obliged to seek a *cosmos* of order and meaningful purpose. Thus, the ego functions as the "one" ordering center of consciousness for its "many" contents, lest they overwhelm. At the profounder level of the collective unconscious, the Self archetype functions as the "one" organizing principle for the "many" other archetypes—lest they merely conflict with each other. Jung even speaks of this archetype in language like Thurman's: "the One who dwells within him, whose form has no knowable boundaries, who encompasses him on all sides, fathomless as the abysms of the earth and vast as the sky." [34]

But even if one were to experience this archetype of Order rather directly—in spontaneous vison or induced by meditation—it is not the "whole" of psychic reality since archetype and ego belong together, in a creative relationship: whereby the Self supports ego consciousness and consciousness actualizes the Self's potential. In other words, the opposites of the "one and the many" belong together and cannot be resolved in favor of one or the other.

Similarly—with regard to the pair, "purity and impurity"—Jung would be wary of judging one side more real than the other. Concerning the related pair, "good and evil," Jung strongly criticized the Christian notion of the *privatio boni* that seeks to define "evil" merely as the absence or privation of what is good. That, he felt, does not give sufficient weight to what is bad or evil—contrary to our own experience, especially in recent centuries of world-wide war. He writes:

> And just as the conscious mind can put the question, "Why is there this frightful conflict between good and evil?" so the unconscious can reply, "Look closer! Each needs the other. The best, just because it is the best, holds the seed of evil, and there is nothing so bad but good can come of it."[35]

This understanding does approach Chinese wisdom, the Taoist image of all opposites as "Yin and Yang"—with a "seed" of each depicted inside the other.

Vimalakīrti

Let us meet our titular hero. Since a Mahāyānist, Vimilakīrti is by definition a Bodhisattva—but a lay Bodhisattva living in the city with a wife and children and engaged in some sort of business, handling money unlike a monk for whom that is forbidden. He is, also, something of a man about town since he visits the local bars and houses of prostitution, off limits even to the thoughts of the ordained. For all that, Vimalakīrti is extraordinarily wise and often put forward—especially by modern lay Buddhists—as a kind of proof that it is possible to become Enlightened without becoming a monk or nun. Reginald Ray thinks the scripture teaches that it is actually "preferable" not to renounce.[36] Indeed, the Arhat Upāli enthuses: "Do not entertain the notion that he is a mere householder! Why? With the exception of the Tathāgata himself, there is no disciple or bodhisattva

---

[34] Jung, *CW* 11, par. 758.

[35] Jung, *CW* 7, par. 289.

[36] Ray, *Buddhist Saints*, 414.

capable of competing with his eloquence or rivaling the brilliance of his wisdom." (31) We see that, at the very least, this man in layman's white rivals Śākaymuni, the Buddha in saffron robes outside of town.

When closely read, however, the text makes it difficult to say who or what Vimilakīrti actually is:

> At that time, there lived in the great city of Vaiśālī a certain Licchavi, Vimalakīrti by name. Having served the ancient Buddhas, he had generated the roots of virtue by honoring them and making offering to them. He had attained tolerance as well as eloquence. He played with the great superknowledges [*abhijñās*, including the *ṛddhis*]. He had attained the power of incantations [*dhāraṇī*, short scriptural formulae; or strings of potent sounds] and the fearlessnesses. He had conquered all demons and opponents. He had penetrated the profound way of the Dharma. He was liberated through the transcendence of wisdom [i.e., the Perfection of Wisdom]. . . . In order to develop living beings with his skill in liberative technique [Means], he lived in the great city of Vaiśālī. (20)

We see why Upāli is excited. This man is not newly converted but has been a Bodhisattva from aeons past, cultivating the Perfections and gaining thereby his own miraculous powers. Although an earthly human being and presumably even "earthy," this lay Bodhisattva might even be as advanced as a Celestial Bodhisattva. Or perhaps more than that since the text reads, "liberated by the Perfection of Wisdom," the goal of the religion.

Fussman cannot resist: "*Vimalkīrti est un tathāgata*."[37] As we read on in scripture, we see why he would say that:

> He wore the white clothes of the layman, yet lived impeccably like a religious devotee. He lived at home, but remained aloof from the realm of desire, the realm of pure matter, and the immaterial realm [the Three Realms of the cosmos]. He had a son, a wife, and female attendants [i.e., a harem], yet always maintained continence. He appeared to be surrounded by servants, yet lived in solitude. He appeared to be adorned with ornaments, yet always was endowed with the auspicious signs and marks. He seemed to eat and drink, yet always took nourishment from the taste of meditation. He made his appearance in the fields of sports and in the casinos, but his aim was always to mature those people who were attached to games and gambling. . . . To demonstrate the evils of desire, he even entered the brothels. To established drunkards in correct mindfulness, he entered all the cabarets. (20-21)

[37] Fussman, *Histoire*, 648.

Vimalakīrti appears to be one thing but, we are told, is really another. This rich man of Vaiśāli, has a wife and child and concubines, yet is somehow always chaste; has many servants yet is always alone; goes into bars but only to preach against going there.

Some of this makes sense, the way that a Methodist minister is "in the world but not of it" and goes into bars to preach against demon drink. As one writer puts it, "Vimalakīrti's own personal ethical conduct is flawless."[38] On the other hand, some of this looks paradoxical as in the phrase, "He seemed to eat and drink, yet . . . ." We are reminded of docetic Nirmāṇa-kāyas who eat and drink but only to conform to what is expected of their human "disguise." True, the force of any contradiction in the text depends on how one translates. Watson's rendering from the Chinese is not quite paradoxical: e.g., "although he ate and drank like others, what he truly savored was the joy of meditation."[39] Still, it is not actually clear what to think of Vimalakīrti.

The scripture maintains all manner of ambiguities until very late. Let us go there:

> The venerable Śāriptutra then asked the Buddha, "Lord, in which Buddha-field did the noble Vimalakīrti die, before reincarnating in this Buddha field?"
> The Buddha said, "Śāriputra, ask this good man directly where he died to reincarnate here." (92)

The Arhat does so but receives a standard "Perfection of Wisdom" answer from Vimalakīrti—namely, that there is "nothing that dies or is reborn," any more than in a magical trick something real appears and disappears. So the Buddha has to intervene:

> "Śāriputra, this holy person came here from the presence of the Tathāgata Akṣobhya in the universe Abhirati." (93)

The text clarifies at last: Vimalakīrti is a Celestial Bodhisattva who usually resides in the eastern Pure Land of Abhirati to serve the Celestial Buddha, Akṣobhya. He has come into our midst as an "emanation" to satisfy his Vow to save all beings, using whatever *upāya* necessary—including seeming to be a mere layman in India—to further that goal.

It follows that Vimalakīrti is and is not a human being, is and is not a householder, a Bodhisattva, a Buddha. We cannot even be certain that he is here. It follows, too, that the *Vimalakīrti Sūtra* is no sure "proof" that it is preferable to be a layperson, rather than a monk or a nun, in order to become Enlightened.

Vimalakīrti's Illness

Early in the scripture, Vimalakīrti determined it would be a good salvific "strategy" to appear ill: "At that time, out of this very skill in liberative technique, Vimalakīrti manifested himself as if sick." (21) That is, he was not really sick but pretended to be in order to get the townsfolk in the

[38] Robinson, et al., *Buddhist Religions*, 113.
[39] Watson, *Vimalakirti*, 33.

thousands to visit him and inquire after his health. It is another one of those holy "lies" that appear in Mahāyāna materials, giving this man an opportunity to teach the following:

> Friends, this body is so impermanent, fragile, unworthy of confidence, and feeble. . . . This body is like a ball of foam, unable to bear any pressure. It is like a water bubble, not remaining very long. It is like a mirage, born from the appetites of the passions. It is like the trunk of the plantain tree, having no core. Alas! This body is like a machine, a nexus of bones and tendons. It is like a magical illusion, consisting of falsifications. It is like a dream, being an unreal vision. . . . Therefore, you should be revulsed by such a body. You should despair of it and should arouse your admiration for the body of the Tathāgata. (22)

This teaching is not in the least paradoxical but Early Buddhist orthodoxy. It exhibits that "revulsion" toward the physical—leading to a psychological detachment—that I have argued is the purpose of such a dim view of the body. By contrast, says Vimalakīrti, there is the "body of the Tathāgata" (nascent Trikāya theory).

Then, Vimalakīrti complains: "I am sick, lying on my bed in pain, yet the Tathāgata, the saint, the perfectly accomplished Buddha, does not consider me or take pity upon me, and sends no one to inquire after my illness." (24) This is humorous, the beginning of a wry streak in what are called the "Reluctance" chapters. Of course, the Buddha across town in Āmrapāli Park has not inquired—because Vimalkīrti is not really sick! Nor should an advanced Bodhisattva be complaining. Nevertheless, the Lord plays along and directs his ten most accomplished "Hīnayāna" disciples to look in on the patient.

Shockingly, they all refuse to go: "reluctant" to encounter a layman who in previous encounters had belittled their ostensibly perfect understanding of the Dharma. Poor Śāriputra is the first to explain:

> I remember one day, when I was sitting at the foot of a tree in the forest, absorbed in contemplation, the Licchavi Vimalkīrti came to the foot of that tree and said to me, "Reverend Śāriputra, this is not the way to absorb yourself in contemplation. You should absorb yourself in contemplation so that neither body nor mind appear anywhere in the triple world. You should absorb yourself in contemplation in such a way that you can manifest all ordinary behavior without forsaking cessation. . . . You should absorb yourself in contemplation in such a way that you are released in liberation without abandoning the passions that are the province of the world." (24)

The Arhat's contemplation had been rudely interrupted by a Mahāyāna teaching on the Nirvāṇa of "no fixed abode." Teaching is, after all, why Vimilakīrti left the ideal world of Abhirati for this Sahā world, why he lives in town.

Rudeness aside, this explanation may make too much rational sense. Cole thinks the "pairs of opposites" are actually at play in order to elude any comprehension. He writes of Vimalakīrti's challenges to all the disciples that they "are of one type":

> they require that opposites be combined. Of course, this matches the description that the omniscient narrator had given Vimalakīrti himself, since he was a layman but behaved like a buddha and so on.[40]

But, Cole adds, combining opposites is actually "impossible," leading to "unthinkability"—i.e., to the eventual goal of seeing "nonduality" beyond all concepts.

We soon learn that Vimalakīrti also interrupted the great Arhat Maudgalyāyana who was teaching the Dharma: "that is not the way to teach the Dharma to the householders in their white clothes . . . . there is no teacher of the Dharma, no one to listen, no one to understand." This sounds like the *Aṣṭa*. Vimalakīrti also scolded Mahākāśyapa who was on his alms round: "You should beg your food in awareness of the ultimate nonexistence of food." For good measure, this mere layman—who is not supposed to know so much—commented on Nirvāṇa in a very clever way: "That which is without intrinsic substance and without imparted substance does not burn. And what does not burn will not be extinguished." In other words, Saṃsāra (being on fire with desires) does not really exist (so one cannot really be on fire); therefore, there is no need for Nirvāṇa (the "blowing out" of fire) nor is it even possible. We will see that kind of relentless demolition of thought in the Madhyamaka philosophy of Nāgārjuna.

These tales of humiliation go on repeatedly until we get to my favorite, featuring Ānanda. He has always been something of a "fall guy" in Buddhism since scriptures often point out that he is "still in training." At the same time, Ānanda is Gautama Buddha's favorite attendant—another play of opposites. In the story, the Lord was physically "indisposed," so he sent his personal assistant to get some milk for his stomach. But Vimalakīrti stopped him on the way to introduce "Dharma-body" theory:

> Reverend Ānanda, the Tathāgatas have the body of the Dharma—not a body that is sustained by material food. The Tathāgatas have a transcendental body that has transcended all mundane qualities. There is no injury to the body of a Tathāgata, as it is rid of all defilements. . . . Reverend Ānanda, to believe there can be illness in such a body is irrational and unseemly!"

Ānanda reported this embarrassing encounter to the Buddha as the reason why he, too, was reluctant to go to the city:

> When I had heard these words, I wondered if I had previously misheard and misunderstood the Buddha, and I was very much ashamed. Then I heard a voice

[40] Cole, *Text as Father*, 257.

> from the sky: "Ānanda! The householder speaks to you truly. Nevertheless . . . go and get the milk!"

There is much religious mischief in all this and a fair amount of fantasy, worthy of the *Chuang Tzu*. And we see why Ch'an (Zen) with its own religious mischief ("the sound of one hand clapping") values this particular scripture—despite claiming to be "outside scripture" (more mischief). Scholars still argue, however, whether any of this is actually funny—which is funny.

Mañjuśrī to the Rescue

Finally, the Celestial Bodhisattva Mañjuśrī agrees to visit (his fellow Celestial Bodhisattva) Vimalakīrti on his sickbed: "although he cannot be withstood by someone of my feeble defenses, still, sustained by the grace of the Buddha, I will go to him and will converse with him as well as I can." (42) Anticipating a grand spectacle, all those surrounding the throne of the Lord rise and accompany this wisest of all Gautama Buddha's followers, heading for the imaginary invalid's room.

By tradition, it measured ten by ten feet—the exact size adopted by certain abbots and "retired scholars" in China for their own private rooms. But how would the hundreds of thousands of visitors fit into such a small space? Easily—because it would be "empty"!

> Then, magically his house became empty. Even the doorkeeper disappeared. And, except for the invalid's couch upon which Vimalakīrti himself was lying, no bed or couch or seat could be seen anywhere. (43)

Unfortunately for him, Śāriputra asked about seats—to which Vimalakīrti retorted: "did you come here for the sake of the Dharma? Or did you come here for the sake of a chair?" (50)

More to the point, what did Vimalakīrti and Mañjuśrī discuss? They discussed the Mahāyāna notion of "emptiness," of course:

> Householder, why is your house empty? Why have you no servants?
> Mañjuśrī, all buddha-fields are also empty.
> What makes them empty?
> They are empty because of emptiness.
> What is "empty" about emptiness?
> Constructions are empty, because of emptiness.
> Can emptiness be conceptually constructed?
> Even that concept is itself empty, and emptiness cannot construct emptiness. (43-44)

Not only is the rich householder's house empty of servants and furniture, it is also void of concepts—even concepts about conceptualization. The story is itself a "means" (an *upāya* or "strategy) to clear the mind of all preconceived thoughts, all "dualism"—opening it to "nondualism," left necessarily undefined. As we know, nondualism cannot be expressed by dualistic language, but—as we have just been witnessing—it can be expressed by fantasy.

That, I think, explains "Vimalakīrti" best: not a model for how to become Enlightened in any of his purported roles but, instead, a fantasy figure of the goal itself. He symbolizes the nondual transcendence of all opposites. Jonathan Silk puts it well:

> Vimalakīrti is an effective spokesman for the principle of non-duality precisely because he himself *embodies* the idea of the paradoxical reality of impossibility. . . . that to really understand the true nature of reality we must transcend such seemingly ordinary dichotomous truths, seeing through the apparent impossibility to the profoundly non-dual, the only true reality, the "really real."[41]

It is this same symbolic mode of expression that we find "embodied" in myth, fairy tale, and dream. Symbolism allows the psyche to say things without "saying" anything at all.

A Transgender Fantasy

Surprisingly—or not at all—a "goddess" (*devatā*) has been living in Vimalakīrti's "empty" house. Suddenly, she appears. And Śāriputra, true to form, asks her why she does not transform herself out of her "female state" since Buddhahood is not open to that gender:

> Thereupon, the goddess employed her magical power to cause the elder Śāriputra to appear in her form and to cause herself to appear in his form. . . . And Śāriputra, transformed into the goddess, replied, "I no longer appear in the form of a male! My body has changed into the body of a woman!" (61-62)

Noting the Arhat's panic, Paul Williams quips: "The poor monk was no doubt concerned about all the Vinaya rules he was unavoidably infringing!"[42] Besides, a female body is inferior in Hīnayāna and Mahāyāna Buddhism and the product of much unresolved "bad karma." Here, then, is yet another humorous play of the pairs of opposites.

Compassionately, the goddess reversed her demonstration of "nondualism," putting Śāriputra's mind and body at rest. Lest her point be missed, she explained about "women" as a conceptual category: "While they are not women in reality, they appear in the form of women. With this in mind, the Buddha said, 'In all things, there is neither male nor female.'" Since that is exactly what the Celestial Bodhisattva Tārā said in the previous chapter—and since we were not sure of her actual religious status—it may be that Tārā is the "Buddha" being quoted. Perhaps She is this household deity. Or not.

The *Vimalakīrti Sūtra* keeps playing with our expectations, loosening the cramp of thinking we can "grasp" the contents bubbling up out of the collective unconscious for our personal benefit.

---

41 Silk, "Taking the *Vimalakīrtinirdeśa* Seriously," 176. Silk's italics.

42 Williams, *Mahāyāna Buddhism*, 154.

Proto-Tantra?

Earlier, I criticized Buddhism's inability to accept the "mud" in which the "lotus" must stay rooted in order to grow into the "light" of consciousness. It is a limitation of all spiritual religions that cannot come to terms with the natural body, sex, emotions, the everyday—except to control what is natural or even deny it. At one point, however, the *Vimalakīrti* appears to correct its own "spiritual" prejudice. Mañjuśrī says to the householder:

> Noble sir, flowers like the blue lotus, the red lotus, the white lotus, the water lily, and the moon lily do not grow on the dry ground in the wilderness, but do grow in the swamps and mud banks. Just so, the buddha-qualities do not grow in living beings certainly destined for the uncreated but do grow in those living beings who are like swamps and mud banks of passions. . . . without going into the great ocean, it is impossible to find precious, priceless pearls. Likewise, without going into the ocean of passions, it is impossible to obtain the mind of omniscience. (66)

These are wise words with which, at first glance, Jung would agree. Vimalakīrti even goes a step farther, transgressively: "when the bodhisattva follows the wrong way, he follows the way to attain the qualities of the Buddha." (64)

Thurman sees Buddhist Tantra in this since that style of the religion, emerging centuries later, is sometimes called the transgressive "path of passion." He writes:

> Vimalakīrti's method in integrating the intellectual and behavior dichotomies is one of the many blatant hints of Tantric ideas in the background of his teaching method . . . . The concept of the adept using paths generally considered evil for the attainment of enlightenment and the Buddha-qualities is basic in Tantric doctrine and practice. (7)

"Integrating" should mean individuation—bringing the opposites of the one and the many, the pure and the impure, good and evil, male and female, closer together so that one's psyche is not always so "split" and in conflict.

Yet the following is what Vimalakīrti actually proposes as the "wrong way":

> Even should he enact the five deadly sins, he feels no malice, violence, or hate. Even should he go into the hells, he remains free of all taint of passions. Even should he go into the states of the animals, he remains free of darkness and ignorance. [etc. through each of the six Destinies] He may follow the ways of desire, yet he stays free of attachment to the enjoyments of desire . . . He may show the ways of the passions, yet he is utterly dispassionate and naturally pure. (64-65)

This is like the scripture's introduction to this wise layman who proved to be in the world but, upon close reading, not really of it.

Vimalakīrti is describing here the compassionate acts of a Celestial Bodhisattva who is able to go into all the Destinies to save others. We have learned from the *Lotus* that this may even require acts of "compassionate violence." But that is not actually a path of integration and more like Docetism. Yes, the highly skilled lay Bodhisattva may show the "way of the passions," but he himself is "utterly dispassionate"—and has not learned how to be, at the same time, a "passionate" man in some way. His behavior remains "flawless" and in no way touched by the "mud."

Besides, the household "goddess" explains that any particular teaching is never true but merely the opposite of a disciple's condition—in order to relativize all teachings and to reveal their "emptiness." She says:

> Liberation is freedom from desire, hatred, and folly—that is the teaching for the excessively proud. But those free of pride are taught that the very nature of desire, hatred, and folly is itself liberation. (60)

And, finally, it is somewhat misleading to refer to "Tantra" in general as a "path of passion." The label suggests antinomian or transgressive acts that are found only in a late form of Buddhist Tantra, called the Anuttarayoga. It is reserved for the very few and not condoned by earlier forms of Buddhist Tantra—forms that succeeded outside India. Tibet, however, did accept the Anuttarayoga while modifying it.

Thunderous Silence

In the chapter called the "Dharma-door to Nonduality," Vimalkīrti asks the many highly advanced Celestial Bodhisattvas who had kindly visited him during his "illness" their own view of "duality." They reply variously and correctly:

> "'I' and 'mine' are two. If there is no presumption of a self, there will be no possessiveness."
> "'Defilement' and 'purification' are two."
> "'Grasping and 'nongrasping' are two."
> "'Good' and 'evil' are two. Seeking neither good nor evil, the understanding of the nonduality of the significant and the meaningless is the entrance into nonduality." (73-74)

And so on. To which Mañjuśrī himself replies correctly:

> Good sirs, you have all spoken well. Nevertheless, all your explanations are themselves dualistic. To know no one teaching, to express nothing, to say nothing, to explain nothing, to announce nothing, to indicate nothing, and to designate nothing—that is the entrance into nonduality. (77)

And turning to Vimalakīrti, the wise Celestial Bodhisattva Mañjuśrī asks the presumably ordinary lay Bodhisattva his own view on nonduality:

> Thereupon, the Licchavi Vimalkīrti kept his silence, saying nothing at all.

This is not the silence of being dumbfounded, like that of Śāriputra who did not know what to say, but of knowing the limits of language. Thus, it is often called the "thunderous silence" of Vimalakīrti—or it is an advanced version of the "Lion's Roar." Unable to contain himself, Mañjuśrī exclaimed in words:

> Excellent! Excellent, noble sir! This is indeed the entrance into the nonduality of the bodhisattvas. Here there is no use for syllables, sounds, and ideas.

Or, as the Taoist *Chuang Tzu* puts it, "The Great Way is not named."[43] Enough said.

"Tathāgatagarbha Sūtra"

Although the *Vimalakīrti Sūtra* teaches at its close an apophatic lesson—one with which we are familiar—it does so within a larger kataphatic "story," more like the *Lotus* with its parables. As Caroline Rhys Davids might say, it proclaims the "Sea." This is also how Joan Sutherland, a Zen Buddhist, understands the scripture:

> In the koan tradition, when we're presented with an apparent duality, we resolve it not by choosing A or B but by looking for C, that unexpected thing that can embrace both A and B and create something new from them. In this sutra, Vimalakirti himself is C, the reconciliation of the opposites.[44]

That sounds like my earlier argument about "three" Truths in Budddhism, with C not expressed in Early Buddhism. In any case, the *Tathāgata-garbha Sūtra* ("Sermon on the Embryo/Womb of the Tathāgata") is itself all C. Composed in the third century, the text is a short compilation of religious images and so unsophisticated philosophically that the word, "emptiness," does not even appear—even though composed later than several Mahāyāna texts that feature the term.

The author(s) would have studied these more complex teachings but chose not to respond: except for the opening image that seems contrived and likely added as a ninth image to an earlier set of eight symbols that express from different angles this scripture's message. The opening ninth image is also treated as analogy—referring to what is already known in other terms—while the set of symbols are more naïve, at once easier to explain and more difficult, crackling with the numinosity of divine revelation. They are what one imagines hearing in the *samādhi* of the *Pratyutpanna* when

---

[43] Burton Watson, trans., *Chuang Tzu: Basic Writings* (New York: Columbia University Press, 1964), 39.

[44] Joan Sutherland, *Vimalakirti and the Awakened Heart: A Commentary on "The Sutra that Vimalakirti Speaks"* (Santa Fe: Following Wind Press, 2016), 8-9.

"face-to-face" with the Lord and hearing new things. According to the *Tathāgatagarbha Sūtra*, the new thing is the Buddha's revelation, "I am within you"—as an "Embryo."

Perhaps, it is not new and what had always been implied by the religion, but the *via negativa* would not say. That there is a Buddha within does not mean that Buddhas are not still residing outside, in Pure Lands far beyond our own. Indeed, a myriad of Bodhisattvas, more numerous than "sixty times the number of sands in the Ganges River," arrive from countless Buddha-fields to listen to the *sūtra*. Nor does the new teaching mean that a Buddha does not reside in history, outside Rājagṛha in India, where this sermon is being taught. It does mean, as one of the text's translators, Michael Zimmermann, writes: "the underlying tendency here is to redirect emphasis to the internalization of religious values."[45]

Unlike the *Vimalakīrti*, the *Tathāgatagarbha* is not *sui generis* but one of a genre of about a dozen Sanskrit texts proclaiming the value of religious "internality." One of these texts is the Mahāyāna version of the *Mahā-parinirvāṇa Sūtra* (not to be confused with the *sūtra* of the same name in the *Digha Nikāya*). That text is also longer and more complex, trying to solve intellectual problems arising from the new symbol. Another scripture in this genre is the *Śrīmālā-devī-siṃhanāda Sūtra* ("Sermon on the Lion's Roar of Queen Śrīmālā") dating from the third century. It is famous not only for its technical discussion of the "Embryo" but for its being taught by a female Bodhisattva of the court. That scripture strongly influenced the *Laṅkāvatāra Sūtra* ("Sermon on the Descent from Laṅka") composed in the fourth century. And, in turn, the *Laṅkāvatāra* became an authoritative scripture for Ch'an Buddhism in China, then Zen in Japan—traditions that rely heavily upon the doctrine (or image) of a *tathāgatagarbha* within.

These East Asian traditions, however, prefer to use a synonym that appears in our text—*buddha-dhātu* ("Buddha-element" or "Buddha-nature")—and that, as we shall see, has influenced their interpretation of what is being taught. Let me note that there is no extant Sanskrit manuscript of the text we will be considering, but there are very early translations of the *Tathāgatagarbha Sūtra* in Chinese and Tibetan. I will be using William Grosnick's rendering from the Chinese when quoting the scripture itself but refer, as needed, to Michael Zimmermann's translation from the Tibetan.[46]

Tathāgata-garbha

We already know that Siddhārtha Gautama preferred the epithet *tathāgata* when referring to himself, suggesting that he was self-conscious of being in a long line of Enlightened Ones. The Sanskrit is ambiguous, however, with two possible meanings: "thus come" (*tathā-āgata*) and "thus gone" (*tathā-gata*)—meaning that all Buddhas have "come" into Saṃsāra and "gone" into Nirvāṇa the same way. Or so it would seem, the Mahāyāna might add.

The second half of this new technical compound is also ambiguous. The primary meaning of *garbha* is "embryo, fetus, child." But it can also mean, "uterus, womb," that which contains and nurtures an embryo. Both meanings derive from biology and belong to a cluster of related

---

[45] Michael Zimmermann, *A Buddha Within: The Tathāgatagarbhasūtra* (Tokyo: International Research Institute for Advanced Buddhology, Soka University, 2002), 33.

[46] Grosnick, *Tathāgatagarbha*, 92-106. To avoid cumbersome citation, I will refer to the text by page numbers.

symbolism in the history of religions: "sacred marriage," "fertility," "gestation," "birth," and especially "rebirth." As true symbols, they point to something known and unknown, yet sacred—for which better expressions cannot be found.

We should sense in the background our previous discussion of symbolic "motherhood": Māyā as the mysterious "Mother" of the historical Buddha and Prajñāpāramitā as the "Mother of all Buddhas." Gautama Buddha himself was said to have "given birth" to his disciples as "sons and daughters." The new genre of Buddhist scriptures could be saying that all this earlier imagery anticipates its own more explicitly "internal" revelation.

To say that *garbha* means "embryo" points to the process of spiritual development—as during the Twelve Acts of a Buddha, through Ten Stages of a Bodhisattva, over three incalculable aeons—an entirely orthodox reference to the Buddhist Path. To say that *garbha* means "womb," however, raises the question of where that "embryo" would be growing. The *Tathāgatagarbha* scripture states that it grows "within sentient beings" in general and, a bit more precisely, "within the body" of sentient beings.

Other texts of the genre are clearer that the nurturing location of the Buddha "embryo" is "within the mind." The Tibetan commentator, Mkhas-grub-rje, summarized the literature by stating: "it has been in the stream of consciousness [*citta-saṃtāṇa*] of all sentient beings since beginningless 'cycles of life' . . . ."[47] We saw much earlier in this book that this ever-changing "stream" was viewed by some as the inherently "luminous" (*prabhāsvara*) mind of Early Buddhist scripture or perhaps the passive *bhavāṅga* mind of Abhidharma. It does not surprise, therefore, that the *tathāgatagarbha* is being added to an ever lengthening discussion of the mental life.

Incidentally, the dome of a Buddhist *stūpa* that contains the Lord's relics within is called in Indian architecture that structure's *garbha* or "womb." In Hindu temple architecture, the inner sanctuary where the image of a god is kept is called the *garbha-gṛha*, "womb house" or, perhaps, "house of the embryo."

Introduction

The scripture begins as usual:

> Thus have I heard. At one time the Buddha was staying on the Vulture Peak near Rājagṛha in the lecture hall of a many-tiered pavilion built of fragrant sandalwood. He had attained Buddhahood ten years previously and was accompanied by an assembly of hundreds and thousands of great monks and a throng of bodhisattvas and great beings sixty times the number of sands in the Ganges River. . . . All could turn the irreversible wheel of the dharma. If a being were to hear their names, he would become irreversible in the highest path. (94)

We actually hear those powerful names—apparently as an act of "grace"—in a long paragraph. Then, as usual, the Lord performs a miracle in the form of a great vision for his worshippers:

[47] Lessing and Wayman, *Mkhas-grub-rje's "Fundamentals,"* 49.

> At that time, the Buddha sat up straight in meditation in the sandalwood pavilion and, with his supernatural powers, put on a miraculous display. There appeared in the sky a countless number of thousand-petaled lotus flowers as large as chariot wheels, filled with colors and fragrances that one could not begin to enumerate. In the center of each flower was a conjured image of a buddha. The flowers rose and covered the heavens like a jeweled banner, each flower giving forth countless rays of light. The petals all simultaneously unfolded their splendor and then, through the Buddha's miraculous powers, all withered in an instant. Within the flowers all the buddha images sat cross-legged in lotus position, and each issued forth countless hundreds of thousands of rays of light.

And the whole assembly "rejoiced and danced ecstatically."

They, also, wondered what it all meant. Specifically, the text says: they "all began to wonder why all the countless wonderful flowers should suddenly be destroyed. As they withered and darkened, the smell they gave off was foul and loathsome." (95) This is the contrived part of the opening image when, otherwise, throughout the history of Buddhism flowers have been entirely positive with showers of them falling at all the great Buddhist moments, the lotus in particular chosen for its outspread beauty. Still, a negative note can appear in the Theravāda ritual of offering flowers before a Buddha image: "I worship the Buddha with these flowers; / May this virtue be helpful for my emancipation; / Just as these flowers fade, / Our body will undergo decay."[48] While that is good doctrine about "impermanence," it is awkward floral symbolism.

The Lord has to explain:

> In a similar fashion, good sons, when I regard all beings with my buddha eye, I see that hidden within the kleśas of greed, desire, anger, and stupidity there is seated augustly and unmovingly the tathāgata's wisdom, the tathāgata's vision, and the tathāgata's body. Good sons, all beings, though they find themselves with all sorts of kleśas, have a tathāgatagarbha that is eternally unsullied, and that is replete with the virtues no different from my own. . . whereas, after the wilted petals have been removed, those tathāgatas are manifested for all to see. (96)

It helps to realize that the vision's innumerable lotuses were closed at first, and it was only when they opened that the seated, meditating "Buddhas" were visible to the congregation.

But, surely, that did not require the flowers' petals to die off—except that the Lord felt obliged to make a point about the *kleśas* or "defilements." They must die off if one is to see what the Buddha sees with his Enlightened "eye." An ethical note is struck as we are told once more that we as sentient beings are impermanent and disgusting. Despite that, we are also told that just inside that outer fragile self, as if within a womb, sits a Great Yogin, the Buddha in eternal contemplation.

---

[48] Wikipedia contributors, "Offering (Buddhism)," *Wikipedia, The Free Encyclopedia*, https://en.wikipedia.org/w/index.php?title=Offering_(Buddhism)&oldid=1031893319.

Readers of my previous book on Hinduism may recall the image of a seated Yogin on a seal from the Indus Valley Culture and a discussion of its relevance for our own more introverted religious future. Readers of Jung will recall his dream of a country chapel with a "wonderful flower arrangement": "in front of the altar facing me, sat a yogi—in lotus posture, in deep meditation. When I looked at him more closely, I realized that he had my face."[49]

The Tathāgatagarbha is the closest Buddhism comes to Jung's discovery of the Self, the "Greater Personality" within the depths of the psyche. It represents for me the "full flowering" of this religion in India.

The Eight Core Similes

There are other ways to express this Buddhist truth, and the *Tathāgatagarbha Sūtra* does so in a standard set of eight similes, i.e., what it is "like," albeit ultimately ineffable. Here is the usual order that displays no internal logic, a fact that probably means that the images were brought together over time. The "Buddha within" is like:

1. honey in a cave or a tree
2. a kernel of wheat still inside its husk
3. gold fallen into a pit of dung
4. treasure hidden under a house
5. the seed or pit inside a mango
6. a gold statue wrapped in filthy rags
7. a king within the womb of a poor woman
8. a gold statue still inside its blackened mold

I will discuss these at the end of the chapter but will change the order since these eight actually express three archetypal motifs: "Food for the Soul," "The Treasure Hard to Find," and the "Divine Child."

Incorrigibles

As wonderful as the new teaching may have sounded at the time, it generated a number of unforeseen controversies. One concerned a category of sentient being called *icchantika* ("wishful"), persons who are inordinately full of desire—thus, not very religious or Buddhist. In fact, these persons are actively opposed to Buddhism; and a looser translation, "incorrigible," fits.[50] Ming-Wood Liu reports that in the *Mahāparinirvāṇa Sūtra* (for short, the *Nirvāṇa Sūtra*) an *icchantika* is described as:

> "devoid of good roots" and as "the most wicked being." He is depicted as "having no capacity for the true Dharma" such that he can never be rehabilitated by the

---

[49] Jung, *Memories*, 323.

[50] See "icchantika," *PDB*, 370.

> instruction of the Buddha and so will never attain supreme enlightenment. . . condemned forever to spiritual darkness . . . . [51]

But we just heard from the *Tathāgatagarbha* that "all beings" innately have within them a "Buddha" and, at the very least, the potential for Buddhahood.

In the Early Buddhist *Aṅguttara Nikāya*, there is a famous pessimistic verse: "whether Tathāgatas arise or not, there persists that law, that stableness of the Dharma, that fixed course of the Dharma: 'All conditioned phenomena are impermanent . . . suffering . . . are non-self.'"[52] In a deliberate parallel, the new text reads much more positively: "Whether or not buddhas appear in the world, the tathāgatagarbhas of all beings are eternal and unchanging." (96)

Let us note that this religious optimism is not entirely new. The *Lotus Sūtra* had already proclaimed, centuries earlier, the existence of countless Bodhisattvas who had taken the Bodhicitta Vow to "save all beings;" the Buddha himself prophesied Buddhahood for numerous persons by their new name in that text, even his evil cousin Devadatta—an *icchantika* if there ever was one. And the parable of the "Prodigal Son" with its happy ending appeared to be meant for us all.

It is true, however, that before the Lord preached the *Lotus*, "five thousand straightway rose from their seats and, doing obseisance to the Buddha, withdrew." The scripture explains that: "This group had deep and grave roots of sin and overweening pride, imagining themselves to have attained and to have borne witness to what in fact they had not."[53] They appear to be *icchantikas*.

Liu informs us that the *Nirvāṇa Sūtra* can go both ways on this issue. In its earlier chapters, we read:

> All sentient beings possess the Buddha-nature. Due to this nature, they can cut off innumerable billions of bonds of defilements, and attain the most perfect enlightenment. The only exceptions are the *icchantikas*.[54]

Then, later in the same scripture (i.e., later in its chronological compilation) we read:

> What is perfect faith? It comprises believing whole-heartedly that the Buddha, the Dharma and the Saṅgha are eternal, that the Buddhas of the ten directions are the skillful manifestations of the one immutable Tathāgata, and that all sentient beings, *including the icchantikas*, possess the Buddha-nature . . . . [55]

And it is this latter, more generous, attitude that became most influential in East Asia.

The controversy persisted, however, as we observe with the famous "Mu" *kōan* of the Japanese Zen tradition:

---

[51] Ming-Wood Liu, "The Problem of the *Icchantika* in the Mahāyāna *Mahāparinirvāṇa Sūtra*," *The Journal of the International Association of Buddhist Studies* 7, no.1 (1984): 58-59.

[52] Bodhi, *AN* 3.136 (p.p. 363-364). Regularized to Sanskrit.

[53] Hurvitz, *Lotus Blossom*, 29.

[54] Liu, "Problem," 64.

[55] Liu, "Problem," 71. Liu's emphasis.

> A student asked: "Does a dog also have Buddha-nature or not? The Master said, "It does not" [Jap., *mu*, "no"].

Then, the commentaries began: Why would the master say that? Everybody knows that all sentient beings, dogs, even trees—and possibly even insentient objects like rocks and roof tiles—have *buddha-dhātu*. Did he just say the opposite of what we expected to hear in order to loosen our attachment to understanding? And on and on.[56]

Sudden or Gradual Enlightenment

A second controversy concerned Enlightenment: Was it experienced gradually or suddenly? We have been witnessing the traditional "gradual" approach for several chapters—how one must make a special vow in the presence of a Buddha, how that vow as seed grows over time to produce its inevitable fruit through Three Trainings or Ten Stages, and in most cases over vast periods of time. True, we also witnessed at the close of Gautama Buddha's first sermons some "sudden" attainments of Arhathood; but they were either exceptional or symbolic of the power of the Lord's voice and charismatic presence.

Now, a faction of Buddhists claimed that a gradual attainment was the wrong way to understand this experience—given their reading of the *Tathāgatagarbha Sūtra*. They noticed that the "lotus petals" of the text's introduction were "withered in an instant" and that the "ecstatic" congregation suddenly saw the new truth of their "Buddha-nature." Why assume the experience is otherwise? Whether or not this issue was important for Indian Buddhists is not clear; but it was very important for Chinese Buddhists.

This we know from a quasi-historical "debate" held at Bsam yas, the first Buddhist monastery of Tibet, in the eighth century CE. The Chinese proponent of the "sudden" position spoke first:

> If you commit virtuous or non-virtuous deeds, because you go to heavens and hells, you still are not liberated from *saṃsāra*. . . . Whoever does not think anything [i.e., has no discriminating concepts during meditation] . . . is instantaneously enlightened. He is the equal to one who has mastered the tenth *bhūmi*.[57]

That *bhūmi* or Stage of a Bodhisattva is, as we have seen, tantamount in Mahāyāna to being a Buddha.

In his response, the Indian scholar Kamalaśīla—recently arrived from his teaching post at Nālandā—pointed out that Gautama Buddha taught a "gradual" Eightfold Path, that meditation was only one of the Three Trainings, and there was real danger of antinomianism in treating "virtuous and non-virtuous deeds" with equal disregard. The Tibetan king who had called the debate declared this Indian "gradual" side the winner and exiled the "sudden" faction, establishing henceforth Tibetan Buddhism's preference for Indian influence. We should note, however, a typical unholy mix of

[56] See Robert Sharf, "On the Buddha-nature of Insentient Things," unfinished essay, University of Michigan, http://www.buddhism.org/kr/koan/Robert_Sharf-e.htm

[57] Williams, *Mahāyāna*, 194.

politics and religion—the king of Tibet was at war with China and could ill afford that the Chinese religious position win.

Recent scholarship on the so-called "Bsam yas debate" has shown a softer polarity on the issues. The "sudden" side was actually argued by monks who had been following a "gradual" path of renouncing family life, following the Vinaya rules, etc; while the "gradual" side never denied that at the end of a long spiritual journey, one finally and "suddenly" realized Omniscence. When Japanese Zen refined its own "sudden" position—derived from the Chinese—they would speak of *kenshō* as an initial "sudden" glimpse into the truth of Buddha-nature, to be cultivated "gradually" over time—with additional *kenshō* experiences—before a more definitive experience of *satori* or Bodhi. This initial "glimpse" reminds us of becoming a "Stream-winner" in Early Buddhism, after which one would eventually "flow" on toward Nirvāṇa.

Although the East Asian refinement shifts the original Indian pattern from "gradual-then-sudden" to "sudden-then-gradual," it reveals a pair of opposites in the religious life that is apparently unavoidable. Calvinist Christians speak of getting "born again" decisively all of a sudden, but then having to mature that experience in a lifelong process of "sanctification." Jungian analysis is not particularly interested in sudden experiences as much as in a gradual change in one's attitude, even one's world view. There are "breakthroughs" along the way, however, that one can even date in a journal.

Tathāgatagarbha as Ātman

The new genre of scriptures stirred yet another controversy that was much more highly charged: Does the revelation of a "Tathāgata-garbha" or "Buddha-dhātu" within all or most sentient beings, seen suddenly or otherwise, imply a "self" when Buddhism had long been committed to "non-self"? The possibility was almost alarming. In the sixth century, the Mahāyānist Bhāvaviveka listed among the attacks by Hīnayānists: "because the Mahāyāna teaches that the *tathāgatagarbha* is all pervasive, it does not relinquish the belief in self."[58]

Recall that, in his Second Sermon, Gautama could not find the "self" (*ātman*) in phenomena because it was a mark of "substantiality"—either as an ontological fact or as an *upāya*. And while the Buddha would not say one way or the other, it was always possible to argue that this was a denial of the Hindu "Self" within the "chariot" of a human being. That is, until now. We read in the *Kaṭha Upaniṣad* that "A certain wise man in search of immortality, turned his sight inward and saw the Self within." Are not the Buddhists now saying the same thing?

The Bodhisattva Mahāmati actually asked the Lord that question in the *Laṅkāvatara Sūtra*:

> Now the Blessed One makes mention of the Tathāgata-garbha in the sutras, and verily it is described by you as by nature bright and pure, as primarily unspotted, endowed with the thirty-two marks of excellence, hidden in the body of every being like a gem of great value . . . Is not this Tathāgata-garbha taught by the

[58] Lopez, "Authority," 22.

> Blessed One the same as the ego-substance [Suzuki's too interpretive translation of *ātman*] taught by the philosophers?

The Lord replied:

> No, Mahāmati, my Tathāgata-garbha is not the same as the [*ātman*] taught by the philosophers; for what the Tathagatas teach is the Tathāgata-garbhas in the sense, Mahāmati, that it is emptiness, reality-limit, Nirvana, being unborn, unqualified, and devoid of will-effort.

In other words, according to this Tathāgatagarbha scripture, traditional teaching has not really changed. Yes, there is new language, but it has a compassionate purpose:

> The doctrine pointing to the Tathāgata-garbha is to make the ignorant cast aside their fear when they listen to the teaching of ["non-self"] and to have them realize the state of non-discrimination and imagelessness.[59]

According to the *Laṅkāvatāra*, therefore, the new teaching is just *upāya* or a "skillful means" to encourage those who might be afraid of the truth of "emptiness."

The *Nirvāṇa Sūtra* is not nearly so cautious; indeed, it throws caution to the winds. Mark Blum translates:

> Good man, "self" is precisely what *tathāgatagarbha* means. All living beings have buddha-nature, and this is what is meant by *this* notion of self. However, the significance of "self" understood in this way has been continuously covered over by an uncountable number of the defilements since the beginning . . ., and that is why living beings have been unable to perceive it.[60]

We could add that it has been covered over by the Buddhist tradition itself—except as we have been able to perceive a "Self" hidden inside its mythology.

The *sūtra* goes on, reminding us of the "Four Distorted Views" that are corrected or inverted in Early Buddhism by the "Three Characteristics" plus the characteristic of impurity: i.e., seeing happiness where there is really suffering, permanence where there is impermanence, seeing self where there is non-self, and purity where there is really impurity. The Lord of the *Nirvāṇa Sūtra* says all this is provisionally true but now needs to be "inverted" again:

> The perception of self in what is nonself and the perception of nonself in what is self, these I also call inversions. Worldly people speak of the existence of a self and we also speak of the existence of a self in the Buddha's dharma, but although

[59] Suzuki, *Lankavatara*, 68-69. Translation altered.

[60] Mark L. Blum, trans., *The Nirvana Sutra (Mahāparinirvāṇa-sūtra)*, vol. 1 (Berkeley: Bukkyo Dendo Kyokai America, 2013), 226. His italics.

> worldly people affirm the existence of self they do not affirm the existence of Buddha-nature. This particular view I call "the perception of self in what is nonself" and this, too, is an inversion. There is a self in the Buddha's dharma but that self is the Buddha-nature.[61]

And the same is true for each of the other Characteristics. This is blatant kataphatic language; and the word "self" in the last sentence should be capitalized. The Lord encourages, "Do not be afraid!"[62]

As we have seen, not all Buddhists agreed with this. In modern times, Matsumoto Shirō—a scholar of Buddhism and a Sōtō Zen priest—really disagrees. He has written an essay whose title, "The Doctrine of *Tathāgata-garbha* Is Not Buddhist," makes his position clear. Thus, he asserts, much of Zen itself is not Buddhist; nor is this author impressed by Vimalakīrti's silence. Instead, that so-called lay "master of the Dharma" should have argued his position—rather than allow to linger the possibility of some transcending "third thing" beyond "empty" opposites, some *dhātu* or "essence" serving as the "primal source of all phenomena" or "existential foundation" (some Truth C).

To Matsumoto, that is all heresy. He writes:

> I wish clearly to reject the idea that Śākyamuni's awakening (and hence Buddhism itself) can be understood in terms of self and existence rather than in terms of no-self and emptiness. For me, the teaching of no-self follows naturally from the notion of *pratītyasamutpāda* [Dependent Origination] to which Śākyamuni was awakened.[63]

The scholar-priest closes his critique with an impassioned appeal:

> For non-Buddhists, none of this is an issue (and indeed for Hindus, the reemergence of *dhātu-vāda* ["following an element"] within the Buddhist tradition might be seen as a fortunate turn of events). But for me, as a Buddhist, there is rather more at stake. Should any of my readers have harbored the notion that the doctrine of *tathāgata-garbha* belongs to the essence of Buddhism . . . I can only plead with them to recognize it as an example of the very thing that Śākyamuni was criticizing and to return to true Buddhist teaching.[64]

This essay appears in a collection entitled, *Pruning the Bodhi Tree*; and one writer has remarked that Matsumoto has severely pruned a Tree that is otherwise lush and beautiful.

But that is speaking symbolically. Indeed, I believe Matsumoto has missed the symbolic dimension of religious expression in favor of the philosophic. Had he relied more on language about

---

[61] Blum, *Nirvana Sutra*, 225.

[62] Blum, *Nirvana Sutra*, 228.

[63] Matsumoto Shirō, "The Doctrine of *Tathāgata-garbha* Is Not Buddhist," in Hubbard and Swanson, *Pruning the Bodhi Tree*, 166.

[64] Matsumoto, "Doctrine," 173.

an "Embryo"—a rich symbol with nuance that is hard to pin down—instead of the more discursive or abstract term, "Element," he might have seen that.

In the same collection of essays, Sallie King counters with her own clear title, "The Doctrine of Buddha-nature Is Impeccably Buddhist." She acknowledges that: "Buddha-nature thought uses some of the terminology of essentialist and monistic philosophy, and thus may give the reader the impression that it is essentialist or monistic"—but that is not what the language really intends.[65] Instead, it is all an "experiment." King writes that:

> Buddhism is not nihilistic but, much to the contrary, holds a promise of something of great value that can be discovered through Buddhist practice. Since emptiness language has these negative effects, and since, after all, śūnyavāda is not the Truth but simply an *upāya*, why not experiment with other ways to communicate the Dharma? And since śūnyavāda had pretty well exhausted the *via negativa*, and language, being dualistic, basically offers only negative and positive options, why not experiment with articulating the Dharma in positive language?

We have already heard from the *Laṅkāvatāra Sūtra* that the "Tathāgatagarbha" is not some great new "Truth" but, instead, a compassionate *upāya* or "strategy" to encourage converts. Now we hear from a scholar of Buddhism that "emptiness" itself is "simply an *upāya*" (my own position).

Nevertheless, the "emptiness of self" for this writer (who is also a Buddhist) has priority. She expresses that in the strange equation: "ātmapāramitā=anātmapāramitā=the true, essential nature of all things"—meaning, apparently, that the "essence" of all things and people is the "lack of an essence," the word "self" meaning somehow the "lack of self."

To be fair, King does see something positive: the world "conceived as dynamic, as a series of processes, rather than constructed of entities."[66] It is what makes "life" possible since "plants are processes, not entities, that grow"—the implication being that anything with "substance" or "self" is, by definition, static and lifeless. In this way, King tries putting "leaves" back on Matsumoto's Bodhi Tree. But she is also avoiding the fact that whatever "changes" for Gautama Buddha is by definition "painful."

A Jungian comment Nor is King addressing the age-old philosophical problem of "being and becoming," a pair of opposites that deserve to be harmonized since they, too, are unavoidable. Psychologically, what "becomes" and forever is in "process" is ego consciousness—and one can hope that it is "growing." What has "being," then, is the collective unconscious with its archetypal structures that function as a Foundation for psychic life. If this sounds "essentialist" (something modern thinkers find abhorrent), it is only symbolically so since we cannot be sure that anything we say about the psyche—from within the psyche—is accurate. All we can do, as Jung has said, is "*dream*

---

[65] Sallie B. King, "The Doctrine of Buddha-Nature Is Impeccably Buddhist," in Hubbard and Swanson, *Pruning the Bodhi Tree*, 174-176.

[66] King, "Impeccably Buddhist," 177.

the myth onwards and give it a modern dress." The composers or compilers of the *Tathāgatagarbha Sūtra* were "dreaming onwards" in their own day.

The Similes

Archetype of "Food" Let us do something similar by treating the core images of our *sūtra* as if they were someone's dreams. It is how we treated the standard set of "dreams" found in the mythic Life of the Buddha shortly before his Enlightenment. Three of the *Tathāgatagarbha* similes, then, contain "food" imagery—telling us in different ways what it is like to have a "Buddha within."

1) First, it is like "honey." The Lord teaches in the Grosnick translation:

> Or, good sons, it is like pure honey in a cave or a tree, surrounded and protected by a countless swarm of bees. It may happen that a person comes along who knows some clever techniques. He first gets rid of the bees and takes the honey, and then does as he will with it, eating it or giving it away far and wide. Similarly, good sons, all sentient beings have the tathāgatagarbha. It is like pure honey in a cave or tree, but it is covered by kleśas, which, like a swarm of bees, keep one from getting to it. With my Buddha eye I see it clearly, and with appropriate skillful techniques I expound the dharma, in order to destroy kleśas and reveal the Buddha vision. (97)

Here, the "Tathāgatagarbha"—"Buddhagarbha," "Buddhadhātu"—is like honey hidden in a cave or tree. But we would not know that if the Buddha had not seen it first, then taught us to see it in scriptures using "skillful techniques" like someone skilled at ridding the hive of bees to reach the food. The teaching even has the power, we are told, to "destroy" our *kleśas* likened to bees.

But interpreters have pointed out that the image does not quite work for a Buddhist—since the bees are not just bad but necessary to make the honey, while dislodging the bees is an act of violence, and taking their honey a kind of theft. But, then, the "Buddha" in the scripture may have explained too much, encouraging thinking about the symbol rather than allowing it to have its own "nourishing" effect.

At the risk of saying too much ourselves, Jung has "seen" that the archetypal psyche is not just structural but dynamic, providing libido for conscious living. Therefore, just as the body needs energy from food to survive, so does ego consciousness need energy from the unconscious for its own survival. Jung writes that "it is the 'nourishing' influence of unconscious contents, which maintain the vitality of consciousness by a continual influx of energy; for consciousness does not produce its energy by itself."[67]

"Honey" says that well. It is a prized food since so delicious, so sweet, and it lasts a very long time. The ancients associated it with abundance of life, even immortality. In the Bible, the Promised

[67] Jung, *CW* 9i, par. 248.

Land of Canaan was said to "flow with milk and honey." In the early Church, the newly baptized were offered a cup of milk and honey to express, ritually, entrance into the Kingdom of Heaven.

But the Book of Proverbs warns that "honey" can also be dangerous: "for the lips of a loose woman drip honey" (NRSV, 5:2). It is here that we find honey's "sweetness" associated with inordinate or misplaced desire—introducing ambiguity into the symbolism.

Still, Edinger reminds us of the adage, "The lure of desire is the *sweetness* of fulfillment," and goes on to say that some persons shrink too much from their desires to avoid life's abundance; they need to respond positively to the symbolism of "honey"—should it show up in their psychology.[68] It is even this "Food" archetype that lures us into the world where we find our "sweetheart," whom we call "honey," even after the "honeymoon." And without experiences of that kind—making mistakes along the way and sometimes being "bad" like some honey thief—there can be no increase in consciousness.

Traditional ascetic Buddhism, however, does not encourage that line of association. For it sounds too much like the "savory earth" at the beginning of the aeon that some greedy person tasted—instigating the Buddhist version of the "Fall." We actually read in an early chapter that the suspicious substance was "very sweet, like pure wild honey."

Nevertheless, in the *Tathāgatagarbha Sūtra*, the Lord wants his "good sons" [and daughters] to see that there is this other "Sweetness within," greater than anything sweet that the external world can offer should one get stuck there. Sujātā offered sweet "food" to Gautama just prior to his breakthrough—special milk-rice that was the "correct thickness, sweetness, and strength." Indeed, it was strong enough to break his attachments to the conventional world even as he returned to the world with his saving message. With that in mind, here are some "nourishing" words from Ralph Waldo Emerson about introversion: "but the great man is he who in the midst of the crowd keeps with perfect sweetness the independence of solitude."[69]

2) A second "food" image is that of a "kernel of wheat":

> Or, good sons, it is like a kernel of wheat that has not yet had its husk removed. Someone who is impoverished might foolishly disdain it, and consider it to be something that should be discarded. But when it is cleaned, the kernel can always be used. In like fashion, . . . I see that the husk of kleśas covers their limitless tathāgata vision. (97)

An "impoverished" person inexplicably does not know that grain needs to be threshed to loosen a hard outer husk—then winnowed in a light wind to separate the edible from the chaff. In other words, the person's "poverty" is ignorance. But the reader is expected to know about cereals and be shocked by the "foolish disdain" of someone who would "discard" such nourishing food. Of course, the point is that everyone tends to undervalue—out of ignorance—the Nourishment that lies within.

---

[68] Edinger, *Anatomy*, 90. His italics.

[69] Emerson, "Self-Reliance," 150.

Zimmermann thinks the "common" existence of grain either in the wild or deliberately cultivated is also the point: "It thus seems in this illustration the author wanted to stress the commonness of the fact that buddhaood is found in all living beings (covered by defilements) and the normality of its manifestation"—and that turning cereal to account is itself an "ordinary process."[70] Thus, the Presence of "Buddha-nature" in what is ordinary in Zen—in a stray dog, in a cup of tea.

Jung notes that what is "ordinary" tends to be undervalued by that very fact:

> The immortal being issues from something humble and forgotten, indeed, from a wholly improbable source. . . . The nourishing character of the transformative substance or deity is borne out by numerous cult-legends: Christ is the bread, Osiris the wheat, Mondamin the maize, etc. These symbols coincide with a psychic fact which obviously, from the point of view of consciousness, has the significance merely of something to be assimilated, but whose real nature is overlooked.[71]

And what is "overlooked" is the reality of the psyche, the inner life—apparently not just today in our own culture but ever since humanity has needed religion to remind them otherwise.

Edinger comments that in Western alchemy the "ubiquity" of the First Matter (*prima materia*) symbolizes where psychotherapy can focus to find what is truly important, namely, within the everyday, the petty, what one is inclined to disdain or have already discarded. Analysis is a bit like "threshing" that beats off a rigid ego's outer shell no longer needed for protection. It is like "winnowing" that sorts in the light wind of discussion what is chaff and what is vital to one's own psyche.

3) There is one more "food" image in this scripture:

> Or, good sons, it is like the pit inside a mango fruit which does not decay. When you plant it in the ground, it grows into the largest and most regal of trees. In the same manner, good sons, when I look at sentient beings with my buddha vision, I see that the tathāgatagarbha is surrounded by a husk of ignorance, just as the seeds of a fruit are only found at its core.

The Teacher seems unsure what point to make here: that the mango is another kind of sweet Enlightenment "food;" or that the invisible "pit" at a mango's core is indestructible unlike the soft fruit surrounding it; or that this seed-pit can grow, if planted, into a very large tree—like a Bodhi Tree—bearing many "nourishing" mangoes. The unconscious, of course, is happy to make all these points at once, as it often does in dreams.

Zimmermann chooses the aspect of "growth" and writes:

---

[70] Zimmermann, *Buddha Within*, 37.

[71] Jung, *CW* 9i, par. 248. For additional associations, see my discussion of the Aztec "maize" god Xipe Totec in *The Body*, 70-73.

> Here, at first glance, it is the process of growing, the ripening of the sprout into a "great king of trees," around which the comparison turns. . . . A closer analysis of the wording will show rather that the essential sameness of sprout and full-grown tree, their alternate generation, and the fact that the tree is contained in its complete but not yet fully unfolded form already in the seed go to make up the focus of the simile. In contrast to most of the other similes no act of purification is needed.[72]

This scholar goes on to say that if the "effect is already in the cause" (one kind of Indian causation theory) and "purification" is not required, that gives the dangerous impression that "serious religious practice is irrelevant."[73] Our *sūtra* even leans that way by advising near its close: "If you exert yourselves / And do not spend a lot of time / Sitting in the meditation hall." (101) This suggests the "sudden Enlightenment" side of the Bsam yas debate—although we know that side reached its conclusion "gradually."

Jung's understanding of the Self is similar: an inner core of the psyche that is "Complete" in itself, yet is unconscious, and needs to "grow" into *conscious* completeness. Thus, he writes of "becoming" the personality one has "always been." As to the process itself, Jung goes both ways. It appears to be happening naturally—collectively, as culture—very, very slowly over the millennia. The scripture, however, speaks of planting the mango pit deliberately and not just allowing it to find its way into the soil. Thus, Jung advises that we deliberately participate in the natural process to accelerate a cultural advance—and to give our individual personal lives a larger purpose.

Archetype of "Treasure" The *Tathāgatagarbha Sūtra* uses four images to express the archetypal motif of the "Treasure hard to attain."

> 4) The first example is quite striking:
>
> Or, good sons, it is like genuine gold that has fallen into a pit of waste and been submerged and not seen for years. The pure gold does not decay, yet no one knows that it is there. But suppose there came along someone with supernatural vision, who told people, "Within the impure waste there is a genuine gold trinket [Zimmermann, "gold nugget"]. You should get it out and do with it as you please." Similarly, good sons, the impure waste is your innumerable kleśas. The genuine gold . . . is your tathāgatagarbha. (98)

Here, the "Buddha within" is "genuine gold." That indicates how valuable or precious it is—in part because it is rarely recognized ("no one knows that it is there"). Nor does gold "decay" just as honey does not spoil. And the yellow color of both alludes to the yellow sun and its light—i.e., to the inner Source of Enlightenment. Psychologically, there does seem to be a "Light" of awareness within the unconscious: it "knows" things, yet different in kind from the "light" of consciousness. Since gold is

---

[72] Zimmermann, *Buddha Within*, 37-38.
[73] Zimmermann, *Buddha Within*, 81.

solid, the text takes no notice of the problem of "substance" in Buddhism and is not careful to refer to a "process" in the way that the motif of "Food" lent itself. Gold is also beautiful, so now we know wherein lies our own true Beauty—releasing us from being overly concerned with external beauty.

This Gold, however, is hidden in a "pit of waste" (a "shit-pit," Alan Cole translates).[74] And the contrast between gold and shit could not be greater; that the "Buddha" is found there is a disconcerting idea. But this excrement is familiar to Buddhists as the *kleśas* or "defilements" of a human being—if not the human body itself (that "stinking machine made of excrement," as Śāntideva describes it).[75] The unpleasant reference is not far from the "disgusting wilted lotus petals" of our scripture's introduction. So, again, morality is emphasized; and it seems all we need do to reach Solid Gold is to "cleanse" ourselves of greed, hatred, delusion, etc.

In this way, our rather late Mahāyāna text is not that different from Early Buddhism's own emphasis on ethical "purity" —symbolically not that far from the "Golden Buddha" in Bangkok that was hidden behind plaster. In fact, Buddhist commentators often equate what is being revealed here with the "luminous mind" of the *Aṅguttara Nikāya*—soiled by "adventitious defilements" that do not really belong to it and that should and can be removed. It sits close to the image of the vowed "Bodhicitta" that acts throughout one's many often-sullied lifetimes like an invisible inner Force for Enlightenment.

About this, Śāntideva is thrilled:

> As a blind man may obtain a jewel in a heap of dust ["dung" is a possible translation], so, somehow, this Thought of Enlightenment has arisen even within me.
> This elixir has originated for the destruction of death in the world. It is the imperishable treasure which alleviates the world's poverty.[76]

Daringly, the *Śrīmālā* says that the Tathāgatagarbha is the "Dharmakāya" within all sentient beings—once it is has been cleaned.[77]

Readers may be familiar with Western alchemy's famous saying that there is "gold in the dung." It led some practitioners of the "Art" to purchase privies and treat the fecal waste found there with chemicals and heat to make actual gold. They failed, of course; but there were fellow practitioners who knew they would. Jung comments:

> There were always a few for whom laboratory work was primarily a matter of symbols and their psychic effect. As the texts show, they were quite conscious of this, to the point of condemning the naïve goldmakers as liars, frauds, and dupes.

---

[74] Cole, *Text as Father*, 220.

[75] Śāntideva, *Entering the Path*, 167.

[76] Śāntideva, *Entering the Path*, 155-156.

[77] Alex Wayman and Hideko Wayman, trans., *The Lion's Roar of Queen Śrīmālā: A Buddhist Scripture on the Tathāgatagarbha Theory* (New York: Columbia University Press, 1974), 98.

> Their own standpoint they proclaimed with propositions like, "*Aurum nostrum non est aurum vulgi*" ["Our gold is not ordinary gold"].[78]

The "extraordinary Gold" they sought, says Jung, was the numinous Self that lies within the depths of the psyche—either as the instigator of individuation or as its goal.

The emphasis in the Buddhist material, however, is on uncovering this Gold by cleansing it of human stain; in the Western material, the emphasis is on making the precious Substance. In fact, it is made from the "dung" itself that is not discarded but called the "Prima Materia" ["first matter"]. Edinger explains:

> Psychologically, this means that the *prima materia* is found in the shadow, that part of the personality that is considered most despicable. Those aspects of ourselves most painful and most humiliating are the very ones to be brought forward and worked on.[79]

Jung remarks about this process: "If I fulfill my pattern, then I can even accept my sinfulness, and can say, 'It is too bad, but it is so—I have to agree with it.' And then I am fulfilled, then the gold begins to glow. You see, people who can agree with themselves are like gold."[80]

> 5) Or, good sons, it is like a store of treasure hidden beneath an impoverished household. The treasure cannot speak and say that it is there, since it isn't conscious of itself and doesn't have a voice. So no one can discover this treasure store. It is just the same with sentient beings. . . . Therefore buddhas appear in the world and reveal to them the dharma store of the tathāgata in their bodies. And they believe in it and accept it and purify their universal wisdom. (98-99)

We have seen this motif twice before, in the *Lotus Sūtra*. The "impoverished" Prodigal Son had no idea that all that wealth of the Rich Man was really his and kept on suffering, almost willfully. Likewise, the man down on his luck did not know there was a precious Jewel sown into his garment and was chided for missing it. A new detail in this "parable" is that the hidden Treasure "isn't conscious of itself and doesn't have a voice"—so as to make itself known.

Here we see the necessity for ego consciousness not only to look for "hidden treasure" but also to give it voice, to express it in some way. Jung wrote in a letter:

> My inner principle is: Deus *et* homo. God needs man in order to become conscious, just as he needs limitation in time and space. Let us therefore be for him limitation in time and space, an earthly tabernacle.[81]

---

78 Jung, *CW* 12, par. 40.

79 Edinger, *Anatomy of the Psyche*, 12.

80 Jung, *Nietzsche's "Zarathustra,"* 803.

81 Jung, *Letters* 1:65-66. His italics.

Buddhism's "impoverished household" is the ignorant ego, not yet aware of its function as an "earthly tabernacle" for the Sacred. That function, when conscious, transforms "poor" egohood into "rich" egohood since it now has some access to archetypal Wisdom. And, as Socrates prayed at the end of the *Phaedrus*: "May I count the wise man only rich."

6, 7) There are two images of hidden "golden statues" that are so close that I will treat them together. The scripture does not identify them as a statues of the Buddha, but we cannot help imagining that to be the case. Let us note that the *Tathāgathagarbha* scripture has to be late enough for anthropomorphic images of the Buddha to exist. Indeed we learn here of the "lost-wax" technique of metal casting. Zimmermann's Tibetan version is the more explicit:

> Sons of good family, again it is like the example of figures of horses, elephants, women or men fashioned out of wax, then encased in clay so that they are completely covered with it and finally, after the clay has dried, melted in fire; and after the wax has been made to drip out, gold is melted. And when the cavity inside the mold is filled with the melted gold, even though all the figures, having cooled down step by step and arrived at a uniform state, are covered with black clay and unsightly outside, their insides are made of gold. Then, when a smith or a smith's apprentice uses a hammer to remove from the figures the outer layer of clay around those figures which he sees have cooled down, then in that moment the golden figures lying inside become completely clean.[82]

The imagery is close to the "removal of a hard husk" covering nourishing grain, of "cleaning" dark dung off shining gold. But it is more elaborate and expresses the creative efforts of culture. We even learn why we need great art—because it shows us what lies within, so we can know our purpose for being here. The beauty of art also points to where Beauty lies.

Then, as if some merchant bought this work of art—and returning now to the Chinese version:

> . . . it is like a man with a statue of pure gold, who was to travel through the narrow roads of another country and feared that he might be victimized and robbed. So he wrapped the statue in worn-out rags so that no one would know that he had it. On the way the man suddenly died, and the golden statue was discarded in an open field. Travelers trampled it and it became totally filthy. But a person with supernatural vision saw that within the worn-out rags there was a pure gold statue, so he unwrapped it and all paid homage to it.

The lesson is what to do when we eventually find the precious Image within the "worn-out rags" of our being—we are to pay "homage" to it. In part, that is to make amends for having trampled on precious values for so long. True, we did not know, but Jung says often that unconsciousness is no real excuse and, indeed, the greatest sin.

---

[82] Zimmermann, *Buddha Within*, 140-141. Slightly altered.

Worshippers of the *Tathāgatagarbha Sūtra* sometimes heralded their scripture as a Third Turning of the Wheel of the Dharma, following the First Turning of the Hīnayāna and the Second Turning of the Perfection of Wisdom. But they also knew it would be rejected by those stuck at the doctrines of "non-self" or "emptiness." We hear that in the story of the first preaching of the new doctrine, when countless Bodhisattvas became Buddhas thereby—except for Vajramati (to whom the Lord told this story) and, to our surprise, Mahāsthāmaprāpta, Mañjuśrī, and Avalokiteśvara. (105)

Yet that is also to be expected since, archetypally, there is an initial "Rejection" of what comes next. Much earlier in this book, we watched the Band of Five reject Gautama Buddha himself, and we should not assume that Gautama had an easy time of that experience. Jung confessed that it was not easy to meet with the general incomprehension that he found the psyche as real as the body containing it, that there is a "God-image" within the collective unconscious that we had best acknowledge and obey. In the last year of his life, he wrote sadly in a letter:

> I have to pay tribute to my old age and accept the beatings lying down. I have to understand that I was unable to make the people see what I am after. I am practically alone. There are a few who understand this and that. But almost nobody that sees the whole. . . . I have failed in my foremost task: to open people's eyes to the fact that man has a soul and that there is a buried treasure in the field . . . ."[83]

But, then, the failure is really ours, not his.

Archetype of the "Child" Only one image among the core set of eight directly reflects the scripture's title, "Womb or Embryo of the Tathāgata": namely, that of a "woman pregnant with a son." It is, also, the only one whose main symbol is truly sentient, in the Buddhist sense of not just being alive like a "seed," but conscious. The word, *sattva*, "sentient being," is rendered by Tibetan as *sems can*, "having mind," a clue to what the Sanskrit intends. And while we could say that the "Buddha" sitting inside a lotus—in the introductory "ninth" image—is sentient, he is fully developed. By contrast, a Buddha "embryo" in the "womb" is in a state of developing, a true "Tathāgatagarbha." That contrast fueled the debate over whether or not Enlightenment had only to be seen as already Present or needed to be gradually matured.

The image of pregnancy, then, clearly supports the gradual development of Buddhahood even as it reveals that the potential for this wonderful outcome is already alive within everyone. Here is the text:

> 8) Or, good sons, it is like a woman who is impoverished, vile, ugly, and hated by others, who bears a noble son in her womb. He will become a sage king, a ruler of all the four directions. But she does not know his future history, and constantly thinks of him as a base-born, impoverished child. In like fashion, good sons, the Tathāgata sees that all sentient beings are carried around by the wheel of saṃsāra,

[83] Edward F. Edinger, *Ego and Self: The Old Testament Prophets*, ed. J. Gary Sparks (Toronto: Inner City Books, 2000), 149.

> receiving suffering and poison, but their bodies possess the tathāgata's treasure store. Just like that woman, they do not realize this. This is why the Tathāgata everywhere expounds the dharma, saying, "Good sons, do not consider yourselves inferior or base. You all personally possess the buddha nature." (101)

The structure of the story is similar to that of the others: something of great value is hidden inside a disgusting or unlikely place. The motif of "impoverishment" is repeated as a metaphor for ignorance. And the Buddha's teaching of the Dharma is required, yet again, to correct this serious error in perception or attitude.

We seem to have read a version of this story earlier in the "Life" of the Buddha where Gautama's mother, Queen Māyā, was pregnant with a child whose future she did not yet know. Could it be that of a Cakravartin, "ruler of all the four directions," as here, or a Buddha? But, then, we learned that the Buddha became a "Cakravartin" of the spirit. So it is not really awkward that in our current story the "sage king" is a metaphor for "Buddha-nature."

Māyā, however, was perfectly virtuous and extraordinarily beautiful like the goddess Lakṣmī, loved by all. This mother is "vile, ugly, and hated by others." One has the impression, nevertheless, that the stories belong together and that the earlier auspicious myth is behind this darker image—revealing what happens when the unwitting ego intervenes and distorts a profound truth. This eighth image, then, is our story; and we are all "vile" mothers, yet all "pregnant" with Something "noble" of which we are not aware.

The Tibetan translation emphasizes the dire circumstances. It reports that the woman took up residence in a "poorhouse": "While staying there she had become pregnant"—by "chance," says another version, and no father is ever mentioned. Nor does the mysteriously pregnant woman ever question, says the Tibetan text, "Of what kind is this life that has entered my womb?"[84] Instead, as we heard, she assumes her impoverishment is shared by the Embryo within her—"a base-born, impoverished child." But it is not the case!

As Zimmermann translates:

> Rather thinking herself poor, she would be depressed, and would think thoughts like "I am inferior and weak," and would pass the time staying in the poorhouse as somebody of unsightly complexion and bad smell."

How sad—yet who can trust any of this? We could not trust Gautama when he was twenty-nine and claimed his palace was like a "cemetery" and the dancing women were all "vile." But, then, he was depressed. Buddhism is giving a profound reason why people get depressed or suffer from an inferiority complex: it is because they are ignorant and out of touch with the divine Child growing within them.

Jung dedicated an essay to "The Psychology of the Child Archetype"—a universal image appearing here and in the stories of Romulus and Remus, the Christ Child, Baby Kṛṣṇa, Young Rabbit of the Sioux, etc. He writes:

---

[84] Zimmermann, *Buddha Within*, 133-136.

> The "child" is born out of the womb of the unconscious, begotten out of the depths of human nature, or rather out of living Nature herself. It is a personification of vital force quite outside the limited range of our conscious mind; of ways and possibilities of which our one-sided conscious mind knows nothing; a wholeness which embraces the very depths of Nature. It represents the strongest, the most ineluctable urge in every being, namely the urge to realize itself. It is, as it were, an incarnation of *the inability to do otherwise* [Jung's italics], equipped with all the powers of nature and instinct, whereas the conscious mind is always getting caught up in its supposed ability to do otherwise. The urge and compulsion to self-realization is a law of nature and thus of invincible power, even though its effect, at the start, is insignificant and improbable.[85]

There is no ethical counsel in this passage—a working hard to rid oneself of "defilements" or the "seven deadly sins"—just as there is none in the Buddhist image of the "pregnant woman." Instead, the emphasis is upon knowing a splendid truth and allowing it to unfold naturally. In fact, Jung says it will "unfold"—even against our will—since it is the "strongest, the most ineluctable urge" in every being.

We might seek a proper balance, nevertheless, between getting out of the way of our "Embryo" and making some effort on its behalf—by providing it, shall we say, with a proper diet of Honey and nourishing Grain; preparing for its future by cleaning Gold and digging up mislaid Treasure; by honoring Images of what it will become after its eventual Birth. This is a symbolic way of saying that we can cultivate an appreciation for the power of religious symbolism itself—"living the symbolic life," as Edinger puts it.[86]

That, I believe, is the most important lesson of this new scripture and its images—as it is of the *Lotus* with its parables and the *Vimalakīrti* with its fantasy. It explains why the Lord of this text claims that even if one worships countless Buddhas in their Pure Lands throughout the universe and honors them with "fifty times more jeweled stūpas than there are sands in the Ganges River"—

> O Vajramati, that bodhisattva would still not be the equal of the person who finds joy and enlightenment in the *Tathāgatagarbha Sūtra*, who accepts it, recites, copies it, or even reveres but a single one of its metaphors." (103)

We have several from which to choose.

---

[85] Jung, *CW* 9i, par. 289.

[86] Edinger, *Ego and Archetype*, 117-130.

Chapter 13
MAHĀYĀNA PHILOSOPHY

Madhyamaka

Since all major religions have developed a philosophy, we can conclude that the psyche desires as much cognitive clarity as possible—alongside its paradoxes and its rich elusive symbolism. Towering thinkers like Origen, Augustine, and Thomas Aquinas became Christianity's answer to Tertullian's anti-intellectual challenge, "What does Athens have to do with Jerusalem?" There is always a risk of too much "Athens," however, the rules of reason obscuring the nonrational truths of "Jerusalem." Carefully worked out conscious schemes may block out the inspiring messages and imagery sent by the unconscious. Philosophy may even claim falsely to be superior to religion, as if they were not both inspired by the archetypal psyche as the matrix of all culture.

Historically, that false split occurred in Western thought beginning in the eighteenth century with the so-called Enlightenment. But it did not occur in India. The philosophies of the Hindu, Jain, and Buddhist religions remained "religious philosophies," i.e., systems of reasoning rooted in their respective scriptures and aiming at their respective salvific goals. They remained more like traditional Western theologies. It is, thus, disconcerting to hear modern Buddhists claim that Buddhism is not a religion but a philosophy. In saying so, they inject into Eastern religious thought a rather recent Western prejudice rooted in anti-clerical, anti-liturgical rationalism.

In Early Buddhism, we witnessed a philosophical attempt to clarify what the Buddha taught, to categorize the many different terms he used in his sermons, and then to interpret the teachings coherently where contradictions persisted. It was called "Abhidharma," the third "basket" of the sacred canon. Of course, the bias of Abhi ("higher")-dharma is that there should be no contradictions (no "Jerusalem," only "Athens"). But it never denied the Sūtra "basket," nor could it. Besides, the Buddha himself was judged in the ancient world to be something of a philosopher—fully aware of the theories of others, having a causal theory of his own called "Dependent Origination," a middle ground between two theories about reality called "eternalism" and "annihilationism." Although wary of metaphysical questions irrelevant to the goal of release from suffering, Gautama did have "right views," that he expressed often enough with clarity and coherence.

Nevertheless, the Abhidharmists felt obliged to distinguish between "Two Truths" in the Lord's sermons: those that expressed "conventional" realties like a chariot or a person as distinct from those that expressed "ultimate" realities like the many parts of a chariot or the five aggregates of a person—that could be analyzed down to their basic constituents, the many impersonal *dharmas*.

I have argued that these seventy-five or eighty-two "building blocks" of reality cannot be "ultimate" but function, instead, as "penultimates" to loosen one's saṃsāric attachments. The Mahāyāna "Perfection of Wisdom" literature appears to agree with that assessment. At least, the

Aṣṭasāhasrikā Prajñāpāramitā claims that followers of the Abhidharma scheme had become "attached" to their theory of *dharmas* and, consequently, were not Fully Enlightened. This newer scripture offered, instead, paradoxical statements and clever stories to loosen everyone's "grasping" tendencies. The problem, we learned, was attributing a substantial *svabhāva* ("own nature," "intrinsic being," "essence") not only to conventional reality but also to the many *dharmas.* Mahāyānists claimed that these would-be "ultimates" were "empty of own nature"—and as ungraspable as foam, a bubble, a dream, etc.

It is important to keep in mind that in these ancient Indian discussions the term "essence" is equivalent to "existence." This is not always the case in Western philosophy where, following Aristotle, substantial "essence" may be distinguished from accidental "existence." In Buddhist thought, Bronkhorst explains: "only that which 'exists' in the highest sense of the term can be or have an own nature. We have already seen [from Dependent Origination] that whatever has originated from causes and conditions does not really exist"—i.e., does not "exist" substantially, eternally, without change.[1]

As we are about to explore Buddhist philosophy in the Mahāyāna, let me warn the reader that much of what follows will be difficult, tedious—and, some would say, beside the point for a book on religion. But the "thinking function" is as valuable as any other and deserves its say. After all, it would be careless in a similar survey of Christian thought to leave out Anselm's proofs for the Incarnation and a famous "ontological argument" for the existence of God or to ignore Thomas Aquinas' brilliant synthesis of theology and Aristotelian philosophy. It is also true that what follows may seem to some not technical enough. But I am a religionist and not a philosopher and will need to rely on others more than usual.

The "Mūlamadhyamakakārikā" of Nāgārjuna

For centuries, the Mahāyāna style of Buddhism was expressed only in the form of *sūtra* ("sermon"), not yet philosophically in the form of *śāstra* ("treatise"). Eventually, however, a Buddhist scholar-monk named Nāgārjuna (probably of the second century CE) decided to argue rationally what the *Aṣṭa* and similar Prajñāpāramitā scriptures were revealing. He was born in the south of India, but taught in the northern monastic complex of Nālandā, and was so successful that he became the founder of an influential school of thought, the Madhyamaka ("Middle Way" school).

It was aptly named since Nāgārjuna's most important work was the *Mūla-madhyamaka-kārikā*, "Fundamental Verses on the Middle Way" (hereafter, the *Kārikā*). The title announces that this Buddhist thinker believed he was in accord with the Buddha's First Sermon on the "Middle Way." No, he would not be arguing the "middle" path between sensual indulgence and mortification of the flesh but that other more philosophical "middle"—the one between own nature and no nature, between eternalism and annihilationism. The word "Verses" in this work's title signals, also, that Nāgārjuna's argument will not be in discursive prose and, instead, be versified in tight, nearly opaque, lines—a style that the ancients loved but that leaves us wondering often what they were trying to say. Fortunately, Nāgārjuna commented on his own obscure verses—in prose! The more

---

[1] Bronkhorst, *Buddhist Teaching*, 145.

expansive Madhyamaka philosopher Candrakīrti (seventh century CE) commented on them, too, so that today scholars of Buddhism are fairly certain what was intended.

I have the impression, however, that Nāgārjuna gets a lot of help from these modern scholars, clarifying what he could not actually clarify. Still, they are following an ancient tradition that praised Nāgārjuna as no less than a "second Buddha." Candrakīrti writes glowingly:

> How the Bodhisattva who courses in the perfection of wisdom sees the true nature of *dharmas* has been clearly taught by the Noble Nāgārjuna, who understood exactly the scriptures, in his Madhyamaka treatise, employing reasoning and scriptural testimony. This true nature of *dharmas* is characterized by their absence of inherent existence.[2]

Robert Gimello says of more recent appraisals of Madhyamaka as the "central philosophy of Buddhism" and "logically unassailable":

> Such judgments abound in the literature of Buddhist scholarship. Nor is it surprising that they should, for they only echo the centuries-old conviction of many eminent Buddhists that Nāgārjuna's thought is the most perfect expression of the Buddha's own middle path.[3]

Yet Gimello wrote that in an essay reminding fellow scholars that there were (and are) other points of view of what the Buddha taught and that Nāgārjuna was not universally praised by all Buddhists. The philosopher's rather withering display of the apophatic approach to religion was not to everyone's taste.

Nearly all writers today agree that Madhyamaka philosophy is "critical philosophy," i.e., aimed at dismantling or "deconstructing" the truth claims of other philosophies. It may even be that Madhyamaka has no views of its own, as claimed by the Prāsaṅgika branch of this school. Indeed, for the sake of consistency, Nāgārjuna also dismantles the truth claims of Buddhism itself. He will state that they are "empty" and that the word "empty" is empty, as well. This led to the charge that this famous monk was not genuinely Buddhist.

Alternatively, it led to the recognition that he was doing what Gautama Buddha had tried to do. We will be witnessing a critique of speculative thought, a dim view of language, and an undermining of all polar opposites that language is required to use in order to make its points. But Gautama, too, tried to rid us of useless speculations and the misleading reifications invented by words—ridding us ultimately of ignorance, the prime cause of suffering (when he was not saying, inconsistently, that the prime cause was craving).

---

2 Williams, *Mahāyāna*, 55.

3 Robert M. Gimello, "Apophatic and kataphatic discourse in Mahāyāna: A Chinese view," *Philosophy East and West* 26, no. 2 (April, 1976), 117.

I will be using the English translation of the *Kārikā* by Jay Garfield even though it is a rendering from the Tibetan translation of the original Sanskrit that is extant.[4] Garfield's language is clear with few neologisms, and he provides an accessible commentary. Furthermore, this scholar is not afraid to make comparisons with Western philosophers, such as Immanuel Kant who is credited with his own "critical philosophy," calling into question the very enterprise of European philosophy due to epistemological limits imposed by the mind's categories. When we need the Sanskrit, David Kalupahana provides that in his own translation and commentary.[5]

Dedication

Nāgārjuna begins his treatise as one would expect with a "Dedication." But it is not just a pious gesture and, instead, an introduction to the entire project. Candrakīrti spent many pages commenting upon it.

> I prostrate to the Perfect Buddha,
> The best of teachers, who taught that
> Whatever is dependently arisen is
> Unceasing, unborn,
> Unannihilated, not permanent,
> Not coming, not going,
> Without distinction, without identity,
> And free from conceptual construction.[6]

Immediately, we see that the philosopher is religious, that he worships a "Perfect" being called Buddha. As a Mahāyānist, Nāgārjuna is by definition a Bodhisattva intent on becoming a Buddha—yet by all accounts he is on a lower Stage of the Bodhisattva Path. Nevertheless, that is a great spiritual achievement, beyond that of an Arhat or a Pratyekabuddha. Still, it means that our thinker is not a Vimalakīrti, a Celestial Bodhisattva merely manifesting himself as a human being for our benefit. Indeed, Nāgārjuna wrote a hymn to the Celestial Bodhisattva Mañjuśrī who is usually at the feet of the Celestial Buddha Vairocana.

This means that the Buddhist cult is in place for this philosopher. It means, also, that Nāgārjuna is not a demythologizer—despite all his dismantling of thought. Indeed, myths grew around him. He was said to have been invited by the Nāga ("serpent") king residing at the bottom of the ocean, to which this Bodhisattva descended; and it was from there that he brought to dry land a copy of a "Perfection of Wisdom" scripture that inspired him. Hence the name, *Nāga-arjuna*," "Clarity of the Serpents."

---

4 Jay L. Garfield, trans., *The Fundamental Wisdom of the Middle Way: Nāgārjuna's Mūlamadhyamakakārikā* (New York: Oxford University Press, 1995).

5 David L. Kalupahana, trans., *Nāgārjuna: The Philosophy of the Middle Way* (Albany: State University of New York Press, 1986).

6 Garfield, *Fundamental Wisdom*, 100.

Although presumably critical of all views, Nāgārjuna appears to have one here in the "Dedication": namely, a view of reality as "dependently arisen" since it was taught by the Buddha. Everything about it, however—as Candrakīrti points out—is stated *via negativa*: "unceasing, unborn, unannihilated, not permanent," etc. That is actually not surprising since the traditional understanding of Dependent Origination is that it solves the problem of thinking "all is" or (its polar opposite) "all is not"—by declaring saṃsāric reality to be neither one nor the other (negatively put). It means that Saṃsāra is not "existent," cannot be pinned down in any way.

The "Dedication" line, "Not coming, not going," gives us pause, however, since that reminds us of the epithet "Tathāgata"—the "One who has thus come and gone." Presumably, Nāgārjuna is even denying the Perfect Buddha's "own nature." In fact, in a devotional hymn to the Lord, he does precisely that—but, to be philosophically consistent, he also does not.

The line, "Without distinction, without identity," anticipates the *Kārikā's* famous twenty-fifth chapter—that we will discuss—where Nirvāṇa is said not to be "distinct" from Saṃsāra. This is often cited as "proof" that the world in which we live is really Nirvāṇa—reminiscent of the miracle in the *Vimalakīrti Sūtra* where we were shown that our land is really a Pure Land. But, then, Nāgārjuna's line says there is no "identity" either. It follows that Saṃsāra is neither distinct from Nirvāṇa nor identical with it. In any case, we as modern persons do not experience the "world" as did ancient Buddhists: with its Three Realms, a Mount Meru at the center of a flat round earth, far distant Buddha-fields, etc.—none of which Nāgārjuna, the pious Buddhist monk, denies.

Perhaps this issue can be resolved by the final line of the "Dedication": "And free from conceptual construction." Being "free" is another positive view, so it is difficult to agree with the Prāsaṅgika position that Nāgārjuna has no views. Still, the Bodhisattva philosopher is saying that we can become a Perfect Buddha if we rid ourselves of "conceptual construction" (Garfield's translation of *prapañca*). The reader will recall that we spent some time exploring this Sanskrit term that is usually translated as "proliferation." It struck me as a candidate for the Buddhist intuition that the mind spreads out and can also be withdrawn—the way that projections externalize unconscious contents, coloring and distorting one's environment.

Kalupahana translates *prapañca,* unexpectedly, as "obsessions;" but that comes closer to a psychological understanding.[7] Because projections "attach" us to objects and quite naturally "obsess" us—since those things and persons carrying our projections are carrying parts of ourselves. Garfield's more "conceptual" understanding of the term is probably due to his being a philosopher himself and due to Nāgārjuna's also having a bias in favor of conceptual explanations.

Chapter 1: "Examination of Conditions"

There are twenty-seven chapters in the *Mūlamadhyamakakārikā*, but I will explore only three of them since not all are germane to this book. Besides, many of the topics—such as "time" and "motion"—are quite abstract. But so as not to make matters too easy, let us examine the first chapter on "Conditions" or "Causation." We read:

---

[7] Kalupahana, *Nāgārjuna*, 101.

> Neither from itself nor from another,
> Nor from both,
> Nor without a cause,
> Does anything whatever, anywhere arise. (vs. 1)

This is not an argument, we are told, but instead a conclusion—in the form of a tetralemma—from arguments that follow in the text. The subject under discussion is "anything" (*bhāva*) that Kalupahana translates more literally as "existent." Thus, we are in the philosophical arena of what has *sva-bhāva*, "own nature," "existence," or—as Garfield often translates—"essence."

First of all, Nāgārjuna disagrees: 1) that anything can be caused "from itself." This has to do with ancient Indian debates about cause and effect, with one position being that the effect resides within the cause. We seemed to find that expressed by *karma* theory and in the previous chapter on the Tathāgatagarbha when relying on the symbolism of a "sprout contained within its seed." Nāgārjuna's disagreement with this position may be relying on agricultural evidence, as well, but in order to arrive at a different conclusion. Garfield explains:

> For example, we might ask a farmer, "Do these seeds have the power to sprout?" as a way of asking whether they are fertile. It would be then perfectly appropriate for him to answer in the affirmative. But if we then asked him to show us where in the seed the power is located, he would be quite justified in regarding us as mad.[8]

Being against "self causation" has a rational basis, moreover, as we learn from Nāgārjuna's next verse in the *Kārikā*:

> There are four conditions: efficient condition;
> Percept-object condition; immediate condition;
> Dominant condition, just so.
> There is no fifth condition. (vs. 2)

Our translator is convinced that Nāgārjuna is distinguishing between "causes" and the "conditions" noted in this verse. After all, the distinction appears early in the language of Dependent Origination. But he admits he is alone in this assessment, so I will not take a position here and let these two terms be close synonyms.

If so, the argument is that there can be no "effect" contained within its "cause"—because there are always *four* causes involved in the production of any effect. Garfield explains: "Rather these phenomena arise as consequences of the collocation of those conditions. To borrow a Kantian turn of phrase, phenomena are not analytically contained in their conditions; rather, a synthesis is required out of which a phenomenon not antecedently existent comes to be."[9]

Put differently by Nāgārjuna:

---

[8] Garfield, *Fundamental Wisdom*, 115.
[9] Garfield, *Fundamental Wisdom*, 110-111.

> The essence of entities
> Is not present in the conditions, etc. . . .
> If there is no essence,
> There can be no otherness-essence. (vs. 3)

That means, on the one hand, that a "sprout" could never be deduced from any of the four conditions for a sprout. It also means that a seed as "condition" (or "cause") cannot logically contain the "essence" of a sprout since its own essence is "seed," not sprout. Thus, the sentence—"The cause contains its effect"—does not make sense.

And that is the point of all this thinking out loud. The philosopher has dismantled the sentence and the thought contained therein, rendering it "empty" in the negative sense of having no meaning.

Nor does Nāgārjuna accept the view that: 2) a "cause" gives rise to a distinctly different "effect" (". . . *nor* from another"). He is attacking the usual way that we understand the relationship of cause and effect even in Dependent Origination: after all, we were told that "ignorance" is the cause or condition of "motivations" which causes "consciousness," etc., through all twelve links of what we took to be a sort of "causal" chain. But we have just learned that caused production is never that simple—since there is a fourfold multiplicity of "conditions." Furthermore, if each member of Dependent Origination "existed" in its own right (either as a cause or as effect), it could neither produce nor be produced. For existence presupposes *svabhāva* which is eternal and cannot have an origin in time, much less a cessation of what is eternal.

Nāgārjuna explains, albeit cryptically:

> When neither existents nor
> Nonexistents nor existent nonexistents are established,
> How could one propose a "productive cause"?
> If there were one, it would be pointless. (vs. 7)
> . . . .
> Since things [*dharma*] are not arisen,
> Cessation is not acceptable.
> Therefore, an immediate condition is not reasonable
> If something has ceased, how could it be a condition? (vs. 9)

He makes the same point elsewhere more clearly:

> Essence arising from
> Causes and conditions makes no sense.
> If essence came from causes and conditions,
> Then it would be fabricated [*kṛtaka*]. (ch. 25, vs. 1)

Indeed, a "fabricated essence" is a contradiction in terms. All one can conclude is that Dependent Origination does not really describe any causes or any effects but only their logical *alternative*, "dependent arising"—which the philosopher claims was Gautama Buddha's actual point.

Nor does Nāgārjuna accept: 3) a compromise between "self causation" and "other causation" implied by the line, "Nor from both." But neither does he accept the last logical possibility: 4) that anything can appear "without a cause" (presumably the position of those materialist Cārvākas encountered early in this book). That he should decline the proposition, "no cause at all," is surprising, since I thought we just learned that causation is impossible. But, then, the regularity of Dependent Origination precludes mere chance implied by "no cause." As well, we are not being handed anything conceptually that we can grasp.

It follows that the notion that causation is logically impossible must be met by its logical opposite: since the idea of a "lack of causation" cannot have *svabhāva* anymore than can the idea of "causation." They are themselves "conceptual constructs" built up by "mental fabrications" supported only by "language." That strikes me as traditional Buddhist thought, if more thoroughgoing than even the Abhidharmists had in mind.

Let us also note that Nāgārjuna's fourfold "causes" are reminiscent of Aristotle's fourfold analysis of causation in Greece in the fourth century BCE. There is no exact correlation between these two schemes. But Nāgārjuna's initial "efficient" condition seems to be equivalent to Aristotle's "efficient" cause (someone "striking a match" is Garfield's example). And the Indian's fourth "dominant" condition appears to be equivalent to the Greek notion of "final cause," since both refer to the goal or purpose (of striking a match, "to produce light."). But, then, Aristotle did not go on to dismantle his own positions.[10]

Nāgārjuna actually does so by saying that his own arguments, for all their logical consistency, are empty of substance. He means that we should not "grasp" onto what he says about causation any more than we should try to grasp conventional causal ideas.

A Jungian comment By now, the reader must see how difficult it is to understand this "second" Buddha and why one might prefer to read the "first" one. It strikes me that we have come a long way from Gautama as the discoverer of causal law for India and far from the saying that converted both Śāriputra and Maudgalyāyana: "For those things that have causes, he has set forth the causes. And he has also set forth their cessation." That was the Buddha's Third Noble Truth—simply put.

Nevertheless, philosophy often hides psychology within itself, like a "sprout" within a "seed." For it is a legitimate question if the archetypal Self (as cause) contains within itself the ego (as effect). If it does, they are very closely related like "milk churned into cream," as expressed by the Upaniṣads. If it does not, then the ego is distinct from the Self like a mythic "hero who slays the dragon." Empirically, the answer appears to be both. It is possible to understand that ego consciousness exists in "germ" within the unconscious and becomes with development the "actualized" manifestation of the unconscious itself—a way to interpret "Tathāgatagarbha" doctrine.

In fact, Jung says that the "egocentrism of consciousness [is] a reflection or imitation of the 'self'-centrism of the unconscious."[11] On the other hand, a developed ego must stand its ground over against too much influence from the unconscious—even disobey or rebel, like a "sinful Adam

[10] For a psychological comment on Aristotle's "causes," see Edinger, *Psyche in Antiquity*, 1:71-72.

[11] Jung, *CW* 14, par. 660.

and Eve"—in order to solidify itself and survive in outer reality. In psychology, then, the conscious effect is contained within the unconscious cause—but it is also by necessity distinct from it.

Chapter 18: "Examination of Self and Entities"

Let us look briefly at Nāgārjuna's discussion of the "self." In advance, let me say that I see nothing new here, although it may be that we have been relying upon this philosopher's interpretations—without quite knowing it—as they have come down through the centuries and have influenced current scholarship. He begins:

> If the self [*ātman*] were the aggregates [the five *skandhas*],
> It would have arising and ceasing (as properties).
> If it were different from the aggregates,
> It would not have the characteristics of the aggregates. (vs. 1)

This seems straightforward since the "self" (or "Self") in ancient Indian thought is, by definition, something blissful (lacking suffering, *duḥkha*), eternal (lacking change), and substantial (not *an-ātman*). The personal aggregates, however, are changing all the time—as we can readily experience in our bodies of "form," our "feelings," etc. They "arise and cease" constantly. Thus an *ātman* cannot be found in the aggregates. If, on the other hand, the "self" (or "Self") were different from the *skandhas*, it would not be subject to suffering, change, etc But, then, we could not know that since all we can know—according to Buddhists—are the "aggregates." That is the standard interpretation of the second half of this verse.

As Garfield explains:

> If, on the other hand, one takes the self to be distinct from the aggregates, the relation between them and the fate of the aggregates becomes irrelevant to the fate of this self. This is because the only objects ever given to us in introspection are the aggregates (a familiar Humean insight), and the self we presumably care about is the one we *know*.[12]

Notice that Garfield is making a choice here by taking *ātman* as a personal "self" (the "charioteer" in the Upaniṣads) and not the transpersonal yet immanent "Self" (the "owner of the chariot" sitting in the back). Perhaps this is Nāgārjuna's own choice, but I think it is as unclear as it has always been in Buddhism. Nevertheless, the ancient philosopher has just "proven" that there is no "self" to be found in experience. Psychologically, of course, Nāgārjuna is not taking into account our own experiences of unconscious forces, personal or transpersonal.

The next verse imagines an opponent:

> If there were no self,

[12] Garfield, *Fundamental Wisdom*, 246. His italics.

> Where would the self's (properties) be?

This is an old cavil: If there is no self, who or what has wholesome or unwholesome properties, who renounces the household life, and who is it that enters Nirvāṇa? Nāgārjuna answers in the following two lines:

> From the pacification of the self and what belongs to it,
> One abstains from grasping onto "I" and "mine." (vs. 2)

The word "pacification" (*śama*, as in "calming" meditation) may seem out of place here, but philosophy in Indian Buddhism is not separate from either the practice of meditation or from worship of Buddhas and Bodhisattvas. In an intellectual context, however, the word probably means that one "sees" that there is no empirical *ātman*, as established in the earlier verse, and its presumed reality is "pacified."

We notice, too, that "I and mine"—an old formula for what is wrong with us—is not identical here with *ātman* but consequent of it. That is Kalupahana's view:

> Through the appeasement of the self-instinct one eliminates the metaphysical notions of a self (*ātman*), and through the appeasement of the object one is able to realize the non-substantiality of phenomena and would not cling to them as "one's own" (*ātmani*). These *culminate* [my italics] in the absence of selfishness (*nir-mama*) and the absence of egoism (*nir-ahaṃkāra*).[13]

This means, I believe, that even in Buddhism "I (*ahaṃkāra*) and mine (*mama*)" are permissible as long as they are not a manifestation of "grasping"—holding on for dear life, lest something change (as inevitably it will). And that is good psychology, presumably "culminating" from having rid oneself of metaphysics in certain areas of one's life (if not all areas).

Verse six reviews different teachings on the "self" that can be found in scripture:

> That there is a self has been taught,
> And the doctrine of no-self,
> By the buddhas, as well as the
> Doctrine of neither self nor nonself. (vs. 6)

Garfield takes this to mean that the Buddha adjusted his teachings as they would be helpful to his particular audience: "self" sermons to the Cārvākas who believed in no self; "non-self" sermons to disciples who had a tendency to "reify" ideas into a self; and "a deeper view of the matter"—neither "self" nor "non-self" in order to teach "emptiness."

[13] Kalupahana, *Nāgārjuna*, 264-265. Slightly altered.

That is because *all* terms are conceptual, and all concepts are empty of substantial "real" referents—despite our persistently assuming that they refer to "entities" and that we are speaking the "truth."

This is Mahāyāna orthodoxy, made clear in the following verse:

> What language expresses is nonexistent.
> The sphere of thought is nonexistent.
> Unarisen and unceased, like nirvāṇa
> Is the nature of things [*dharmatā*, literally, "dharma-ness"]. (vs. 7)

That agrees with the *Aṣṭa*, and the Madhyamaka intends to do so. But I see little argument or "proof" here and, instead, an affirmation of what has been revealed by scripture. This, then, would be a specific instance of what the Christian thinker Paul Tillich has called the "theological circle," from which the religious thinker cannot (nor even wish to) escape. In other words, Nāgārjuna knows the "answer" before he applies his so-called "unassailable logic."

Chapter 25: "Examination of Nirvāṇa"

We have just heard Nāgārjuna use the word, *nirvāṇa*, so let us explore that topic in the famous twenty-fifth chapter of the *Mūlamakhyamakakārikā*. Nāgārjuna begins with his imagined opponent's voice (although without a commentary, one would have no idea who is speaking):

> If all this [i.e., *saṃsāra*] is empty,
> Then there is no arising or passing away
> By the relinquishing or ceasing of what
> Does one wish nirvāṇa to arise? (vs. 1)

Our philosopher answers with the very opposite position:

> If all this is nonempty,
> Then there is no arising or passing away.
> By the relinquishing or ceasing of what
> Does one wish nirvāṇa to arise? (vs. 2)

Nāgārjuna means, of course, "empty" or "nonempty" of *ātman* or *svabhāva*—unchanging essence. The logic is transparent.

Garfield explains:

> Nirvāṇa would be precluded not by the emptiness of saṃsāra, but rather by its inherent existence. For then it could not pass away. Nor could an inherently grasping grasper relinquish grasping, or an inherently existent delusion be alleviated. The

> achievement of nirvāṇa requires dependence, impermanence, and the possibility of change, all of which are grounded in emptiness.[14]

Notice that we are no longer looking upon *saṃsāra* as "disgusting" because it changes—the Early Buddhist model—but are instead looking upon *saṃsāra* as "empty" and capable of dissolving, the Mahāyāna model. The tone has shifted from an affective one to a cooler, more philosophical one. It is still true, however, that Nāgārjuna is looking upon *saṃsāra* and *nirvāṇa* as distinct from one another—as in Early Buddhism. In the Jātaka material, Sumedha put that well: "Just as there is, in this world, pleasure which is diametrically opposed to pain. . . so there must be Nirvāṇa that extinguishes the fires of lust," etc.

Then, in the next many verses, Nāgārjuna shifts to a description of Nirvāṇa as beyond distinction and as something that could never be expressed positively (i.e., as something that could be "attained" or that could "arise"). Reflecting the language of the new Prajñāpāramitā texts of his day, he writes:

> Unrelinquished, unattained,
> Unannihilated, not permanent,
> Unarisen, unceased:
> This is how nirvāṇa is described. (vs. 3)

That same apophatic language was used in the "Dedication" to refer to Dependent Origination, but now it is applied to Nirvāṇa.

Furthermore, Nāgārjuna will "prove" the necessity of speaking that way by examining a tetralemma: that Nirvāna "exists," "does not exist," "both exists and does not exist," "neither exists nor does not exist." In Indian logic, this fourfold formula was considered to cover all logical possibilities (although in Aristotelian logic the third possibility violates the law of the excluded middle).

We encountered a tetralemma very early in this book where, in the *Majjhima Nikāya*, the monk Mālunkyāputta grumbled that the Lord did not explain if—after death—a Tathāgata exists, does not exist, both does and does not exist, or neither does nor does not. Whereupon, that same Lord taught the parable of the man "wounded by a poisoned arrow"—who asked too many questions and would die before he got his answers. Undaunted, Nāgārjuna presses on with his critical philosophy. He begins:

> Nirvāṇa is not "existent."
> It would then have the characteristics of age and death.
> There is no existent entity
> Without age and death. (vs. 4)[15]

---

[14] Garfield, *Fundamental Wisdom*, 323.

[15] For clarity, I have added quotation marks to Garfield's translation in this section.

This is a bit odd since "age and death" remind us of the twelfth member of Dependent Origination, and there are no substantial "existents" in that formula since they are all "dependent" upon each other by definition. So we must be expected to take age and death conventionally here, the way that someone might say, "Devadatta grew old and died"—with the conventional assumption that he "existed" in the first place.

Nirvāṇa, however, has long been declared by scripture to be the "Deathless," free from disease, old age, and death. So it follows, first of all, that Nirvāṇa does not "exist."

The second possibility, that Nirvāṇa does "not exist" is rejected this way:

> If nirvāṇa were "not existent,"
> How could it be appropriate for it to be nonexistent?
> Where nirvāṇa is not existent,
> It cannot be a nonexistent. (vs. 7)

The point seems to be that the very notion of "existence" in the previous discussion depends on its contrast with the notion of "nonexistence" to make any sense. Since Nāgārjuna has just proven that Nirvāṇa does not "exist," its paired opposite—"nonexistent"—cannot be true.

Then, there are these verses:

> That which comes and goes
> Is dependent and changing.
> That, when it is not dependent and changing,
> Is taught to be nirvāṇa. (vs. 9)
>
> The teacher has spoken of relinquishing
> Becoming and dissolution.
> Therefore, it makes sense that
> Nirvāṇa is "neither existent nor nonexistent." (vs. 10)

Garfield comments:

> Nirvāṇa is here again explicitly characterized only by contrast with saṃsāra. While it therefore cannot be an entity of the kind with which saṃsāra is populated, it is, as the release from saṃsāra, not completely nonexistent. So it can neither be conceived of conventionally or ultimately as a thing, nor coherently asserted not to exist.[16]

We hear in this explanation an allusion to the very early Buddhist argument against "either eternalism or annihilationism," that the Buddha answered with "dependency" as a kind of existence between

[16] Garfield, *Fundamental Wisdom*, 328.

the two. But these verses come close to solving the "fourth" case of the tetralemma while solving this "second" case, namely, that Nirvāṇa does *not* "not exist."

The third case is easier to demonstrate as impossible. Nāgārjuna writes:

> If nirvāṇa were "both
> Existent and nonexistent,"
> Passing beyond would, impossibly,
> Be both existent and nonexistent. (vs. 11)

The point is that this would be "impossibly" a contradiction. Garfield states, "We don't want to say that one does and does not pass into nirvāṇa upon release from saṃsāra."[17] Well, we do not unless a devotee of the "holy book" called, *Aṣṭasāhasrikāprajñāpāramitā*—with all its contradictions or paradoxes. In other words, Nāgārjuna chooses the argument that fits his purpose even if he has to ignore other arguments.

He even turns to simile for help:

> How could nirvāṇa
> Be both existent and nonexistent?
> These two cannot be in the same place.
> Like light and darkness. (vs. 14)

In any case, the *Kārikā* has now proven that Nirvāṇa does not "both exist and not exist."

Finally, with equal ease:

> Nirvāṇa is said to be
> "Neither existent nor nonexistent."
> If the existent and the nonexistent were established,
> This would be established. (vs. 15)

This argument rests upon previous arguments that proved Nirvāṇa does not "exist" and does not "not exist." It follows that the combined negation of both does not make logical sense. Hence, Nirvāṇa does not "neither exist nor not exist." The entire scaffold of the tetralemma falls.

Yet it all seems to be for the purpose of Nāgārjuna's arriving at verses 19 and 20 of this twenty-fifth chapter of the *Kārikā*. They are his most famous and most controversial:

> There is not the slightest difference
> Between cyclic existence [*saṃsāra*] and nirvāṇa.
> There is not the slightest difference
> Between nirvāṇa and cyclic existence. (vs. 19)

---

[17] Garfield, *Fundamental Wisdom*, 329.

> Whatever is the limit of nirvāṇa,
> That is the limit of cyclic existence.
> There is not even the slightest difference between them,
> Or even the subtlest thing. (vs. 20)

Nāgārjuna is emphatic here, repeating himself in different ways, to make his point.

But what is the point? Modern Buddhists have decided that it "proves" what they have known all along, that Buddhism has no transcendent dimension in any sense—is not a religion, perhaps not even a philosophy—and is an unqualified secular humanism. Saṃsāra, the everyday here and now, is itself Nirvāṇa and there is nothing to seek and almost nothing to do to find oneself "enlightened" except to realize this basic fact. As many web sites happily announce, "You're already Enlightened, you just don't know it." Mark Epstein, a Buddhist "Mindfulness" psychologist, writes:

> Yet it has become a fundamental axiom of Buddhist thought that nirvana is samsara—that there is no separate Buddha realm apart from worldly existence, that release from suffering is won through a change in perception, not through a migration to some kind of heavenly abode.[18]

We know, however, that any "identity" of Saṃsāra and Nirvāṇa is not an "axiom" since our many chapters demonstrate different Buddhist positions on almost every issue. As for there being no Buddhist "heavenly abode," the author is simply ignoring the many "heavens" of traditional Buddhist cosmology, not to mention the countless ones of Pure Land Buddhism. I am not saying they exist; I am saying that Buddhism says they exist.

Besides, Nāgārjuna is careful with words and did not say that Nirvāṇa and Saṃsāra are "identical" but said they are "not different." In the "Dedication," he even announced the logical impossibility of the pair, "identity and difference," since they condition each other. Thus, Kalupahana writes somewhat caustically of the purported "identity" of Saṃsāra and Nirvāṇa:

> This assertion may appear to be correct, if we are to ignore all that has been said by Nāgārjuna regarding the metaphysical doctrines of identity (*ekatva*) and difference (*nānatva*) . . . . Those who upheld the view that this statement is an assertion of the identity of *saṃsāra* and *nirvāṇa* do not seem to have paused for one moment to reflect on the question regarding the nature of the identity they were implying; nor have they attempted to place that conception of identity (if there is one) in the historical context.[19]

The historical context includes the fact that Nāgārjuna is a pious monk who prays to the Celestial Bodhisattva Mañjuśrī, hoping to be in his holy presence after death.

---

[18] Epstein, *Thoughts Without a Thinker*, 18.

[19] Kalupahana, *Nāgārjuna*, 366.

Jay Garfield, our translator, stays closer to the text and concludes that the *Kārikā* is saying here that all pairs—including "Saṃsāra and Nirvāṇa"—are logically suspect. Their members make no sense as independent terms ostensibly referring to independent entities. In this regard, no Buddhist terms are actually "different" from one another—even if saying so runs the risk of appearing to criticize Buddhist teachings. But Nāgārjuna believes he is a Mahāyānist merely criticizing "substantialist" Abhidharma teaching and not the teaching of the Buddha who refused to answer Mālukyaputta's fourfold complaint.

Indeed, it is my own view that Nāgārjuna stops "philosophizing" where Gautama (not to mention Vimalakīrti) stops speaking—having proved the instability of all statements. That, for me, explains the variety of interpretations of the *Kārikā* that actually intends to demonstrate the impossibility of making any viable interpretation of the *Kārikā*. Garfield seems to agree by saying that Nāgārjuna "emphasizes that all discourse is only possible from the conventional point of view."[20]

But Garfield goes on—and I am surprised that he does so—to say, "Seeing the conventional as conventional . . is to see it as it is ultimately." This means for him that: "the ultimate truth is merely the essenceless essence of those conventional things." I personally doubt that the founder of Madhyamaka would permit the phrase, "essenceless essence," to stand unchallenged. It is, however, a conclusion shared by many scholars of Buddhism, namely, that the religion's highest truth is that there is no highest truth—and not just as a thoughtful strategy to loosen one's attachments, but as an accurate description of "reality as it is." As our translator states clearly, like Epstein: "To be in nirvāṇa, then, is to see those things as they are—as merely empty, dependent, impermanent, and nonsubstantial, but not to be somewhere else, seeing something else."

To be consistent, one would have to add that anyone who "sees" things this way is himself or herself "merely empty, dependent, impermanent, and nonsubtantial." As would be the "seeing" itself, a "merely empty" experience. Paul Williams cautions that interpreting Buddhism this way is close to saying, "Everything is foam which dissolves into nothing."[21] As a religionist, and not just a philosopher, Williams knows that Buddhism would not have transformed India, much less have spread to transform other Asian cultures, if its greatest insight was to perceive life as a water bubble on the Ganges.

A Jungian view I grant that one does not need to be "somewhere else" to become a more conscious human being and that a change in "perception" or attitude is critical. It is also true that one can no longer believe in metaphysical locations like "heavens" and "hells." But the Buddhist religion did believe in those locations and did keep open the meaning of Nirvāṇa as somehow "transcendent," beyond Saṃsāra. Even the "immanent" divine Tathāgatagarbha transcends ordinary experience by being "hidden" in so many ways.

This is important to Jungian psychology, because its own perceptions are rooted in and shaped by "recognition of 'the ancient' and the continuity of culture and intellectual history"—as Jung puts it.[22] The Buddhist religion is part of that history, and depth psychology can ill afford a misinterpretation

[20] Garfield, *Fundamental Wisdom*, 330-333.

[21] Williams, *Buddhist Thought*, 112.

[22] Jung, *Memories*, 235.

of such an important cultural achievement—a misunderstanding that denies Buddhism the symbolic equivalent of a collective unconscious and a wholeness transcending consciousness. Equating reality with just "foam" denies not only outer reality but also—critically, for the continuity of meaning—the reality of the psyche and its very real demands.

As suggested at the outset, Nāgārjuna himself was more than an intellectual intent on demolishing others' intellectual arguments. We know this from four hymns (*Catuḥstava*) attributed to Nāgārjuna, the last of which is entitled, "Hymn According to the Supreme Truth [*paramārtha*]."[23] It integrates—wonderfully, I might add—what the philosopher knows to be the limits of truth statements with what his religious feeling tells him about the eternal Presence of the Buddha. It begins:

> How shall I praise you, the Lord who has not been born, who remains nowhere, who is beyond all comparison proper of the world, something beyond the path of words?
> Anyhow—be you whatever you may be in the sense of the true reality—I, abiding by the world's conventions, shall praise the Master out of devotion [*bhakti*].
> Since there is not a forthcoming with an own being, there is not forthcoming for you, neither going nor coming, O Lord, I pay homage to you devoid of an own being.
> You are neither an existing being nor a non-existing being, nor liable to destruction nor eternal, nor permanent nor impermanent. I pay homage to you devoid of duality.
> . . . .
> You are not either far or near, either in space or on the earth, either in the *saṃsāra* or in the *nirvāṇa*. I pay homage to you who are in no place.
> Praised in this way, so may you be praised—but have you been praised in truth? Since all the *dharmas* are void, who is praised? By whom is he praised?

The prayer goes on, but the "second Buddha" is confessing here that the "first Buddha" still exists—even though he does not exist. It strikes me that Nāgārjuna "dreamed the myth onwards" with his logic but felt obliged to stay within the myth as we are all obliged to do.

Yogācāra

Within two hundred years of the success of Madhyamaka thought—which is, actually, a very long time—a new Buddhist philosophy emerged. It did so while claiming to be a " Third Turning of the Wheel"— not of *sūtra*, but of systematic thinking. First, there was the Abhidharma, then the Madhyamaka, and now the Yogācāra ("Practice of Yoga") as the definitive understanding of what the Buddha taught. The name, however, does not sound like philosophy and more like meditation. As we shall see, it even looks like psychology or, more accurately, a "philosophy of psychology." In any case, this new approach returns the focus of Buddhist thought to issues of the mind.

---

[23] Fernando Tola and Carmen Dragonetti, trans., "Nāgārjuna's Catustava," *Journal of Indian Philosophy* 13 (1985): 35-36.

Accordingly, its language is more positive. Thus, the Madhyamaka school would criticize the Yogācāra for its many declarative sentences, saying it ran the usual risk of reifying concepts, making "real" what is merely conceived or imagined. Perhaps the Madhyamaka noticed that the word "yoga" in the name of this second major school of Mahāyāna philosophy was a favorite of Hinduism and thought the "Yogācāra" was too concerned with a resurgent Hindu religion during the rise of the Gupta dynasty, too worried about patronage.

The scholar, Dan Lusthaus, has only praise for the Yogācāra since it:

> provided perhaps the most sophisticated examination and description in all of Buddhism of how the mind works—in psychological, epistemological, logical, emotional, cognitive, meditative, developmental, and soteriological modes. At once a rigorous, rational philosophy and an elaborate system of practice, it provided methods by which one could identify and correct the cognitive errors inherent in the way the mind works, since enlightenment meant direct, immediate, correct cognition.[24]

This is a long way of saying what was quoted at the beginning of this book, that Buddhism is "all about the mind" (or a lot about the conscious mind). Obviously, this writer agrees with Yogācāra's claim to be the crowning phase of Buddhist religious thought. From it came creative ideas about the "Three Bodies" of the Buddha, as well as a more restrained formal Buddhist logic in the thought of Dignāga (sixth century).

Notice that Lusthaus is not saying that this new (historically, last) Buddhist philosophy of India is different from what went before but is a more "sophisticated" expression of it. It can even feel when reading its texts that one is merely reviewing what was already said in Gautama's sermons. This is particularly noticeable in Yogācāra's other names.

Other Names

1) Another name for this philosophy is "Citta-mātra" ("thought-only"). We encountered the word *citta* at an early stage of our study as the third member of the phrase, "body, speech, and mind," a description of a karmic human being who performs "actions" of these three kinds. We also learned that acts of *citta* (or *manas*, another word for "mind") had priority over acts of body and speech as their "intention" (*cetanā*, derived from the same Sanskrit root as *citta*). We learned, too, that if one deliberately intended to become Enlightened, that planted a seed called "Bodhi-citta" that would eventually bear its fruit—provided one perfected the Buddhist virtues, called the Perfections.

The word *citta* was used to describe the Early Buddhist "stream of consciousness" (*citta-saṃtāna*). This expressed with an image a degree of karmic continuity into which one was "planting" the Bodhicitta—a "stream" that would carry one's intention through innumerable lifetimes. Although metaphors are mixing here, implying a "stream of seeds," it was necessary to offset the notion of radical discontinuity implied by the Abhidharma theory of discrete momentary *dharmas*.

---

[24] Dan Lusthaus, "Yogācāra School," *EB* 2:914-921.

So important was this word *citta* that one might conclude from this other name that "only thought" exists in Yogācāra. This is what many have taken to be Gautama's meaning by telling the shining young god Rohitassa that the origin and cessation of the "world" could be found "in just this fathom-high carcass endowed with perception and mind." It has even led to a fairly standard interpretation of Yogācāra as philosophical "idealism," i.e., the view that objects appearing to exist in the external world do not actually exist and are "only" (*mātra*) thought or mind. This is the opposite of philosophical "materialism," the view that the mind does not exist or is at best an epiphenomenon of matter (or the brain).

George Berkeley, the eighteenth-century Irish philosopher, is often mentioned at this point as an idealist who also denied the existence of externals with the famous question, attributed to him: "If a tree falls in the forest and no one is there, does it make a sound?" This question makes us doubt our assumptions about reality, our experience of the outer world.

The current Dalai Lama says:

> The fact that our inner experiences of pleasure and pain are in the nature of subjective mental and cognitive states is very obvious to us. But how those inner subjective events relate to external circumstances and the material world poses a critical problem. The question of whether there is an external physical reality independent of sentient beings' consciousness and mind has been extensively discussed by Buddhist thinkers. Naturally, there are divergent views on this issue among the various philosophical schools of thought. One such school [Cittamātra] asserts that there is no external reality, not even external objects, and that the material world we perceive is in essence merely a projection of our minds.[25]

Here is the word "projection" again without reference to an unconscious mind that projects. But the Dalai Lama's point is that he disagrees with the Cittamātra. As the head of the Dge-lugs-pa ("Gelugpa") order of Tibetan Buddhism, he agrees instead with that order's founder, Tsoṅ-kha-pa—namely, that the Madhyamaka is superior to Yogācāra.

Nevertheless—as we shall soon learn from the the *Triṃśikā* of Vasubandhu—the "mind only" school does not actually teach philosophical idealism any more than does Madhyamaka. It is just not very interested in the outer object, that it never denies, nor is it interested in the material sense organs that everyone possesses.

Let me note that Jung seems like an idealist himself when he says, "Not only does the psyche exist, it is existence itself."[26] But he never denies the outer object, only our ability to know it outside the mind's categories for knowing—both the categories of consciousness and the structures of the archetypal psyche. Jung is also showing here his introverted bias toward the inner "subject" as opposed to our culture's extraverted bias toward the outer "object." But that bias does not keep him from looking both ways while crossing the street.

---

[25] Dalai Lama, "Buddhist Concept of Mind," 15.

[26] Jung, *CW* 11, par. 18.

2) Another name for Yogācāra is "Vijñāna-mātra" ("consciousness-only"). That is because the Sanskrit word *vijñāna* is very important to the system. We know the term already as the fifth of the five *skandhas*—and took it to mean "consciousness of" a sensory object with which it is always associated. Thus, the alternative translation, "perception," has merit. In Buddhism, there are six "sense organs" that perceive objects: the usual five physical organs of eye, ear, nose, tongue, and body or skin; plus the sixth mental organ of mind (*manas*). Their objects are, accordingly, visibles, sounds, smells, tastes, and tangibles; plus thoughts or ideas.

It is important to keep in mind that, according to Buddhist sensory theory, when an organ makes contact with its object, there arises a corresponding kind of *vijñāna* or "consciousness." Thus, "sight-consciousness" is produced when the eye organ sees something, a "taste-consciousness" arises when the tongue tastes something, etc.—and a "mind-consciousness" (*mano-vijñāna*) is produced when the "mind" (*manas*) perceives a thought. Altogether, these factors are listed in the Abhidharma as the "eighteen realms" (*dhātus*) consisting of six organ, six corresponding objects, and six consequent forms of perceptual consciousness.

From an early date, however, the mental organ *manas* and its associated *mano-vijñāna* were treated a bit differently. And the Yogācāra will exploit or re-work this fact. William Waldron explains the original position:

> When a cognitive awareness of a sensory object occurs, it is often followed by an awareness of that awareness, that is, a reflexive awareness "that such and such a sensory awareness [*vijñāna*] has occurred." This is one of the "objects" of mental cognitive awareness [*mano-vijṅāna*]. Mental cognitive awareness, however, also arises in conjunction with cognitive objects that occur independently of the sensory cognitive system, such a thinking, reflection, or ideas.[27]

This means that *manas* or "mind" is aware of its own contents or ideas but is also aware that the other organs are aware of their contents. Bhikkhu Bodhi adds in a note to the *Saṃyutta Nikāya* that *manas* "coordinates the data of the other five senses" while cognizing its own special objects.[28] It enjoys, therefore, a certain priority in sensory functioning, the way that *citta* enjoys priority in karma theory.

To anticipate our discussion, *manas* as "coordinating sense" is somewhat like Aristotle's "common sense" that coordinates sense data from the five sensory organs—and somewhat like the ego's role in modern psychology. Although the ego often lacks good "common sense," in the popular meaning of that phrase.

We also know *vijñāna* as the third member of Dependent Origination, conditioned by "karmic dispositions" or *saṃskāras*. Trying to explain transmigration, Buddhists said that the first three members of this formula—namely, 1. ignorance, 2. karmic dispositions, and 3. consciousness (*vijñāna*, and sometimes *mano-vijñāna*)—represented the "prior life" about to enter into a new

---

27 William S. Waldron, *The Buddhist Unconscious: The Ālaya-vijñāna in the Context of Indian Buddhist Thought* (London: RoutledgeCurzon, 2003), 29. Slightly altered to reflect Sanskrit.

28 Bodhi, *SN*, p. 769.

existence. This was conceived as a *gandharva* that descends into the womb at conception. This, too, gave special significance to *vijñāna* as the "linking consciousness" between past and present lives. It would then establish itself in 4. "name-and-form," around which other features developed into the next human being.

It would even be said that at 12."death" it was *vijñāna* that departed the body (in Buddhist Tantra, through one of the "nine orifices," the crown of the head being most propitious for the next Destiny).[29] In this way, "consciousness" was even associated with the body's "life and warmth" as a necessary ingredient for sentience.[30]

3) Finally, the Yogācāra can be called "Vijñapti-mātra" ("representation-only"). The term seems new but only because it has been isolated by this new philosophy from its early use in the Sautrāntika sect of Early Buddhism. Jadunath Sinha explains:

> The Sautrāntikas also hold that the external world exists [as multiple momentary *dharmas*]. But according to them it is not an object of direct perception. The external objects produce presentations [*vijñapti*] in the mind through which we infer the existence of external objects. From the epistemological point of view . . . [Sautrāntikas] are advocates of indirect realism or representationism.[31]

Sinha goes on to say, however, that the "Yogācāras do not believe in the existence of extra-mental objects"—the standard "idealist" interpretation. We can see that this is a misunderstanding, even from this scholar's own words, since "representationism" raises the question: "re-presentation of what?" And the answer is: of an object, either externally or internally perceived. Indeed, the term *vijñapti* is best translated not as "presentation," but as "representation."

Wayman writes of *vijñapti* as a "picture in the mind which the mind attributes to the external world. It is impossible that this picture or aggregation could exist in the external world, since it is representation-only. The vulgar interpretation—that this denies external objects—is nonsense."[32] He is saying that it is nonsense to deny externals (including "external" ideas) simply because they are not identical with the "re-presentations" that externals stimulate. Wayman is also saying, in agreement with the Yogācārins, that the opposite is nonsense: equating what is only the subjective reflection of an object with that external object itself, as if what we think of an object is identical with that object. This throws us back into the "problem" of the snake and the rope discussed earlier in this book.

Thus, it should be clearer that the word "only" (*mātra*) in these various Yogācāra titles means something pejorative—"merely" or "just" or "nothing but." As Lusthaus puts it, "The inability to distinguish between our interpretations of the world and the world itself is what Yogācāra calls

---

[29] Wayman, *Buddhist Tantras*, 140-141.

[30] See Alex Wayman, "Vijñāna," *ER* 15:260-264.

[31] Jadunath Sinha, *Indian Psychology*, 2 vols. (Calcutta: Sinha Publishing House, 1958), 1:104.

[32] Alex Wayman, "Yogācāra and the Buddhist Logicians," *The Journal of the International Association of Buddhist Studies* 2, no. 1 (1979): 70.

vijñaptimātra. This problem pervades ordinary mental operations and can be eliminated only when those operations are brought to an end."[33] That is orthodox Buddhism.

As for the "picture-making" function of the mind, Jung says often that it is only imagery that we experience directly: "We can make only the dimmest theoretical guesses about the nature of matter, and these guesses are nothing but images created by our minds."[34] This psychological fact, however, does not deny matter.

The Founders

The founders of Yogācāra Buddhist philosophy were Asaṅga (late fourth century) and his younger half-brother Vasubandhu (to mid-fifth century). For many years, they had been monks ordained in Early Buddhist sects. The elder was a Mahīśāsaka but unhappy with his religious progress until, according to tradition, he had visions—during a long retreat—of the Celestial Bodhisattva Maitreya who taught him the Mahāyāna point of view. Or perhaps Asaṅga used his supernormal *ṛddhis* to visit this future Buddha in Tuṣita heaven. Some scholars, however, take Maitreya (or Maitreyanātha) to be a human teacher antecedent to the brothers since several Yogācāra texts are attributed to an author of that name. Asaṅga would eventually write large compendia, like his *Yogācāra-bhūmi*, that explicated seventeen "Stages" of the Buddhist Path since he included not only the ten Stages required of a Bodhisattva to become a Buddha but also what a Śrāvaka or a Pratyekabuddha would need to achieve in order to become a Bodhisattva in the first place.

We know Vasubandhu from earlier chapters since he, too, was inclined to write compendia. His very large *Abhidharmakośa* became a classic presentation of the Early Buddhist Sarvāstivāda sect in which he was ordained while his *bhāṣya* or "commentary" on his own text introduced arguments from the Sautrāntika sect's opposition. Vasubandhu was severely criticized by Sarvāstivādins for suggesting that there was another way of seeing things. But we can read his autocommentary as a sign of dissatisfaction with "Hīnayāna" in general—anticipating his conversion to his brother's different style of Buddhism, the Mahāyāna.

Saṃdhinirmocana Sūtra

Both the Madhyamaka and Yogācāra are philosophical attempts to systematize or state coherently what Buddhist scriptures express less rationally, often with story and imagery. Thus, religious philosophies address the "head" more than the "heart." Still, a heartfelt choice of scriptures to systematize must be made. Nāgārjuna chose to explain primarily the "Perfection of Wisdom" literature with all its strange paradoxes. Asaṅga and Vasubandhu were more interested in scriptures like the *Saṃdhinirmocana Sūtra* ("Sermon Explaining the Hidden Meaning") dating perhaps from the third century CE.

The text opens typically, "Thus have I heard at one time. The Bhagavan ["Blessed One"] was dwelling in . . . " a fabulous place. By the fifth chapter, however, the *sūtra* begins to sound more like

---

[33] Lusthaus, "Yogācāra," 917.

[34] Jung, *CW* 8, par. 623.

a treatise or *śāstra*. This may be evidence of a conscious re-working of an original vision. We hear the Lord teaching, as translated by John Powers from the Tibetan (since the original Sanskrit is lost):

> Viśālamati, consciousness [Sanskrit, *vijñāna*] is also called the "appropriating consciousness" because it holds and appropriates the body in that way. It is called the "basis-consciousness" [*ālaya-vijñāna*] because there is the same establishment and abiding within those bodies. Thus they are wholly connected and thoroughly connected. It is called "mind" [*citta*] because it collects and accumulates forms, sounds, smells, tastes, and tangible objects. Viśālamati, the sixfold collection of consciousness—the eye consciousness, ear consciousness, nose consciousness, tongue consciousness, body consciousness, and mind consciousness—arise depending upon and abiding in that appropriating consciousness. An eye consciousness arises depending on an eye and a form in association with consciousness. Functioning together with that eye consciousness, a conceptual mental consciousness [*mano-vijñāna*] arises at the same time, having the same objective reference.[35]

These lines are almost a review of Early Buddhist sensory or perceptual theory—but with some obscure changes.

Asaṅga and Vasunbandhu concluded from passages of this kind that the Buddha actually taught that the mind operates through "eight forms of consciousness (*vijñāna*)"—the usual six "perceptual" forms that we know, plus two additional forms that we will now study. To make it easier to follow the discussion, here is a list of Yogācāra's standard eight *vijñānas* in order of increasing significance for the system:

1. *cakṣu-vijñāna* (eye-consciousness)
2. *śrota-vijñān*a (ear-consciousness)
3. *ghrāna-vijñāna* (nose-consciousness)
4. *jihvā-vijñānas* (tongue-consciousness)
5. *kāya-vijñāna* (body or skin-consciousness)
6. *mano-vijñāna* (mind-consciousness)
7. *manas* (mind; also, *kliṣṭa-manas*, "defiled mind")
8. *ālaya-vijñāna* (storehouse-consciousness)

Let me observe that listing in this way can be misleading—since it does not include what else belongs to a human being's experience. We are missing "speech" in the formula, "body, speech, and mind," and missing a keen awareness of *skandhas* like "feeling," and the physical body itself with its "disgusting" substances—not to mention the worldly objects stimulating all this *vijñāna*.

Furthermore, the eighth form of consciousness may seem, from its place in the list, to lie very deep within the mind; but that may not be the case in Buddhism. Perhaps it would be better to list

[35] John Powers, *Wisdom of Buddha: "The Saṃdhinirmocana Sūtra"* (Berkeley: Dharma Publishing, 1995), 71.

them in reverse order (since the "storehouse-consciousness" operates first in human psychology) or to list them horizontally (to see what occurs in experience at every instant).

The "Triṃśikā" of Vasubandhu

Fortunately, Vasubandhu could also write in brief. So I am taking the liberty of ignoring his more prolix brother Asaṅga in the following analysis. In fact, the materials on Madhyamaka and Yogācāra, both ancient and modern, are voluminous and difficult to control, the conclusions often at variance. Thus, as with Nāgārjuna and his fairly short *Kārikā*, I will consult a short treatise by Vasubandhu, his *Triṃśikā-vijñapti-kārikā* ("Thirty Verses on Vijñapti"). Extant in Sanskrit—albeit in those terse verses that India prefers—it is sometimes called a "textbook" on Yogācāra and should help us to arrive at a particular understanding if not quite a definitive one.

There are several translations of the "Thirty Verses" in English. But I have chosen that of Stefan Anacker who also provides the Sanskrit. It is also of some interest to me that he subtitles his collection of several works by Vasubandhu, "The Buddhist Psychological Doctor."[36] I will also use the translations from parallel Chinese materials provided by Dan Lusthaus in his long study, *Buddhist Phenomenology*[37] Again, the reader is forewarned that this material is obscure and can be tedious to explore; consulting it, however, will prevent us from "merely" imagining what Yogācāra is trying to tell us.

We see already from the title of this treatise that *vijñapti* (as in "Vijñapti-mātra") is at issue. Anacker translates it as "perception" but "representation" is preferable so that the image-making—the "picture-making"—feature of experience is preserved. Also, the translator's first verse makes choices that I must interrupt with the Sanskrit in order to get our bearings for what comes later.

> Verse 1. The metaphors of "self" and "events" [*ātman* and *dharmas*] which develop [*pravartate*, "evolve"] in so many different ways take place in the transformation [*pariṇāmo*, "process, change"] of consciousness [*vijñāna*]: and this transformation is of three kinds.

At the outset, Vasubandhu is telling us that "consciousness" is something that develops or unfolds in "three kinds." That may remind the reader that both Freud and Jung discuss the "unfolding" of mental life in a threefold way—as Id, superego, and ego or as collective unconscious, personal unconscious, and ego, respectively—suggesting that the archetype of "Three" becomes constellated when we try to speak of psychological development.

Although the word "transformation" appears here, we should not take it to have the nuance of "transformative" but merely that of an unfolding or change from one mental state to another in ordinary experience. At its farthest extent—the text says—notions of "self" and "events" (i.e., the duality of subject and object) arise in the mind, even though they have no more substance than

[36] Stefan Anacker, trans., *Seven Works of Vasubandhu: The Buddhist Psychological Doctor* (Delhi: Motilal Banarsidass Publishers, revised 2005), 183-190.

[37] Dan Lusthaus, *Buddhist Phenomenology: A Philosophical Investigation of Yogācāra Buddhism and the "Ch'eng Wei-shih lun"* (London: RoutledgeCurzon, 2002).

"metaphors," i.e., images. It is important to notice that the philosopher is describing an intra-psychic process.

> Verse 2. Maturation [*vipāka*], that called "always reflecting" [*manana*], and the perception [*vijñapti*, "representation"] of sense-objects. Among these, "maturation" is that called "the store-consciousness" [literally, "*vijñāna* called *ālaya*"] which has all the seeds.

Thus, the three main categories of psychological unfolding are, as Anacker translates: "maturation," "reflecting," and "perception." In Yogācāra discussions, these comprise the eight forms of "consciousness" as follows: "maturation" refers to the eighth called ālaya-vijñāna; "reflecting" refers to the seventh called *manas*; while "perception" or representation points to the remaining six sensory consciousnesses (including *mano-vijñāna*) appearing since earliest Buddhism. The "sense objects" (*viṣaya*) are perceived. But Vasubandhu makes no special point about it since these outer objects are assumed.

"Maturation" Consciousness

(8) *ālaya-vijñāna* The second half of this verse introduces the all-important eighth consciousness of ālaya-vijñāna, nearly a Yogācāra neologism. Powers translates it in the *Saṃdhinirmocana* as "basis consciousness" while others prefer "foundational consciousness." Anacker translates "store-consciousness." That is closer to what is now the standard English translation as "storehouse consciousness" since the idea or image of storage is involved (e.g., ālaya is in the name of the Himalaya Mountains as a "storehouse of snow"). One translator suggests "granary consciousness" to cover the fact—as this verse states—that "all the seeds" of karmic intention are stored there. Somehow, these "seeds" ripen or mature at this level of mental life or, perhaps better, "mature" from there. Thus, the ālaya-vijñāna is, by definition, a "maturation" consciousness.

We can see that the Yogācāra is making a fresh attempt to understand the Law of *karma*: Where do karmic "seeds" go once they are "planted" and how do they "ripen," mature, or fructify into experience? Later in the text, verse 19 adds that the "seeds" are "perfumed" (*vāsanā*) with latent tendencies that have yet to fade, something we learned earlier in this book.

> Verse 3. Its appropriations, states, and perceptions [*vijñapti*] are not fully conscious, yet it is always endowed with contacts, mental attentions, feelings, cognitions, and volitions [*cetanā*].

The focus will now stay on this "storehouse consciousness" for several verses. It appears to be responsible for every mental process: representations, the contacts with sensory objects that make them possible, and the feelings and cognitions that follow, even conscious "volitions" or intentions. The point is that this foundational form of *vijñāna* is not just a karmic "holding" place but a dynamic reality that "unfolds" into all else within mental life, coloring it with the positive, negative, or neutral quality of its seeds coming into fruit.

In Yogācāra materials, all that unfolds from the *ālaya* is often labeled *pravṛtti-vijñāna* ("evolving consciousness"). Sometimes, however, that term is reserved just for the final more perceptual six forms. But let us note that Vasubandhu likes words derived from the Sanskrit root, *vṛt*, "to turn or roll"—leading to notions of "evolution," and (as we shall see) "devolution" at the moment of Enlightenment. There it will fit nicely with the Western religious image of "con-verting"—actually, from the same Sanskrit root *vṛt*—as our term for salvation. The Buddha, too, liked the image of "turning"—his teaching was called "Turning the Wheel of the Dharma."

This important verse states that the *ālaya-vijñāna* is "not fully conscious" (*a-saṃ-vidita*), i.e., it is somewhat unconscious. Or, as Richard Robinson translates, "not discerned consciously" since somewhat unconscious.[38] In the sixth century, the Indian scholar Paramārtha—famous for his translations into Chinese—asked, as Lusthaus informs us:

> If it cannot be discerned, how do we know it exists? His answer is, By inference from what it produces. One infers what is the case from its effects. The ālaya-vijñāna, he says, is not known itself; it is never an object of knowledge.[39]

In comments like this, the foundational "consciousness" is beginning to look like the modern notion of the unconscious.

A Jungian parallel? As Jung himself often states, the unconscious is by definition "unconscious" and cannot be known, at best hypothesized to exist from its effects. True, he does not call it a form of "consciousness," as do the Yogācārins—but their *vijñāna* is somewhat unconscious. It is true, also, that Jung's collective "unconscious" is somewhat conscious with its peculiar wisdom visible in our dreams. Indeed, Jung said in his Tavistock lectures: "To Freud the unconscious is chiefly a receptacle for things repressed. He looks at it from the corner of the nursery. To me it is a vast historical storehouse."[40]

The similarity of language is not an identity of meaning, however, since Jung's "storehouse" does not assume the metaphysical Laws of *karma* and transmigration—while the Buddhist "storehouse" of karmic "seeds" does. There is also in Jung's comment on Freud the distinction of a personal unconscious of repressed contents and an impersonal collective unconscious whose patterns have been laid down by all of humanity over the ages. To which "unconscious," then, is the *ālaya-vijñāna* closer?

The answer is ambiguous. On the one hand, Buddhist texts say clearly that our everyday actions plant "seeds" of personal karmic recompense. On the other hand, they say these seeds may have been planted long ago in former lifetimes—giving them a kind of impersonal quality, although they are still somehow "ours" (the way that "Gautama" was somehow "Sumedha" aeons earlier).

---

[38] Lusthaus, *Buddhist Phenomenology*, 277. Lusthaus uses the Robinson translation from the Sanskrit.

[39] Lusthaus, *Buddhist Phenomenology*, 306.

[40] Jung, *CW* 18, par. 280.

Nevertheless, writers frequently detect an exact "correspondence" between the ancient and modern here, with priority of discovery belonging to the ancient Buddhists. Radmila Moacanin, a practitioner of Tibetan Buddhism, tells us in the language peculiar to her tradition:

> In the view of one school of Buddhist tenets there are six kinds of consciousness . . . . Then there is the afflicted, or deluded, consciousness responsible for the misconception of the ego. And underlying all of it is the "store consciousness" (*alaya-vijnana*), the source of all consciousness, the Universal Mind, in which primordial forms and all experiences since beginningless time are stored. Its latent contents appear to the other kinds of consciousness when aroused by the corresponding conditions and associations. The notion of store consciousness clearly corresponds to Jung's concept of the unconscious.[41]

Shortly, however, she thinks better of the matter and writes:

> We are dealing here with two different categories: philosophical and metaphysical on the one hand, and psychological on the other hand, and consequently no real comparison could be made.

This second comment, I believe, is more accurate.

That is not to deny the possibility that Vasubandhu is speaking, in a brilliant prescient way, out of that same unconscious "Wisdom" from which Jung speaks to us today. But the philosopher has given us no hint thus far that his *ālaya-vijñāna* is numinous as is the collective unconscious—filled with images of all the "gods" (of India and elsewhere) still influencing our lives. These archetypal "god-images," furthermore, are not mere karmic "seeds" waiting to mature into everyday experience where they cease to exist; instead, they are eternal structures of the psyche itself that cannot cease.

Granted, the parallel is uncanny, acting as a hook for projecting "Jung" onto the Buddhist discussion. The archetypal psyche, after all, is a kind of storehouse; and it does unfold into other levels of psychic life.

Within Buddhism, I think it best to consider Yogācāra's "storehouse consciousness" as a re-working of the "stream of consciousness" image used in Abhidharma to solve the problem of karmic continuity. In fact, Verse 4 tells us that, "it develops like the currents in a stream." Not surprisingly, the *ālaya-vijñāna* was sometimes associated in this school with the "rebirth" *vijñāna* as the third member of Dependent Origination, influenced as that member is by the second member of karmic "predispostions." Wayman writes of this third member: "Since it is supported by the 'store consciousness'—a store of habit–energy (*vāsanā*) and (underlying) traces (*anuśaya*)—this store must go along with it"—providing continuity from one lifetime to another.[42]

---

[41] Radmila Moacanin, *Jung's Psychology and Tibetan Buddhism: Western and Eastern Paths to the Heart* (London: Wisdom Publications, 1986), 75. Slightly altered.

[42] Wayman, *Untying the Knots*, 129.

"Reflecting" Consciousness

> Verse 5. Its de-volvement [*vyā-vṛti*] takes place in a saintly state: Dependent on it there develops a consciousness called "manas," having it as its object-of-consciousness, and having the nature of always reflecting

(7) *manas* The first part of this verse pertains to Enlightenment or the "saintly state," so let us discuss that later. The rest of the verse, then, introduces *manas* or "mind" as the seventh "consciousness" in the Yogācāra system. It is "dependent," we learn, on the foundational eighth and actually "develops" or "evolves" (*pravartate*) out of it; often, it is called the first "evolute" of the *ālayavijṇāna*. Furthermore, we are told that *manas* is always "reflecting" ("thinking" is an acceptable translation of *mananā*)) and takes the "storehouse" as its "object-of-consciousness." That introduces the" duality" of subject and object into this intra-psychic description of experience.

Of course, "duality" is suspect in "nondualist" Mahāyāna. But matters only gets worse, according to the next verse.

> Verse 6. It is always conjoined with four afflictions, obstructed-but-indeterminate, known as view of self, confusion of self, pride of self, and love of self.

What *manas* thinks it sees when it perceives the *ālayavijñāna* is a "self" (*ātman*), here in four iterations. It might even think this "self" is the divine Self of the Upaniṣads. But that is because this first evolute of the psyche is structurally defiled—"afflicted," says this verse. Indeed, the Yogācārin Sthiramati (sixth century) calls it *kliṣṭa-manas*—its specific defilement being not really lust or hatred but, instead, delusion.

It follows, as we learn in Verse 7, that *manas* "doesn't exist in a saintly state," i.e., when one is Enlightened. Technically, the verse goes on, it does not even exist "in the attainment of cessation, or even in a supermundane path." What is meant is the fourth *samāpatti* trance, called "attainment of cessation" (*nirodha samāpatti*) that "touches Nirvāṇa" yet eventually ends—bringing the meditator back from the top of the Formless Realm to the Realm of Desire.

But if that person's "feeling and ideas" actually "ceased" while in trance—yet "continued" somehow karmically—where were those feelings and ideas during "cessation"? An Early Buddhist answer was within an underlying (but not very deep) "stream of *bhavāṅga*." Now the answer is within an eighth form of consciousness called a "storehouse." Nor does *manas* exist in the "supermundane path" of a Bodhisattva who has reached the highly advanced Eighth Stage.

Unfortunately, we are ignoring a serious problem If the reader glances back at the list of the "eight consciousness" within the Yogācāra system, it will be obvious that each member in the list has "*–vijñāna*" as the second qualifying member of a compound—except for *manas*, at Number 7. In fact, if this *manas* were so qualified, it would appear identical with Number 6, *mano-vijñāna*. Is Vasubandhu just trying not to repeat himself?

We have been told by classic Buddhist materials that the first six *vijṇānas* (eye-consciousness, etc.) in the list are the products of an organ (the eye, etc.) making contact with an object (something visible, etc.)—but the first five of these sensory organs do not appear in the list, nor do their objects.

They do not appear since not at issue for an intra-psychic "philosophy of psychology." Yet *manas* as the *organ* of "mind"—in support of *mano-vijñāna* as "mental consciousness"—does appear, unexpectedly. As D. T. Suzuki remarks, we are confronted here with the problem of the "treacherous interpretation" of Yogācāra's *manas* with a variety of possible solutions.[43]

Suzuki himself simply takes Number 7. *manas* to be the sensory organ behind Number 6. *mano-vijñāna*—but makes use of Early Buddhism's considering it in a special way as a kind of "common sense" coordinating all sensory data. He writes of the use of *manas* in the *Laṅkāvatāra Sūtra*, a scripture associated with Yogācāra philosophy, as follows:

> Manas is conscious of the presence behind itself of the [eighth] Ālaya and also of the latter's uninterrupted working on the entire system of the [six more external] Vijñānas. Reflecting on the Ālaya and imagining it to be an ego [*ātman*], Manas clings to it as if it were reality . . . . In other words, Manas is the individual will to live and the principle of discrimination. The notion of an ego-substance is herein established, and also the acceptance of a world external to itself and distinct from itself. . . . Manas sits at the headquarters and like a great general gathers up all the information coming from the six ["external"] Vijñānas. For it is he who shifts [sifts?] and arranges the reports and gives orders again to the reporters according to his own will and intelligence. The orders are then faithfully executed.[44]

Some of this we have already established from the *Triṃśikā*—although, as usual, it is dubious to translate *ātman* as "ego" (as *manas*' misinterpretation of the *ālaya-vijñāna*).

Besides, Suzuki really wants *manas* to be the "ego"—as the "individual will to live and the principle of discrimination." It is this ego "consciousness," then, that acts like a "great general" in the psyche sorting out the data (like a "common" sense) and sending "reports" of its findings to the other more sensory *vijñānas*. But it sends false reports, getting them to believe in external objects with *svabhāva*—because *manas* is inherently "defiled," something all spiritual religions say about egohood. This does explain why *manas* "doesn't exist" in a saintly state—if not as ego, then as egotism. It explains why *manas* does not exist in the higher trances when the ego dissolves.

William Waldron thinks otherwise about 7. *manas*. Working with the *Yogācārabhūmi* of Asaṅga, he argues for two distinct kinds of *manas* in the Yogācāra: 1) the traditional one implied by 6. *mano-vijñāna* (but unlisted) that is a sensory organ of experience but not inherently defiled; and 2) a "newer level of mental activity," *manas* as a "deep-seated, even unconscious, self-centeredness"—the inherently "defiled" nature of which not only misreads the *ālaya-vijñāna* (behind it) but influences nefariously the six "perceptual" *vijñānas* (ahead of it). Thus, the six sensory consciousness are tempted to read their own respective sensory objects incorrectly—as real objects of a real subject. Waldron summarizes:

---

[43] Suzuki, *Lankavatara*, xxiii.

[44] Suzuki, *Lankavatara*, xxiii-xxiv.

> It is only when this form of mentation (*manas*) has finally come to an end that mental cognitive awareness itself will be "freed from the bondage of perception in regard to phenomena." In other words, only when the latent afflictions are finally and fully eradicated at their basic, subliminal level will they cease adversely affecting our perceptions of the world and thereby cease instigating the afflictive activities that continue to perpetuate samsaric existence.[45]

This interpretation eliminates *manas* as a candidate for "ego" that, by definition, is not at a "subliminal level" of the mind.

A Jungian thought Waldron's interpretation of *manas* points to a Jungian personal unconscious—a "deep-seated, even unconscious, self-centeredness," as this writer puts it—that the ego is unwilling to acknowledge and represses out of sight as the "shadow." Yogācāra, insists, however, that this feature of the mind completely disappears at Enlightenment, since emptied of all defilements. Waldron is forced to agree.

It is one thing, however, to say that "self-centeredness" can be overcome as one develops psychologically and quite another to say that the shadow completely disappears. We know this is unlikely from personal experience but even from the "shadow" figures of Buddhism: although "still in training," Ānanda can win an argument with the Buddha; Devadatta can still do his worst; and Māra just will not go away. The Puritan claim is primed for failure.

"Perception" Consciousness

(6-1) "perceptual" *vijñānas* The rest of the system is straightforward:

> Verse 8. This is the second transformation; the third is the apprehension of sense-objects of six kinds: it is either beneficial, or unbeneficial or neither.

As Vasubandhu announced at the outset of his treatise, he has described 1) a basic "maturation" consciousness; then 2) its "second" transformation as a problematic "reflecting" consciousness; and will now present 3) a "third" transformation as the perceptual "apprehension" of sense objects with positive, negative, or neutral karmic consequences. This presentation goes on for several verses with no real surprises—and is a review of standard Buddhist sensory theory, along with a list of the defilements.

There is at Verse 15, however, an important image:

> In the root-consciousness, the arising of the other five takes place according to conditions, either all together or not, just like waves in water.

This image of "water and its waves" appears throughout Indian religious thought. Here, in Buddhism, it means that the standard six sensory *vijṇānas* are like "waves" and, thus, merely modifications of

---

[45] Waldron, *Buddhist Unconscious*, 122-123.

the "root-consciousness" of *ālayavijñāna* as "water." It would be foolish, therefore, to take the superficial experiences of consciousness as essentially different in kind from the deepest level of consciousness from which they come—just as it would be to say that the waves are different from the water.

While it is tempting to conclude that "all is water" as in idealist philosophy, Anacker reminds us in a note that it is the "agitation" of external sense-objects that act as a kind of "wind" to stir up the waves of our experience.[46] The Yogācāra position is clear: we are only ever reading "representations" or "pictures" within the mind that have reached us from the "storehouse"—intrapsychically.

Thus, Verse 17 states:

> This transformation of consciousness is a discrimination, and as it is discriminated,
> it does not exist, and so everything is perception-only.

And Verse 18 makes the same point:

> Consciousness is only all the seeds, and transformation takes place in such and such a way, according to a reciprocal influence, by which such and such a type of discrimination may arise.

It is no surprise that the "seeds" within the *ālaya-vijñāna* find themselves coming to "fruition" at the level of the sensory *vijñānas* where new "representations" are stimulated by objects. The new karmic "seeds" produced by those (generally erroneous) perceptions are a "reciprocal influence"—refilling the "storehouse" with karmic consequences in a vicious cycle. This is the way the mind operates within itself at every moment.

It is even, as we read in Verse 25, the "ultimate truth":

> It is the ultimate truth [*paramārtha*] of all events, and so it is "Suchness" [*tathatā*],
> too, since it is just so all the time, and it's just perception only.

Obviously, this is how Yogācāra got its other names, "mind-only" and "representation-only."

What we have described at some length, however, is only the "ultimate truth" of how the mind operates when not Enlightened, when in Saṃsāra. And capitalizing "Suchness" (or "Thatness") obscures that important distinction. So let us listen to a warning from Vasuandhu himself at Verses 26 and 27:

> As long as consciousness is not situated within perception-only [*vijñapti-mātra*],
> the residues of a "dual" apprehension [*grāha*, "grasping"] will not come to an end
> [*vinivartate*, "not turn back"].
> And so even with the consciousness: "All this is perception only,"
> because this also involves an apprehension.

[46] Anacker, *Seven Works*, 189.

> For whatever makes something stop in front of it
> isn't situated in "this-only [*tan-mātra*]."

He is saying—granted, obscurely—that we are not to take this philosophy as an idea "in front" of ourselves as something to be "grasped" intellectually: "Oh, now I know that everything is subjective!" The warning is akin to Nāgārjuna's stating that even his ideas about "emptiness" are empty of substance—to which one should not become attached, helpful though they may be along one's religious path.

The Breakthrough

We must now ask of the Yogācāra, what happens if one does not fall into that intellectual trap and actually "sees" (perhaps through the practices of yoga) that all one's experience is mental, *citta-mātra*? Vasubandhu's answer is contained in the final three verses of the *Triṃśikā*:

> Verse 28. When consciousness [*jñāna*, "knowledge"] does not apprehend any object-of-consciousness, it's situated in "consciousness-only" [*vijñāna-mātra*], for with the non-being of an object apprehended, there is no apprehension of it.
>
> Verse 29. It is without *citta* ["thought"], without apprehension, and it is supermundane knowledge [again, *jñāna*];
> It is revolution [*parāvṛtti*, "turning back, devolution"] at the basis, the ending of two kinds of susceptibility to harm [i.e., the usual two Mahāyāna "obscurations" of defilement and misunderstanding].
>
> Verse 30. It is the inconceivable [*a-cintya*], beneficial, constant Ground [*dhruva*, "immovable"], not liable to affliction [*an-āśrava*], bliss, and the liberation-body called the Dharma-body of the Sage.

The language is charged, indicating that the experience of Nirvāṇa is what happens next.

At his own breakthrough, Gautama had proclaimed, "This is the way leading to the cessation of the taints" (*an-āśrava*), the same Sanskrit term found here. Nirvāṇa is also signaled by the removal of the "two obscurations" and by the attainment of the "Dharma-body" of the Buddha. And by the word "bliss" (*sukha*), the opposite of saṃsāric "suffering" (*duḥkha*). The attainment is somehow solid, expressed here by the word, "immovable"—that our translator capitalizes (correctly, I think) as "constant Ground," not something we hear often in this religion. Beyond that, however, Vasubandhu says little—noting that what he is telling us is actually *a-cintya* or "inconceivable." His reticence is a reminder of many other occasions of holy "silence" in Buddhism.

Still, there is some special Yogācāra language describing what occurs just prior to the ineffable breakthrough. We heard it earlier at Verse 5 as the "de-volvement" (*vyāvṛti*) of the "storehouse consciousness" in a saintly state. Here, in Verse 29, it is translated by Anacker as, "revolution at the basis" (*āśrayasya parāvṛtti*)—a controversial and, therefore, famous phrase. It would be better, however, to translate "of the basis" (rather than "at") to honor the Sanskrit genitive case in both of these verses. Others render the phrase, "transformation" or "transmutation" of the *ālaya-vijñāna.*

Vasubandhu appears to be saying that upon Enlightenment the entire saṃsāric superstructure of mentality collapses, and what has previously "evolved"—as habitual karmic functioning, and as the naive belief in real objects out there (without a subjective component and to which one is likely to become attached)—"devolves." The previously misinformed "perceptual" *vijñānas* no longer function in that way. The *manas* that has misinformed them while misconstruing a "self" ceases to "exist" (as we have heard) in this "saintly state." Critically, I believe even the *ālaya-vijñāna* collapses since the vicious cycle that feeds it with karmic "seeds" has been broken.

There is controversy, however, over whether or not the "storehouse" somehow remains when everything else is gone. To me, it seems unlikely that it could exist without seeds—just as in Buddhist cosmology a heaven does not exist without its divine inhabitants. And that conclusion seems confirmed by what was stated at Verse 18: "consciousness is only all the seeds." By contrast, the state of Nirvāṇa is free of the "seeds" of karmic recompense and, thus, from transmigration—free of everyday *citta-mātra*—and deserving of Anacker's capitalization as the "Dharma-body" of the "Great Sage."

Another clue is Vasubandhu's shift in terminology. He now writes of a non-grasping "knowledge" (*jñāna*) and not just of evolving perception or "consciousness" (*vi-jñāna*). These words are related etymologically, of course, but the latter carries the prefix *vi-* that can signify "separation, distinction." Illusory dualistic consciousness, therefore, has been displaced by nondual knowledge about which one can say nothing.

Some modern psychology This thoroughgoing "devolvement" confirms what Lusthaus said earlier—that "mind-only" is the problem in Yogācāra and not the solution. Now, he writes:

> Everything we know, conceive, imagine, or are aware of, we know through cognition, including the notion that entities might exist independent of our cognition. The mind doesn't create the physical world but it produces the interpretive categories through which we know and classify the physical world, and it does this so seamlessly that we mistake our interpretations for the world itself. . . A deceptive trick is built into the way consciousness operates at every moment. Consciousness projects and constructs a cognitive object in such a way that it disowns its own creation—pretending the object is "out there"—in order to render that object capable of being appropriated. . . . Realization of *vijñapti-mātra* exposes this trick intrinsic to consciousness's workings, catching it in the act, so to speak, thereby eliminating it. When that deception is removed one's mode of cognition is no longer termed *vijñāna* (consciousness); it has become direct cognition (*jñāna*).[47]

[47] Lusthaus, *Buddhist Phenomenology*, 538.

Some of this sounds like Yogācāra, and some of it like a scholar's attempt at a more modern understanding of how the psyche functions. Lusthaus accurately grasps the "interpretive" character of mental life, as well as the general "mistake" or failure even to suspect it. He understands that if we catch this error "in the act," it eliminates or softens it by definition. But, again, we find the strange notion that "consciousness projects"—as if I consciously make up a "snake" where there is only a rope.

What is lacking—and generally lacking in Buddhism—is an explicit reference to an unconscious psyche that actually "does" the projecting without our knowing it.

Waldron, as we have seen, thinks Yogācāra does finally acknowledge an unconscious dimension of the mind: with *manas* as a "deep-seated, even unconscious, self-centeredness" and with the "not fully conscious" *ālaya-vijñāna*. But he follows Vasubandhu's view that they are eliminated at Enlightenment—although the ancient philosopher is not entirely clear. Asaṅga, however, is clear:

> As soon as the basis is revolved, the ālaya-vijñāna must be said to be have been abandoned; because it has been abandoned, it must be said that all the defilements also have been abandoned.[48]

Waldron, therefore, lauds the Yogācāra for its "ambitious project—tantamount to emptying out or utterly transforming the contents and structures of the unconscious mind."[49] But this naively overstates what is actually possible in psychology.

Lusthaus also overstates:

> For Kant a thing-in-itself is ultimately unknowable as it is in itself; i.e., it is noumenal. For Yogācāra the way things happen (*yathābhūtam*) is eminently knowable, and seeing things as they truly are is one of the goals of the system.[50]

Yet again a writer confuses what Buddhism itself does not confuse—the "way things are" in Saṃsāra as opposed to the way things are in Nirvāṇa. The former is described, even by Vasubandhu; but the latter is left unstated. Besides, Jungian psychology is grateful to the Western philosopher Kant for seeing that we can never know the noumenal "thing-in-itself"—nor need we pretend to do so in order to live increasingly more consciously.

"Tricks" of the Mind

As a kind of check on our interpretation of Yogācāra, let me cite two other texts where Vasubandhu recounts stories of delusion. The first comes from the *Trisvabhāvanirdeśa* ("Teaching of the Three Own-Beings"). There, the philosopher describes the scene of an Indian magician who has on stage a contraption of wood. Using a *mantra*, the magician hypnotizes his audience into believing they see an elephant that is not actually there. Then, the magician makes the "elephant"

[48] Waldron, *Buddhist Unconscious*, 126-127.

[49] Waldron, *Buddhist Unconscious*, 123.

[50] Lusthaus, *Buddhist Phenomenology*, v.

disappear, to everyone's amazement. Vasubandhu says: "Suchness is like the wood . . . and duality is like the elephant itself."[51] Obviously, the wood on stage—as external object—is real and does not disappear. But the "duality" between the would-be "objective" elephant and the audience's "subjective" perception is revealed to be an illusion—all of it mental or *citta-mātra*.

Then, in the very short *Viṃśatikā-kārikā* or "Twenty Verses," Vasubandhu refers in passing to "the *pretas* in the seeing of pus-rivers, etc." Alex Wayman explains:

> This alludes to the Buddhist mythological theory of five or six destinies (*gati*), including the hungry ghosts as those disembodied spirits that are perpetually hungry and thirsty because their own consciousness pollutes what is inherently pure, making it so repulsive as to be uneatable and undrinkable. Jñānagarbha's commentary on the Maitreya chapter of the *Saṃdhinirmocanasūtra* illustrates the mis-reported nature of the external object with the standard example of the stream of water which animals, hungry ghosts, men, and gods all see differently, the hungry ghosts seeing it full of pus, the gods seeing it as lapis lazuli, and so on. The stream itself is not denied.[52]

In these examples—that are images, really, not rational thoughts—we are being encouraged to question the accuracy of our experience of the "world" and to wake up to the fact that the world we see is the one we get. What others see is what they get. It is the philosophical end product of Gautama's having experienced the palace women as wonderful and then—all of a sudden—like bodies in a cemetery. How could that be? To which experience should he commit himself, to which dare he be attached? He claims that he detached from all of it. He was reluctant to say, however, what it was like to live unattached.

A "Ninth" Consciousness

Paramārtha, to whom we have been introduced, heard these teachings and was dissatisfied. He said it could not be that when the "storehouse consciousness" ceased, there was little more to say. Nor could its cessation be the only reason for "bliss." So he posited a "ninth consciousness" called *amala-vijñāna* ("immaculate consciousness") as the pure basis of the "eighth consciousness" at every moment of its defiled saṃsāric activity. And it was into this "Immaculate" level of mind that Paramārtha claimed the "storehouse" level returned at the "revolution of the basis."

For those in agreement, this new idea actually maintained an old Buddhist tradition of an inherently "luminous" and "pure" mind. Furthermore, it expresses a religious *via positiva* that appealed to the Chinese with whom this scholar was residing to translate Sanskrit texts he had brought with him as a missionary from India. It may even be that the Chinese inspired this innovation since the new technical term has not been attested in any Sanskrit text.[53]

---

[51] Anacker, "The Teaching of the Three Own-Beings," in *Seven Works by Vasubandhu*, 294.

[52] Wayman, "Yogācāra and the Buddhist Logicians," 67.

[53] See "amalavijñāna," *PDB*, 33.

The *Laṅkāvatāra Sūtra*, however, is a Sanskrit text composed at the start of Yogācāra thinking. As we know from the previous chapter, it teaches the kataphatic sacred "element" of the Tathāgatagarbha. While preaching on this topic, the Lord makes an extraordinary connection:

> let those Bodhisattva-Mahāsattvas who are seeking after the exalted truth effect the purification of the Tathāgata-garbha which is known as the Ālayavijñāna.[54]

It is not quite Paramātha's point, but the scripture is proclaiming that something positive does remain in Nirvāṇa when Saṃsāra collapses: namely, a purified "Embryo of the Buddha" which is the same as an emptied "storehouse consciousness"—for which Paramārtha provides a new name.

From a philosophical perspective, the identity is ambiguous (an "Embryo" that does and does not need to develop? a "Storehouse" that no longer stores seeds?). If we take these terms as symbols, however, they can appeal to the religious temperament as the revelation that, when all else fails, there is in fact an immovable Ground—ineffable and inconceivable though that may be. Jung called it the archetype of the Self.

A closing Jungian thought Jung never heard of Vasubandhu or his brother Asaṅga, but he did write "Yogācāra-like" sentences such as these:

> It is my mind, with its store of images, that gives the world color and sound; and that supremely real and rational certainty which I call "experience" is, in its most simple form, an exceedingly complicated structure of mental images. Thus there is, in a certain sense, nothing that is directly experienced except the mind itself. Everything is mediated through the mind, translated, filtered, allegorized, twisted, even falsified by it.[55]

Nor did Jung know directly of Nāgārjuna, but he continues in the same paragraph in a "Madhyamaka-like" way:

> We are so enveloped in a cloud of changing and endlessly shifting images that we might well exclaim with a well-known sceptic: "Nothing is absolutely true—and even that is not quite true."[56]

Nevertheless, it was Jung's advice that we explore our own "relative" experiences of the external world, even sensory ones, to see where they lead.

They might lead us to explore what lies behind experience: ego consciousness; then the shadow; then the archetypes that are guiding us (and even misguiding us) and about which we need to be morally discriminating. Possibly, we will be able to see that the psyche is in a state of unfolding or "evolving" from an unconscious Foundation to a more conscious manifestation of itself. We might

---

[54] Suzuki, *Lankavatara*, 81.222 (p. 192).

[55] Jung, *CW* 8, par. 623.

[56] Jung is quoting Multatuli, pen name of the Dutch writer, E. D. Dekker.

even feel morally obliged to assist in this unfolding. None of this ever collapses, however, nor should it. But our ignorance does, our unconscious projections do, our general inflation subsides. And if Buddhist philosophy encourages that kind of "devolution," then it has fulfilled a most important task.

PART VI

TANTRIC BUDDHISM

Chapter 14
TANTRA

Introduction

Five centuries after Nāgārjuna and three centuries after Vasubandhu, new scriptures appeared that these great Buddhist thinkers had never seen. Yet these new texts claimed to be sermons of the Buddha preached long ago. They usually opened in the traditional way: "Thus by me it was heard. At one time, the Lord was dwelling at . . . "—as if recited by Ānanda at the First Council. We know, however, that these new texts were composed in India from the seventh to the eleventh century CE.

But, then, the followers of Early Buddhism had never seen the Mahāyāna scriptures that began to appear in the first century CE and that also claimed to be very old—upon which Nāgārjuna and Vasubandhu commented as authentic. Those scriptures, as we have seen, were somewhat more miraculous than earlier ones. They revealed the Lord preaching a *Lotus Sūtra* on the small mountain of Vulture Peak outside Rājagṛha, yet surrounded by hundreds of thousands of followers that included not only human beings but Celestial Bodhisattvas and all the gods. It was as if "Vulture Peak" was not actually in India and not a real place. And when Vimalakīrti took over the preaching of the *Vimilakīrtinirdeśa Sūtra*, it was as if—along with all the miracles—he was not really a Buddhist layman and not really living in a house.

One of the newer scriptures (from the eighth century), the *Mañjuśrī-mūla-kalpa* ("The Primary Ritual Ordinance of Mañjuśrī"—or MMK, for ease of reference) makes it clear that its Buddha Śākyamuni is, in fact, *not* preaching on earth. It opens with the standard *nidāna* or "introduction," as Glenn Wallis translates from the Sanskrit:

> Thus have I heard. At one time the Blessed One was dwelling in the vault of sky above the Śuddhāvāsa ["Pure Abode"] heaven, in the pavilion of the assembly of inconceivably, miraculously, wondrously distributed *bodhisattvas*. There, the Blessed One spoke to the *devaputras* ["young gods"], the inhabitants of the Śuddhāvāsa: "Hear, O *devaputras*, about that upon which all beings depend: the inconceivable, wondrous, miraculous transformation of the *bodhisattva*, the use of the *maṇḍala*, for superior liberation, purity, contemplation, proper conduct; hear about the *mantras* of that great being, the princely *bodhisattva* Mañjuśrī, which completely fulfill one's wishes for power, health and long life."[1]

---

[1] Glenn Wallis, *Mediating the Power of the Buddhas: Ritual in the "Mañjuṣrīmūlakalpa"* (Albany: State University of New York Press, 2002), 55-56.

As we already know, the "Pure Abode"—the location of this text—is a set of five heavens at the top of the Realm of Form. Countless long-lived deities reside there, as do Early Buddhist "Nonreturners" spending their last long lifetime before passing into Nirvāṇa. It is there in Mahāyāna Buddhism that some very advanced Bodhisattvas spend much more time and from which they compassionately send *nirmāṇas* or "emanations" to bring about the salvation of all sentient beings. Now we learn that the Buddha preaches sermons there. And his topics include what are called *maṇḍalas* and *mantras*. Somewhat surprisingly, he promises health and a long mundane life in Saṃsāra.

Śākyamuni, we are told, is residing in a divine "pavilion" or palace surrounded by his own divine retinue. That reminds us of the Buddha-fields of mainstream Mahāyāna that exist mysteriously far from our world. As we explore technical terms in the MMK's introduction, it will remind us of the structure of the *maṇḍala* with its central Buddha and surrounding *devatās* within a palace. So exalted is this opening scene that the Buddhist commentaries are certain Ānanda could not have "heard" it—not being sufficiently advanced along the Path—so it must have been heard by the scripture's interlocutors, the Celestial Bodhisattva Mañjuśrī or the newly promoted Celestial Bodhisattva Vajrapāṇi.

In fact, Tibetan translations of these new texts punctuate the opening phrases of the *nidāna* so that one reads, "Thus have I heard at one time" (instead of, "Thus have I heard. At one time")—suggesting that the entire sermon had been heard all at once, outside of ordinary time, mystically. Indeed, Mañjuśrī had been residing in a different Buddha-field but arrived in this new one instantaneously when summoned by a ray of light emanating from the Teacher.[2]

Another new text (from the seventh century), the *Mahā-vairocana-abhisaṃbodhi* ("The Higher Complete Enlightenment of the Great Vairocana"—hereafter, VAT) dispenses with the standard introduction altogether. An important commentator from the following century, Buddhaguhya, explains—as Stephen Hodge translates from the Tibetan—that the lack of a *nidāna* is due to the "fixed nature of the teacher, time and place, and because the audience and compilers are such Bodhisattvas as Samantabhadra, Vajrapāṇi and so on who are mainly realization oriented."[3] He means there are no "hearers" in the audience (i.e., "Śrāvakas" like Ānanda) who could have heard it, only highly accomplished tenth-stage Bodhisattvas. It means that the Lord's location is "fixed"—which is to say he "perpetually dwells" on the "seat of Enlightenment."

He resides, that is, beyond such "un-fixed" variable locations as Akaniṣṭha, Mount Meru, and Rājagṛha that are named in other texts. Buddhaguhya adds, "such *sūtras* have the words 'at one time' because the time and place are not fixed." Shortly, we read that this Lord Buddha who dwells perpetually outside place and time is not really Śākyamuni but a Buddha named Vairocana ("very shining," "resplendent")—who merely "emanates" as a being called Śākyamuni.

The very early seventh-century *Su-siddhi-kara* ("Producing Good Success"—hereafter, SSK) dispenses with the standard introduction, also, and opens instead with praise from a Bodhisattva. He asks the Lord, who is here named not Śākyamuni, nor Vairocana, but Vajradhara ("holding the *vajra*") about particular practices. Rolf Giebel translates from the Chinese:

---

2 Wallis, MMK, 79-80.

3 Stephen Hodge, trans., *The Mahā-Vairocana-Abhisaṃbodhi Tantra: With Buddhaguhya's Commentary* (London: Routledge, 2015), 47.

> What are the characteristics of *mantras*? And the characteristics of an *ācārya* ["master"]?
> What are the characteristics of an adept [*siddha*]? And explain the characteristics of an associate [to a master].
> Which localities are excellent for performing rites?
> . . . .
> Which flowers bring success easily? How does one use unguents?
> How does one make offerings of food? And which incense does one burn?[4]

Questions of this kind go on for the remainder of the first chapter. Thus, scholars conclude that all these new sermons taught by a "Lord" of whatever name and wherever are not primarily about doctrine. Instead, they assume the doctrine already established by Buddhism in prior centuries and introduce new methods or techniques.

These methods are called "rites" (*vidhi*), "practices" (*caryā*), "evocations" (*sādhana*), and "worship" (*pūjā*)—that belong to the practical Means (*upāya*) half of the traditional Mahāyāna pair, "Means and Wisdom." A tantric Buddhist devotee will still need both to become Enlightened.

The Meaning of "Tantra"

Texts of the kind we have just cited often call themselves *sūtras*, as one would expect since they are "sermons" of a Buddha. But the VAT is self-conscious of being different and calls itself a *tantra*. In fact, over time all these texts will be labeled *tantras* by Buddhism—if not for their titles, then for their content. There is not much difference, however, between the two labels.

As we know, *sūtra* derives from the Sanskrit root *siv*, "to sew," and alludes to a "thread" of thought or argument which shapes the "fabric" of a text of any kind. The word *tantra*, then, derives from the root *tan* which means "to weave," from which one gets the same sense of a fabric of thought or argument shaped by the interlacing of threads. Both kinds of text, therefore, put together a coherent religious world view. As we shall see, the vision of the *tantras* is really the same as previous styles of Buddhism—but its perspective is different. That is how we arrive at the name "Tantra" or "Tantrism" for this new kind of Buddhism and why its adherents are often called *tāntrikas*.

Let me observe at the outset that work in this field is extremely difficult—and not just because it is hard to keep track of the names or where it is exactly that the Lord is preaching. As Michel Strickmann comments, "For the scholar of comparative religions, Tantrism must represent the ultimate challenge."[5] One reason is that there is no scholarly consensus, no master description of Buddhist Tantra. And one reason for that is the plethora of Sanskrit manuscripts—well over a thousand—that sit unedited for errors and, thus, not yet translated into a Western language for easy

---

4 Rolf W. Giebel, trans., *Susiddhikara Sūtra*, in *Two Esoteric Sutras* (Berkeley: Numata Center for Buddhist Translation and Research, 2001), 125.

5 The quotation appears as the epigraph for Christian K. Wedemeyer, *Making Sense of Tantric Buddhism* (New York: Columbia University Press, 2013).

access. Some of the early Sanskrit has been lost. Fortunately, many texts do exist in Chinese or Tibetan translation; and we are forced to rely heavily upon them.

The Tibetan Buddhist canon is especially useful since that country converted to Buddhism late, beginning in the eighth century, when all Buddhist scriptures were new to them and *tantras* were accepted—if not always indisputably—as "Buddha word." But ancient translations do not necessarily reflect the original Sanskrit works at every turn. This means that the field is in the hands of a limited number of scholars who can move about these materials despite their rough state.

Another difficulty is that the available Buddhist *tantras* are obviously compilations. They read in a disjointed way and defy catching the "thread" of argument, if there even is one. But, then, these texts are primarily instructions for how to "do" Tantra, not how to "understand" it. They read often like cook books that are not known for their narrative flow and make little sense if one does not intend to follow the recipe.

Secrecy

Then, again, some of the "ingredients" of Tantra have intentionally been left out of the written recipe! Tantric Buddhism, unlike the other styles of Buddhism we have studied, is not intended for the general public. If it is true that the historical Gautama Buddha taught whoever would listen—although not insisting that the listener follow his advice—and if it is true that the Great Bodhisattvas are compassionately available to all who suffer, it is no longer the case in Tantra. Buddhist Tantra is "esoteric" or secret—not "exoteric" or public like Early Buddhism and mainstream Mahāyāna. It is intended only for superior candidates who have been initiated into the practices of a particular tantric cycle of texts by a qualified *guru* ("teacher") or *ācārya* ("master"). Tāntrikas are expected to follow the usual Buddhist Precepts and Vinaya rules that we have studied, but there are an additional "Fourteen Root Violations" that must be avoided. And the seventh violation is: "revealing secrets to non-initiates or those not ready to receive them."[6]

To protect that secrecy, what was written down was often intentionally left incomplete—or, in late *tantras*, put into a sort of "code" called "twilight language" (*saṃdhā-bhāṣā*)—so that the uninitiated could not follow precisely. The Tibetan historian, Bu-ston (d. 1364) puts it baldly:

> In order to stop people from becoming involved with tantras of their own accord, tantras are set forth in an incomplete way, in an unclear way, and with confusion.[7]

There was a note of compassion in doing so since practices could be dangerous for the uninformed. But this means tantric texts were surely not intended for the eyes of the disinterested modern scholar—anymore than tantric art was intended for modern museums.

---

6 See "fourteen root violations of the tantric commitments," *PDB*, 1088-1089.

7 Cited by Steven Neal Weinberger, "The Significance of Yoga Tantra and the *Compendium of Principles* (*Tattvasaṃgraha Tantra*) within Tantric Buddhism in India and Tibet" (Ph.D. dissertation, University of Virginia, 2003), 46, http://www.libra2.lib.virginia.edu/public

If one visits an exhibit of tantric Tibetan Buddhist *thaṅ kas* (hanging painted scrolls) one might notice still intact at the top of a scroll a bit of cloth that can be let down to veil the image when not in use—or to protect it from prying eyes. We can assume a similar care for ancient Indian tantric images painted on cloth or paper (called *paṭa*, in Sanskrit)—now lost due to the fragility of the materials.

Thus, it is somewhat misleading to say, as we sometimes read, that Buddhist Tantra became "popular" in India after the fall of the Guptas—since it could not be popular, by definition. Besides, we have been told in an earlier chapter that Mahāyāna itself was probably not very popular; and Tantra claims to be part of Mahāyāna Buddhism. Much is made of the fact that the Chinese pilgrim Hsüan-tsang, who visited India as late as 645 CE, said nothing about Tantra despite thoroughly reporting upon his travels. Just thirty-five years later, however, another Chinese pilgrim named Wu-hsing reported on the widespread "acceptance" of the esoteric path within the monasteries.[8] While this Buddhist devotee's observation suggests a rather swift emergence of Tantra, it tells us little of how it was actually practiced: by large or small monasteries as a whole, by esoteric groups therein, or by individuals who set themselves apart for tantric practice while affiliated with a monastery, or even by unaffiliated "heretics" who had their own disciples.

That is not to say Tantra was not studied in the monasteries. Indeed, that is how we possess Buddhaguhya's helpful commentaries. It is as if the esoteric nature of tantric Buddhism—its attempt to confine what was happening to the private relationship between teacher and student—actually stimulated in compensation a rather large exoteric project to explain the basic or "root" scriptures. The eleventh-century commentaries of Abhayakaragupta are invaluable as are those of the ninth-century tantric Candrakīrti (not to be confused with the earlier Candrakīrti who wrote commentaries on Nāgārjuna's works). In Tibetan Buddhism, the brilliant Tsoṅ-kha-pa (d. 1419) valued both Candrakīrtis and wrote penetrating studies on both Madhyamaka and Tantra. His student, Mkhas-grub-rje, produced a work that has been translated as "Fundamentals of the Buddhist Tantras" that one of its translators, Alex Wayman, believes may have served as a brief lecture course.[9] We will refer to it often since it teaches or tries to communicate.

With regard to all this more public commentarial literature, Wayman adds:

> It should be recognized that the followers of the Tantric cults, including many Tibetan monks, would *never* presume to interpret a Tantra from the language of the revealed text alone. These invariably require the assistance of a commentary, perhaps one written by their *guru*.[10]

And if the commentary of one's *guru* were written like a "recipe," one could ask in private what he left out and what he really meant.

---

[8] Davidson, *Indian Esoteric Buddhism*, 118.

[9] Lessing and Wayman, *Mkhas Grub Rje's "Fundamentals,"* 12.

[10] Alex Wayman, "Esoteric Buddhism," *ER* 2:475. His italics.

A Jungian comment Jung wrote often about "secrecy." But, first, let us listen to a warning from the current Dalai Lama who refers to Buddhist Tantra as "Secret Mantra":

> If Secret Mantra is practiced openly and used for commercial purposes, then accidents will befall such a practitioner, even taking his life, and conditions unfavorable for generating spiritual experience and realizations in his continuum will be generated. . . . Furthermore, if the fault of proclaiming the secret to those who are not ripened is incurred, there is danger that instead of helping, it will harm.[11]

These are strong words, and their meaning will become clearer as we continue.

Jung said something similar in a letter when asked if he had any "secret knowledge" beyond what could be found in his books:

> Beyond that I have had experiences which are, so to speak, "ineffable," "secret" because they can never be told properly and because nobody can understand them (I don't know whether I have even approximately understood them myself), "dangerous" because 99% of humanity would declare I was mad if they heard such things from me, "catastrophic" because the prejudices aroused by their telling might block other people's way to a living and wondrous mystery. . . .[12]

That "mystery" is a higher level of psychological development than one's fellow human beings.

When discussing esoteric tantric Hinduism, Jung repeats the point:

> The real secrets are secrets because nobody understands them. One cannot even talk about them, and of such a kind are the experiences of the Kundalini yoga. That tendency to keep things secret is merely a natural consequence when the experience is of such a peculiar kind that you had better not talk about, for you expose yourself to the greatest misunderstanding and misinterpretation.[13]

The same principle applies to analysis. After telling the spouse what transpired in therapy, the analysand soon learns that what actually transpired cannot be communicated—or, if told, dampens its impact because somehow devalued by this attempt at sharing. This brings us back to Gautama Buddha's reluctance to teach since he was certain no one would understand. Well, perhaps a few, he decided eventually.

---

[11] Dalai Lama, "Introduction" to Jeffrey Hopkins, trans., *Tantra in Tibet: The Great Exposition of Secret Mantra by Tsong-ka-pa* (London: George Allen and Unwin, 1977), 17.

[12] Jung, *Letters* 1:140-141.

[13] Jung, *Kundalini Yoga*, 28.

Gautama's "Tantric" Enlightenment

Despite deliberate obscurities, Buddhist Tantra does have some controlling mythic narratives. The most important is a revision of Siddhārtha Gautama's actual Enlightenment. We encountered that religious story in a very early chapter and saw that it functioned as a paradigm for certain doctrines and practices within the religious institution. Now we learn from the eighth-century scripture, *Sarva-tathāgata-tattva-saṃgraha* ("Compendium of the Principles of all the Tathāgatas"—hereafter, STTS) that what we were told is not really what happened.

In this tantric version, Gautama is in India at the end of his three aeons of practicing the Mahāyāna Perfections and in the tenth Stage of Bodhisattvahood, sitting on the *bodhimaṇḍa* (presumably under the Bodhi Tree that is not mentioned). He is in a deep state of concentration or *samādhi*. The *tantra* reads, as Rolf Giebel, again, translates from the Chinese:

> All the Tathāgatas gathered as if in a cloud and betook themselves to where the Bodhisattva and Mahāsattva Sarvārthasiddhi [similar in meaning to "Siddhārtha"] was seated at the place of enlightenment. Manifesting the body of enjoyment [*saṃbhoga-kāya*], they spoke all together as follows: "Good sir, how will you, who endure ascetic practices without knowing the truth of All the Tathāgatas, realize unsurpassed perfect enlightenment? Thereupon the Bodhisattva and Mahāsattva Sarvārthasiddi, having been aroused by All the Tathāgatas, arose from the *āsphānaka-samādhi* [Giebel says this is a state of mind "characterized by a complete absence of mental activity"], made obeisance to All the Tathāgatas, and said, "World-honored Tathāgatas, please instruct me! How should I practice? What is the truth?"[14]

How extraordinary—Gautama on the night of his breakthrough does not know what to do! He must ask for instruction: and that justifies mythically not only Buddhist Tantrism but also its reliance upon the teacher-student relationship.

Buddhism had always encouraged spiritual guidance from someone older and wiser—for help with the rules of the Order, and for advice on what to study and how to meditate—but now that is emphasized. It means Tantra—like exoteric Pure Land Buddhism—has moved away from the "self-reliance" model of Early Buddhism.

The text goes on:

> When he had finished speaking thus, All the Tathāgatas addressed the bodhisattva in unison, saying, "Good sir, abiding in the *samādhi* of observing one's mind, you should chant as many times as you please with the following mantra, which is effective of its own nature: *Oṃ cittaprativedhaṃ karomi* ["*Oṃ*, I know my own mind."] Then the bodhisattva said to All the Tathāgatas, "World-honored Tathāgatas, I have understood it completely. I see my heart to be like a lunar

[14] Giebel, trans., "The Adamantine Pinnacle Sutra," in *Two Esoteric Sutras*, 23.

> disc in shape. All the Tathāgatas addressed him all together, saying, "Good sir, the mind is by nature radiant. It is just as, when you make extensive efforts, the result obtained is in proportion to the action, or when you dye a white garment, it changes color according to the dye."

Gautama learns that the correct "practice"—i.e., the tantric practice—is to go into a different kind of *samādhi*, not one absent of mental activity but one with specific content. And he learns a short Sanskrit phrase, a *mantra*, that is said to have power in and of itself. Chanting or repeating it many times, perhaps thousands of times, induces a vision: Gautama sees his "heart" (*hṛdi*, a synonym for *citta*, "thought or mind") as a round, white, shining moon. The Tathāgatas explain: "the mind is by nature radiant"—but obscured or "colored" by karmic "action" the way that a white garment can be dyed.

This explanation is classic non-tantric Mahāyāna doctrine reflecting what we learned about the "cleansed" Tathāgatagarbha. As we know, Buddhists associate it with the Bodhicitta or "Mind of Enlightenment" as the goal but also with the "luminous mind" of the early *Aṅguttara Nikāya*. On the eve of his "tantric" Enlightenment, Gautama is learning this—and learning the power of *mantra* as the Method (*upāya*) for doing so. That is why Tantra, even before it solidifies as a new movement in Buddhism, is called *mantranaya*, the "way of the *mantra*."[15]

The story continues:

> Then, in order to increase his knowledge of the mind radiant by nature, All the Tathāgatas again commanded the bodhisattva, saying, *"Oṃ bodhicittam utpādayāmi"* ["*Oṃ*, I generate the Bodhicitta"], and caused him to generate the mind of enlightenment with this mantra, which is effective by nature.[16]

Here, the *mantra* produces the "Bodhicitta" itself which deepens Gautama's self-knowledge of the nature of his mind. Of course, he must have already generated the "Mind of Enlightenment" as an aspiration aeons ago; and so there might be here only a kind of liturgical affirmation of that fact. But if the Bodhicitta and the Radiant Mind are being equated, then the *mantra* is actually generating the eventual truth about which this meditating man is to become Enlightened.

That is a step beyond using a *mantra* to evoke a helpful Bodhisattva (like Avakokiteśvara or Tārā—as in mainstream Mahāyāna) since it now has the power to evoke one's very own Buddhahood.

The Tathāgatas tell Śākyamuni that he has just generated the "mind of Samantabhadra ("completely auspicious")." This is the name of a Celestial Bodhisattva and occasionally the name of a Buddha. Here it seems to be a personification of the Bodhicitta that has been generated, deepened, and now needs to be stabilized or made "firm." Thus the command: "contemplate the form of a *vajra* [here, "diamond"] on the lunar disk in your heart with this mantra: *Oṃ tiṣṭha vajra* ["*Oṃ*, stand, O *vajra*"]. Then:

---

[15] Anthony Tribe, "Mantranaya/vajrayāna—tantric Buddhism in India," in Williams, *Buddhist Thought*, 146.

[16] Giebel, STTS, 23-24.

> All the Tathāgatas addressed him all together, saying, "Make firm the *vajra* in the mind of Samantabhadra of All the Tathāgatas with this mantra: *Oṃ vajrātmako 'ham* ["*Oṃ*, I am of the nature of a *vajra*"].

Although these passages are difficult, it is actually getting clearer that Sarvārthasiddhi is not just having spontaneous visions but is being instructed to contemplate specific contents or images even though in *samādhi*.

Therefore, it is not so much that he saw his mind ("heart") as a "lunar disk" but that he actively imagined in his mind the round shape of the moon, and then a certain shape inside that. Now he imagines—with the help of a powerful *mantra*—that his own nature is as "firm" as that *vajra* or "diamond." This is kataphatic imagery, expressing positively what is achieved upon Enlightenment. There is more than a nod in Tantra to the usual Buddhist view of life as an ephemeral "bubble," to the "emptiness" of all phenomena, and to the Madhyamaka critique of thought and language as so many insubstantial distinctions. But tantric symbolism very often points beyond the "emptiness" of Saṃsāra to something "Real" and "Solid"—if not real or solid in the ordinary sense—in Nirvāṇa.

Now, all the Tathāgatas "consecrate" this man who is becoming a Buddha. The ritual action is important since paradigmatic for sets of consecrations (also called "initiations") in tantric practice. Technically, "consecration" is *abhiṣeka*—literally, "sprinkling," as in pouring water from the sacred rivers of India over the head of a new king. We already observed this rite in Early Buddhism when images of the Buddha were consecrated to "enliven" them. Following the Tibetan translation, *dbaṅ bskur* ("to confer power"), scholars often render the Sanskrit as "empowerment"—since that is the effect of a tantric consecration. We read:

> Then All the Tathāgatas consecrated the Bodhisattva and Mahāsattva Sarvārthasiddhi with an adamantine name, calling him "Vajradhātu, Vajradhātu." Then the Bodhisattva and Mahāsattva Vajradhātu said to All those Tathāgatas, "World-honored Tathāgatas, I see All the Tathāgatas as myself.

This is the specific "name initiation" (the last of a set of five standard initiations). The new name symbolizes and even causes a new status—in this case, the name means, "Realm of Vajra."

We are witnessing a Buddhist pattern. Very early in this book, we heard of a Brāhmaṇa ascetic named Sumedha receiving his prediction of a new name—"He will become a Buddha named Gautama." In the later *Lotus Sūtra*, Gautama Buddha predicts new Enlightened names for many of the Bodhisattvas in his retinue. Here, "Bodhisattva Mahāsattva Sarvārthasiddhi" becomes "Bodhisattva and Mahāsattva Vajradhatu," which does not sound like much of an advance since still a "Great Being" Bodhisattva. But apparently it is since he can now see "All the Tathāgatas as myself," a status very close if not identical to the goal.

It needs to be made "firm," however: "World-honored Tathāgatas, I beg you to empower me and make this actual realization of enlightenment firm."[17] They do so in a few more obscure steps:

---

[17] Giebel, STTS, 25.

and this Indian man who is presumably meditating at Bodhgayā "became a Tathāgata, one worthy of worship, and a perfectly all-knowing one (*samyaksaṃbuddha*)."

In the next paragraph of the STTS, this new Complete Buddha is called, "Tathāgata Vajradhātu," as we might expect since no longer merely Bodhisattva Vajradhātu. But he is also called, "Tathāgata Śākyamuni," as we would expect for non-tantric Buddhism. Still, in the paragraph after that, he is called what must be his most exalted and truest name, "Tathāgata Vairocana"—Lord of the *Sarvatathāgatatattvasaṃgraha* scripture itself. Oddly, he is now seated on top of Mount Meru (in the heaven of the "Thirty-three" gods) in a "pavilion" on a lion-throne surrounded by all the other Tathāgatas. Since there are so many Buddhas—as many as there are sands in the Ganges River—they are symbolized by the standard set of non-tantric Mahāyāna Buddhas of the four cardinal directions: Amitābha representing all the Buddhas in the west; Akṣobhya, all the Buddhas in the east; Amoghasiddhi in the north; and Ratnasambhava in the south. The *tantras* are often call them the "four Buddhas." When Vairocana "centers" them, visually and metaphysically, they are called the "five Buddhas" reigning over the entire cosmos—and representing all the Tathāgatas everywhere.

Mkhas-grub-rje could see that this account of the Buddha's Enlightenment is somewhat confusing. He lists several authoritative interpretations, among which Buddhaguhya's is clearest. This commentator explains that when Gautama at Bodhgayā asked the Tathāgatas, "How shall I proceed?"—"They guided him to the Akaniṣṭha heaven":

> Moreover, while his maturation body [*vipāka-kāya*, the body ripened by *karma*] stayed on the bank of the same Nairañjanā River, the mental body [*manomaya-kāya*, "body made of mind"] of the Bodhisattva Sarvārthasidda proceeded to the Akaniṣṭha heaven."[18]

And it is actually there that Gautama receives not only the "name" consecration but also two others called the "garment" and "diadem" initiation. He is then taught a sequence of specifically tantric meditations and, thereby, becomes a "Manifest Complete Buddha as Mahāvairocana, the Saṃbhoga-kāya."[19] Buddhaguhya continues:

> Having become a Buddha, he performed the four kinds of marvel. He proceeded to the summit of Mt. Sumeru and pronounced the Yoga Tantras [like the STTS itself]. Thereupon, he proceeded to the world of men and re-entered his maturation body on the bank of the Nairañjanā. Then he arose, defeated Māra, and taught the methods of Manifest Complete Buddhahood, and so forth.

This explanation is, at least, somewhat more coherent.

Gautama had been trying unsuccessfully to become Enlightened while in India; when prompted, he ascended in a "body made of mind" to Akaniṣṭha heaven at the top of the Realm of Form. There, he won the Three Bodies of Buddhahood (that must have included the *dharma-kāya* of Vairocana).

[18] Lessing and Wayman, *Mkhas-grub-rje's "Fundamentals,"* 27.

[19] Giebel, STTS, 103.

He then descended (in Vairocana's *saṃbhoga-kāya*) to Mount Meru in the Realm of Desire to teach the gods there. And eventually, this divine Being descended (in Vairocana's *nirmāṇa-kāya*) back down to India where—with the name Śākyamuni in an ordinary "physical" body—he demonstrated the traditional Twelve Acts of becoming a Buddha.

Buddhaguhya offers, as well, a new definition of the two kinds of Nirvāṇa: "Nirvāṇa without remainder [of the body] is the attribute of Tathāgatahood, which is to become perfectly enlightened in Akaniṣṭha, devoid of even the subtle idea of emptiness. Nirvāṇa with remainder is the attribute of Perfect Buddhahood, which is to become perfectly enlightened under the Bodhi-tree in the Realm of Desire"—but with a trace of the "idea" of emptiness still to be abandoned.[20] In this comment, we hear an attempt to keep the tantric account of Gautama's Enlightenment somewhat related to the non-tantric account.

Tantric and Non-tantric Buddhism

A Superior Path

Tantric Buddhism of early medieval India needed more than this "origin myth" to justify its existence. Mainstream exoteric Mahāyāna had that challenge centuries earlier and justified its existence in relationship to the established "Hīnayāna" in both a conciliatory and a more antagonistic manner. In one argument, non-tantric Mahāyāna gave Early Buddhism credit for removing the "obscuration of defilements" (*kleśāvaraṇa*)—a moral achievement—but not the "obscuration of the knowable" (*jñeyāvaraṇa*)—a cognitive achievement close to the very notion of Enlightenment.

Buddhaguhya, in his commentary on the VAT, agrees but goes on to say that there are actually "two types of Bodhisattvas: those who engage in the practice of the Perfections, and those who engage in the practice of the Mantra Method." He adds, however, that each type often engages in the practices of the other "as a subsidiary."[21] Here we see Buddhist Tantra understanding itself, in a conciliatory way, to be a kind of Mahāyāna Buddhism and that there need not be a conflict between tantric and non-tantric Mahāyāna. They can be understood as different Paths or methods toward removing the "obscuration of the knowable."

Indeed, the *Vairocanābhisaṃbodhi* spends much of its first chapter demonstrating mastery of the "knowable." Vairocana Buddha addresses the Celestial Bodhisattva Vajrapāṇi:

> Lord of the Secret Ones! What is Enlightenment? It is to know your mind as it really is [a Yogācāra point]. . . . Therein there is neither that which becomes enlightened nor that to which one is enlightened [something Madhyamaka would say] . . . . Because the mind is utterly pure by nature [a Tathāgatagarbha point].[22]

In fact, this section of the *tantra* is particularly clear about accepted Buddhist wisdom:

---

[20] Hodge, VAT, 181.

[21] Hodge, VAT, 95.

[22] Hodge, VAT, 56-57.

> The mind has not been seen, is not seen, nor will be seen by any of the Tathāgata Arhat Samyaksaṃbuddhas. It is not blue, not yellow, not red, not white, nor purple, not transparent, not short, not long, not round, not square, not bright, not dark, not male, not female and not neuter. . . . Because the mind has the same attribute as space and so it is free from all thought and conceptualization. Why? Because the nature of space is the nature of the mind. The nature of the mind is the nature of Enlightenment. Lord of the Secret Ones! Therefore the mind, the realm of space and Enlightenment are without duality [*advaya*, "nondual"] and cannot be separated.

Early Buddhism and non-tantric Mahāyāna have already taught this view—along with requiring ethical behavior and the study of scriptures.

Nevertheless, despite continuity, Gautama's "tantric" Enlightenment demonstrates that Wisdom cannot be achieved without the Mantra Method. After all, the non-tantric Bodhisattva under the Bodhi Tree did not know what to do. He did not yet know the power of a *mantra* sound that is "effective of its own nature." It functions like a Roman Catholic sacrament that is effective *ex opera operato* ("from the work performed")—and not dependent on one's understanding or even a pious attitude.

Gautama certainly did not know the power of the famous "100 syllable *mantra*" that we will encounter below. Of it, the STTS claims:

> By means of this mantra, even if one commits the five sins that bring immediate retribution [i.e., murdering one's father, mother, etc.], slanders All the Tathāgatas and the true Dharma of the vast Great Vehicle [like an *icchantika*], or performs all manner of misdeeds, one will still obtain success [*siddhi*]. Owing to the firm state of Vajrasattva ["Diamond Being"], he who practices the seals [*mudrās*, sacred "gestures"] of All the Tathāgatas will obtain in this present lifetime quickly and at his pleasure all supreme accomplishments, including the attainment of the supreme *siddhi* of the Tathāgata—thus spoke the Lord Vajrasattva of All the Tathāgatas.[23]

Officially, tantric Buddhism is just a subdivision of mainstream Mahāyāna Buddhism. But here it announces its superiority to all non-tantric approaches to emancipation. We learn that its esoteric practices include in theory all sorts of disciples—even those who have committed the heinous "five Great Sins"—provided they have been initiated. This is a controversial position, one that will be exploited by late tantric materials advising that one actually should "sin greatly" in order to be saved. It is something that even St. Paul pondered—in order to receive more Grace—but then rejected as a heretical notion.

---

[23] Giebel, STTS, 99.

A Quick Path

We have just heard that tantric Enlightenment can be achieved "in this present lifetime quickly." The *tantras* say that frequently. It must have been good news for mainstream Bodhisattvas facing three incalculable aeons of practicing the Mahāyāna Perfections inside *saṃsāra*. It also makes contact with Early Buddhism that showed Arhathood to be available almost immediately upon hearing Gautama preach.

But the tantric claim of "quickness" may have been something of a selling point. After all, one needed much past good *karma* (even if currently sinful) to bring one along, through many lifetimes, to this new purportedly speedy approach. And why hurry if mainstream Mahāyāna's "selling" point was that there is not much difference between a Buddha and an advanced "compassionate" Bodhisattva who emanates helpful manifestations? Some texts do say, however, that getting to Buddhahood in a hurry is itself compassionate since "eternal" Buddhas themselves are forever sending helpful emanations—like their *saṃbhoga* and *nirmāṇa* "bodies"—into the world. In the eighteenth century, the seventh Dalai Lama said of those suffering but trapped in Saṃsāra: "How nice it would be if I could achieve right now a means to free them!"[24]

Let us note, however, that the *Hevajra Tantra* (from the eighth century—hereafter, HVT) preaches "quickness" right alongside the usual slow, steady progress:

> First there should be the public confession, then they should be taught the ten rules of virtuous conduct, then the *Vaibhāṣya* teaching and then the *Sautrāntika* [all of this a nod to Early Buddhism], after that the *Yogācāra* and then the *Mādhyamika* [i.e., non-tantric Mahāyāna]. Then when they know all *mantra*-method [*tantras* earlier or preliminary to what the HVT teaches], they should start upon Hevajra. The pupil who lays hold with zeal, should succeed there is no doubt.[25]

This text expresses confidence in the new method, but one wonders if all that mastering could be achieved "in this present lifetime."

A Path of "Accomplishment"

Another way in which Tantra distinguishes itself is a preference for technical terms derived from the Sanskrit root *sidh*, "to accomplish." Its human Bodhisattvas tend increasingly to be called *siddhas* ("adepts") who as tantric *sādhakas* ("practitioners") follow accurately the *sādhanas* ("means of accomplishment," "evocations"). If all goes well, the *siddha* is one who achieves the ultimate *siddhi* ("accomplishment"), namely, Buddhahood. And so we read in the STTS:

> I shall now explain of all the teachings that which accomplishes (*sādhana*), that which is accomplished (*siddhi*),

---

[24] Hopkins, *Tantra in Tibet*, 207.

[25] D. L. Snellgrove, trans., *The Hevajra Tantra*, 2 vols. (London: Oxford University Press, 1959), 1:116.

> And the great action of the accomplished ones (*siddha*).[26]

But there are two levels of *siddhi*: the "transmundane" one of becoming a Tathāgata, and several "mundane" *siddhis*.

We already saw this latter kind in Early Buddhism as the miraculous *abhijñās* (like clairvoyance) that included *ṛddhis* (like flying)—as spontaneous by-products of mastering the fourth *dhyāna*. They were possible because that level of meditation allowed one to pull out of the "gross" material body a "subtle" body called *mano-maya-kāya*. This, of course, is the same "body made of mind" that Sarvārthasiddhi used at his tantric Enlightenment to ascend to Akaniṣṭha heaven. In fact, the mundane *siddhis* of Tantra include all the *ṛddhis* of previous forms of Buddhism. But the list gets longer and more worldly: the ability to heal disease, produce rain, find lost treasure, to attract a woman for a client, or even kill the enemies of a king, etc.

Here, we sense a different ethos in a different historical context for Tantric Buddhism. Davidson writes:

> The evidence supports a position that is curiously both astonishing and reassuring: the Mantrayāna is simultaneously the most politically involved of Buddhist forms and the variety of Buddhism most acculturated to the medieval Indian landscape.[27]

He is pointing to the fact that when the Gupta Empire collapsed in the sixth century, India fragmented politically and socially. That meant patronage of monastic Buddhism could no longer be assumed either from a sympathetic emperor or from wealthy merchants whose trade routes and contracts were now disrupted. New petty kings had to be wooed, and the religion had to offer not only Nirvāṇa but also more immediate, more worldly, benefits. This, after all, had been the Buddhist experience in foreign lands like China where welcoming rulers were less interested in Enlightenment than in the protection or power that the new "Indian god" could provide. In post-Gupta medieval India, a local ruler was mostly interested in good harvests for his people and victory in war; personally, he wanted freedom from disease and a long life, and beautiful women in his harem. Wealthy householders wanted some of these same benefits.

Tantric *siddhas*, functioning increasingly as sorcerors in the society, apparently offered "mundane" services in exchange for support of their religion. It is a development, as Davidson puts it, both "astonishing and reassuring"—something of which earlier forms of Buddhism would not have approved, nor would they have had to consider in order to survive. We will encounter this issue again as the "four Actions" (*caturkarma*) or rites that look just like "white and black" magic.

Vajrayāna

Tantric Buddhism did survive for five centuries before the onslaught of Muslim Turks made it impossible for any style of Buddhism to survive in the land of its origin. Part of that late success

---

[26] Giebel, STTS, 85.

[27] Davidson, *Indian Esoteric Buddhism*, 114.

was due to the emergence of a delimited dynasty in the Bengal region of the northeast (what is today Bangladesh and the Indian state of West Bengal). It still included Magadha to the west with its holy site of Bodhgayā and the monastic complex at Nālandā. The Pāla kings ruled this region from the eighth to the twelfth century and supported both non-tantric and tantric Buddhism—along with Hinduism that elsewhere in India was now dominant. They did so despite incursions and were able to establish what the art historians Susan and John Huntington have called "one of India's most brilliant phases of intellectual and artistic activity."[28]

The phase was, also, derivative. Its polished steles in dark stone and its inlaid metal sculptures are technically impressive, but they are also visually busy—with decorative details that can overwhelm both the Buddhist subject and the religion's contemplative attitude. As Rowland remarks, the classical Gupta "sense of plastic conception is lost under the intricacy of surface detail."[29] (See, for example, the "Tārā" relief at Figure 11.3.) Pāla tantric subjects, however, would serve as models for tantric Buddhist art elsewhere, especially in Tibet. And it is with the Tibetan version of Buddhist Tantra that most people are familiar.

Increasingly, Tantra saw itself as a distinct *yāna* or "Vehicle" within Buddhism. The religion had long favored the notion of "three Vehicles." The *Lotus* preached them as 1) the Śrāvaka-to-Arhat, 2) Bodhisattva-to-Pratyekabuddha, and 3) Bodhisattva-to-Buddha Vehicles. Philosophy emphasized a threefold distinction within Buddhist thought as 1) Abhidharma, 2) Madhyamaka, and 3) Yogācāra. And one can read, also, of 1) Madhyamaka, 2) Yogācāra, and 3) Tathāgatagarbha as three ways to understand the mind. Now the "way of the *mantra*" made its own three-fold claim: the three Vehicles to Enlightenment are really the Śrāvakayāna, the Mahāyāna, and the Vajrayāna.

Calling itself the "Vehicle of the Vajra" expressed openly Tantra's superiority in what Anthony Tribe has called the "vajra-isation of Buddhism."[30] The reader has no doubt observed how often the word *vajra* appears in the tantric passages cited and how frequently tantric names begin with "Vajra."

Vajra

This Sanskrit word, *vajra*, has a long provenance in India. As early as Vedic Hinduism, Indra—chief of the Thirty-three—was said to wield a *vajra*. He was the weather god, and the *vajra* was his "lightning" or "thunderbolt" accompanying the fertile rain. It also accompanied destructive flood. Since Indra was also the Aryan war god, his lightning was the mythical weapon that struck down enemies. Perhaps in actual battle it was the name of a throwing weapon or maybe just a club. With the rise of kingship within India, *vajra* became the name of a monarch's "club" of authority, his scepter of power. That was his symbolic proof of being in league with the god Indra and a guarantee to his people that they would have good harvests and security in exchange for their loyalty and their taxes.

---

28 Susan L. and John C. Huntington, "Leaves from the Bodhi Tree: The Art of Pāla India (8th-12th Centuries) and Its International Legacy," *Orientations* 20, no. 10 (October, 1989), 2.

29 Rowland, *Art and Architecture of India*, 232, 257.

30 Tribe, "Mantranaya," 165.

In Early Buddhism, the *vajra* appears in the hand of Gautama's divine bodyguard, a "tamed" converted *yakṣa* or tree deity who was not only fertile but fierce. Eventually, he would be called Vajrapāṇi ("*vajra* in hand"). We read in the *Majjhima-Nikāya* of a debate between the Buddha and a Jain on the topic of the *ātman*. When his opponent refused to answer a question twice, Gautama challenged: "Now is not the time to be silent. If anyone, when asked a reasonable question up to the third time by the Tathāgata, still does not answer, his head splits into seven pieces there and then." And that is because: "a thunderbolt-wielding spirit [*yakṣa*] holding an iron thunderbolt that burned, blazed, and glowed, appeared in the air" . . . saying, "If this [Jain] when asked a reasonable question up to the third time by the Blessed One, still does not answer, I shall split his head into seven pieces here and now."[31]

Figure 14.1 Vajrapāṇi Protecting the Buddha

An early Ghandāra relief depicts the Buddha with an unlikely topknot and behind him the bearded Vajrapāṇi dressed in a "Roman" tunic protecting his Lord with a fly whisk in one hand and a *vajra* club in the other (see Figure 14.1). The device is long with curved ends and, oddly, narrow in

[31] Bodhi, *MN*, 35.13 (p. 326).

the middle. Is that how lightning was imagined? Or how an actual weapon was shaped? Let us note that "lighting" as an image carries other meanings in Buddhist literature: negatively, as an image for what is short-lived or "impermanent;" positively, as an image of the "light of Wisdom" that can slice through the darkness of human ignorance.

The word *vajra* also means "diamond." Perhaps that is due to the folk notion that when lightning strikes a rock, it becomes adamantine. Whatever the connection, both the lightning bolt and the diamond are powerful, the latter the strongest mineral on earth, capable of cutting all other stones and itself uncuttable except by another diamond. "Vajra" appears in the name of the popular Mahāyāna scripture called the "Diamond Sūtra" (composed as early as the 2nd century CE). Its full title is *Vajrac-chedikā-prajñāpāramitā Sūtra*, "The Diamond-cutter Perfection of Wisdom Sermon." As Gregory Schopen comments:

> According to its original title, the "wisdom" it refers to does not explain or describe. It cuts or shatters. This in turn might suggest that a religious text of this sort was not meant to convey ideas or doctrine, but was rather designed to affect, rearrange, or shatter established ways of seeing oneself, the world, and conventional religious practices.[32]

That may be why this particular text was valued by antinomian Ch'an with its stories of unconventional behavior.

The meaning brings lightning and diamond together as "destructive" agencies. But surely Buddhists heard "diamond" and thought, also, of the precious jewel of Wisdom hidden within all human beings—as in the *Lotus* parable of a gem hidden in the garment of a poor man.

In Buddhist Tantra, *vajra* as "lightning" points primarily to the destructive (yet creative) power of Wisdom—eliminating the *kleśas*, destroying *avidyā*. While *vajra* as "diamond" refers not so much to Wisdom's cutting ability but instead to its own "uncuttable" realization, its indivisibility. This is expressed in scriptures as "firmness." We saw that in the story of Sarvārthasiddhi who needed to make "firm" his vision of a lunar disk and stabilize his Bodhicitta vow: "*Oṃ*, stand, O *vajra*." This, in turn, led to his becoming "firm" himself like a diamond: "*Oṃ*, I am of the nature of a *vajra*." Thus, as "Vajradhātu" and "Vajrasattva," he could function in his role as Vairocana Buddha who "eternally abides . . . and is the *vajra* of all body, speech, and mind." This means that the "Diamond" Body, Speech, and Mind of the Buddha is behind or within the "body, speech, and mind" of all ordinary human beings (a Tathāgatagarbha point).

David Snellgrove quotes the eleventh-century tantric commentator, Advayavajra, on Enlightened knowledge:

> Firm, substantial and solid, of uncuttable and unbreakable character,
> Unburnable, indestructible, the Void is said to be Vajra.[33]

---

[32] Gregory Schopen, "Diamond Sūtra," in *EB* 1:227-228.

[33] David Snellgrove, *Indo-Tibetan Buddhism: Indian Buddhists and Their Tibetan Successors*, 2 vols. (Boston: Shambhala, 1987), 1:134.

That last phrase in the translation maintains a certain ambiguity: as if Vajra were not "substantial" itself but "void" of substance; or—as we sometimes hear—the "substantial" Truth of insubstantiality. But that would be an Abhidharma or Madhyamaka interpretation. Instead, I find Tantra leaning toward kataphatic imagery for a religious reason, namely, that it wishes to express in symbols "Something" that is Real and Solid. Snellgrove agrees, saying that Vajra is distinctively tantric and joins other positive imagery—such as the Wheel, the Tree, the Lotus, and the Footprint—as "major symbols" of the Sacred in Buddhism.

A Jungian observation The symbols of "lightning" and "diamond" appear often in dreams and imagination at critical points of psychological development. One of Jung's patients complained of being "stuck" in her life and painted a fantasy picture to express how that felt. It showed her stuck to a group of round boulders close to a shoreline. But the next picture anticipated the future of her therapy: "One of the round forms has been blasted out of its place by a golden flash of lightning."[34] This eventually reminded Jung that:

> The liberating flash of lightning is a symbol also used by Paracelsus and the alchemists for the same thing. Moses' rock-splitting staff, which struck forth the living water and afterward changed into a serpent, may have been an unconscious echo in the background. Lightning signifies a sudden, unexpected, and overpowering change of psychic condition.

The hardness of the "diamond," however, appears much more often in Jung's writing. For one thing, the ego must achieve a certain "hardness"—to withstand inevitable assaults from outer and inner events that have their own obdurate character. Indeed, a genuinely developed consciousness, says Jung, is "inflexible, hard, detached, immortal, and can no longer be changed"—back into its malleable infantile beginnings.[35] Awareness of one's "shadow" gives the personality a certain stony weight: "for the inferior and even the worthless belongs to me as my shadow and gives me substance and mass."[36]

Most important, the "diamond" as the hardest, most precious, and clearest stone symbolizes both the unconscious beginning (the archetypal Self) and the conscious goal (the realized Self) of individuation. Since the outcome of that process is a unique "individual," Edinger writes:

> The word *individual* derives from the two Latin roots, *in* = not, and *dividere* = to divide. Its basic meaning is therefore something that is indivisible. . . . It seems that in attempting to describe such a basic fact as individuality we must resort to the same procedure as used in describing deity; since it is a fact that transcends

---

[34] Jung, *CW* 9i, pars. 525-533.

[35] C. G. Jung, *Children's Dreams: Notes from the Seminar Given in 1936-1940* (Princeton: Princeton University Press, 2008), 223.

[36] Jung, *CW* 16, par. 134.

> our categories of conscious understanding, we can no more than describe it in terms of what it is not, the so-called *via negativa*.[37]

In this way, Jungian "in-dividuality" and Buddhism's "un-cuttable" Wisdom of "non-duality" approach each other.

Sometimes, becoming a more conscious undivided (i.e., whole) personality requires "putting a lid" on a compulsive desire. Jung likens it to the alchemist putting his "devil" into a bottle:

> Of course, he will rumble in your entrails, but you can always see that it is right after a while. You slowly get quiet and transform, and you discover that in that bottle grows the stone, the amber or the *Lapis*. In other words, that solidification or crystallization means that the situation has become habitual, and inasmuch as the self-control or nonindulgence, has become a habit, it is a stone. The more it has become a habit, the harder, the stronger, that stone will be, and when it has become a *fait accompli* it is a diamond.[38]

In this way, we gather "precious stones" not just at the End of an authentic life's journey but along the way. One man dreamed he hit a golf ball errantly into the rough; but when he went looking for his ball, he found instead a "diamond in the rough." He was delighted by the pun as he told me the dream, but the image makes it clear that he still had the task of polishing his Stone. That puts the matter positively, according to a *via positiva*.

Ritual Instruments

Functioning as a true symbol, *vajra* combines within itself the many meanings of lighting/weapon/scepter/diamond/light, etc. defying simple definition and even thorough discussion. Indeed, each of these meanings expands into others. The ritual object by this name, however, unites them all visually and even physically—so that we can hold it in our hand, like Vajrapāṇi. This is a double-sided instrument usually of brass while its length can vary from four inches to over a foot long (see Figure 14.2). Tribe describes it:

> Generally made of metal, it is comprised of a central sphere from which two prongs emerge at 180 degrees to each other. These prongs may each be surrounded by a number of other prongs—usually four [as in our Figure] though occasionally two or eight—that also emerge from the central sphere, curving away from and then back towards the central prongs. Held alone, usually in the right hand, the *vajra* stands in general for the non-dual and indestructible nature of awakened awareness. In particular, the unity of the two sets of prongs in the central sphere are seen as representing the unity of wisdom (*prajñā*) and compassion (*karuṇā*).[39]

---

[37] Edinger, *Ego and Archetype*, 162-163.

[38] Jung, *Visions,* 1:614.

[39] Tribe, "Mantranaya," 165.

As a ritual object, the *vajra* is visually double. Thus, it can carry the meaning of the "union" of "Wisdom and Compassion," says Tribe—a frequent alternative for the pair, "Wisdom and Means." But, increasingly, Wisdom and Means came to express all twofold realities that the Enlightened Buddhist must transcend or unite. The "twofold" *vajra* device, therefore, "unites" all the pairs of opposites.

Figure 14.2 Ritual Vajra and Bell

The small sphere in the middle, however, may signify Wisdom alone, specifically the wisdom of "Emptiness" that transcends the two sides of this object. But there are lotus forms on either side of this "empty" sphere that remind us of the "lotus seat" upon which the Buddha can be found. Not surprisingly, then, the prongs that curve away from these "lotuses" on either side refer (twice) to the standard four directional Buddhas (Amitābha, etc.)—curving back at the points of the *vajra* to signify their union as the central Buddha (Vairocana).

In late Tantra, this fifth or quintessential Buddha is sometimes called the Ādi-Buddha ("Primordial Buddha") who gives rise to the others, as we observe if we read this object in the opposite direction back toward the middle. This is "emanation" imagery and not explicit in Buddhist doctrine—but it is implicit in the "unfolding" of the Lotus in Buddhist symbolism. And we see it here in the *vajra*.

Since the ritual lightning or diamond is held in one's right hand while chanting *mantras*, that leaves the other hand free to hold a ritual bell (*ghaṇṭā*) (see Figure 14.2). It is rung for the same reason bells are tolled in all religions—to chase away obstructive demons—and, as Anne Morse explains for Buddhist Tantra: "To gain the attention of the deity, entertain it with sound, and then to provide it with melodious accompaniment upon its departure. Bells are also used to awaken the enlightened mind of the practitioner."[40]

When these two instruments appear together in tantric ritual, it is regularly the case that the *vajra* is held in the right hand: symbolizing Means as masculine (in part, due to its association with an assertive phallic Indra). The *ghaṇṭā* is held in the left hand: symbolizing Wisdom as feminine (since the bell's curved and open bottom alludes to receptive femininity). Together, of course, the Vajra and the Bell symbolize the "nondual" union of Means and Wisdom. But, then, the clapper inside the bell may associate to the masculine "inside" the feminine—much like a *lingam* within the *yoni* of Hinduism. Thus, the opposites unite within the bell itself. They also unite if the handle of the bell is a *vajra*, as in our Figure. What a richness of meaning in these ritual objects!

The "Subjugation" of Śiva

Hindu Tantra

Another controlling myth of Buddhist Tantra is the "subjugation" (i.e., the conversion) of the Hindu god Śiva. We learned in my previous volume, *The Snake and the Rope*, that the impersonal Brahman-Ātman of the Upaniṣads became personified over time as the great gods Viṣṇu, Brahmā, and Śiva. As the Trimūrti or "Three Forms" of Brahman, they carried out the cosmic duties—respectively—of Creation, Preservation, and Destruction of the cosmic cycles. When Brahmā was replaced by Devī, the "Goddess," much of this dynamic remained the same. But each of these divinities also stood alone in their cults in a kind of monotheism whereby each god performed all three functions—albeit with an emphasis upon their role in the Hindu "Trinity." Each functioned to maintain the coming and going of *saṃsāra* but also inspired their renunciant devotees to leave cyclical existence altogether for what was often called, even in Hinduism, *nirvāṇa*.

These cults flourished during the Gupta "Golden Age" as did Buddhism. They also developed tantric forms. In fact, it appears that the followers of Śiva developed their Tantrism earliest of all, in the fifth or sixth century, before the Gupta empire was entirely dismantled.[41]

This indicates that tantric practices are not in origin a response to what has been called post-Gupta "medieval feudalism" even if they eventually fit feudalism's somewhat fragmented world. Instead, the tantric movement appears to integrate religious practices that were already extant—in the background of Indian "high" culture, perhaps in village or hill tribe India—but not considered

---

[40] Anne Nishimura Morse, "Ritual Objects," *EB* 2:729.

[41] David B. Gray, "Tantra and the Tantric Traditions of Hinduism and Buddhism" (April, 2016), *Oxford Research Encyclopedia of Religion,* https://doi.org/10.1093/acrefore/9780199340378.013.59.

orthodox. Indeed, since Vedic times, Śiva (-Rudra) had been heterodox. He did not quite belong to the Thirty-Three and was not quite welcome as a divine guest at the sacrifice. Śiva himself was an upsetting paradox: at once the divine Yogin who wears ashes as a sign of renouncing the world and the divine Phallus as a sign of creatively engaging it—the "Erotic Ascetic," as Wendy O'Flaherty puts it.[42]

His devotees still wear an image of his phallic *lingam* around their necks but also "bathe" their naked, renounced bodies in ashes—that they gather from the cremation grounds, when not sitting on corpses at charnel sites. Eventually, a tantric form of worshipping Śiva—called the Mantramārga ("Path of the Mantra")—emerged. It must have been highly influential since tantric Buddhism perceived it to be a threat. The story of the "Subjugation of Śiva" confirms this.

Cosmic Battle

The myth features Vajrapāṇi, the fierce bodyguard of Gautama Buddha. By the time of the *Aṣṭa*, he had become the bodyguard of advanced Bodhisattvas ("Vajrapani, the great Yaksha, constantly follows behind the irreversible Bodhisattva").[43] The *Lotus* informs us that the Bodhisattva Avalokiteśvara himself sometimes "preaches Dharma by displaying the body of the spirit who grasps the thunderbolt."[44] And, then, in the STTS, Vajrapāṇi himself is listed as one of the Mahāsattva Bodhisattvas; he even stands at the head of them all ("Lord of the Secret Ones")—with Avalokiteśvara second, and Mañjuśrī third. Snellgrove writes of this great Yakśa-Bodhisattva: "I confess to finding him by far the most interesting divine being throughout the whole history of Buddhism, for he has a personal history and considerable personal character."[45]

That character is on display in the following version of the "Subjugation of Śiva." The Buddha Vairocana asks Vajrapāṇi to assemble all the gods, but the Bodhisattva refuses, as Snellgrove translates from the STTS:

> Placing his vajra on his heart, he said to all the Buddhas: "O all you Lord-Tathāgatas, I do not comply." They said: "O why?" and he replied: "O Lords, there are evil beings, Maheśvara ["Great Lord," i.e., Śiva] and others, who have not been converted by all of you Tathāgatas. How am I to deal with them?"

With a *mantra*, Vairocana summons all the unconverted Hindu deities.

> Then Vajrapāṇi raised his vajra away from his heart and waving it, he surveyed the whole circle of the threefold world to its limits. He spoke: "Come, my friends, to the teaching of all the Tathāgatas. Obey my command!" They replied: "How should we come?" Vajrapāṇi said: "Having sought protection with the Buddha,

42 Wendy Doniger O'Flaherty, *Śiva: The Erotic Ascetic* (Oxford: Oxford University Press, 1973).

43 Conze, *Eight Thousand*, 205.

44 Hurvitz, *Lotus Blossom*, 315.

45 Snellgrove, *Indo-Tibetan Buddhism*, 1:134.

> the Dharma, the Community, approach, O friends, so that you may gain the knowledge of the Omniscient One."

All the Hindu *devatās* obeyed . . . except for Śiva:

> Then Mahādeva, the Lord of the whole threefold world in this worldly sphere, proud of his overlordship of the whole threefold world, appeared very wrathful and said: "Listen you *yakṣa*, I am Īśvara, Lord of the threefold world, Creator, Destroyer, Lord of all Spirits, God of Gods, Mighty God. So how should I carry out the order of a *yakṣa*?

Davidson translates this final taunt: "How should I take orders from you, a local tree spirit?"[46]

Tantric Buddhism and tantric Hinduism are clashing here, Vajrapāṇi with his "blazing *vajra*" and Śiva with his cosmic "flames":

> Then Vajrapāṇi, waving his vajra and laughing, said, "Approach, you eater of corpses and human flesh, you who use the ashes of funeral pyres as your food, as your couch, as your clothing, and obey my command!"

Śiva still refuses—so he is killed by a powerful *mantra.*

Vairocana Buddha compassionately pleads for the God's life, however, so that in the far distant future in a far-off Buddha-field even this deity of the Śaivites will become a Tathāgata named "Soundless Lord of Ashes." So Vajrapāṇi revives Śiva with another powerful *mantra*. But he stands on his body with one foot, his other foot on Śiva's divine wife, Umā. This is, as Davidson remarks, "the greatest insult in India as the feet are the most polluted limb."[47]

Nevertheless, the divine insult is a blessing:

> from the contact with the sole of Vajrapāṇi's foot he became the recipient of consecrations [*abhiṣeka*], powers of meditation, salvation, mnemonics [long *mantras* called *dhāraṇis*], faculties of knowledge and magical powers, all of the highest perfection, tending even to Buddhahood.

We are reminded of "conflict" motifs in Hinduism, and especially the goddess Durgā's fierce defeat of the buffalo-demon, Mahiṣa, upon whose back she placed her foot. As we learned in *The Snake and the Rope*: "if one is touched by the feet of the Maiden, the Mother of the three worlds, can there be any doubt that *māyā* will be destroyed?"[48] In this Buddhist version, Śiva is not only "subjugated,"

---

[46] Ronald M. Davidson, "The Bodhisattva Vajrapāṇi's Subjugation of Śiva," in Donald S. Lopez, Jr., ed., *Religions of India in Practice* (Princeton: Princeton University Press, 1995), 552.

[47] Davidson, *Indian Esoteric Buddhism*, 151.

[48] Elder, *Snake and the Rope*, 110, 308.

he is also initiated into the practices of Tantra. Or, as Davidson aptly remarks: "all beings will be included in the sacred reality, whether they want to or not."[49]

An Expanded Pantheon

There were always many gods in Indian Buddhism, and they were worshipped or propitiated by Buddhists for their mundane benefits: large families for the laity, good crops, freedom from illness and danger, etc. But these male and female *devas* and *devīs* ("gods" and "goddesses") or *devatās* ("divinities") did not belong to a specifically Buddhist pantheon. Gautama Buddha did not deny their existence or their blessings and needed them on occasion. But he did not encourage reliance upon these saṃsāric deities—and taught, instead, freedom from the vagaries of *saṃsāra* altogether. For his own religious achievement, however, the Buddha himself was revered and nearly worshipped in his lifetime—as in the ritual manner that devotees approach him in scriptures. But, again, he specifically denied being a "god." He also denied being a "human being"—since a "Buddha" is beyond all ordinary categories.

Nevertheless, when Gautama died, his relics and the memory of his "Presence" were increasingly valued as divine. He became the main figure in a specifically Buddhist pantheon and not just revered but worshipped. Maitreya, the Bodhisattva waiting in Tuṣita heaven for his turn as Buddha, was already a member of this specifically Buddhist pantheon—that sat beside the other pantheon or above it in a kind of divine hierarchy.

Sixteen "Great Arhats" were also objects of reverence and prayer. They had been asked by Gautama Buddha on his deathbed to "remain in the world" to preserve the doctrine until Maitreya's descent—thousands of years from now. Said to reside in mysteriously remote mountain caves, this sacred group was the object of a popular cult in Buddhist China—where they conflated with Taoist immortals.

As we know, all this expanded greatly with Mahāyāna Buddhism and the emergence of "countless" other Celestial Buddhas preaching in Buddha-fields or Pure Lands surrounded by "countless" Celestial Bodhisattvas. Whether or not they were called *devatās*, these sacred Buddhist beings functioned in the religion as divinities, just as divinities function in other religions.

With the "conversion" and inclusion of the vast Hindu pantheon in Buddhist Tantra, however, the pantheon becomes nearly unrecognizable as specifically "Buddhist." It is one reason why scholars say that Buddhism increasingly was absorbed by Hinduism (even though the myth of the "Subjugation of Śiva" claims it was the other way around).

The Feminine

The most important Hindu gods had long been imagined by their worshippers to be divine kings and, accordingly, had divine wives or consorts. Thus, when Śiva and even Viṣṇu became "Buddhist," they brought with them female deities. Perhaps Buddhists already considered Prajñāpāramitā to be

[49] Davidson, "Subjugation of Śiva," 549.

a female deity—Tārā was certainly one—but now they had, along with more gods, more goddesses to acknowledge, fear offending, propitiate, and from whom to ask for help.

In late *tantras* like the HVT, we find powerful independent female deities who appeared first in tantric Śaivism—and from which they seem clearly to have been borrowed by tantric Buddhists. They are often called "Yoginīs," a name that would otherwise belong to human female practitioners—and with whom they can be confused while reading a *tantra*.

They are joined by strange female divinities called "Ḍākinīs" often found in sculpture in a "dancing pose" (see Figure 14.3 for an eighteenth-century Tibetan rendering). The Sanskrit is obscure, so we rely upon the Tibetan translation, *mkha' 'gro ma*, "sky goer." Other translations, "fairy" or "angel," are too benign since *ḍākiṇis* were originally flesh-eating ogres and only later spiritual beings, retaining a certain ambivalence. Jacob Dalton says they appear in Buddhism in both dangerous "mundane" and helpful "transmundane" manifestations with a "tendency for each type to blur into the other, so that a gnostic *ḍākinī* can suddenly become dangerous."[50] Indeed, our dancing Figure is not just charming but daunting, being entirely naked with a scowl on her face and three eyes.

Figure 14.3 Ḍākinī

[50] Jacob P. Dalton, "Ḍākinī," *EB* 1:192.

It seems to have dawned on the followers of this new style of Buddhism that Celestial Buddhas themselves were a lot like "kings"—Cakravartins really, "universal monarchs," ruling over their Buddha-fields—and deserved to have wives. Thus, for the directional Buddhas: Pāṇḍarā became the tantric consort of Amitābha; Locanā became Akṣobhya's wife; Māmakī belonged to Ratnasaṃbhava; while Tārā was raised in status from Celestial Bodhisattva to the tantric companion of Amoghahasiddhi Buddha. Vairocana's divine consort was sometimes named Vajradhātviśvarī when not named Mārīci.

The Celestial Bodhisattvas were also matched with consorts as the assembly of *devatās* fairly explodes in number and their many names begin to confuse us. Superficially, we could say that these "feminine" additions to the Buddhist pantheon are just a response to resurgent Hinduism in the religious environment. More profoundly, Buddhism had to be "ready" for it, willing to take on female deities. I see it as more evidence that part of this religion's cultural task was to recover the Feminine for India.

A Sociological Note

As with non-tantric Mahāyāna and its apotheosis of "Prajñāpāramitā," women did not directly benefit from this development in Buddhist Tantra. This is almost surprising since the last of the tantric "Fourteen Root Violations" reads: "verbally or mentally denigrating women." Unfortunately, the commentaries say this means, "not lusting" after them—nothing actually new in Buddhism. Davidson has examined the "epigraphic, ethnographic, and textual sources" of these centuries and says:

> they indicate that women's numbers precipitously declined during the period of esoteric Buddhism, particularly in high status and authoritative religious positions. Far from being supportive of women's participation, the Mantrayāna was decidedly deleterious to the religious aspirations of those women desiring participation as independent and equal persons.[51]

Thus, we witness again how difficult it is for religious ideals (i.e., for new "revealed" contents) to be actualized in everyday life.

This fact is reflected in Jung's considering the papal declaration in 1950 of the "Assumption of Mary" to be "the most important religious event since the Reformation"—since, officially, a "Bride" (the Virgin) has joined the "Bridegroom" (Christ) in heaven. It represents a union of the opposites, "Feminine and Masculine," in anticipation of all the opposites becoming united in some way. It even proclaims a *hieros gamos* of "Mother and son," irrationally, as if integrating a motif from the Greco-Roman Mysteries. Yet not much has come of it here on "earth," i.e., among conscious human beings.[52]

---

[51] Davidson, *Indian Esoteric Buddhism*, 91.

[52] Jung, *CW* 11, par. 752.

The "Wrathful"

When Śiva became a "Buddhist," he did not lose his wrathful character, nor did other dangerously powerful Hindu deities admitted into the pantheon. This, too, was a new development in tantric Buddhism. But Bodhisattva Vajrapāṇi had to prove himself even more wrathful in order to win his contest with the "Destroyer." It is not that Gautama had not conquered Māra in order to win Enlightenment—as we saw in the "Life"—but he conquered his opponent by meditating on the Perfections and by silently "touching Earth," demonstrating thereby the virtue of "nonviolence" (*ahiṃsā*). By contrast, in this eighth-century myth, the Buddhist hero Vajrapāṇi is demonstrating the "virtue" of violence.

We should not be surprised, therefore, when Vairocana Buddha himself is described in the STTS as having a "wrathful" side:

> He is without beginning, without end, the quiet one, the violent one,
> the wrathful one, and of great calm patience.
> He is a *yakṣa*, a *rākṣasa*, the valiant one, the majestic one,
> the fierce one, and of great opulence.
> He is Lord of the goddess Umā, [i.e., he is also Śiva!], lord of the world, Viṣṇu,
> the victorious one, and the great silent one.[53]

As so often occurs in actual conflict, Buddhism appears to be absorbing—in its "fight" with a rival religion—the opponent's own darker features, perhaps a reflection of the increasingly more violent character of Indian society itself.

We should not forget, however, that mainstream Mahāyāna had already introduced the motif of "compassionate violence" in its re-writing of Buddhist ethics. If through clairvoyance a Bodhisattva knew that a son was about to murder his parents, it was permissible to kill the son to spare the parents and to spare the son's falling into Avīci hell. Indeed, the tenth of the "Fourteen Root Violations" in Buddhist Tantra is failing to do so: "having the ability to perceive the mental continuum of others and recognizing that someone will commit great harm to others, but not taking action"—is not just an option but a sin.[54]

Should all the Buddhist *devatās* have the capacity for violence as needed? The answer was a resounding, yes. Thus, the Celestial Buddhas and Celestial Bodhisattvas not only gained celestial "wives," they also had added to their traditional "peacefulness" (*śāntika*) the attribute of "wrath" (*krodha, abhicāra*). For example, Akṣobhya Buddha is considered peaceful under his usual name but wrathful under the name of Hevajra or Heruka. His wife, Locanā, is lovely but expresses her wrath as Nairātmyā or Vajravārāhi. It is hard to imagine that the compassionate and feminine Bodhisattva Avalokiteśvara has a wrathful side—but there he is as Mahākāla, sculpted in stone from twelfth-century Orissa with flaming hair, a flaying knife, and standing on a corpse (see Figure 14.4).

---

53 Giebel, STTS, 21-22.

54 See "fourteen root violations," *PDB*, 1089.

Figure 14.4 Mahākāla

While Tārā's role seems fluid—a Celestial Bodhisattva, a Buddha's Consort, or even an independent deity—she is recognizably wrathful as Bhṛkutī whom we already learned may stand beside Tārā with her eponymous unfriendly "frown." Just as often, Tārā's wrath appears as Kurukullā, a dangerously seductive dancing *ḍākinī*. Of course, all of this means that the tantric pantheon of *devatās* kept growing over the centuries in a bewildering complexity.

A Jungian thought Jung was not very aware of an Indian form of Buddhist Tantra, largely because scholarship on the subject was just beginning. What he learned from his Indologist friend, Heinrich Zimmer, pertained almost entirely to a late form of Tantra we have yet to discuss; and what the archeologist Giuseppe Tucci conveyed at the Eranos conferences—scholarly gatherings in Switzerland attended by Jung—focused on Tibet's version. Accordingly, Jung often identified Buddhist Tantra with "Tibetan Buddhism," as some still do. That is wrong on two counts: Buddhist Tantra was Indian before it was Tibetan, and Tibetan Buddhism is not entirely tantric.

One exception in Jung's materials is a set of lectures on a text he called, the "Shrī-Chakra-Sambhāra Tantra," given in 1938-1939. Originally in Sanskrit, this text had been translated into Tibetan—with an English version made available by John Woodroffe in 1919. Unfortunately, the seminar by Jung has not been published. But I have seen it, and it does not say much more than is available elsewhere. Besides, it is not really a *tantra*. David Gray explains in his recent translation of the actual *Cakrasamvara Tantra* that Woodroffe had merely published a "series of Cakrasamvara ritual texts" based upon the "root" scripture (hereafter, CST).[55]

In any case, Jung was led to the conclusion that tantric Buddhism long ago had begun to address—with its "wrathful" deities—the very serious problem of the "dark side" of God. He writes: "In Tibetan Buddhism all gods without exception have a peaceful and a wrathful aspect, for they reign over all the realms of being."[56] Jung himself addressed this issue with regard to the Judeo-Christian "God-image" in his *Answer to Job*.[57] His thoughts are important because we must eventually realize that the "problem of Evil" is not just personal, something we can solve by trying harder to be good. Instead, Evil is archetypally built into the human psyche—and we cannot survive under the traditional illusion that: *Omne bonum a Deo, omne malum ab homine* ("All good from God, all evil from humanity").[58] God is not "all Good," says Jung, and one's dreams—not to mention one's own unintended evil and the news—confirm that.

Tantric Buddhist "deities," however, are actually "all Good." True, Vajrapāṇi's "wrath" is dark, but it is compassionate—intended only to "tame" those who have yet to submit to the Light of the Dharmakāya. Rob Preece, a Buddhist who writes with Jungian terminology, tries to explain why the deity Yamāntaka—the "wrathful" side of the otherwise "peaceful" Bodhisattva Mañjuśrī—looks dangerous:

> Archetypally, Yamantaka is a personification of the dark angel. He is of the same order as the forces of the underworld, the Shadow that is to be transformed. . . . The deity appears in a wrathful form because it embodies this potent power, and the object of this force is not projected outside blaming outer enemies. Having recognized that the true enemy is the ignorance and ego-grasping that lies within us all, there is a change of direction. All the destructive demonic characteristics exemplified in the deity are directed at the ultimate destruction of stupidity, selfishness, and ego-grasping.[59]

This is Buddhist theodicy ("justifying deity") on the same level as Christian theodicy, since the "true enemy" in this passage is human "ego-grasping"—and never any of the Bodhisattvas or Buddhas. Granted, the imagery of Buddhist Tantra "looks" otherwise, as if the collective unconscious were trying to make Jung's point through its religious symbolism.

---

[55] David B. Gray, trans., *The "Cakrasamvara Tantra": The Discourse of Śrī Heruka* (New York: American Institute of Buddhist Studies at Columbia University, 2007), 4.

[56] Jung, *CW* 11, par. 380.

[57] Jung, *CW* 11, pars. 553-758.

[58] Jung, *CW* 9ii, par. 81.

[59] Rob Preece, *The Psychology of Buddhist Tantra* (Ithaca: Snow Lion Publications, 2006), 186-189.

Families of Deities

Finally, on this topic of the expanded Buddhist pantheon, Tantra tried to get some control over its unwieldy character by organizing divine beings into "Families." In this way, a Buddha could be named the "father" of a whole set of deities, his consort their "mother," one of the sixteen major Celestial Bodhisattvas could be the "son" of that family, etc. And their wrathful sides could all be included in the "family." By the time of the STTS—with the standardization of the "five Buddhas"—five "Families" also become standard: 1) Vairocana is father of a "Tathāgata" family; 2) Amitābha is father" of the "Padma" family with the Bodhisattva Avalokiteśvara as his chief son and, here, Tārā as his consort; 3) Akṣobhya head of the "Vajra" family with Vajrapāṇi as his son; 4) Ratnasaṃbhava father of the "Ratna" family; and 5) Amoghasiddhi head of a "Karma" family. Eventually, all the other deities could be assigned places in one or another Family—even as "guardians," and what are called "offering deities," etc. And while there is no limit to the actual number of Buddhist *devatās*, as Mkhas-grub-rje reminds us, "there are practically none of them that are not comprised in the various five Families."[60]

There is opportunity here for a system of tantric gods. But it is difficult to find one that does not shift from text to text or even within a single *tantra*. If we had a *guru* and were initiated into a tantric cycle, perhaps it would all make more sense. Then, again, the eighth century *Saṃpuṭa Tantra* (hereafter, SPT), does not offer much hope: "The Families are said to be five-fold; there is also a hundred-fold division and an infinity of Families."[61] "Infinity" is hardly an organizing principle. We see, nevertheless, that Tantra is seeking some order or regularity in the Buddhist pantheon. The *maṇḍala* as a "circle" of deities will be another way to find it. Indeed, there is an archetypal urge within the psyche to seek Order, manifest at the level of consciousness as the ego's need for "law and order."

Mantrayāna

While it is "Vajra-yāna," tantric Buddhism remains emphatically "Mantra-yāna." The tradition's reliance upon the power of *mantras* is obvious in all of its literature—in every literary "cycle" of a "root" scripture, associated "explanatory" scripture, *sādhana* practice manual, and commentary. We saw Gautama as a very advanced Bodhisattva, on the eve of his tantric Enlightenment, still having to learn certain *mantras* in order to become a Buddha. All those who follow him must do the same.

We saw that a *mantra* is, usually, a short Sanskrit phrase or formula—with elements that may or may not make sense, yet are considered effective. That was apparent in mainstream Mahāyāna when the Celestial Bodhisattva Avalokiteśvara could be praised and even evoked by "*oṃ, maṇi padme hūṃ*." When scholars of exoteric or esoteric Buddhism translate *mantra* as "spell," "incantation," or "charm," they catch the magical dimension of the practice that makes things happen. But that

---

[60] Lessing and Wayman, *Mkhas grub rje's "Fundamentals,"* 317.

[61] George R. Elder, trans., *The Saṃpuṭa Tantra: Edition and Translation, Chapters 1-4* (Ph.D. dissertation, Columbia University, 1978), 169. Unpublished.

is balanced by a sacred dimension in the use of *mantras* that requires selection and training of practitioners, the proper religious attitude and feeling for each formula—that is ultimately mysterious.

Tantric "Buddhas" are often said to comprise the "Three Mysteries" (*guhya*, "secret") of a Vajra Body, Vajra Speech, and Vajra Mind. When "Vajra Speech" manifests in sound, it is called *mantra*—and when someone repeats it, he or she sounds like a Buddha.[62] It is probably best, then, that we not try to translate this word.

Mantras can also be long as in the famous "100-syllable" *mantra* found in the STTS, of which we have already heard. It reads in Sanskrit:

> *Oṃ vajrasattva samayam anupālaya, vajrsattvatveopatiṣṭha, dṛḍho me bhava, sutoṣyo me bhava, anurakto me bhava, supoṣyo me bhava, sarvasiddhiṃ me prayaccha, sarvakarmasu ca me cittaśreyaḥ kuru, hūṃ ha ha ha ha ho, bhagavan sarvatathāgatavajra mā me muñca, vajrībhava, mahāsamayasattva āḥ.*[63]

Most of this can be translated, but I have left it in Sanskrit momentarily to make the point that Giebel (who is translating this text from the Chinese) was obliged to retain the Sanskrit since the Chinese manuscript had already done so. That is because the *mantra* is effective only in the language in which it was revealed to some Indian tantric adept. Its "sound," therefore, matters more than its meaning.

For the record, here is an English translation that Giebel provides:

> *Om*. O Vajrasattva, keep your pledge! Be close at hand as Vajrasattva! Be firm for me! Be well-pleased in me! Be attached to me! Be well-nurturing for me! Grant me all success and bring about happiness of mind for me in all actions! *hūṃ ha ha ha ha ho*! O Lord, Vajra of All the Tathāgatas, do not abandon me! Be like a *vajra*! Great pledge-being! *āḥ*!

One can feel the power of this *mantra*. Indeed, it is a moving prayer. So who can fault the translator for inserting so many exclamation points when there is no punctuation in the original language?

When *mantras* are very long, they tend to be called *dhāraṇīs*. The word derives from the Sanskrit meaning "to hold, retain"—and may have originally been intended as a relatively long passage of scripture helping one to "retain" the whole. That is why Snellgrove translates the word as "mnemonic." In Early Buddhism, the Dharmaguptaka sect included a collection of *dhāraṇīs*—along with its Tripiṭaka canon—as if it were a fourth "Basket." In mainstream Mahāyāna, then, the twenty-sixth chapter of the *Lotus Sūtra* is devoted to "*Dhāraṇī*" where we read that the Celestial Bodhisattva Bhaiṣajyarāja ("Medicine King"): "gave to the preachers of Dharma a *dhāraṇī*-charm for their protection." It begins: "*anye manye mane mamane cite carite same samitā . . .*" and goes on in that rhyming way at some length. Hurvitz, our translator of the *Lotus* writes of this "charm":

---

62 Wayman, *Buddhist Tantras*, 31. "Mystery" here translates *guhya*, usually "secret."

63 Giebel, STTS, 99.

"Most of the words are Indic, some pure Sanskrit and some just mumbo-jumbo"—so he declines to translate.[64]

Now we learn that *dhāraṇīs* are not just mnemonic but have an apotropaic or "protective" purpose. That is true for *mantras* in general. Let us note that in Early Buddhist scripture Gautama himself taught formulas for "protection" (*paritrāṇa*; Pāli, *paritta*) although they tended to make sense.

And *mantras* can be mono-syllabic. These are what Anthony Tribe calls "mantra particles." As sounds, they have no connotation, but their "meaning" is in their function: "Thus, deities are summoned by *jaḥ*, drawn in by *hūṃ*, bound by *vaṃ*, and made to pervade the *maṇḍala* by *hoḥ*. The particle *phaṭ* can be put to use as a weapon *mantra* to deal with obstacles and foes."[65] Ordinary *mantras* often have a mono-syllabic prefix or suffix: *oṃ . . . hūṃ*. In this case, "*oṃ*" may be called a *bīja* ("seed")-syllable since it is the seed from which the rest of this particular *mantra* grows. Of course, that kind of "seed" is not to be confused with karmic "seeds" planted in one's "stream of consciousness."

In Tantra, deities have their own "*bījas*." These are the single syllables that express who or what a particular deity is in "essence;" they must be imagined or recited before that god can unfold—from its "seed"—into his or her anthropomorphic form. And we will see that in a *sādhana* evoking Tāra below. Sharf explains:

> The mantra of a particular deity is consubstantial with the deity-itself (that is, it bears the same relationship to the deity that, according to certain Mahayana scriptures, the title of a *sūtra* bears to the *sūtra*). Thus to grasp the mantra is to grasp the deity, just as to intone the title of a *sūtra* is tantamount to reciting the entire *sūtra*.[66]

When drawing a *maṇḍala* to invite the gods and goddesses, it is permissible to draw only seed-syllables, often depicted on lotuses as if the deities were seated there. In one system, "A" invites Vairocana, "Ba" invites Amitābha, etc. These syllables, however, must be sounded (*japa*)—aloud, softly, or silently in the mind—to be effective, since they are primarily sonic realities.

Regarding the number of recitations, Mkhas-grub-rje quotes the SSK:

> In general, if there be of syllables
> The number of fifteen or fewer,
> One must mutter each syllable 100,000 times;
> Up to thirty-two syllables, it is said
> The muttering of the entire formula must be done 300,000 times;
> When the syllables are more than that,
> Do the preliminary service of the entire formula 10,000 times.[67]

---

[64] Hurvitz, *Lotus Blossom*, 320.

[65] Tribe, "Mantranaya," 169.

[66] Robert H. Sharf, "Visualization and Mandala in Shingon Buddhism," in Robert H. Sharf and Elizabeth Horton Sharf, eds., *Living Images: Japanese Buddhist Icons in Context* (Redwood City: Stanford University Press, 2002), 185.

[67] Lessing and Wayman, *Mkhas grub rje's "Fundamentals*," 191.

This Tibetan commentator goes on:

> When during the recitation one becomes drowsy, yawns, sneezes, coughs aloud, breaks wind, or feels an urge to ease nature, etc. he immediately sets aside his chaplet [i.e., a string of beads or *japa-mālā* that helps one keep count], interrupts the service, makes ablutions, and starts again from the beginning of the count.

The procedure does seem mechanical, but it is not easy.

None of this use of sacred sound, however is particularly Buddhist nor is it particularly tantric except when emphasized. That is because Indian religious culture itself is committed to the "sonic" dimension of the holy. Thomas Hopkins explains Vedic religion—an early form of Hinduism—from around 1500 BCE:

> Many Vedic hymns contain identities such as, "You, O Agni, are Indra," originally intended as statements of praise. In the developing ritual, these came to be considered formulations of the truth in sound. Such ritual formulations were called *mantras*, formulas which embodied in their sound the special power to bring into reality the truth they expressed. . . . Sanskrit words were not just arbitrary labels assigned to phenomena; they were the sound forms of objects, actions, and attributes, related to the corresponding reality in the same way as visual forms and different only in being perceived by the ear and not by the eye.[68]

Tantric Buddhism, then, honors this deeply Indian perception.

Tantra may even be a revaluing of it since Buddhism had long been criticizing language as a distortion of truth, as merely reifying "permanence." Nāgārjuna is said to "deconstruct" the distinctions made by words. But that cannot be the whole truth. After all, the Buddha taught in words; and his "Buddha-word" (*buddha-vacana*) is Truth itself. *Mantra* expresses or symbolizes that fact in the religion, the fact that certain kinds of words can point to and connect one to the "Vajra Speech" of the Lord. It is the same connection to the Divine that explains why people read the words of the Bible, why calligraphic roundels hang prominently at Hagia Sophia, why some people read Jung's words in the morning.

Mudrā

The Buddha's "Vajra Body" manifests in the human realm as certain gestures of the hands. And when a yogin enacts them, he or she is behaving symbolically like a Buddha. They are called *mudrā* (from the Sanskrit for "seal") and involve either one or both hands, a few or all of the fingers, during tantric practice. We have already seen some of them in the iconography of non-tantric Buddhist sculpture: the Buddha's *mudrā* of "fear not" at Mathurā, the *mudrā* of "teaching the Dharma" at

[68] Thomas J. Hopkins, *The Hindu Religious Tradition* (Encino: Dickenson Publishing Company, 1971), 19-20.

Sārnāth, and the popular gesture of "touching Earth." On reliefs, we saw devotees in the *mudrā* of "reverence" with outstretched closed palms.

It is only natural for Buddhism to use a kind of "sign language" to communicate meaning, since we do that in everyday conversation. But these are sacred gestures standardized to signify certain activities of Buddhas, Bodhisattvas, and worshippers. They should not be confused, however, with what in the literature are called "hand symbols" (*hasta-cihna*) that refer to a standard set of objects to identify the image of a Buddhist deity in art—a lotus blossom, a sword, a book, etc.

For religious practice, Tantra multiplies the number of *mudrās* into the hundreds. They can be simple, as in this instruction from the VAT:

> Also the wise one should make both of his hands into fists, and insert both thumbs inside. This symbol is the great *mudrā* which purifies the continuum of reality.[69]

Or they can be complex:

> Likewise, you should link together both your hands into a fist and raise up both your middle-fingers, then crooking both your forefingers, place them at their sides like a *vajra*. Raise both your thumbs and little-fingers and holding them thus, insert both of your ring-fingers within your hands.

Obviously, we need a *guru* to demonstrate. But the text goes on: "This great *mudrā* is the *vajra* symbol which destroys the citadel of ignorance." In other words, *mudras*—like *mantras*—are not just expressive but effective (see Figure 14.5 for a demonstration of ritual hand gestures from a twelfth-century Japanese scroll).

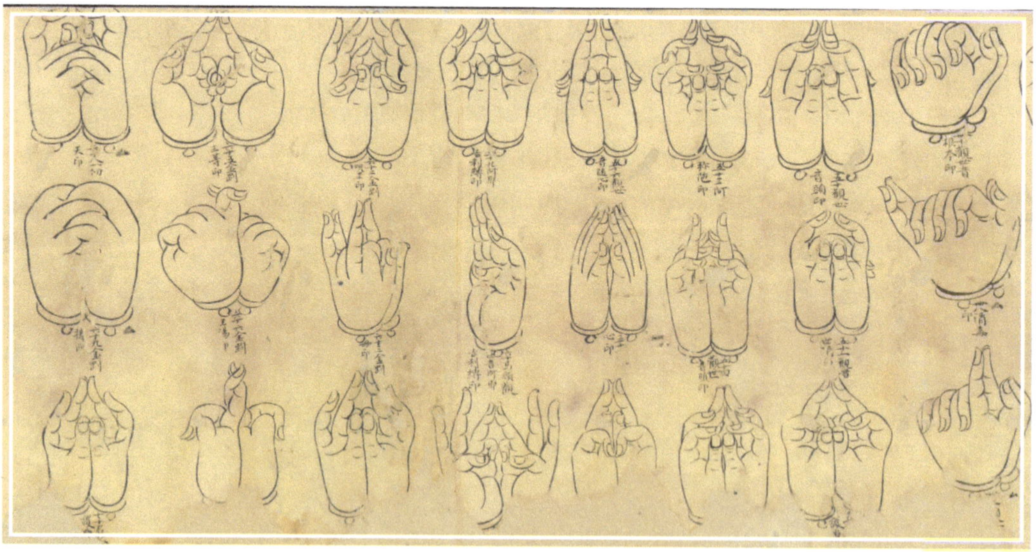

Figure 14.5 Mudrās

[69] Hodge, VAT, 234-235. Slightly altered.

Together, *mantras* and *mudrās* are considered very powerful techniques. In fact, *mantras* are seldom recited without an accompanying *mudrā*. Wallis writes: "In the *Mmk*, these gestures invariably accompany verbal actions. The two, *mudrās* and *mantras*, are in fact so closely bound that they can be said to form a single instrumental act." He cites his text:

> The *mudrās* are the seals of the *mantras*; and with the *mantras* they are well-sealed. There is no *mantra* without a *mudrā*, devoid of the *mudrā*, there is no seal.[70]

Here, the *tantra* is making use of the basic meaning of *mudrā* as "seal." We discussed seals in *The Snake and the Rope* as small stamps, beautifully carved, used in the very early Indus Valley Culture to secure trade goods. Stamped images authenticated those goods and prevented tampering. Eventually, Indian kings would hold a "seal" of office, an image or object authenticating their reign. That helps to explain tantric gestural *mudrās* as authenticating a rite or the tradition as a whole. Buddhaguhya suggests a "protective" purpose: "It is just as in the world, where a person who bears the king's seal will be untroubled by people," i.e., not be harmed.[71]

When reading a tantric text, however, the word *mudrā* can be ambiguous (like *yoginī*). It can mean not just a sacred gesture of the hand but, instead, a female deity. Or it can mean a human female partner who appears in late Anuttarayoga materials. When that partner is actual, she is called a *karma-mudrā* (probably because a body of flesh and blood matures by *karma*); and when that partner is imagined she is called a *jñāna-mudrā* (with the emphasis upon "knowledge" or mental reality). In that late form of Tantra, Enlightenment itself may be called "*Mahā-mudrā*" or "Great Mudrā." Why the word has this much range is not clear, but it is part of the difficulty of tantric studies. Perhaps there is some great "Seal" holding all these meanings together.

A psychological note Since the primary meaning of "seals" is that they secure what might otherwise come loose, one gets the impression that a verbal *mantra* requires the physical *mudrā* to secure it or make it "firm" (the same symbolic function of the *vajra*). Psychologically, that relates to an issue in analysis.

At the outset, the analysand discovers that there is a big difference between having certain things in mind and expressing them in words to the analyst. They become more real, more difficult to deny (to oneself). There soon follows the challenge of making these expressed thoughts and feelings—and the insights gained by discussing them—really "firm" by doing something, actually changing one's behavior. This is what Jung calls the "morality of analysis." And progress in psychological development often founders or is delayed by that requirement.

Edinger puts this matter strongly. He says about new contents emerging in psychotherapy from dreams or dialogue:

> One must also respond to the emerging content by asking the question: "What does this content demand of me ethically? What must I do with it?" If I don't engage

70 Wallis, MMK, 41.

71 Hodge, VAT, 232.

> that question of what I do with it, if I'm just satisfied with enjoying the image aesthetically or just satisfied with an intellectual "enjoyment" of its meaning, the whole relation to the unconscious can turn negative—dangerously negative.[72]

As the Buddhist material suggests, "words" and "gestures" belong together.

Homa

Mudrā—like *mantra*—points back to fire altar ritual in Vedic Hinduism: priests used stylized gestures to signify stress and rhythm in a language that eventually became Sanskrit. Thus, it is not surprising that fire sacrifice itself reappears in tantric Buddhism. As in Hinduism, it is called *homa* and means the act of "offering gifts into a fire" for the gods.

For many centuries in India, that was an elaborate public ceremony involving three fires and two kinds of offering: animals such as cattle, goats, and horses; or "vegetarian" offerings like water, milk, ghee (butter "purified" of its milk solids), rice and barley cakes. But there had long been a simpler domestic *homa* (or *yajña*) with one small fire and no animal offerings. Both, however, honored the fire god Agni first of all—as mediator between the sacrificer and the other Thirty-three gods who received their gifts on high in the subtle form of smoke.

Gradually—under pressure from the renunciant movement and its virtue of "nonviolence" (*ahimsā*)—public animal sacrifices became relatively rare in the religions of India. By contrast, the "vegetarian" kind could be found daily at a Hindu temple or at home—and usually without fire but now in the presence of an image of a deity toward whom the sacrifice was addressed. When devotional and not just propitiatory, this kind of religious practice was called *pūjā*, "worship." And it is that kind of worship, when private, that appears as *homa* in tantric Buddhism.

Although Modern Buddhists claim the historical Siddhārtha Gautama was opposed to all sacrifices, early scriptures show him opposed only to sacrifices involving the killing of animals. The Buddha says in the *Aṅguttara Nikāya*:

> I do not praise all sacrifice, *brāhmaṇa*, nor do I withhold praise from all sacrifice. I do not praise a violent sacrifice at which cattle, goats, rams, chickens, and pigs are slain, at which various creatures are led to slaughter. . . . But I praise a nonviolent sacrifice at which cattle, goats, rams, chickens, and pigs are not slain, where various creatures are not slaughtered, that is, a regular giving, a sacrifice offered by family custom. . . . For one who makes such sacrifice it is indeed better, never worse. Such a sacrifice is truly vast and the deities too are pleased.[73]

It is good, therefore, to sacrifice to the gods in the right way. It pleases them and leads to an auspicious rebirth. Granted, Gautama preaches elsewhere in the Nikāyas that there are more advanced and better sacrifices: such as "giving gifts" to the Saṅgha instead of to the gods and, especially, "giving

[72] Edinger, *American Jungian*, 55.

[73] Bodhi, *AN* 4.4.39 (pp. 429-430). Slightly altered.

up" one's wife and children as a renunciant monk. But his position is not extreme, and there was room for sacrifice eventually in Buddhist Tantra. See Figure 14.6 for a picture of a private *homa* in the Shingon tradition, the Japanese form of tantric Buddhism.

Figure 14.6 Shingon Homa Ritual

In the SSK, the Lord Vajradhara instructs in that typically "cookbook" style of tantric texts:

> Next, I shall explain in detail the rules for *homa*, which cause the reciter to quickly obtain *siddhi*. In front of an image of the deity make a hearth [a fire pit] for *homa* that is one cubit square, has a rim on all four sides, and is a half-cubit deep; the measurements are also the same if you make the hearth circular. If the place of recitation is indoors, you should go outside and dig the hearth where you can see the figure of the deity inside. . . . Place things such as fuel sticks, as well as incense and flowers [all three are considered offerings], on the right-hand side and place the *homa* vessels [for additional offerings] on the left-hand side. . . . In order to remove pollution, you should recite the *mantra* of Kīlikīli [a converted *rākṣasa* forest demon] and also make his seal [*mudrā*], and in order to protect the ritual recite the *mantra* of Kuṇḍalin [a wrathful Bodhisattva] and sprinkle some water to purify it. Then use fuel sticks to light the fire, and once you have lit the fire, first invoke Agni [just as in Vedic religion], saying, "I now respectfully request Agni,

> who is foremost, seer among the gods, and esteemed among those who perform Brahman practices, to descend to this place and receive *homa*.[74]

It is gratifying to read a tantric passage that is not only clear but confirms what we have already learned about this new style of Buddhism. As expected, several *mantras* follow, including one to "mantrafy"—as Giebel aptly puts it—the "five grains, ghee, curds, and other things" to be offered in the fire.

Then:

> Having made sacrifices of food to Agni, mentally visualize that you lead Agni back to his seat in the heavens. Then recite the *mantra* of Kīlikīli, make his hand-seal, and again purify the fire. All *homa* should be performed in this manner. Next, invite your own deity [this is one's personal *iṣṭa-devatā* or "tutelary deity"]: first recite your deity's *mantra* once and install him on his seat and, after you have worshipped him as prescribed, ask him to deign to accept the *homa*.

After gaining merit thereby and the benefit of being in that deity's presence, the sacrificer must ask the deity to leave: "Remove the word 'descend' in the invocatory *mantra* and substitute the word 'return.'"

Some psychology of "fire" It should be obvious by now why tantric Buddhism is said to be ritual Buddhism. What is not so obvious today is that all these rites were powerfully moving, at least to many, in the ancient world. Richard Payne argues that in our own culture the Protestant criticism of Roman Catholic *hocus pocus* (in the sixteenth century) and the European Enlightenment's subsequent criticism of all things liturgical (in the eighteenth century) have stifled our appreciation for the power of ritual action when it is alive and well. Today, the word "ritual" often means just "meaningless ritual."

Yet Payne confides his own response to the *homa* ceremony in tantric Japanese Buddhism: "From the first time I saw it, I knew what I wanted. The raw emotional power of the Shingon ritual was so moving that it has given definition to my practice"—so much so that Payne, the scholar, felt obliged to become a Shingon priest.[75] Here is living proof of the SSK's ancient claim: "If, on hearing of mantra rites for the first time, a person's hair should all stand on end and his heart dance for joy, such a person is a Dharma-vessel for the fruits of success."[76]

By temperament and by virtue of his level of consciousness, Jung could not become a Buddhist priest like Payne, but he could understand that man's experience—as having been gripped by the "Fire" of the *numinosum* that resides within the archetypal psyche. Indeed, since Vedic times, India had felt that the religious life required some kind of intense "heat" (*tapas*). Thomas Hopkins tells us:

---

[74] Giebel, SSK, 237-240.

[75] Richard K. Payne, "Burning with the Fire of Shingon," *Lion's Roar: Buddhist Wisdom for Our Time*. https://www.lionsroar.com/burnng-with-the-fire-of-shingon.

[76] Giebel, SSK, 137.

> A belief in the independent power of *tapas* gradually developed. *Tapas* or heat was the effective power in the activities credited to Indra, but men could also create *tapas*—in the sacrifice by the fires, and in themselves by devotional fervor.[77]

We witnessed this "fiery energy" as *tejas* at the consecration of a Buddhist statue in an earlier chapter.

Acknowledging its manifestation elsewhere in the history of religions, Jung says it:

> glows in the burning bush and in the countenance of Moses; in the Gospels it descends with the Holy Ghost in the form of fiery tongues from heaven. In Heraclitus it appears as world energy, as "ever-living fire;" among the Persians it is the fiery glow of "haoma," divine grace; among the Stoics it is the original heat, the power of fate.[78]

Psychologically, then, the *numinosum* is immanent within the unconscious as its libido or "Energy." It can flame out into one's conscious life unawares or be ignited more deliberately—yet is always part of the individuation process.

It is no easy experience, however, to be exposed to the "sacrificial fires" of psychological transformation. At the very least, individuation burns away cant. That is why Jung quotes the "esoteric Christ" from a Gnostic scripture as if in warning: "He who is near unto me is near unto the fire."[79] Yes, there is that other "Fire"—of desirousness—against which Gautama Buddha preached an early famous sermon. Seeing both, T. S. Eliot writes toward the close of his "Four Quartets": "We only live, only suspire / Consumed by either fire or fire."[80]

---

[77] Hopkins, *Hindu Religious Tradition*, 26. See also Elder, *Snake and the Rope*, 105.

[78] Jung, *CW* 7, par. 108.

[79] Jung, *CW* 12, par. 157.

[80] Eliot, *Norton Anthology*, "Little Gidding," 2:1805.

Chapter 15
TANTRA (CONTINUED)

Visualization

In the previous chapter, we learned that Buddhist Tantra is not a breakthrough in new doctrine (Wisdom) but, instead, a discovery of new techniques (Means) by which to seek Enlightenment. They included the use of *mantras*, of *mūdras*, and ritual fires or *homas* by which to make offerings to, and receive blessings from, an expanded tantric pantheon.

Another new technique often listed in the scholarly literature is "visualization." What we seldom learn, however, is what Sanskrit word is being translated as "visualization," even though other technical terms are carefully specified. We know this method is important since Sarvārthasiddhi's Enlightenment required him to "see" certain things: e.g., "visualize yourself in the form of a Buddha."[1] One would expect some "seeing" word here, but that is not usually the case (although forms of *paś*, "to see," do appear). Instead, we find Sanskrit words related to meditation.

One is *bhāvanā*: literally "cultivation" but more generally "contemplation" or "meditation." Thus, when Giebel is not translating that word as "visualization" in the STTS (i.e., from the Chinese that is rendering an original Sanskrit manuscript), he will more carefully write with brackets, "cultivate [visualization of] . . . ."[2] Another word for this practice is *dhyāna* that in Early Buddhism refers to "trance" states in the Realm of Form or to "meditation" generally. Wallis renders *dhyāna* in the MMK as "contemplative visualization."[3]

I am not saying that visualizing is not taking place; but the language used by *tāntrikas* shows they do not consider their "visualizations" to be all that different from the "meditations" that have gone before. Whatever the terminology, visualizing in tantric Buddhism expresses the "Vajra Mind" of the Buddha who "sees" or understands reality in an Enlightened way—just as the *mantras* sound "Vajra Speech" and *mudrās* gesture the "Vajra Body" of the Lord.

"Visualization" may be a tantric revaluing of "imagination." We see this when Snellgrove translates *purato vibhāvya* in the HVT unexpectedly as "imagine before one"—instead of "visualize" or "contemplate" in front of oneself.[4] Elsewhere, the connection is more direct with words derived from the Sanskrit root *kḷp*, "to imagine." Thus, Christopher George translates in the *Caṇḍamahāroṣaṇa Tantra* (hereafter, CMT): "Then, concentrating [*dhyātvā*] on the syllable *bhruṃ*, he should imagine [*prakalpayet*] a celestial palace." George, incidentally, does not translate

---

1 Giebel, STTS, 24.
2 Giebel, STTS, 95.
3 Wallis, MMK, 3.
4 Snellgrove, HVT, 57.

"visualize" when encountering words related to *bhāvanā* and renders more conservatively, "meditate in front of him," "meditate that his own body is pellucid," etc.[5]

The reason why this may be a revaluing of imagination is because words derived from *klṛp*—such as *parikalpa* ("imagination") and *vikalpa* ("discursive thought")—were used by earlier phases of Buddhism for the error of reification, of falsely imagining a snake where there is only a rope, or seeing substance (*ātman*) where there are only parts (*anātman*).

In the VAT, Vajrapāṇi himself has difficulty accepting a practice that makes use of "imagination." He questions the Buddha:

> Buddhas are without perceptual forms,
> And reside in the *dharmakāya*;
> If the Dharma they reveal is
> Without attributes, unconditioned, unequalled,
> Then why, O Great Hero, is
> This ritual with perceptual form
> Taught for the mantra practice?

The Lord answers:

> The Dharma is free from concepts,
> And devoid of all imagining;
> . . . .
> But this is unknown to the stupid
> Who wrongly conceive of their environments.
> Objects, time, perceptual forms and so on
> Are asserted by those who are enveloped in darkness.
> So in order for them to be helped,
> I teach this ritual.[6]

In other words, tantric "imaginative" practices are another *upāya*, a compassionate stratagem—like the controversial "lies" in the *Lotus Sūtra* of non-tantric Buddhism.

We should not forget, however, that many of Buddhism's earlier practices required a certain skill in visualizing, understood as imagining. The use of a round disk (*kṛtsna*; Pāli, *kasiṇa*) trained one to see it mentally, very clearly—with eyes closed. During meditations on the "Foulness" of the body in a charnal ground, one had to imagine one's own eventual decomposition. The four "Divine Abidings" were called the four "Immeasurables" because one had to imagine during meditation an immeasurable number of sentient beings toward whom one extended love—since they were not actually there. In "Recollecting the Buddha" to worship him, one trained to "see" him with all of his

---

5 Christopher George, trans., *The Caṇḍamhāroṣaṇa Tantra: A Critical Edition and English Translation, Chapters 1-8* (New Haven: American Oriental Society, 1974), 58.

6 Hodge, VAT, 89

Thirty-two Marks with the mind's eye. And Pure Lands had to be visualized first in order to plant seeds of merit—and assure rebirth—therein. It follows that *parikalpa* did not just falsify but was already a creative feature of the Path. Tantra exploits it, develops it.

Deity Yoga

In fact, "Recollecting the Buddha" in Early Buddhism became over time in Tantra the practice of "deity yoga" (*devatā-yoga*). We can see that in a *sādhana* or set of instructions for contemplating (visualizing, imagining) the deity Tārā whom we met first as a Celestial Bodhisattva. In this excerpt from the eleventh-century *Sādhana-mālā* ("Garland of Sādhanas"), she is more than a Bodhisattva. Indeed, the longer version of this instruction calls Tārā "great mother of the conquerors, who is totally free from fault or defect"—as if she were herself Prajñāpāramitā, "Mother" of all Buddhas. The technique has two parts, the first of which does not seem very esoteric or distinctively tantric; the second part, however, breaks new religious ground.

a) **Generation in front** Gómez translates from the shorter version:

> First, one meditates on her as Tārā, the Remover of the Eight Perils [a saving capacity we observed in her mainstream manifestation], visualizing her in the middle of the sky [i.e., in the air "up to six feet" away, says Tsoṅ-kha-pa]. After one has worshipped her mentally, then one should confess one's transgressions.[7]

This begins a standard "seven-branched worship" (*saptāṅga-vidhi*) first outlined in exoteric Mahāyāna by Śāntideva. It includes such traditional acts as Taking Refuge, rejoicing in the merits of others, and beseeching the deity to "remain in the world, without entering Nirvāṇa." For Tārā is—at least, during this visualization—present in the world to save.

So real is she that the meditator makes offerings of water, flowers, perfumes, etc. Mkhas-grub-rje comments:

> If the oblation and the succeeding offerings cannot be actually provided, it is taught that they may be offered mentally by visualizing them vividly. Indeed, it is taught that even when the offerings are actually provided, they are first to be passed mentally in review, for the mental offering is the chief thing.[8]

Receiving so much honor, accompanied by the appropriate *mantras* and *mudrās*, the deity is pleased—and particularly pleased, we learn, by "imaginary" offerings. She confers her blessing upon the meditator who can now expect a longer life, a happier one, along with other *siddhis*—on the way to the transmundane *siddhi* of Buddhahood.

---

[7] Luis O. Gómez, "Two Tantric Meditations: Visualizing the Deity," in *Buddhism in Practice*, ed. Donald S. Lopez, Jr. (Princeton: Princeton University Press, 1995), 320. See Wayman, *Buddhist Tantras*, 147.

[8] Lessing and Wayman, *Mkhas grub rje's "Fundamentals,"* 183.

b) **Self-generation** The second half of deity yoga is called "self-generation" whereby the deity imagined in front "dissolves" into the meditator—i.e., is imagined to be identical with the worshipper. That is so distinctly tantric or esoteric that Tsoṅ-kha-pa claimed it to be the essential difference between the Path of the Perfections and the Path of Mantra. As he comments in his famous *Sṅags rim chen mo* ("Great Exposition on the Stages of Mantra"): the mind of a Buddha is "vast," and the "vastness of this system is deity yoga."[9] Hence, he calls Tantra the "Vast Path." Elsewhere, he distinguishes between the exoteric "Causal Path"—that uses the Perfections as "causes" to slowly reach the goal—and the "Result Path" of Tantra that uses imagery of the goal or "result" to get there more quickly.[10] John Powers explains:

> Underlying the theory of this system is the idea that the more one familiarizes oneself with something the more likely one is to manifest it. Thus, if one engages in lying, lying becomes progressively more natural and spontaneous. If, however, one becomes familiar with visualizing oneself as having the body, speech, and mind of a buddha—and as performing the activities of a buddha—one will gradually come to approximate the state of buddhahood. . . .[11]

This sounds like a kind of religious "conditioning" in order to become divine—not something one hears in Western religions but does hear in the Mystery religions of ancient Greece and Rome.

The actual procedure of "self-generation" begins with a contemplation of "emptiness," i.e., Buddhism's traditional view that all phenomena (including the meditator) lack "substance" (*ātman*). This clears the air, as it were—even the air in front of oneself where the *devatā* has been imagined and worshipped conventionally—as the focus shifts from outside to within the mind of the practitioner where Tārā reappears "out of voidness." The *Sādhana-mālā* instructs:

> Thereupon, one should visualize an eight-petal lotus flower in full bloom, within the moon in one's heart [i.e., within one's "mind"].
> In the middle of this lotus, one imagines the syllable "Tāṃ," [a *bīja* or "seed" syllable] and, then, within this syllable, a blue-colored lotus.
> In the middle of this lotus, one visualizes again the syllable, now shining with the flames of a burning fire.
> With this, he generates a mental image of the deity Tārā, adorned with all of her ornaments and features [as described by manuals in iconographic detail: posture, color, number of arms, etc.].[12]

Note that these verses describe an ever increasing interiority: like nesting Russian dolls or, closer to India, like the "sheaths" (*kośa*) of Hindu mystical physiology that when unpeeled from the gross to the very subtle reveal the divine Self at the deepest layer of one's being. Here, one imagines an

---

9 Hopkins, *Tantra in Tibet*, 126-127.

10 Hopkins, *Tantra in Tibet*, 105.

11 John Powers, *Introduction to Tibetan Buddhism* (Boston: Snow Lion, revised 2007), 272

12 Gómez, "Two Tantric Meditations," 320.

image of the moon, and within the moon a lotus, within the lotus a syllable, etc.—until one arrives at the goddess or, at least, the imagined goddess.

Somehow—in a way not clear to me—the meditator becomes Tārā (regardless of his or her personal gender that is irrelevant). The *sādhana*, then, requires the following reflections:

> "All things without exception are by nature and in their own being perfectly pure. I too am by nature perfectly pure." . . .
> "Everything here, moving and unmoving, is in itself nothing but the varied manifestations of the nondual, obscured by conceptualizations and discursive thought based on constructed oppositions such as that between subject and object."
> . . .
> "Om, I in my true self [*svabhāva-ātmaka*] am of the nature of this diamond of the knowledge of emptiness." . . . [13]

Presumably, if one keeps imagining such things (that are actually exoteric, at least in the Tathāgatagarbha tradition), they become real—or so Powers, who is a Buddhist, explains.

In any case, the "visualization" practice closes dramatically: "Emerging from trance, the yogin sees the whole universe in the form of Tārā, and moves about freely, seeing himself as the blessed Tārā."[14] The HVT describes similarly a "continuous practice" when identified with the goddess Nairatmyā:

> Moreover at all times whether washing the feet or eating, rinsing the mouth or chewing betel-nut, rubbing the hands with sandal-wood, or girding the hips with the loin-cloth, going-out, making conversation, waking, standing, in wrath, in laughter, the wise man should honor the Lady, strong in his vows, he should meditate upon the Yoginī. (2.2.5-6)[15]

The statement is reminiscent of Gautama's early description of a *bhikṣu* as one "who acts in full awareness when walking, standing, sitting, falling asleep; waking up, talking, and keeping silent" (*MN* 10.8). Tantra claims it is not just a matter of being "mindful" of these activities but of being mindful or aware that one is acting as a "deity" while doing them.

Divine Pride

A consequence of identifying with divinity is "divine pride." As Tsoṅ-kha-pa explains: "With such a yoga of method and wisdom in which one cultivates the pride of a Buddha such as Vairochana [or Tārā, etc], one attains the state of a Buddha without the passage of a long time as in the Perfection Vehicle."[16] The STTS instructs:

---

[13] Gómez, "Two Tantric Meditations," 324-325.

[14] Gómez, "Two Tantric Meditations," 327.

[15] Snellgrove, HVT, 1:89.

[16] Hopkins, *Tantra in Tibet*, 120.

> Visualizing oneself in the form of a Buddha, one should recite, "Adamantine Realm". . . .
> Brandishing the [*vajra*]-pestle with haughty air and maintaining adamantine pride [*māna*] . . . .[17]

Although the word for "pride" here is *māna*, it is not the same as ordinary pride (also, *māna*) that appears in some lists of the Defilements—especially as, *asmi-māna*, "I am pride." Thus, instead of this ordinary egocentricity, the Buddhists now have in mind its very opposite, "*vajra*-pride."

The current Dalai Lama comments:

> The most important and difficult of the Mantra disciplines is to meditate at all times on one's body as a divine body and to view whatever appears as a deity's sport. . . . With the disappearance of the ordinary body and mind there is no longer a sense of I, but in place of that impure body and mind the mind which earlier realized emptiness is used as the basis of emanation and itself manifests as a divine form with a face, arms, and so forth.[18]

This clarifies the earlier "emptiness" meditation—at the outset of deity yoga—as specifically "emptying" one's mind of an ordinary "sense of I." To the extent that was intended by the Early Buddhist teaching of *an-ātman*, this advice is entirely orthodox. What we did not know earlier is that a divine "Ego" replaces it—or does so in imagination.

A Jungian critique The imaginative practices taught by Buddhist Tantra will remind some readers of "active imagination" in Jungian psychology. Although not fond of techniques in psychotherapy—lest they attempt to manipulate the psyche—Jung did advise the following for "actively" getting in touch with the unconscious:

> One concentrates one's attention on some impressive but unintelligible dream-image, or on a spontaneous visual impression, and observes the changes taking place in it. Meanwhile, of course, all criticism must be suspended and the happenings observed and noted with absolute objectivity. Obviously, too, the objection that the whole thing is "arbitrary" or "thought up" must be set aside, since it springs from the anxiety of an ego-consciousness which brooks no master besides itself in its own house.[19]

As in Tantra, this practice revalues the act of "imagining" for Western culture. Historically, Judaism and Islam are aniconic, prohibiting the image (Greek, *eikon*) produced by the imagination. Christian art is friendlier toward the image, but all three traditions obey to some degree the second of the Ten

---

[17] Giebel, STTS, 84-85.

[18] Dalai Lama, *Deity Yoga: in Action and Performance Tantra*, trans. Jeffrey Hopkins (Ithaca: Snow Lion, 1981), 12.

[19] Jung, *CW* 9i, par. 319.

Commandments that reads: "You shall not make yourself a carved image or any likeness of anything in heaven or on earth" (Exodus 20:4).

Like Tantra, Jungian active imagination is only for those we can call "superior candidates"—persons in analysis who already have some sense that consciousness is not the only resident in the "house" of the psyche. Nor does the tantric Buddhist (who imagines a deity) or the Jungian analysand (who imagines how a dream might continue) consider the practice mere "day-dreaming." Instead, each has learned from experience that deliberate fantasy is an effective means toward Enlightenment or toward psychological wholeness.

Jung even criticizes the "European" who—unlike the Buddhist—can "easily explain away these deities as projections" but is "quite incapable of positing them at the same time as real."[20] Jung's point is that the psyche in all of its manifestations is real and that the *tāntrikas* know this. That is implied by the *sādhana* statement—"Everything here, moving and unmoving, is in itself nothing but the varied manifestations of the nondual." One could almost translate this psychologically as, "All that we consider real is nothing but the varied manifestations of the psyche that at bottom is the reality of the 'nondual' collective unconscious."

The difference between deity yoga and active imagination, however, must be obvious. For one thing, the former belongs to a religious tradition, built up over many centuries by countless individuals, and standardized into imagery detailed in the *sādhana* manuals. By contrast, Jungian psychology has existed for only a hundred years and is still far from "popular" even in the tantric sense. As for standards, there is only the model of the psyche that Jung has sketched for us and about which, given his epistemology, Jung cannot be entirely sure.

Even more different is the fact that tantric Buddhist "visualizations" are guided imaginations—set forth precisely in the manuals from which one should not deviate in some misguided "creative" way. By contrast, active imagination is spontaneous and different in almost every case—due to the aim of discovering one's authentic uniqueness. Indeed, when I do "active imagination" with a dream figure, it will be for the very first time ever! No one will have seen that image quite the same way, even if archetypal. And whether I let it just unfold (as Jung suggests) or engage it in imagined conversation, or draw or paint the image with as much care as I can manage, or even dance with it alone—that is entirely up to me and private. The analyst can make suggestions, but the analysand must find his or own way along what Jung calls a "razor-edged path, to be trodden for God's sake only, without assurance and without sanction"—from anyone else or any collective organization.[21]

In addition, it is never the case that a Jungian intentionally identifies with an unconscious content—in fact, the point is to dis-identify in order to become less unconscious and more conscious. This is especially true for archetypal "divine" contents with which one is tempted to identify in order to feel (unconsciously) Omnipotent and Omniscient. The problem is, as Jung explains while discussing Hindu Tantra, that we already "think we are gods"—"and therefore the tantric yoga idea that one becomes a god is dangerous for us. We start with that prejudice."[22] Put differently, we are already inflated.

---

20 Jung, *CW* 11, par. 833.

21 Jung, *CW* 9i, par. 399.

22 Jung, *Kundalini Yoga*, 99.

Jeffrey Hopkins, a scholar and practitioner of tantric Tibetan Buddhism, has written an essay entitled, "Jung's Warnings Against Inflation." While basically just quoting Jung, Hopkins is "impressed with his insights."[23] Nevertheless, as a Buddhist, he disagrees that there is danger and claims the preliminary meditation on the "emptiness" of *asmi-māna* ("I am pride") is adequate protection before "identifying" with divinity:

> Because the empty status of the person is being realized, . . . deity yoga serves to counteract the conception of oneself as inherently existent and thereby prevents afflicted pride, a version of ego-inflation. . . .

He adds:

> Also, I have observed in Tibetan monastic communities how the community serves to exert pressure on persons who have become too grandly public in their virtues—through teasing, mild derision, mimicry, and so forth.[24]

That still does not address the danger of inflation for Westerners trying to be Buddhist.

The issue, however, is also complex. Jung follows Luther by saying, first there is Christ, the divine Son of God, and now there is the "Christification" of many. More than once, Jung cites John 10:34, "Ye are gods," as scriptural warrant that we share in divinity. What Jung has in mind, however, is the logic of individuation, the "mutual rapprochement" between consciousness and the collective unconscious: "God will be humanized, man will be 'divinized.'"[25] While this means the archetype of the Self and the ego increasingly approximate each other, it is far from identity. Instead, one learns thereby one's proper psychological size and weight (and it might be quite large) but in the presence of what is always the "Greater Personality."

What is "Really" Happening in Deity Yoga?

I ask this question because there appears to be an additional step missing from the *sādhana* we explored—although included in the commentaries. This step involves the distinction between a "symbolic being" (*samaya-sattva*) and a "knowledge being" (*jñāna-sattva*). We know it is important since Mkhas-grub-rje says: "one generates the self into a god, draws in the *jñāna* beings," etc. Alex Wayman writes that these notions are "among the most difficult and important ideas of the Buddhist Tantric literature." Indeed, after consulting other commentaries, Wayman arrives at the following significant conclusion:

> The above explanations indicate that the *samaya-sattva* is the yogin who has identified himself with a deity he has evoked or imagined, while the *jñāna-sattva* is either a human Bodhisattva or a celestial Bodhisattva or Buddha . . . Again, by

[23] Jeffrey Hopkins, "Jung's Warnings Against Inflation," *Chung-Hwa Buddhist Journal* 21 (2008), 171.

[24] Hopkins, "Jung's Warnings," 159, 172-173.

[25] Jung, *CW* 18, par. 1684.

> the term *jñāna-sattva* these contexts generally refer only to the celestial beings among the two kinds of *jñāna-sattva*.[26]

This means that the tantric meditator who has become identified with a god through the power of imagination is only a *samāya-sattva* or "symbol" of a deity.

He is at this point like a Buddha statue that has yet to have its "eyes" opened, yet to be infused with the numinous Presence of an actual Buddha. That actual Buddha or Bodhisattva is understood by Tantra to be a *jñāna-sattva* who, by definition, possesses divine "knowledge." The "symbolic being" functions, nevertheless, to attract this "knowledge being"—from some far-off Buddha-field to render the two of them increasingly "non-dual." As Jung might say, the ego and Self increasingly approximate each other.

This is quite different from saying, as Powers does, that the yogin conditions himself into becoming a Buddha, as if the "self-help" model were still intact—a kind of deliberate euhemerism whereby the "gods" are just human beings writ large. Snellgrove appears to agree with this other more difficult understanding:

> The high point of any such rite is the descent of the actual divinity (known as the "wisdom-being" or *jñānasattva*) into the symbol of the divinity (the "sacramental being" or *samayasattva*), which has been prepared for this mystical (or magical) conjunction.[27]

This interpretation does a greater justice, I think, to Buddhist Tantra as religion. It does justice to the "100-syllable mantra" wherein the yogin prays with much feeling: "Be close at hand as Vajrasattva! Be firm for me! Be well-pleased in me! . . . *hūṃ ha ha ha ha ho*! O Lord, Vajra of All the Tathāgatas, do not abandon me!"

Initiation

Tantric Guru

A *tāntrika* is not "permitted" to practice without being initiated, consecrated, or empowered—i.e, "sprinkled" (*abhiṣeka*) with Vajra-water. For that, one needs the services of a qualified tantric initiator who has himself been initiated by a special *vajra-ācārya* ("*vajra*-master") ceremony. The SSK describes the master's qualifications:

> What are his characteristics? His limbs are sound, and he is adorned with merit; he must fully comprehend matters mundane and supramundane; he always abides by the Dharma and does not do anything that is contrary to the Dharma; he is endowed with great compassion and takes pity on sentient beings. . . moreover,

[26] Lessing and Wayman, *Mkhas grub rje's "Fundamentals,"* 162.

[27] Snellgrove, *Indo-Tibetan Buddhism*, 1:131.

> his virtue has been extolled by his teacher with these words: "You may go now, having proven yourself fit to be conferred initiation and become an *ācārya*."[28]

His qualifications are said to be comparable to a Buddha. The initiator puts this strongly in his own words in the STTS as he addresses the candidate:

> "Henceforth you will look upon me as Vajrapāṇi. You must do as I say, and you must not treat me with contempt. Do not bring calamity upon yourself such that you die and then fall into hell!"[29]

Indeed, the very first of the "Fourteen Root Violations" is, "contradicting one's *guru*." In a sense, it means that the student will really be consecrated by "Vajrapāṇi." And it is to this Celestial Bodhisattva or some other divine being that one is actually pledging full obedience.

A Jungian response One can assume that on occasion the *guru* was not actually worthy. In fact, a commentary on the late *Kālacakra Tantra* (perhaps 11th century—hereafter, KCT) advises potential disciples to be wary of "corrupt" teachers. Vesna Wallace informs us:

> In contrast to the qualified tantric teacher, a corrupt spiritual mentor is said to be full of conceit, which is of many kinds: conceit in one's own learning, in one's own wealth, seeing others as beneath oneself, and so on. His absence of humility is seen as an indication of his lack of compassion. . . . Similarly, a *vajrācārya* who is greedy and attached to mundane pleasures, or who is an uneducated fool, ignorant of the true path and not initiated into the *tantra*, or who is fond of liquor or sex, is to be avoided, for he leads his disciples to hell.[30]

This ancient warning has not always been heeded in modern times. The case of Chögyam Trungpa—who was "fond of liquor and sex"—is striking in this regard. A Tibetan Buddhist in exile and founder of a meditation center at Boulder, Colorado, Trungpa taught what he called the "crazy wisdom" of Vajrayāna—while having promiscuous sex with adoring disciples and drinking heavily, eventually dying at age forty-eight with cirrhosis of the liver. He was seldom criticized for this behavior, and even today is revered by Buddhists for the "mystery" of his life style.[31]

Jung might be surprised by this account since he was convinced that Westerners would not be so "obedient." He wrote: "Who among us would place such implicit trust in a superior Master and his incomprehensible ways? This respect for the greater human personality is found only in the

---

28 Giebel, SSK, 135.

29 Giebel, STTS, 76.

30 Vesna A. Wallace, *The Inner Kālacakratantra: A Buddhist Tantric View of the Individual* (Oxford: Oxford University Press, 2001), 8.

31 See Fabrice Midal, ed., *Recalling Chögyam Trungpa* (Boston: Shambhala Publications, 2005).

East."[32] But he was not thinking of gullible Americans. Nor was he considering, for the moment, the dynamic of psychological transference.

In analysis, the analysand almost always projects onto the analyst his or her own unconscious—that eventually needs to be acknowledged and integrated. This particular form of projection is called "transference," since what needs to be discovered for one's healing has been temporarily transferred to someone who—fortunately—understands the dynamic and can assist in self-discovery.

When archetypal contents are transferred, there is even the equivalent of a "god" in the room. In Tantra, the *guru* encourages that kind of projection—"look upon me as Vajrapāṇi." In a modern analysis, it is not encouraged but simply happens—and, if all goes well, acts as bridge to the suffering person's realization that true healing comes from the transpersonal dimension of the psyche. Of course, the analyst might be "corrupt" in any number of ways. That is a very good reason for both parties to pay close attention to dreams that reveal what is really going on in the analytic relationship. The actual "gods" tend to be jealous and will not long tolerate substitutes.

Preparatory Rite

The "master's initiation" often appears as the seventh in a list of initiations but is considered "uncommon" or special. The other six are "common" and required of all practitioners of Tantra. But the first one of these six is "preparatory"—which leaves five standard consecrating ceremonies that are happily correlated with the Five Buddhas of the Five Families of all the gods. The preparatory consecration is called the "Flower Garland" initiation. It is named for the ritual drama of determining the particular deity—among the vast Buddhist pantheon—who will be the candidate's primary guide along the Path. It is performed blindfolded before a *maṇḍala* depicting the deities—upon which the candidate tosses a flower. Where it lands determines one's *iṣṭa-devatā*—literally, one's "wished for divinity" but usually translated, "chosen deity." Much subsequent deity yoga will be directed toward this particular god or goddess.

Let us be clear, however, that the candidate does not "choose" this guiding god but that it is chosen for him or her by an act of divination (like the casting of lots or consulting the *I-Ching*). The practice would have been frowned upon by Early Buddhists who taught that geomancy, astrology, and palmistry were "debased" and to be avoided by the laity—not to mention by monks and nuns (*SN* 3.28). Yet today, one can request one's astrological "chart" from a Tibetan Buddhist adept.

After determining what we might better call the tutelary ("guardian") deity, the master puts the tossed flower into the candidate's hair. And, as Mkhas-grub-rje tells us: "The guru makes the disciple understand that by relying in the direction of the deity on whom the thrown flower falls, he will reach Complete Enlightenment in the Family of that Tathāgata."[33]

Initiations Proper

The candidate is now prepared for the main ceremony:

---

[32] Jung, *CW* 11, par. 902.

[33] Lessing and Wayman, *Mkhas grub rje's "Fundamentals,"* 315.

1) The first initiation is called the "water (*jala*) consecration"—for which, technically, all the initiations (as a kind of "sprinkling") are named. A jar of mantrified water is solemnly raised by the *guru* who pours some of its contents on the head or hands of the disciple. Specific *mantras* and *mūdrās* accompany the ritual. Although symbolic action, it is effective; Mkhas-grub-rje says it "is able to wash off the defilement" that obstructs Enlightenment.

But it does not just cleanse; it empowers with a foretaste of Nirvāṇa as the "deathless" (*amṛta*). There are references in the *tantras* to "drinking" this water, so as to imbibe the Wisdom symbolically contained in the jar. Indeed, Mkhas-grub-rje refers to it as "*vajra-āmṛta*"—translated by some as "diamond ambrosia" since ambrosia was the "food of immortality" of our own Greek gods.[34] Others translate this *āmṛta* as "nectar" since that was specifically the Olympians' "drink" of immortality.

2) Then comes the "diadem (*mukuṭa*) consecration" whereby a small crown or band of cloth is placed upon the candidate's head. Thus, he begins to look like a Buddhist deity who—in Mahāyāna iconography—is not shown as a shaved monk but as a "Universal Monarch" with a jeweled crown on a full head of hair, and otherwise royally adorned. After all, the goal is to become not only an "inconceivable" Dharmakāya—lacking "conceivable" attributes—but also a grand Saṃbhogakāya with "attributes," sitting within a celestial palace and surrounded by a princely retinue of Celestial Bodhisattvas. We have heard that the tantric Path is the Result Path, and this ceremony is making the "Result" present "here and now"—in a symbolic way.

It so happens that these same acts of sprinkling and crowning were performed by the kings of the day during their own inaugural "consecrations"—evidence, therefore, of social influence or even compromise. Mkhas-grub-rje comments, however, that the "crown" really points to whatever Buddhist meaning had accrued to the "invisible *uṣṇīṣa*" or bump on the head of the Lord as one of his Thirty-Two Marks. That cranial protuberance, as we already saw, burst into flames (iconographically) in Thai Buddhist art as a visible expression of Enlightenment. In some Mahāyāna scriptures, it could send out light rays—just like the *ūrṇā* or tuft of hair at the middle of a Buddha's forehead—to illuminate the universe and thereby bless it.

3) The third initiation is called the "*vajra* consecration" whereby the *vajra* ritual device is placed in the right hand of the purified and crowned candidate. This rite, too, may have been influenced by Indian royal scepter symbolism. But Mkhas-grub-rje assures us that holding the *vajra* instills the "capacity for accomplishing the non-discursive knowledge" of a Buddha. The *Vajrapāṇy-abhiṣeka-mahātantra* provides more detail:

> Now, O possessor of the vajra, this Dharma of vajra has been explained for you, and the vajra arisen from meditation has been actually placed in your hand by all the Buddhas. So, from today, all the magical ability of Vajrapāṇi in the world is just yours. It is yours to tame those insufferable beings harming the Dharma and

[34] Lessing and Wayman, *Mkhas grub rje's "Fundamentals,"* 289.

> to kill those afflicted with anger—that is why the guides of the world have given you the vajra.[35]

Here, the candidate is granted explicit permission to use "compassionate violence."

4) Then the "bell consecration" puts a ritual bell in the left hand of the candidate. Its ring "accomplishes the speech" that will allow the proper sounds to "teach the Dharma." It also completes the symbolic achievement of "nonduality"—since the candidate is holding both *vajra* and bell, in right and left hands, grasping the masculine and feminine pair that stands for all the other pairs, symbolically expressing both Means and Wisdom.

5) Climactically, the "name initiation" is the standard Buddhist prophecy to Enlightenment pronounced by the *ācārya* (that is, by "Vajrapāṇi" or some other Bodhisattva or Buddha he is imagined to be): "You will be a Tathāgata of such a [*vajra-*] name when becoming a Buddha in that Family." Here are a master's concluding remarks to a group of initiates:

> The Buddha, together with Vajradhara,
> Indeed, all the Buddhas have consecrated you.
> So you will be, from this day forward,
> Great Kings of the triple world,
> Lords among the Victors.
> From this day on, you are victorious over Māra.
> You have entered the most excellent city;
> And you will, from this day on,
> Obtain Buddhahood, of that there is no doubt.[36]

All of these actions had been secret but are now on gracious display for the candidate who requested permission to practice Tantra and who met the requirements—and he is deeply moved. For he has been "chosen" by a god and not only allowed to practice but also empowered to become a Buddha. There is, of course, some ambiguity. On the one hand, the initiate is already "victorious over Māra;" on the other hand, he "will" someday obtain Buddhahood. It is the function of ritual, however, to achieve symbolically in the present what will be achieved in actuality in the future. That explains why a disciple is advised to be consecrated often, by a *guru* in the flesh or in imagination.[37]

A Jungian thought Although specifically Buddhist and tantric, this set of initiations belongs to a pattern in the history of religions. The Greco-Roman "Mysteries," for example, were forms of antique religion distinct from the public cult. Esoteric, requiring initiation, they demanded secrecy so well kept that even today we are not sure what happened in them. We do know that the rites of Demeter at Eleusis, of Dionysus throughout the Mediterranean, Mithras among the Roman soldiers, etc. conferred a saving knowledge. We know, too, that these initiations conferred immortality,

---

[35] Davidson, *Indian Esoteric Buddhism*, 126.

[36] Davidson, *Indian Esoteric Buddhism*, 113.

[37] Davidson, *Indian Esoteric Buddhism*, 127.

resolving the ancient world's increasing anxiety about fate and death by promising an Afterlife. In anticipation, the initiates were identified with an immortal deity.

Kurt Rudolph writes of Apuleius's initiation into the cult of the goddess Isis (from what little is revealed in that Roman lawyer's novel, *The Golden Ass*):[38]

> the actual mysteries began with preliminary rites such as baptism (sprinkling), a ten-day fast, and being clothed in a linen robe . . . and a vesting of the initiate as the sun god (*instar solis*); the initiate was *renatus* ("reborn") and became *sol* ("the sun"), or in other words experienced a deification (*theomorphosis*).[39]

While the *tāntrika* is also deified, Apuleius becomes "divine" for the immediate purpose of properly worshipping Isis as the Mother of the cosmos.

It might be worth mentioning, then, that Indian religion contains a principle occasionally invoked, as Heinrich Zimmer translates: "No one who is not himself divine may successfully worship the divinity" (*nādevo devam arcayet*).[40] That might even protect one against inflation since no longer merely human, presuming to address the Divine.

While traditional rites no longer touch many of us, they are necessary lest we lose any sense of our place in the "divine drama of life"—as Jung puts it. He writes:

> Life is too rational, there is no symbolic existence in which I am something else, in which I am fulfilling my role, my role as one of the actors in the divine drama of life. . . . That gives the only meaning to human life; everything else is banal and you can dismiss it. A career, producing of children, are all *maya* compared with that one thing, that your life is meaningful.[41]

Fortunately, a modern version of sacred "empowerment" is available. Jung expresses it somewhat emotionally:

> But one thing I will tell you: the exploration of the unconscious has in fact and in truth discovered the age-old, timeless *way of initiation* [Jung's italics]. . . . Now it is not merely my "credo" but the greatest and most incisive experience of my life that this door, a highly inconspicuous side-door on an un-suspicious-looking and easily overlooked footpath—narrow and indistinct because only a few have set foot on it—leads to the secret of transformation and renewal.[42]

---

38 Apuleius, *The Golden Ass*, trans. Jack Lindsay (Bloomington: Indiana University Press, 1960), 251. See Marie-Louise von Franz, *A Psychological Interpretation of "The Golden Ass" of Apuleius* (Irving: Spring Publications, revised 1980).

39 Kurt Rudolph, "Mystery Religions," *ER* 10: 235-236.

40 Zimmer, *Philosophies*, 581. No citation is given other than *Gandharva Tantra*—yet more of a hint than given by other writers who refer to this religious principle.

41 Jung, *CW* 18, pars. 628, 630.

42 Jung, *Letters* 1:141.

Here is the same attitude, the same language even, that we have witnessed among the ancient initiates, East and West.

Maṇḍala

Initiation in Buddhist Tantra cannot take place without a *maṇḍala*. The basic meaning of this Sanskrit word is "circle," a geometrical form with a center and circumference. It can also mean a disk like the full moon, a wheel (*cakra* is another word for "wheel"), or even a sphere like a ball. *Maṇḍala* appears in Sanskrit political writing as the sphere of a monarch's influence. By extension, the word indicates anything "complete" like a complete section of scripture, the entirety of a group, even the universe—hence, offering a Buddha or one's *guru* a *maṇḍala* is to offer "everything." But a *maṇḍala* can also be a square, perhaps because that is a geometrical figure with a defined center—with four sides equidistant from it. Thus, a square palace with a courtyard is a *maṇḍala*.

As one might expect, any combination of these geometrical forms can carry the same label—thus, a square within a circle or a circle within a square is a *maṇḍala*. We saw that combination in Early Buddhist cosmology with the round earth centered by Mount Meru with its square base, four continents in each of the cardinal directions. The combination of circle and square shows up in the *stūpa* with its round dome and usually round base, surrounded by a square sacred space marked by four gateways. Any celestial Buddha-field or Pure Land implies a *maṇḍala* since its Lord resides in a square palace encircled by worshipping Bodhisattvas. Even the saṃsāric "Wheel of Existence" (*bhava-cakra*) is a *maṇḍala* "circle." And so is every open "Lotus" blossom, as seen from above, and upon which all Buddhas serenely sit at its center.

In tantric Buddhism, the *maṇḍala* is the sacred space "inside" which initiations take place—depicted or imagined. There is reason to believe that, originally, the tantric *maṇḍala* was complete as a circle surrounded by a square.[43] With time, however, this combination was itself encircled: thus, the classic design is a circle, surrounded by a square, surrounded by a larger circle. We may observe different *maṇḍalas*, moreover, with additional concentric squares and concentric circles, as well as circles elsewhere.

Most *tantras* give instructions for diagramming a basic *maṇḍala* on the ground using colored powders finely crushed from natural rock or even gems. The MMK says it might be as large as twenty-four feet across and take either a night or several days to complete.[44] The modern Tibetan Buddhist version of this powdered *maṇḍala* is about five feet across and made of sand, created from white rock that has been crushed and dyed with brilliant hues.

The current Dalai Lama has allowed it to be crafted in public on a floor or a table by monks in the presence of Western onlookers. In that context, the tantric *maṇḍala* has nothing to do with initiation and is no longer esoteric or secret—but intended to promote a general awareness of the Tibetan political and religious plight. This religious leader may be relying upon a distinction made

[43] Christian Luczanits, "On the Earliest Mandalas in a Buddhist Context," in *Mahayana Buddhism: History and Culture,* eds. Darrol Bryant and Susan Bryant (New Delhi: Tibet House, 2008), 118-119.

[44] Wallis, MMK, 132-134.

long ago by Tsoṅ-kha-pa: that the "fault" in revealing secrets is "in what is revealed to the ear, not in what is revealed to the eye."[45]

It remains true, however, that all powdered forms are temporary. So there are rituals of dispersal, no matter how carefully constructed or beautiful the design—as a Buddhist lesson in "impermanence."

Painted *maṇḍalas* are more permanent but smaller—and, also, portable and more capable of being kept secret. Scriptures call for special brushes and specially woven cloth upon which the image of consecratory space is depicted. The finished scroll could be rolled and unrolled, laid on the ground or hung on a wall, and was called a *paṭa* in Sanskrit (literally, "cloth;" the Tibetan *thaṅ ka*). Painting, of course, allowed for greater detail than did powder; and, as we know from Tibetan "t'ankas" in museums, allowed for the display of an artist's skill. Let us note that a *maṇḍala* image was sometimes painted on monastery walls, and that would have allowed a degree of permanent, and somewhat public, display.

So far, we have been describing what Mkhas-grub-rje calls the "*maṇḍala* of residence," the sacred arena. It is merely preparation, however, for the "*maṇḍala* of residents," i.e., images of the Buddhist deities who will be asked to be Present at the consecration to receive the tossed flower, to hold the flask, and prophesy the new name.[46] If, as seems likely, the powdered *maṇḍala* could not allow precision of anthropomorphic divine forms—as prescribed by the *sādhanas*—it was always permissible to use statues of the gods or to symbolize their presence by the location of their "seats" alone (drawn as lotuses), or by their "hand symbols" (a lotus flower, a sword, etc.), or just their "seed syllables"—the essential sounds from which they evolved in meditations.

Still, the VAT instructs for its *maṇḍala* of powdered colors complex forms such as this:

> To the south of the Lord Vairocana,
> Vajradhara [i.e., Vajrapāṇi] should be drawn;
> he fulfills all wishes,
> and in color he is like a *priyaṅgu* flower,
> greenish-yellow, or like an emerald.
> This Lord has a crown and is adorned
> with all the ornaments of a Great Being;
> he holds a vast *vajra* which penetrates all places,
> and he is encircled with rays of light.[47]

That would have been very difficult to reproduce. The result, nevertheless, would be a genuine icon, a "sacred image."

---

[45] Wayman, *Buddhist Tantras*, 67.

[46] Lessing and Wayman, *Mkhas grub rje's "Fundamentals,"* 291.

[47] Hodge, VAT, 111.

Figure 15.1 Nine-Deity Maṇḍala of Amitābha

The Nine-Deity Maṇḍala of Amitābha

To get our bearings, let us "read" a fairly simple *maṇḍala* art historically (see Figure 15.1). This is a nineteenth-century Tibetan rendering of a *maṇḍala* described in an ancient Sanskrit text; all original Indian renderings, however, are now lost. It is a painting on cloth that has been glued to wood and is just a foot square—intended, we are told, to be put on top of a table for appropriate ceremonies.[48] The square of the frame accentuates visually the powerful square form at the center—that, we have noted, may have been the earliest outer shape of a tantric *maṇḍala*. But square-ness is balanced by the large outer circle that touches the frame and by the innermost concentric circles. And while the flaming auras surrounding the several figures here are not quite round, they emphasize what is round. The over-all effect is one of harmony between square and circle.

Visually, the icon is flat; it makes little attempt at three-dimensional perspective. Nor is anything "moving." The centeredness, the square's orientation in the four directions, and the precise symmetry wherever one looks keeps the image visually calm and stable. Even the four triangles within the square—usually considered dynamic—point inward toward the center and hold the eye there.

The colors, however, do excite. They even clash a bit—but that may be a Tibetan aesthetic preference along with the delicate swirling floral forms filling all the spaces in what seems to be *horror vacui*. There are not many hues: the standard five of red, yellow, green, black (or dark blue), and white are on display here. As with many categories in Tantra, they are correlated with the "Five Buddhas" that represent all the Buddhas in the universe.

There is also the visual excitement of so many details forcing us to ask, "What are we seeing?" The *tantras* tell us that we are looking down, from a birds-eye view, on a square palace—its four walls enclosing a large courtyard. Each wall is pierced by a doorway in the cardinal directions indicated by the "T" shape. That shape should remind us of the monumental gateways at the Sāñcī *stūpa* with their heavy architraves extending beyond the uprights. In addition, there sits over each lintel the traditional form of a Wheel of Dharma flanked by deer, reminding us that what we are exploring here began at Deer Park where Śākyamuni taught his first sermon.

And there he is in the upper left corner near the frame, a saffron robed monk with his begging bowl sitting in meditation in *bhūmi-sparśa-mudrā*—albeit surrounded by an orange flame and backed by stylized white clouds. Gautama, however, is outside the sacred space of the *maṇḍala* and not featured here, any more than he is featured in Indian Mahāyāna tantric Buddhism as a whole. He is, as we know, just an emanation of Vairocana.

Let us note that the walls of the palace are symbolically "rising," as indicated by concentric squares of different colors that reach a "roof line" with decorative banners and jars full of gems. But this is all laid flat. It is why writers sometimes refer to the *maṇḍala* as a "blueprint," although one could hardly build from these visual clues. Instead, the palace is primarily an abstract design.

That fact is apparent from the large curved form over each "doorway" that comes to a point: these are the protruding prongs of an enormous "crossed *vajra*" (*viśva-vajra*) lying invisibly underneath

---

[48] Art history by Jeff Watt, Himalayan Art Resources. https://www.himalayanart.org.

the palace. That gives it a "firm" foundation like a Diamond. Yet under that is an even larger open Lotus whose stylized colored petals surround the palace and its adamantine base. Since a lotus sits beneath all the Buddha images we examined, we know this image is something of an architectonic Buddha (as is the early *stūpa*).

All this deserves to be protected from the profane. Thus, a thin black ring—upon which appear at intervals tiny gold *vajras*—surrounds those lotus petals. That increases the "firmness" of the image but also, like a "wrathful" Vajrapāṇi, dispels any attempts by demonic forces to obstruct the initiations performed within. Completing what amounts to a tripartite circumference—added over time but standard, at least, in Tibet—is a wide band of multi-colored flames. Buddhists often say they represent the "fiery light" of Wisdom. More likely, this ring of fire is added "protection," establishing the boundary or threshold so that nothing inappropriate gets into the sacred interior—and nothing appropriate gets outside.

And now for the divine "residents." The main and largest figure appears at the center of the palace courtyard. In this case, it is Amitābha Buddha whose skin is iconographically red—to distinguish him from Akṣobhya Buddha who is blue, Ratnasaṃbhava who is yellow, etc. With his legs crossed in "full-lotus" posture, the Lord's hands are in *dhyāna mudrā*. They also hold a vase containing *amṛta* ("deathless"), the elixir of immortality—Nirvāṇa in "liquid" form.

That fluid is not only at the ready for a Water consecration but also signals this Buddha's other name. Yes, he is Amitābha ("immeasurable light") with stylized "light rays" emanating from his body, a solar halo behind his head, and an aurole of radiance surrounding the entire figure. But he is also called Amitāyus ("immeasurable lifespan"), the Immortal One. Dressed in royal silks, a high "Cakravartin" crown upon his head, this eternal Buddha is seated upon a circle of stylized lotus petals and surrounded by his own colorful concentric circles. He is, indeed, Lord of the *maṇḍala*.

Amitābha reappears identically eight more times inside a larger concentric circle touching the courtyard's sides (mimicking the outer circle touching the frame). There are four in each of the cardinal directions (named for four Families—""Ratna" Amitābha. etc.) and four more in the intermediate directions (named for this Lord's attributes—"Jñāna" Amitābha, etc.). It is not standard, however, for the central Buddha of a *maṇḍala* to multiply in this way. Instead, we would expect one of the "Five Buddhas" at the center with the other four arranged around him, along with Bodhisattvas at the intermediate points. But the arrangement we see does suggest visually what is merely implied in the texts—that the central deity is "emanating" himself or herself as all the other divine beings within the palace, regardless of their names.

Referring to Indian *maṇḍalas* in general, David White states:

> The practice of the maṇḍala generally involves . . . an implosion of the entire grid into its center point. Here, the underlying assumption is that this implosion is a reversal of the original cosmogony—that is, of a primal impulse or flow (*saṃsāra*) into manifest existence—back into the source of energies mapped on the grid.[49]

---

[49] David Gordon White, *Tantra in Practice* (Princeton: Princeton University Press, 2000), 11.

This is an understanding better suited to Hindu metaphysics than to Buddhism that prefers to claim a "beginningless" universe with no First Cause. Yet we are actually observing a kind of "cosmogony" here in a Buddhist *maṇḍala*.

We see that tantric Buddhists have discovered with the *maṇḍala* yet another way to "organize" the plethora of deities, how to rank them hierarchically, and to do so in a visually attractive way. For the record, that is Maitreya near the upper right corner of the frame. In the lower right corner, one of the Four Great Kings guarding the world sits contemplatively. And in the lower left corner another red Amitābha appears—but as a Bodhisattva and not yet a Buddha. We see he has kept his "Bodhisattva Vow" by becoming in manifold form an Incomparably Complete and Perfect Buddha.

Figure 15.2 Vajradhātu Maṇḍala

The Maṇḍala of Vajradhātu

Let us look briefly at one of those more elaborate *maṇḍalas* to which Snellgrove refers (see Figure 15.2). This is called the "Vajradhātu ('Diamond Realm') Maṇḍala," as found, for example, in the STTS. This version is Central Tibetan, painted on cloth about a yard square and from the 14th century. We see all the basic elements of a *maṇḍala* but in a much more complex fashion. Indeed, it is nearly overwhelming with so much detail and so much color—it is also very beautiful.

Although difficult to see here, that is a white Vairocana at the center in his four-faced (Omniscient) eight-armed (Omnipotent) manifestation. His circle "expands" into eight other circles: containing the four "directional" Buddhas, and then four goddesses in the intermediate directions making offerings to the Lord of this *maṇḍala*. They are all embraced by a larger circle. At the corners of the palace are four more offering goddesses in their own circles.

And what are the tiny figures filling in the four sides of the courtyard? One thousand Celestial Bodhisattvas, 250 per wall, in four different colors—all in rapt *samādhi* listening to the word of the Lord. Indeed, wherever we look—inside or outside the great circumference of protective flames—there are more circles, more deities, more of the same attentive awareness of a Center.[50]

The "maṇḍala" in Jungian psychology We know from the second chapter of this book that Jung borrowed two Sanskrit terms from Indian religion. One is the translation of *ātman* as "Self," signifying in the Upaniṣads the identity of the divine and the essence of the human being. The other term, left untranslated, is *maṇḍala*, whose basic meaning is "circle" in both Hinduism and Buddhism. For Jung, both terms point to the same thing: the one a verbal symbol, the other a visual symbol, for the psyche as a whole centered by a "divine" archetype called the Self.

This central, "controlling," archetype is expressed in the world's religions in different ways: a) anthropomorphically, as a personal God (Puruṣa, Buddha, Christ, etc.); b) organically, such as a natural Tree (the Tree of Life or the Bodhi Tree); c) inorganically, such as a special Stone (Rock of Ages, Diamond), etc. But Jung was particularly attracted to the impersonal imagery of d) the Circle and the Square—and their combination in the *maṇḍala*—since each is whole and centered. As geometrical figures, they hint at principles or "laws" of the psyche that—like the law of gravity—are true no matter what we believe and with which we had best cooperate to live well or even to live at all.

As early as 1929, Jung wrote the following about "psychic development":

> Historically, this process has always been represented in symbols, and today the development of personality is still depicted in symbolic form. . . . When the fantasies take the form chiefly of thoughts, intuitive formulations of dimly felt laws or principles emerge, which at first tend to be dramatized or personified. . . . If the fantasies are drawn, symbols appear that are chiefly of the *mandala* type. *Mandala* means "circle," more especially a magic circle. Mandalas are found not only throughout the East but also among us. The early Middle Ages are especially rich in Christian mandalas: most of them show Christ in the center, with the four

[50] Art history from The Metropolitan Museum of Art. https://www.metmuseum.org/art/collection/search/42605.

> evangelists, or their symbols, at the cardinal points. This conception must be a very ancient one, because Horus and his four sons were represented in the same way by the Egyptians. . . . Most mandalas take the form of a flower, cross, or wheel, and show a distinct tendency towards a quaternary structure reminiscent of the Pythagorean *tetraktys*, the basic number. Mandalas of this sort also occur as sand paintings in the religious ceremonies of the Pueblo and Navaho Indians. But the most beautiful mandalas are, of course, those of the East, especially the ones found in Tibetan Buddhism. . . . [51]

Despite these "collective" cultural occurrences, Jung was much more interested in the *maṇḍalas* of individuals as found in their dreams and fantasies. He admits that in comparison they are "poor in form, poor in ideas"—yet they express the "individual attitude of the patient far more clearly than the Eastern pictures, which have been subjected to a collective and traditional configuration."[52]

Thus, in the late essay, "Concerning Mandala Symbolism," Jung includes pictures of fifty-four *maṇḍalas*—but only nine come from collective culture (and only two of those are Buddhist).[53] Of the remaining forty-five individual *maṇḍalas*, four were actually painted by Jung himself (without attribution)—including an abstract rendering of his moving "Liverpool" dream that we discussed at the beginning of this book. We know that Jung's archetypal dream of a city "square" with a "circular" pool of life at its "center" brought him relief from his depression—and taught him personally the function of this kind of symbolism. He wrote similarly of his patients' experience:

> Without going into therapeutic details, I would only like to say that a rearranging of the personality is involved, a kind of new centering. . . . Patients themselves often emphasize the beneficial or soothing effect of such pictures.[54]

As we quoted much earlier concerning variations on the *maṇḍala*:

> Their basic motif is the premonition of a center of personality, a kind of central point within the psyche, to which everything is related, by which everything is arranged and which is itself a source of energy. The energy of the central point is manifested in the almost irresistible compulsion and urge to *become what one is* [Jung's italics] . . . . This center is not felt or thought of as the ego but if one may so express it, as the *self.* Although the center is represented by an innermost point, it is surrounded by a periphery containing everything that belongs to the self—the paired opposites that make up the total personality.[55]

---

[51] Jung, *CW* 13, par. 31.

[52] Jung, *CW* 9i, par. 647.

[53] Jung, "Concerning Mandala Symbolism," CW 9i, pars. 627-712.

[54] Jung, *CW* 9i, par. 645.

[55] Jung, "Concerning Mandala Symbolism," in *CW* 9i, par. 634. His italics.

Buddhists themselves do not say these things, but their imagery does. The VAT has put it strikingly: "What is Enlightenment? It is to know your mind as it really is."[56] And there it is in the *maṇḍalas* of "Amitābha" and "Vajradhātu." The pictures show us that the mind is divine at its core, that there is a "God" present there—radiating outwardly in an orderly way to reveal or manifest as other "gods," all attending to that center. This depicts, first of all, the orderly nature of the collective unconscious—and if one feels disordered, if life has become chaotic, the imagery reveals that is not the case at one's deepest reaches. It can be very helpful to know that, to feel it as a psychological fact.

Jung adds that it can also be very helpful to "see" that—just as the many features of a *maṇḍala* belong to the image as a whole, from its center to its periphery—so does everything within one's own psychology "belong," all the myriad details and the many colors of one's life. True, the Self may be "rearranging" those details, accounting for some of the chaos being experienced. But it is for the sake of creating an engaging, beautiful "picture"—one that includes all that we actually are.

But where are we actually in these Buddhist *maṇḍalas*? Tantra emphasizes "divinity" so much—the initiator and initiates themselves "generated" as gods—that we are hard put to find any "human being" here, any sign of the carrier of consciousness. I believe it is the "square"—an image of wholeness just as visually strong as the "circle" in these religious paintings. It is possible, as we have already suggested, to take circle and square as alternative images of centered totality. But it is also possible to say that the "circle" (as a geometrical figure of original unconsciousness) becomes—over the long course of psychological development—the "square" (as a figure of actualized consciousness).

That explains Jung's interest in the pseudo-problem of "squaring the circle" in alchemy. It is not something one can do mathematically but something one can try to do psychologically—namely, to become, in the language of tantric Buddhism, an adequate "residence" for the divine "residents" of the soul.

Jung expresses this passionately in a letter:

> God wants to be born in the flame of man's consciousness, leaping ever higher. And what if this has no roots in the earth? If it is not a house of stone where the fire of God can dwell, but a wretched straw hut that flares up and vanishes? . . . Let us therefore be for him limitation in time and space, an earthly tabernacle.[57]

In this way, we arrive at the art historical necessity of a rather elaborate "palace" within a *maṇḍala* full of "gods."

We also begin to understand why "circle" and "square" must share the same Center, why they are drawn in perfect harmony. For the goal of psychological development is, on the one hand, to bring increasingly into consciousness what lies in the unconscious and, on the other hand, to "harmonize" the relationship of consciousness with what will remain forever unconscious as the psyche's archetypal foundation. That may even explain the eventual art historical appearance of the

---

[56] Hodge, VAT, 56.

[57] Jung, *Letters* 1:65-66.

larger outer circle—first the "circle" of the unconscious; then the "square" of consciousness; and finally the "outer circle" that holds them together, symbolizing their harmony.

Visually, that means that the human and the divine are found within the same "sacred space" defined by that outer circle. Perhaps it is a way of expressing the logic of individuation: "God will be humanized, man will be 'divinized.'" In any case, the "golden *vajras*" at the periphery encourage us to hold "firm" and be well-defined as individuals. The outermost "flames" encourage us to protect ourselves—allowing into our "sacred precinct" only what genuinely belongs, and holding within all that is precious—i.e., all that we uniquely are.

Little wonder, then, that Jung would say in *Memories, Dreams, Reflections*: "I knew that in finding the mandala as an expression of the self, I had attained what was for me the ultimate. Perhaps someone else knows more, but not I."[58]

Maṇḍala Ritual

Nāgabodhi, an eighth-century *mahā-siddha* ("great achiever"), lists twenty-one steps in the standard *maṇḍala* ritual. They begin with "clearing the site" and "seizing the site" and go on to a preparatory "pitching the lines with chalk," "beseeching the gods," "preparation of the disciple," then "putting in the colors" and "inviting the gods." He lists the various initiations we have already discussed—and the concluding acts such as "conferral of permission" and "dismissal of deities, along with a burnt offering."[59]

The VAT fleshes out the steps, as we read:

> When he knows the trainee is firm, the Master should search out a good site. Pure and pleasing places with water, having fruit and flowers, these are praised by all Buddhas for the task of drawing the Mandala. . . .Then in order to purify the site, he should clear away stones, broken pottery, pebbles. . . . Such a place from which all impediments have been removed is pleasing to the deities.[60]

Buddhaguyha notes that permission had been granted seven days earlier by the local authorities. They include not only the king but also the local gods who would otherwise be "harmed by the radiant glare of the wrathful deities of the Mandala."[61]

Additional protections are named. The "calendar, constellations, planets, hours and minutes" must all be auspicious as the Master calls upon the "Earth Goddess, Pṛthivī":

> O Goddess! You are a witness
> to the Levels and Perfections,
> the special methods of practice

---

[58] Jung, *Memories*, 197.

[59] Alex Wayman, "The Ritual in Tantric Buddhism of the Disciple's Entrance into the Mandala," *Studia Missionalia* 33 (1984): 41-42.

[60] Hodge, VAT, 87-88. Slightly altered.

[61] Hodge, VAT, 92.

> of all the Protector Buddhas.
> Just as the Protector Śākyasiṃha ["Lion of the Śākyas"]
> Overcame the armies of Māra,
> Likewise I shall be victorious over Māra
> And draw a mandala here!
> Then touching the ground with his hand,
> He should call on her many times . . . . [62]

This is an extraordinary gesture. The *ācārya* is performing the *bhūmi-sparśa-mudrā* ("touching the earth gesture")—assimilating himself to "Act 9" in the Life of the Buddha and, at the same time, assimilating into Tantra earliest Buddhist tradition.

Premonitory Dreams

The value of auspicious premonitory dreams had long been part of Buddhism, as illustrated by the Life. But Serinity Young informed us that in Early Buddhism "only unenlightened people dream"—since dreams were just another example of the "illusions" we all take to be real while we are asleep, physically and spiritually.[63] That view has been changing over time, apparently, as we see here in Buddhist Tantra. For the Master of the rite is instructed to go to sleep on the west side of the site:

> Then the *mantrin* will see a dream, either of renowned Bodhisattvas, or of Buddhas and the Blessed Ones, who exhort him to undertake the task of drawing the Mandala in order to benefit beings. . . .[64]

Even Vairocana, who is teaching this in the VAT, instructs the initiator to say to his candidates for initiation:

> "Therefore tomorrow you will be born into the Mahayāna!" If in dreams they see temples, fine groves. . . beautiful women dressed in white . . . then such dreams as these are divined to be auspicious. The wise one should know that dreams opposite to these are bad. "O you fine trainees! In the morning, you should recount all to me!"[65]

Thus, strict obedience toward the *guru* includes paying attention to one's dreams.

---

[62] Hodge, VAT, 88-89.
[63] Young, *Dreaming*, 30.
[64] Hodge, VAT, 93. Slightly altered.
[65] Hodge, VAT, 96-97. Slightly altered.

Drawing the Maṇḍala.

Before actually drawing the *maṇḍala*, the Master imagines a *maṇḍala* "in the sky." The Lord teaches:

> Then the *mantrin* should arise, and in the middle, imagine myself upon a white lotus throne, with topknot and crown, spreading out in all directions light rays of various colors. Then the wise one should imagine the four perfect Buddhas in their places . . . . and entering into *samādhi* he should reverently utter these words: "Pay heed to me, all you Lords who have compassionate natures! Please take possession of this site with your sons [Bodhisattvas], after noon tomorrow!"[66]

Buddhaguhya comments that the teacher is "imagining the deities of the intrinsically existent Mandala [*svabhāva-maṇḍala*] who have been gathered together. . . . [He] imagines the Five Buddhas in the sky." This is an important comment because it is making a threefold distinction: an "intrinsic" or self-existent *maṇḍala* not yet present, an imagined *maṇḍala* in the sky, and one yet to be drawn on the ground. The drawing begins:

> The Master should make prostrations to all the Buddhas [in the air] and then taking a thread of five different colors, he should transform himself [by deity yoga] into the Bhagavat Vairocana. To make out a line to the east, the cord should be held in the air, level with the navel [etc., through each of the four directions]. . . . In that way the *mantrin* should make a complete square [i.e., the outline of the palace].[67]

As we see here, the *ācārya* is identified with "Vairocana" himself—thus, the Lord is constructing his own "residence." Although the "cord" is held high, we know that cords were made "wet" with powder and with the aid of an assistant snapped on the ground to determine the main lines of the *maṇḍala* image.[68]

More instructions follow. For example:

> In the four directions, the wise one should make portals in each portion with care and restraint, as the places of the Lords of the deities. When he has finished all this careful division into sections, he should draw an excellent white lotus in the center. . . . it should be sixteen inches or more. It is complete with eight petals, and has very beautiful stamens. In between all the petals, he should draw *vajras*.

And when the "residence" is completed, the "residents" are drawn:

---

[66] Hodge, VAT, 90-92.

[67] Hodge, VAT, 102. Slightly altered.

[68] Lessing and Wayman, *Mkhas grub rje's "Fundamentals,"* 285.

> In the center of the matrix, he should draw the most excellent Lord of the Jinas, golden in color, blazing in light, with his topknot and crown. He is completely surrounded by pure light. The Lord free from all ills should be depicted residing in *samādhi*.

The text goes on, with instructions for several other deities, Locanā as "Mother of all the Protectors" to the north, Avalokiteśvara to the north and right of Vairocana, etc.

What is "Really" Happening?

I asked this question earlier as a way to explore the "symbolic" and the "actual" in Deity Yoga. It is pertinent again for the *maṇḍala* ritual. When the complex and colorful image is completed, Vajrapāṇi "looked at the entire assembly and then looked at the Bhagavat for a long time with unwavering eyes" and exclaimed: "If any evils one has done throughout many millions of aeons will all be cleansed away merely by seeing such a mandala as this, then what can be said when one abides in this most glorious method of mantra practice?"[69] In other words, if merely seeing the *maṇḍala* is so powerful, how much more powerful will be the subsequent practice of *mantras*, *mudrās*, and meditations after "entering" it. Surely, it will lead to Buddhahood in a single lifetime.

Nevertheless, it is not quite clear what Vajrapāṇi is seeing and why he is thrilled. Yes, there is a beautiful powdered *maṇḍala* on the ground (or a painted one on cloth). But there are two other *maṇḍalas* to be considered—the imagined one "in the sky" still hovering, and what was called the "intrinsically-existent" one that has *svabhāva*.

Mkhas-grub-rje's commentary points to a solution: "After finishing the drawing and adorning in that way of the *maṇḍala* of residence and residents, one must 'accomplish' it."[70] Since that is not easily explained, Mkhas-grub-rje reports what his fellow Tibetans have said, along with two different schools of the "great men of India." Here are some of the clearer sentences:

> Regarding the entry of the Knowledge Beings [*jñāna-sattvas*], the Knowledge Beings who have been previously invited from their natural abode [*svabhāvika-sthāna*] are caused to enter. Next, the *maṇḍala* which previously had been lifted to the sky is brought entirely down.[71]

This is called the "three-fold merger"—although there are obscure references to a four-fold and even a seven-fold merger.

I think we can conclude from this that the *maṇḍala* that has been drawn on the ground is a *samaya maṇḍala* or "symbolic *maṇḍala*"—just like the yogin who is a *samaya-sattva* or "symbolic being" when imagining himself to be a deity. We saw earlier that a yogin who becomes a symbolic being attracts the Presence of an actual god, called the *jñāna-sattva* or "knowledge being." It follows

[69] Hodge, VAT, 120-121.

[70] Lessing and Wayman, *Mkhas grub rje's "Fundamentals,"* 291.

[71] Lessing and Wayman, *Mkhas grub rje's "Fundamentals,"* 297-298.

that the *maṇḍala* drawn carefully on the ground attracts a *svabhāva-maṇḍala* of actual deities who arrive as *jñāna-sattvas* to perform the initiations.

This suggests that the main purpose of drawing or painting a *maṇḍala* is not—as nearly all writers say—to "aid in meditation." Instead, the main function of the image is to attract the Celestial Buddhas, the Celestial Bodhisattvas, their consorts, and the offering deities to be Present here and now. That is what it means to "accomplish" the *maṇḍala*. And that is why Vajrapāṇi is thrilled!

This even has to be the case, as Robert Sharf argues, since in most tantric ceremonies there is just not enough time to meditate on an elaborate *maṇḍala*. He writes of Japanese Tantra:

> Like all Buddhist icons, a Shingon mandala is not so much a representation of the divine as it is the locus of the divine—the ground upon which the principal deity is made manifest . . . To come into the presence of a mandala is to enter the presence of the Tathāgata—one literally "sees the Buddha" and partakes of his *kaji*, or empowerment.[72]

Granted, we have not adequately explained the *maṇḍala* "hovering in the sky." Perhaps that is merely an imaginary template for drawing the "symbolic" *maṇḍala* so exactly and beautifully that it evokes the "actual" *maṇḍala* of the gods. But Snellgrove sums up what we do know:

> Thus as means toward the result he must first place in position in the maṇḍala the *samaya*-beings, the symbols or guarantors of the divine beings who are identified in their ultimate state as pure wisdom. At a second stage he induces the descent of pure wisdom, which then pervades the *samaya*-beings, transforming them into "wisdom beings" (*jñana*-sattva). . . . It will be now more readily understood how this term *samaya*, which means literally a coming together or conjunction, may in some contexts be suitably translated as sacrament.[73]

The translation, "sacrament," reminds me of the heated argument between Martin Luther and Huldreich Zwingli of Zurich concerning the Christian sacrament of the Eucharist. The more humanistic and rational Swiss stated that the "signs" of Bread and Wine were merely a "remembrance" of a sacred event long ago. The more passionately religious German insisted that Christ's Body and Blood were "really present" in those signs—and that is what made them effective for our salvation. Jung would say that is what made them "symbols" and not mere signs, capable of attracting the Reality of the collective unconscious, closing the gap between ego and archetype.

Initiations in the Maṇḍala

The ceremony can now begin. The *Vairocanābhisaṃbodhi* informs us:

---

[72] Sharf, "Visualization and Mandala," 191.

[73] Snellgrove, *Indo-Tibetan Buddhism*, 222.

> After the offerings have thus been made, the trainees are led before the Mandala, and are sprinkled with water by the *mantrin*. . . . they are transformed into Vajrasattvas ["Diamond-beings"]. . . Then with a compassionate mind, he should blindfold them. . . In the presence of all the protectors, he then makes them throw their flower, and wherever their flower falls, that deity should be given to them.[74]

This, of course, is the "preparatory" initiation with the other "common" initiations to follow. Accordingly, the master of the rite implores the tutelary deity: "May you assist this disciple who belongs to your family up to the time of his enlightenment!"[75] Let us observe here that the disciples are not Enlightened—yet have already been imaginatively "transformed into Vajrasattvas."

Discussing the ceremonies as a "*rite de passage*, a movement from one mode of being to another," Per Kvaerne writes:

> It is important to point out that even before they are performed, the aspirant is identified with a divine being . . . It would be beside our purpose to discuss whether this rite . . . represents a genuine, as opposed to a merely simulated state of possession, and to what extent it may—in psychological terms—be held to contribute to, or be involved with, the subsequent attainment of mystical insight; what *is* significant, is the fact that the neophyte is from the very outset regarded as a being enjoying divine status.[76]

In other words, in Buddhist Tantra all the actors are "gods." At least, they are not merely human beings. We know that the "Result" Path is being practiced in this way. But it may be part of that general Indian religious notion that, "In order to worship a deity, one must become a deity."

It is then that the initiate receives the five empowerments we discussed: Water, Crown, Vajra, Bell, and Name. When they are completed, the ceremony comes to a close, according to the VAT:

> Then taking those trainees the *mantrin* should instill a compassionate frame of mind in them, and teach the *samaya* commitments to them: "From this day forward, you should never abandon the holy Dharma and *bodhicitta*, even for the sake of your life."[77]

Here, *samaya* does not mean "symbol" but "pledge" and is often paired with "vow." As we read in Mkhas-grub-rje: "At the time of entering, it is necessary to take the pledges (*samaya*) and vows (*saṃvara*)."[78] There is little difference, however, since the former is usually a specific requirement related to a certain text while the latter is general and includes such precepts as the "Fourteen Root Violations" that the newly initiated promise they will never incur.

---

[74] Hodge, VAT, 138. Slightly altered.

[75] Wayman, "Ritual in Tantric Buddhism," 50.

[76] Per Kvaerne, "On the Concept of Sahaja in Indian Buddhist Tantric Literature," *Temenos* 11 (1975): 165, 173.

[77] Hodge, VAT, 147.

[78] Lessing and Wayman, *Mkhas-grub-rje's "Fundamentals,"* 309.

Here again is a reference to "entering" a *maṇḍala*. Let me clarify, should it not be obvious, that no physical entrance occurs during these ceremonies. First of all, it would ruin a powdered *maṇḍala*, even if large enough to enter into; and it is nearly impossible to enter a smaller painted *maṇḍala* sitting on the floor or a table. But it is entirely impossible to enter a painted textile *maṇḍala* hanging on a monastery cell wall.

Instead, "entrance" is symbolic as a disciple sits at the "east gate" and imagines entering into the Presence of "all the Buddhas"—from whom he takes initiation and before whom he makes his solemn commitments. Yet it is all quite real. Jung makes this point psychologically: "If you put yourself into the icon, the icon will speak to you. Take a Lamaic mandala, which has a Buddha in the center, or a Shiva, and, to the extent that you can put yourself into it, it answers and comes into you."[79]

Figure 15.3 Borobudur

Borobudur

The disciples do not even imagine "entering" a flat colorful *maṇḍala*—and, instead, a three-dimensional palace constructed from the two-dimensional "blueprint." We know this from sculptures of *maṇḍalas*, complete with four gates, an underlying *viśva-vajra*, etc. But the largest three-dimensional *maṇḍala* in the world was actually constructed on the Indonesian island of Java. This is the monument of Borobudur, built in the eighth century and architecturally unique within Buddhism (see Figure 15.3).

This massive structure identifies itself at once as: 1) Mount Meru that mysteriously flew over from India; 2) a giant *stūpa* containing an image of the Buddha at its very top complete with a three-

[79] Jung, CW 18, par. 413.

tiered parasol *chattra* (now dismantled), and surrounded by seventy-two smaller *stūpas* housing Buddhas; and 3) a *maṇḍala* with a rectilinear "square" base or boundary (as in the earliest *maṇḍalas*) and five square walkways to a plateau, where we find three concentric "circles" rising toward an imposing dome at the summit.[80]

Of course, Buddhist pilgrims never "entered" the architectural marvel of Borobudur literally. But they did enter the stairway at the east and begin to circumambulate, rising past thousands of bas reliefs showing them the religious meaning of their ascent—that, at the same time, was a movement toward the center—until coming into the Presence of "all the Buddhas." We can do the same today, as tourists. Perhaps we can even "put ourselves into" this *maṇḍala* in active imagination and allow its meaning to "enter" into us.

Post-initiatory Practice

Tantric practice following initiation involves not only keeping the vows and pledges but keeping alive the spirit of what was just experienced. Glenn Wallis outlines a "bare ritual" that is actually similar to practice in other Indian religions. Wallis goes on to delineate features peculiar to Buddhism, and I have put them in brackets:

> Early in the morning, a man [and sometimes a woman], who has previously received initiation and instruction [in secret] by a master [who is never criticized], carries a rolled-up cloth painting [depicting a *maṇḍala* of Buddhist deities, "the animated 'circle' of beings generating both the authority and power sustaining the practices"] and a bag containing small lamps, bottles of camphor and sandalwood oil, incense, rice and other implements [for offerings to one's tutelary deity] to a desolate field. There, after bathing in a nearby pond [for ritual "purification" from defilements and in anticipation of meditating on "emptiness" to "purify" the mind of conventional views], he cleans the area and arranges the cloth on the ground. Sitting on a mound of grass in front of this cloth, he repeatedly recites [perhaps thousands of times] a short phrase, a *mantra* [accompanied by *mudrās*]. With a pleasant voice he sings hymns of praise to visualized enlightened beings and deities [while holding the *vajra* and bell]. Finally, he may light a small fire before the cloth and make oblations [the Buddhist version of sacrifice or *homa*] of wooden sticks or flowers.[81]

From this activity the practitioner gains much merit, receives blessings from the deities evoked and worshipped, and becomes an increasingly advanced *siddha*—moving ever closer and "quickly" to his or her Buddhahood.

---

[80] Alex Wayman, "Reflections on the Theory of Barabuḍur as a *Maṇḍala*," in *Barabudur: History and Significance of a Buddhist Monument*, eds. Luis O. Gómez and Hiram W. Woodward (Berkeley: University of California, 1981), 139-172.

[81] Wallis, MMK, 4.

The *Susiddhikara* says these actions should be repeated throughout the day: "If you wish to seek *siddhi*, you must recite three times daily and wash yourself three times daily."[82] In addition, the *tantrika* maintains a close relationship with the *guru* as "mundane" spiritual guide, and continues to learn both doctrine and new *sādhanas*—new *mantras* and *mudrās*, new *maṇḍalas* with different arrangements of Buddhist deities. More important, the relationship with one's "supramundane" spiritual guide—one's *iṣṭa-devatā* or tutelary deity—deepens, as it is not just imagined but becomes increasingly "Real." And like the Bodhisattva of the mainstream *Pratyutpanna*, the *siddha* is able to ask questions of this other Guide, "and is gladdened by the elucidation of those questions."

Worldly Goals

Post-initiatory mundane *siddhis* are also sought and practiced. Many *tantras* list a set of three or four special procedures—sometimes called "magic rites" (*karma*)—that reveal a certain prominence of worldly goals in Buddhist Tantra, absent in other styles of Buddhism. The SSK names: 1) "pacifiying" (*śāntika*), 2) "increasing" (*pauṣṭika*), and 3) "destroying" (*abhicāruka*); while the VAT adds, 4) "controlling" (*vaśikaraṇa*). Here are instructions for 1) "pacifying" in the SSK:

> If you would do *śāntika* recitation and perform the *homa* rite for the elimination of calamities [such as illness or bad weather], then take refuge in the Three Jewels, arouse deep thoughts of compassion, and at dusk on the first day of a bright half-month commence recitation, whereupon you will succeed in the *śāntika* rite, for at this time the Gods of Pure Abode descend and roam about among humankind, and with the assistance of the gods you will quickly obtain *siddhi*.[83]

Some scholars call this magic or sorcery, but the need for assistance from the *devas* makes it (at the same time) a religious act. Put differently, magic and religion are never far apart: magic emphasizes "works" by will power, while religion is more aware of the need for "grace"—i.e., the cooperation of divine forces that cannot be compelled and only implored. Nevertheless, this rite's technical features for the sake of earthly benefits seem particularly "magical": the practitioner must wear white, should sit near a *stūpa* at an auspicious time, recite "peaceful" *mantras* beginning with *oṃ* and ending with *svāhā*, etc. As in sorcery, success is certain.

The rite of 3) "destroying" carries the same promise but is darker. The SSK explains that it is meant to punish those "who harbor wicked thoughts toward the Three Jewels" or who, if not stopped, would end up in Avīci. Thus, what looks bad may be actually good, the way that Wrathful deities are destructive only for the good of the religion. On the other hand, this rite may be performed for a king to destroy an enemy army. The practitioner should wear red, feel anger, recite "wrathful" *mantras* beginning with *hūṃ* and ending with *phaṭ*, and preferably do so in a charnal ground at midnight—when the "*piśācas, bhūtas, and rākṣasas* [classes of demons] gather in one place" and can assist.

---

[82] Giebel, SSK, 148.

[83] Giebel, SSK, 181-187.

When we examine the other two rites—2) "increasing," for the sake of a longer life or increasing wealth by finding buried treasure; and 4) "controlling," for example, a man and woman to become attracted to each other—it becomes apparent that the Buddhist practitioner of these mundane *siddhis* has other people in mind, even clients or local rulers willing to pay a fee. Geoffrey Samuel writes:

> By the ninth and tenth centuries, it is clear that both Buddhist and Śaiva practitioners were in the business of selling aggressive and destructive rituals (and also, one might add, healing rituals and rituals for prosperity) to their secular employers, and that there was a market for both Buddhist and Śaiva versions.[84]

It is Tantra's response to the uncertainty of royal patronage to which we have already alluded. Let us acknowledge, however, that all of these rites are only ever performed by advanced *tāntrika* Bodhisattvas whose actions have one underlying intention: to help others compassionately here and now, with eventual Enlightenment as the final supramundane goal.

A final Jungian thought Jungian analysts, also, have paying clients who expect "mundane" results. But the experienced analyst must be wary of playing the magician who promises a cure. That may work up to a point, as long as the client's problems are strictly personal ones having to do with ego adaptation. It is then that the more psychologically mature, more adapted, therapist can help determine the actual problems and offer advice.

But as soon as the person seeking help requires advice from the "gods" (i.e., the cooperation of the transpersonal psyche) as determined by dreams and by the progress of therapy—or by the failure of a personalistic approach—nothing can be promised. Indeed, at this point the analysand is no longer a "client" deserving results but a genuine "patient" (from Latin, *pati*, "to suffer," with the extended meaning of "being self-restrained, lenient"). Otherwise, there is the risk of antagonizing the unconscious with an impatient attitude.

The ancient *siddhas* seemed willing to risk the danger of coercing the gods to do their bidding, but they were protected by a cosmology filled with heavens and hells, celestial Bodhisattvas, Buddhas, *ḍākinīs*, etc. That paid attention, albeit indirectly, to the other side of the psyche. That honored the gods.

Jung seems to have that in mind when he writes of willful religious acts:

> A great many ritualistic performances are carried out for the sole purpose of producing at will the effect of the *numinosum* by means of certain devices of a magical nature, such as invocation, incantation, sacrifice, meditation and other yoga practices, self-inflicted tortures of various descriptions, and so forth. But a religious belief in an external and objective divine cause is always prior to any such performance.[85]

---

[84] Geoffrey Samuel, *The Origins of Yoga and Tantra: Indic Religions to the Thirteenth Century* (Cambridge: Cambridge University Press, 2008), 349.

[85] Jung, *CW* 11, par. 7.

In the modern West, we no longer enjoy the "prior" protective belief in an "objective divine cause" and cannot help but participate in the general inflation that "where there's a will, there's a way."

Thus, the analyst and the analysand must together find the proper balance between "magic and religion." Which is not to say that "mundane" benefits are not forthcoming. Jung writes of the "experiment" that the Self is making of each of us:

> And if you do something which rather serves your experiment, you will have the blessing of heaven and the angels will come to dance with you. You are helped along. You have ungodly health, and you develop powers which you have not had before because you have obeyed, not the ego, but that will of the [S]elf.[86]

[86] Jung, *Nietzsche's "Zarathustra,"* 1:403.

Chapter 16
ANUTTARA-YOGA TANTRA

Classes of Tantra

None of what we have learned thus far about Buddhist Tantra appears particularly deviant from Buddhism's history. It is also the form of Tantra primarily accepted outside India, especially in China and cultures influenced by it. Critics of the day did question the presence of myths and techniques that had not been part of Gautama's own teaching—but Early Buddhist Abhidharma and mainstream Mahāyāna had already found ways to justify new scriptures. Besides, Tantra could claim that it was just a new *upāya*; it could say that Śākyamuni approved whatever "strategy" worked to free a person from *saṃsāra*. It was perhaps more difficult to justify the increase in "Wrath" within this new movement. Surely, the *abhicāruka* rite—for "making close friends hate one another, or making your foe seriously ill"—was open to abuse.[1] Yet only the initiated under the guidance of a *guru* would ever hear or read of such "secret" things.

So there is nothing alarming here, nothing that could lead to the accusation by Rajendralal Mitra, a nineteenth century Sanskritist, that tantric Buddhism was "at once the most revolting and horrible that human depravity could think of."[2] Christian missionaries and Victorian scholars (the few who knew), were likewise appalled by these "particularly abominable excrescences of South Asian superstition."[3] But, then, they were referring not to Buddhist Tantra in general but to a late class of tantric texts—composed from the eighth to the eleventh centuries—called, the Anuttara-yoga ("incomparable discipline").

I have deliberately avoided referring to "classes" of *tantras* so as not to influence the reader's expectation of what belongs to any one class. It is a fact, however, that at some early stage of Buddhist Tantra, Indian commentators began categorizing texts into classes to give order to the surfeit of tantric materials. The earliest distinction was that between Kriyā ("action") *tantras* and those called Caryā ("practice") *tantras* if not, actually, Yoga ("discipline") *tantras*. As we can see from the translations, there is not much difference in the names—nor was there always much difference in the content of the texts categorized in this way. But if we allow these to be the first three classes of tantric scriptures, there begins to be a real difference in content in a fourth category called Mahāyoga ("great discipline") *tantras* and a final fifth category called Yoginī ("female tantric deity") *tantras*. Since these last two are so similar, the Tibetans (and perhaps also the Indians) combined them into the single class of Anuttarayoga Tantra to make just four main classes of tantric texts. I will do

---

1 Giebel, SSK, 185-187.

2 Wedemeyer, *Making Sense*, 2.

3 David Gordon White, *Tantra in Practice* (Princeton: Princeton University Press, 2000), 4.

this, as do most scholars, to avoid unnecessary complication and to allow us another glimpse of the archetypal pattern of "Three and the Fourth," whereby the fourth is somehow different.

Let me observe that the issues we discussed already can be found everywhere within Buddhist Tantra—I cited all classes in the previous two chapters—so there is a certain "mainstream" esoteric doctrine and practice that can be found in the earliest Kriyā *tantras* as well as in the latest Anuttarayoga *tantras*. Nevertheless, the SSK and MMK belong to the Kriyā; the VAT is the chief text of the Caryā; the STTS is the chief text of the Yoga Tantra; while the Anuttarayoga includes such *tantras* as the *Hevajra* (HVT), *Saṃpuṭa* (SPT), and the *Caṇḍamahāroṣaṇa* (CMT)—all of which were quoted in support of a general view of tantric Buddhism. I should add to this list the *Guhyasamāja Tantra* (hereafter, GST) as an important text in the fourth class.[4]

A Transgressive Nidāna

With the Anuttarayoga, however, we know we are in new religious territory from the *nidāna* found at the opening of many of its scriptures. The SPT (like the HVT) begins: "Thus I heard at one time. The Bhagavat was dwelling in the sex organs [*bhaga*] of the Vajra-women [Locanā, etc.], the heart of the Body, Speech, and Mind of all the Tathāgatas."[5] First of all, I have followed the Tibetan punctuation by putting "heard" together with "one time." This makes sense of the SPT's own comment that the "hearing" occurs, not historically, but timelessly in a "*samādhi* of inconceivable liberation."[6] What is alarming, however, is that the Lord is no longer abiding in the Indian city of Rājagṛha or nearby on Vulture Peak, not even in a high heaven called Akaniṣṭha, but is "dwelling" in sexual union with "Diamond" women.

If it had been difficult to allow violence (however compassionate) in the Buddhist religion that from the outset advocated nonviolence, and difficult to worship female Buddhist *devatās* when females had long been denigrated by ascetic monks, the religion now has the added difficulty of embracing sexual imagery and—as we shall see—sexual behavior for renunciants who had taken a solemn vow of chastity.

Indeed, the art expressing this controversial development depicts male and female Buddhist deities who are both wrathful and in coitus. See Figure 16.1 for an eighteenth-century Tibetan painting of Hevajra Buddha standing in fiery sexual union with his divine Consort, Nairātmyā.

---

4 Francesca Fremantle, trans., *A Critical Study of the Guhysamāja Tantra* (Ph.D. dissertation, School of Oriental and African Studies, University of London, 1971). Scribd.com/doc/29906080.

5 Elder, SPT, 161.

6 Elder, SPT, 191.

Figure 16.1 Hevajra in Union with Nairātmyā

It gets worse. One of those Vajra-women asks in the CMT: "Can you bear, my dear, to eat my filth—and feces, urine, and suck the [menstrual] blood from inside my Bhaga?"[7] Some verses later, the wrathful Caṇḍamahārosana Buddha proclaims: "This diet is the best, eaten by all Buddhas."[8] Sexual transgression, we discover, has spread into dietary transgression—and even into rules of commensality since one is often required to "dine" with a *caṇḍālī* or *ḍombī*, a low-caste or outcaste woman.

Not to be outdone, Hevajra Buddha counsels in his own *tantra* that one should break all Buddhist moral rules:

> You should slay living beings.
> You should speak lying words.
> You should take what is not given.
> You should frequent others' wives.[9]

As Mitra would have it, "horrible and revolting." This verse is even modeled after the standard "Five Precepts" that name these very acts as the ones all Buddhists condemn and must avoid. We see why tantric Buddhism—but, actually, only its most extreme expression in Anuttarayoga—is called antinomian ("against the law").

Interpretation

What is going on here? If we follow Tsoṅ-kha-pa's fifteenth-century Tibetan commentary, perhaps nothing. He does use erotic imagery to distinguish the classes of texts but then explains it in an entirely orthodox way. Alex Wayman summarizes from the *Sṅags rim*: The Kriyā category is akin to "deities laughing," the Caryā to their "mutually gazing," the Yoga class to their "holding hands," and the Anuttarayoga to "deities united" in sexual intercourse. Yet these stages of increasing erotic attraction are really referring—says Tsoṅ-kha-pa—to tantric practice that goes increasingly inward.

Thus, the Kriyā Tantra (like the SSK) is for trainees "who delight mainly in external ritual over inner *samādhi*." The Caryā Tantra (like the VAT) is for "those who delight in external ritual and inner *samādhi* equally." The Yoga Tantra (like the STTS) is for candidates "who delight predominantly in inner *samādhi* over external ritual." While the Anuttarayoga Tantra is for "those who delight in inner *samādhi* completely."

Let us note that Tsoṅ-kha-pa is supporting here Anuttarayoga's own claim to "superiority" among the classes—something with which the so-called "lower tantras" would not agree.[10] Nevertheless, it follows from this scheme that whatever we find in scriptures like the *Guhyasamāja* (technically, in the Mahāyoga class) or in the *Hevajra* or *Saṃpuṭa* (technically, in the Yoginī class)—however

[7] George, CMT, 56.
[8] George, CMT, 64.
[9] Snellgrove, HVT, 1:97.
[10] See George R. Elder, "Problems of Language in Buddhist Tantra," *History of Religions* 40, no. 3 (February, 1976): 234-235.

offensive—is mental, imaginary at worst as some kind of *upāya* or perhaps entirely symbolic of the intensity of a practitioner's "inner *samādhi*."

Even so, Geoffrey Samuel informs us that the great Tsoṅ-kha-pa was forced to agree that sexual practices "had to be performed in some form for the attainment of Buddhahood."[11] His own emphasis on "interiority" may have been an effort to reform transgressive practices having already arrived from India.

There is ambiguity, nevertheless, in the SPT's own *nidāna*. The *bhagas* or "sex organs" are glossed as the "heart" of the "Body, Speech, and Mind" of the Tathāgatas—suggesting that they refer not just (or not at all) to coitus but to something like the "essence" of Tathāgatahood. In a later chapter of that text, we encounter a play on words:

> "Bhagavat" ["Blessed One," often translated as "Lord"] is explained as follows: He possesses lordliness, a beautiful form, fame, glory, knowledge, and exertion toward the goal. These are called the "*bhagas*" [meaning both "female sex organs" and "blessings"] of six kinds. Since he possesses them, he is called "Bhaga-vat." Or, he is called "Bhagavat" because he is the one who has "broken" [*bhagna*, a word playfully close to *bhaga*] those discordant *dharmas* [i.e., the defilements].[12]

Verses later, we read: "Wisdom is called *bhaga*. Every Tathāgata dwells in that *bhaga* accompanied by his Lady"—his Bhagavatī, the feminine form of Bhagavat.

So what seems offensive at first glance may just be colorful language for inoffensive mainstream truths. In Early Buddhism, no one seems to have taken offense at verse 294 of the *Dhammapada*: "Having slain mother, father, two warrior-kings, and destroyed a country together with its treasurer, ungrieving goes the holy man." Everybody knew it meant that an Arhat "kills" craving and conceit, the two extreme views, etc.[13]

Antinomian Rites

Nevertheless, antinomian behavior does exist in Indian Anuttarayoga Tantra—in a new set of initiations and in post-initiatory practice. Of course, it will be practiced for the sake of Enlightenment and (tellingly) for the sake of eliminating all desire for transgressive behavior, including sexual intercourse. We could have even anticipated this from the tantric Enlightenment story of Gautama Buddha according to this class.

Let us recall that all the Tathāgatas had challenged Sarvārthasiddhi, "You cannot become a Manifest Complete Buddha by this *samādhi* alone." And he implored, "Then, how shall I do it?" Tsoṅ-kha-pa's own disciple, Mkhas-grub-rje, reports without elaborating: "Thereupon all the Buddhas of the ten directions summoned the daughter of the gods Tilottamā"—an *apsaras* or "celestial nymph"

---

[11] Samuel, *Origins,* 264n.

[12] Elder, SPT, 192. These same lines appear in the "root" *tantra* HVT 1.5.15.

[13] Buddharakkhita, *Dhammapada*, chapter 21, vs. 294.

from among the Realm of Desire gods, known for their ability to seduce ascetics.[14] This suggestive twist in the myth—not found in the other *tantra* classes—will function as a paradigm, then, for erotic tantric Buddhist practice.

Lest there by uncertainty about this matter, a commentary states that the Buddha "taught the blissful state that arises from sexual union, but concealed it out of his great compassion for the sake of the spiritual maturation of simple-minded people."[15] Ordinary folk just would not understand—especially since the Buddha taught clearly in the Vinaya that it would be better if a disciple's "penis be stuck into the mouth of a black viper than into a woman's vagina."[16] And since they had heard of the four "Defeats" that require immediate expulsion from the Order—the first of which is sexual intercourse, defined with exquisite precision.

Let me say at the outset that the relationship of this fourth class of *tantras* to the "lower" three is, in general, to accept them and then to add its own "higher" procedures. Thus, there are four Anuttarayoga initiations. 1) The first one, however, includes all of those belonging to the Kriyā, Caryā, and Yoga Tantra classes that we have already discussed. They are now collectively called the "Vase" (*kalaśa*) in recognition of the initial "Water" initiation among those five (six or seven) earlier rites. 2) The second initiation, then, is distinctly Anuttarayoga and called "Secret" (*guhya*); 3) the new third consecration is called "Knowledge of Wisdom" (*prajñā-jñāna*) or just "Wisdom;" and 4) the final one is merely called the "Fourth" (*caturtha*)—about which, not surprisingly, there is much disagreement.

Similarly, post-initiatory practice accepts what we have already observed about "mainstream" deity yoga as a) "generation-in-front" of an imagined god, followed by b) "self-generation" or identification with that god. But the Anuttarayoga calls this entire two-fold procedure the A) "Stage of Generation" (*utpatti-krama*) for which candidates must receive the "Vase" initiations. Those who receive the three additional "superior" consecrations, then, can go on to practice B) a subsequent "Stage of Completion" (*saṃpanna-krama*) as the Anuttarayoga's contribution to an "unexcelled" path. By building on what had already been established, and not denying it, even this controversial form of Tantra demonstrates a principle observed frequently in the history of religions, namely, that whatever is new can last only if rooted in the past.

2) "Secret" initiation

Having already explored in previous chapters the **1) "Vase" initiations**, let us proceed directly to the new "Secret" initiation. Without examining it, we know that a *maṇḍala* is in place on the ground or in a painting, that the Buddhist *devatās* are "resident" there in a "palace," and that it is they who will actually "administer" the empowerment. We know, too, that the residents are as likely to be female as male, as "Wrathful" as they are "Peaceful." We can even anticipate—from what we have been learning—that the male and female deities of the Anuttarayoga *maṇḍala* may be naked,

[14] Lessing and Wayman, *Mkhas grub rje's "Fundamentals,"* 37.

[15] Samuel, *Origins of Yoga and Tantra,* 331.

[16] Ṭhānissaro, *Monastic Code*, 14.

standing or sitting in sexual intercourse. They may hold skull bowls filled with disgusting food. Thus, Hevajra ("O Vajra")—the tantric expression of Akṣobhya—proclaims:

> There at its center am I, O Fair One, together with you. The Joy Innate I am in essence, and impassioned with great passion. I have eight faces, four legs, and sixteen arms, and trample the four Māras under foot. . . Fearful am I to fear itself with my necklace made of a string of heads, and dancing furiously on a solar disk. Black am I and terrible with a crossed *vajra* on my head, my body smeared with ashes, and my mouths sending forth the sound *hūṃ*. But my inner nature is tranquil, and holding Nairātmyā ["She who is Non-self"] in loving embrace, I am possessed of tranquil bliss.[17]

In art the male usually faces us when in "divine coitus" with a slightly smaller female's back toward the viewer. But, occasionally, when a female divinity occupies the center of a *maṇḍala*, that arrangement is reversed. The "necklace of heads" and "ashes" here are evidence of Hindu Śaivite influence, with its charnel ground and cremation ground practices.

A Female Participant

Dramatically, a human female enters the sacred initiation arena. Kvaerne comments:

> For while there were only two actors in the minor consecrations, the neophyte and the preceptor, there now enters a third, the heroine, one might say, of the sacred drama, namely, a young woman variously known, to quote but the most common of her titles, as *mudrā* ("Seal"), *vidyā* ["Knowledge"] or *prajñā* ("Wisdom"), or simply *devī* ("Goddess").[18]

Both the master and the disciple will eventually have sex with her. Yet all three will do so as imagined *devatās* and not as mere human beings. They will perform a specific instance of what, in the history of religions, is called a *hieros gamos*, a "divine marriage" or sacred sexual union.

This "young woman" in the rite is very young, either twelve or sixteen years old, according to many *tantras*. Wayman cites passages that associate age sixteen with puberty—making sense of references to menstrual blood—but he cannot explain the alternative age of twelve in this way. Since Saraha, a *mahāsiddha* or "great adept," lists acceptable ages of 8, 12, 16, 20, and 25, Wayman ventures the interpretation that the "age" is not actually about the woman but the number of years that the initiate has been practicing Buddhism. Alternatively, the "ages" predict the number of years the practitioner will need in order to reach transmundane *siddhi*.[19]

---

[17] Snellgrove, HVT, 1:110.

[18] Kvaerne, *Sahaja*, 166.

[19] Wayman, *Buddhist Tantras*, 195-198.

At least, that symbolic meaning allows for the woman's ideal features (despite often being an outcaste *caṇḍālī*). According to the HVT:

> She is neither too tall, nor too short, neither quite black nor quite white, but dark like a lotus-leaf. Her breath is sweet, and her sweat has a pleasant smell like that of musk. Her *pudenda* [Skt., *padma*, "lotus," a common euphemism in Indian literature] give forth a scent from moment to moment like different kinds of lotuses or like sweet aloe wood. She is calm and resolute, pleasant in speech and altogether delightful, with beauteous hair and three wrinkles in the middle of her body. By vulgar men, in fact, she would be classed as first-rank [i.e., in the first of "four types" of Indian women]. Having gained her, one gains that *siddhi*, the nature of which is the Joy Innate [*sahaja-ānanda*].[20]

Finally, this woman is strangely highly advanced along the Path and has become so in a very short amount of time.

The text addresses the *ācarya*:

> Taking this girl, who has wide-open eyes and is of age and endowed with youth and beauty, he should consecrate [*saṃskaret*, "prepare"] her with the seed of enlightenment [i.e, the Bodhicitta vow]. Beginning with the ten rules of virtuous conduct, he should expound to her the Dharma, how the mind is fixed on the divine form, on the meaning of symbolic forms and concerning one-pointedness of mind, and in one month she will be fit, of that there is no doubt. And so the girl is there, now freed from all false notions, and received as though she were a boon. Or else he should produce a Mudrā by conjuring her forth by his own power [*prakalpayet*, "imagine"] . . . .[21]

These extraordinary features tempt one to conclude that the woman herself is imagined and not a woman of flesh and blood. But the last Sanskrit line makes it clear she is preferably—at least, for the Secret initiation—an actual karmic creature, a *karma-mudrā*.

Besides, Mkhas-grub-rje regrets that, "Nowadays, we do not find such hierophants, neophytes, along with a *vidyā*, that possess the complete characteristics as have been set forth"—so all this can merely be performed mentally in the Tibet of his day.[22] That is not what he said in the previous chapter when advising "mental offerings" to deities in what is now called the Stage of Generation.

---

[20] Snellgrove, HVT, 1:116.

[21] Snellgrove, HVT, 1:90.

[22] Lessing and Wayman, *Mkhas grub rje's "Fundamentals,"* 218-219, 323.

Sacred Coitus

The CMT informs us that the master and the woman engage in sexual intercourse:

> Then there is the following Secret Consecration. The student should give clothing, etc. to his teacher, and present to him a delightful woman adorned with beauty and youth . . . Then, having paid respect to his teacher, the student should go outside and remain there, repeating the mantra: "*Oṃ*, O Caṇḍamahāroṣaṇa, *hūṃ, phaṭ!*" The teacher, moreover, should worship himself with intoxicants, meats, etc. and having satisfied Wisdom, being in her embrace, he should place the resulting white and red on a leaf, shaped into a funnel, etc. Then, having summoned the student, he should take that substance with his ring-finger and thumb, and write the letters, "*Hūṃ, phaṭ,*" on the student's tongue. Then he should have the student pronounce the words, "Ah! Pleasure!"[23]

Small details in this instruction—the disciple's going outside to allow for privacy, the use of a leaf funnel, the ancient ritual gesture of touching the fourth finger and thumb—are clues that this Indian tantric scene is not imagined but externally enacted.

In addition, the *guru* consumes "intoxicants and meats, etc." These refer to the "five M's" (*pañca-makāra*) or five words associated with the sexual act in Indian erotics: alcohol (*madya*), meat (*māṃsa*), fish (*matsya*), and dry-roasted grain (*mudrā*, yet another meaning of this prolific word) that are aphrodisiacs to enhance the pleasure of the fifth "M," coitus (*maithuna*).[24]

There is nothing wrong with them in the household life where the pleasures of sex and the reproduction of children are expected and even a duty. In Hinduism, the second "goal" of life (after worldly "success") is "pleasure" (*kāma*) for which the Kāmasūtras were composed. But the "five M's" are shockingly associated here with a Buddhist master whose duty—so we have been taught—is to avoid such things. Yet he goes on to "satisfy" the Prajṇā, "being in her embrace" (*saṃpuṭī-bhūya*, a "kind of sexual intercourse," according to the Monier-Williams Dictionary).

Granted, we are not told that the master actually enjoys the act of inserting his *vajra*—a new erotic meaning of this important word—into the woman's *padma*. Indeed, the HVT cautions:

> Then taking her, one should perform the practice with the realization of one's own composure. For this practice, which is called terrifying [or "terrible," *bhīma*] in appearance, is not taught for the sake of enjoyment, but for the examination of one's own thought, whether the mind is steady or wavering.[25]

With (or without) pleasure, the man does ejaculate his semen while the woman produces the secretions of her arousal.

---

[23] George, CMT, 55.

[24] Flood, *Hinduism*, 189.

[25] Snellgrove, HVT, 1:91. I have changed "waving" to "wavering."

Sacred "Food"

These two sexual fluids are called the "white and the red" in Indian materials generally, and not just in Tantra. True, semen is actually white, but it is also symbolically "white;" while the woman's clearer sexual fluid is, by contrast, considered "red" even if not tinted by menstrual blood. Some texts do advise, however, that the *vidyā* of this consecration should be menstruating. That is because in ancient physiology the "white and red" signify the "vital essence" of a man and a woman. Food was thought to be digested into ordinary circulating blood, then flesh, fat, bone, marrow, and finally into white semen or red menstrual blood. They combine, it was thought, at conception to form an embryo. But biological fertility is not at issue here; nor have I read of any concern that the tantric woman might become pregnant.

Instead, the "vital fluids" produced by the sexual act are collected as a special kind of "food"—and fed to the candidate who has been called back into the room. This feeding is done ritually with thumb and ring finger (see *Bṛhadāraṇyaka Upaniṣad*, 6.4.4) and presumably in the shape of "wrathful" or transgressive *mantras*, i.e., *hūṃ* and *phaṭ*.

Whether or not he actually likes this unexpected "food," the initiate is told to respond to the taste, "Ah! Pleasure [*sukha*]!" This word, we know, has long been associated with the "happy" or "blissful" state of Nirvāṇa, the very opposite of "suffering" (*duḥkha*) that characterizes Saṃsāra. Yet now it is an answer to the Diamond Woman's question, "Can you bear, my dear, to eat my filth?" Because in Buddhism her "red" is, indeed, filthy as is the "white" of the *guru*—both listed in Early Buddhism among the body's excrescences for meditating on "Foulness." The philosopher Nāgārjuna himself wrote: "Lust for a woman mostly comes from thinking that her body is clean. But there is nothing clean in a woman's body."[26]

In the Anuttarayoga, however, the human body's semen, blood, urine, feces, and marrow or flesh are called, for the sake of practice, the "five ambrosias (*amṛta*)." They are often found in tantric rites in a bowl made from a human cranium retrieved from the charnel ground or left over from an incomplete cremation. The skull bowl is the very antithesis of the Buddha's wooden begging bowl, long revered as a sacred "relic of use." It holds disgusting substances called *amṛta* (literally, "deathless") even though this had long been a name for the experience or "taste" of Nirvāṇa.

Interpretation

Again, we must ask, what is going on here? Christian Wedemeyer affirms that this rite is actually being performed in tantric Indian Buddhism—as opposed to the opinion of some, even today, that Buddhists would not actually do such things. Wedemeyer adds, however, that these acts are entirely compatible with mainstream Mahāyāna and even some aspects of Early Buddhism, if correctly understood. He writes:

> What does it mean, then, for a practitioner of the Mahāyoga Tantras, having gone through the process of self-creation as an enlightened Buddhist divinity, to eat

[26] Snellgrove, *Indo-Tibetan Buddhism*, 1:288.

> from a skull a foul soup of polluting meats and bodily fluids? . . . [It signifies] the attainment of the enlightened state of nondual gnosis (*advayajñāna*), called in some sources communion (*yuganaddha*)—the ultimate goal of the practitioner in which the deluded perception of things as having an intrinsic nature (pure or polluting, good or evil) is transcended.[27]

The point is that the male *guru* has compassionately consented to sexual union with a low-caste woman to show concretely and dramatically—and not just with words or concepts—that there is no real distinction between male and female, high class and low class, chastity and sexual intercourse, following monastic rules and disobeying them—i.e., between the symbolic opposites of the "Red and White" that are here united in a sexual act between a man and a woman and combined as food. Graciously, the *guru* "feeds" that essentially orthodox Buddhist insight to the candidate for his "ingestion."

True, it is all an "act," but a ritual act that in a living religion has a salvific effect. Thus, the CMT instructs the *ācārya* to say to the initiate while feeding him:

> "Today I cause to be produced the Buddha-Knowledge, the very same means by which the past, future, and present Buddhas, Lords, obtained independent Nirvāṇa."[28]

Elsewhere, that special "food" is called "Bodhicitta," either as the Vow that causes one's eventual Enlightenment or as a symbol of the vow's intended outcome, the Mind of Enlightenment—beyond all distinctions.

It makes sense, then, that the candidate responds, "Sukha!"—to the "one taste" (*samarasa*) of the voidness of all phenomena (to put it negatively) or to the "single flavor" of Buddha-nature lying within everything (put positively).

The eleventh-century Indian adept Jñānasṛī confirms this, as Wedemeyer translates from the Tibetan:

> The five meats and the five ambrosias. Rely on these as appropriate, in order to dispel conceptuality. Because concepts such as "this is pure, this is impure" are fetters, if one methodically consumes sin-free meat of extremely base sorts such as human, horse, cow, dog and elephant, and the death-cheating ambrosias such as semen, blood, feces, urine, and human flesh, considering them void of intrinsic reality by the appropriate method and repeatedly conserving those very things as if they were divine ambrosia, if one enjoys [experiences?] them without passion, gradually concepts such as pure and impure will not arise.[29]

---

27 Wedemeyer, *Making Sense*, 121-122.

28 George, CMT, 55.

29 Wedemeyer, *Making Sense*, 148.

The word "gradually" here suggests that this is advice for post-initiatory practice in the following months and years. It indicates a "conditioning" of one's experience over time, as some writers suggest. The idea is to overcome one's disgust at filthy substances by swallowing them, says the text, "as if they were divine ambrosia."

A *mahāsiddha* named Nāgārjuna—not the philosopher of the same name—describes the results sharply in verse:

> As oneself, so an enemy . . . .
> As one's mother, so a whore . . . .
> As urine, so wine.
> As food, so shit.
> As sweet-smelling camphor, so the stench from the ritually-impure.
> As words of praise, so revolting words. . . .
> As pleasure, so pain.[30]

Getting to this "nondual" attitude is called the "path of passion"—as scholars often remind us. Indeed, we read in the HVT: "That by which the world is bound, by that same its bonds are released."[31]

We see, however, that the goal is not to embrace passion or to become thereby a passionate person but, instead, to become indifferent. A "great adept" is telling us here that highly advanced tantric Buddhists experience life with no emotional reaction to praise or blame, to pleasure or pain—seeing "gold and gravel" in the same way without any labels, as expressed by the VAT, a lower *tantra*.[32]

We are reminded of Gautama's former birth as Viśvantara who naturally felt bad at having given away his children to a scoundrel, but said: "I must quiet this affection and be calm." He succeeded at becoming indifferent even toward their mother's distress—although he must have allowed himself to feel some compassion.

3) "Wisdom" initiation

Kvaerne observes: "in any case, the essential point of the Consecration of the Secret is the transfer of the Thought-of-Enlightenment of the preceptor to the neophyte."[33] One might even say this transfer of Bodhicitta (in symbolic form) is sufficiently empowering for the disciple to practice on his own. In fact, historically, these new consecrations may have developed independently and were brought together artificially. The dramatic introduction of sexual intercourse in the new second consecration, however, has the weakness of being vicarious for the disciple and only for the production of sexual fluids.

---

30 Wedemeyer, *Making Sense*, 122.

31 Snellgrove, HVT, 1:80.

32 Hodge, VAT, 337.

33 Kvaerne, *Sahaja*, 171.

That changes with 3) the consecration called "Prajñā-jñāna" ("knowledge of wisdom"). Now, the disciple himself embraces the "ideal" outcaste woman. The CMT instructs:

> Then he should entrust that very Wisdom to the student . . . . the teacher should whisper in his ear the division of the Four Blisses [*ānanda*, "joy"]. Then the teacher should go outside. And then Wisdom having become naked, and squatting, should indicate her secret place with the forefinger, and ask: "Can you bear, my dear, to eat my filth . . . ." Then the candidate must say: "Why should I not bear to eat your filth, O Mother? I must practice devotion to women until I realize the essence of Enlightenment. . . . Then the candidate should concentrate that he himself has the form of Caṇḍamahāroṣana; and, embracing Wisdom in the form of Anger Vajrī, he should aim at the Four Blisses.[34]

The sexual union of the *guru* and the woman—identified with the central god and goddess of the *maṇḍala*—is now enacted by the candidate and the woman. As in the *nidāna* of the *Saṃpuṭa*, the "Buddha" is now "dwelling in the *bhaga*" of "Wisdom."

We see that the rite includes another "eating" of sexual fluid. The focus, however, has shifted to her fluid ("my filth") and away from his semen or even the combination of the two. That is confirmed by the HVT that informs us: "With his tongue he must receive the ambrosia for the increasing of his strength."[35] Calling the woman, "O Mother," adds to this new emphasis as does the vow to practice "devotion to all women." Thus, we read long lists of females worthy of devotion, as in the SPT:

> Mother, sister, daughter and female kin, Brahman maid, Kṣatriya maid, Vaiśya maid, and Śūdra maid, dyer, and dancer, outcaste, and *caṇḍālinī*—these one should worship by the ritual of means and insight with devotion to their reality.[36]

We find a similar list in the CMT that says the point is that there is no "distinction" among them.[37]

Emanation

One gets the impression, however, that these "many" indistinct women are worthy of devotion because they are all manifestations of the "One" divine Prajñāpāramitā. That, however, would be more of a Hindu notion than a Buddhist one, what we would hear in a cult of the Goddess or Devī that solves the perennial problem of the "One and the Many" in that particular way. At the same time, one has the impression that all ordinary men are many sacred manifestations of the Supreme Buddha. The CMT confirms this, as Miranda Shaw translates:

> I am the son of Māyā [i.e., Śākyamuni],

[34] George, CMT, 56-57.

[35] Snellgrove, HVT 1:104, note.

[36] Elder, SPT, 167. See HVT for similar verses, 1.5.16-18 and 2.5.59.

[37] George, CMT, 66.

Now in the form of Caṇḍamahāroṣaṇa.
You are the exalted Gopā [wife of Śākyamuni],
Identical to Lady Perfection of Wisdom.
All women in the universe
Are your embodiments, and
All men are my embodiments.[38]

This suggests Creation by "emanation," something Buddhism has avoided since its cosmology of "beginningless time" obviated creation of any kind.

Yet we suspected emanationism in our discussion of the *maṇḍala* where the central Deity manifested itself as all the other deities within that sacred space. That was particularly apparent in the "Ninefold Maṇḍala of Amitābha" wherein the central Lord multiplied himself identically in eight directions. Snellgrove agrees that these ideas are "awkward" for Buddhists for whom "all notion of a creating divinity and created beings is anathema."[39] Yet Hinduism is influencing Buddhism so much now that Heruka Buddha declares:

The whole of existence arises in me,
In me arises the threefold world,
By me pervaded is this all,
Of nought else does this world consist.[40]

That is exactly what Viṣṇu, Śiva, and Devī say.

The Joy of Sex

Another shift of focus in this third initiation is away from the mere production of sexual fluids for ritual ingestion toward the "blissful" experience of sexual intercourse itself. The disciple is told to "aim at the Four Blisses." This means there is no longer ambiguity (as in the previous initiation) about enjoying coitus. Indeed, the Indian penchant for categorizing has divided this sexual pleasure into four stages of feeling. The word ānanda has been translated as "bliss" by George but as "joy" by Snellgrove—who reserves the stronger English word, "bliss," for the affective side of Nirvāṇa. Thus, we read in the HVT of the "four Joys":

First is just Joy (ānanda),
Secondly is Joy Supreme (*parama-ānanda*),
Thirdly is the Joy of Cessation (*virāma-ānanda*),
Fourth is the Joy Innate (*sahaja-ānanda*).[41]

---

38 Miranda Shaw, *Passionate Enlightenment* (Princeton: Princeton University Press, 1994), 28.
39 Snellgrove, *Indo-Tibetan Buddhism*, 1:264, 131.
40 Snellgrove, HVT, 1:77.
41 Snellgrove, HVT, 1:82.

Explaining them as increasingly exquisite experiences of delight, this scripture resorts to an image: "The first is represented by a smile, the second by a gaze, the third in an embrace, and the fourth in union. This fourfold set of consecrations is for the purpose of perfecting living-beings."[42] Now we know where Tsoṅ-kha-pa got his imagery for the Four Classes of Tantra claiming that "union" is meant for candidates who "delight in inner *samādhi* completely."

The HVT claims, also, that its "Four Joys" are correlated with the Four Consecrations of the Anuttarayoga—so that one experiences the first "Joy" during the "Vase" initiation, the second during the "Secret" initiation, etc. But the CMT clearly disagrees by placing them all within this third "Wisdom" consecration; indeed, the CMT does not even mention a "Fourth" consecration with which a fourth "Joy" could be correlated.

Despite the increasing intensity of pleasure during sexual intercourse—for the yogin, at least, if not also for the woman who seems to be forgotten—the fourth Joy is different in kind from the other three. The HVT comments: "The first Joy is of this world, the second Joy is of this world, the third Joy is of this world, but the Innate exists not in these three."[43] Harunaga Isaacson takes this statement to mean that the fourth (climactic) Joy is experienced during orgasm and interprets it as a "foretaste" of Nirvāṇa:

> Now for it to be possible to meditatively cultivate in the *mantranaya* the non-dual, transcendent and supremely blissful goal that is that which is called the Dharmakāya, it is necessary first to have some sort of cognition or experience of it. We might put it that a glimpse of this transcendent target must be had, in order that one can later firmly set one's meditative sights on it. It is the function of the *prajñābhiṣeka* to provide this glimpse . . . . in the brief interval between the moment in which the initiand's *bodhicitta*, that is his semen, is in the center of the *maṇi* ["jewel"], that is the glans of his penis, and the moment of emission.[44]

We see here an orgasmic emission of semen that is called "*bodhicitta*." This is a restricted use of the term and not the nondual "combination" of semen and vaginal discharge, the "white and the red."

Yet Isaacson interprets the sexual intercourse between the male and female exactly as in the earlier consecration: it offers a foretaste of "nonduality" beyond conceptual opposites, and a "glimpse" of what it feels like to go beyond the ordinary joys "of this world." In fact, none of these joys can compare to the "Joy" of Buddhahood. As the CST puts it: "the happiness of the divine [i.e., worldly gods] and human states do not amount to one sixteenth of Vajradhara's."[45] In the Farrow and Menon translation of the HVT, we read: "erotic pleasure is not the real bliss."[46]

---

42 Snellgrove, HVT, 1:95-96.

43 Snellgrove, HVT, 1:82.

44 Harunaga Isaacson, "Tantric Buddhism in India (from c. A.D. 800 to c. A.D. 1200)" (revision of a lecture originally given in 1997), 9, http://www.buddhismuskunde.uni-hamburg.de/pdf.

45 Gray, CST, 26, 162.

46 See G. W. Farrow and I. Menon, trans., *The Concealed Essence of the Hevajra Tantra: With the Commentary "Yogaratnamālā"* (Delhi: Motilal Banarsidass, 1992), 134.

"Sahaja"

The real bliss is symbolized by the "fourth Joy," *sahaja-ānanda* ("innate joy"). We have seen it mentioned earlier when Hevajra proclaimed, "The Joy Innate I am in essence," and in a reference to transmundane *siddhi*, "the nature of which is the Joy Innate."

What is being translated as "innate" is a technical term that literally means, "together" (*saha*)-"born" (*ja*). Roger Jackson states that it is such an important term for the "great adepts" of Buddhist Tantra that it serves as a synonym for a long list of other important terms: "great bliss" (*mahāsukha*), "knowledge," "stainless mind," "nondual mind," "the union of wisdom and method," "tasting the same" (*samarasa*), "the real" (*tattva*), the "pure," yet "beyond" purity and impurity, etc.—"so many terms, so many images, so many predications for a concept reputed to be ineffable!"[47]

The HVT even reads: "So the whole world is the Innate, for the Innate is its essence. Its essence too is *nirvāṇa* when the mind is in a purified state."[48] One thinks of the Tathāgatagarbha that lies innately, although invisibly, within all things.

Since *sahaja* can also be rendered as "simultaneously-arisen," it alludes to the ability to see that all paired opposites arise together and are only apparently distinct or independent from each other. Kvaerne quotes Guenther: "Essentially it refers to the spontaneity and totality of the experience in which the opposites such as transcendence and immanence, subject and object, the noumenal and phenomenal indivisibly blend"—in other words, the "Joyful" experience of *advaya* or "nonduality." Being more exact, the GST says: "neither duality nor nonduality" (*na dvayaṃ na-advayaṃ*)—a nod to the thoroughness of Madhyamaka.[49]

It follows that the "Fourth Joy" at orgasm during the Wisdom initiation symbolically anticipates the actual "Joy"—yet to be achieved—of being Enlightened. This means, also, that the Anuttarayoga of Buddhist Tantra is merely extending into the behavioral sphere what non-tantric Mahāyāna already expressed philosophically.

4) "Fourth" initiation

The standard presentation of this fourth and final consecration in the Anuttarayoga Tantra class—when it appears—is that it is entirely verbal. Mkhas-grub-rje says somewhat awkwardly: "In the phase of completely conferring the fourth initiation, when one is certified by not less than conviction of the third one, that very one is made the example, as the *guru* imparts to the disciple an understanding of the 'coupling' (*yuganaddha*) symbolized thereby."[50] In other words, the master of the rite supposedly explains in this Fourth consecration rite the true meaning of the third one. As Isaacson remarks, however, what one "expects to be the culminating or crowning empowerment of

---

47 Roger R. Jackson, trans., *Tantric Treasures: Three Collections of Mystical Verse from Buddhist India* (Oxford: Oxford University Press, 2004), 21-22.

48 Snellgrove, HVT, 1:92.

49 Wedemeyer, *Making Sense*, 255 note.

50 Lessing and Wayman, *Mkhas grub rje's "Fundamentals,"* 325.

consecration could well seem an anti-climax."[51] Indeed, the CMT and GST ignore it; while the HVT and SPT are committed to the principle that "everything goes in fours."[52]

The ancient commentaries provide various solutions to this problem, but Kamalanātha gives a somewhat convincing one, as described by Isaacson: "This is the notion that the fourth empowerment, understood as the state (or the realization of the state) which is the goal, is experienced directly by some few (fortunate, or rather advanced) disciples during the [third] *prajñājñānābhiṣeka*. For others, however, it must be revealed with words thereafter."[53] That allows for a Fourth initiation while acknowledging it is not always needed. Let us accept it, then, as one more instance in India of the problem of the "Three and the Fourth," a motif toward which religious thought is innately inclined.

Jungian thoughts Jung was not aware of Anuttarayoga Tantra and its transgressive practices. What he heard from Heinrich Zimmer and read in John Woodroffe hinted at this late form of Buddhist Tantra but in a "softened," more conventional form (closer to Tsoṅ-kha-pa). In his study of early Hindu Tantra, David White calls this form "soft core" Tantra as opposed to what we are now exploring, "hard core" Tantra.[54] Hinduism itself makes the distinction between "right hand" tantric practices as opposed to the less savory "left hand" practices—referring to the hand used by Indians for polluting acts such as washing one's feet and cleaning after defecation.

I doubt, however, that Jung would have been offended by the "left" side of tantric Buddhism. After all, that side associates to the unconscious that contains (within the shadow) our undeveloped, devalued, and weak side. It is, understandably, felt to be "sinister" (Latin for "left") but with which we need to "unite" if there is to be anything resembling psychological honesty or wholeness.

If a man identifies "one-sidedly" with ego consciousness—denying his shadow, not to mention the archetypal dimension of the psyche—his unconscious "Other" side is often symbolized, by contrast, as "female" (what Jung calls that man's "anima," Latin for "soul"). It would be understandable, then, that the woman brought into the room for the Secret and Wisdom initiations be an "outcaste"—yet also highly valuable, as symbolic of what is required to "complete" this man. If the Buddhist rituals are initiating an ascetic into that missing part of his personality—even without awareness of its modern psychological meaning—so much the better. The candidate intuits that he is doing the "right" thing by embracing the "left." And the psychological opposites of "left and right" come closer.

Granted, that is not the same as a slow, difficult, process of individuation in real life—whereby the opposites in the "split" personality of a modern man or woman come closer—but the ritual expresses it for us to ponder. A modern woman identified with only conscious ideas and plans would need to reflect upon her own "outcaste," unconscious "animus" (her "soul" mate)—who also deserves to be brought into the "room" of her psychology for some kind of "union."

---

[51] Isaacson, "Tantric Buddhism," 12.

[52] Snellgrove, HVT, 1:49.

[53] Isaacson, "Tantric Buddhism," 12.

[54] White, *Tantra in Practice*, 6-7.

Transgressive food Let us observe that the Anuttarayoga initiations are not unique in the history of religions by offering special or proscribed "food" to their candidates to bring about a union with the Divine. Examples extend from the earliest totemic meals that allowed the tribe to eat the flesh of a taboo animal and "ingest" its sacred power; to the Dionysian *omophagia* ("eating of raw flesh") in rites called *orgia* (its English derivative preserving memories of antinomian behavior); to the Christian ritual of eating and drinking the "body and blood" of their incarnate God. It is considered ambrosia in the Gospel of John 6:54: "Anyone who does eat my flesh and drink my blood has eternal life." Although the Church's rite uses red wine and white bread—their version of the symbolic opposites, "Red and White"—the very idea was offensive to the Jews of the first-century who had long avoided consuming blood even in cooked meat.

Today, no one is offended by this "disgusting" alimentary Christian ritual but neither is it effective, says Jung—to bring about a "communion" with the archetypal depths on the "Other Side" of the psyche. Yet one can try to bring the meaning of all these examples back to life, Jung suggests, by their psychological equivalent: "He must celebrate a Last Supper with himself, and eat his own flesh and drink his own blood, which means that he must recognize and accept the other in himself."[55] He adds, "there is no meal worse than one's own flesh."[56]

Transgressive sex Of course, the Anuttarayoga sacred acts are also conspicuously sexual—the "food" consisting of sexual fluids, accompanied eventually by the actual "joy" of sex. It is an historical fact, however, that India had never quite kept the sexual and the sacred apart—until the arrival of the Mughals, then the British. Even then, temples at Konārak (13th century) and at Khajurāho (14th century) were constructed with sculptural programs of erotic *maithuna* decorating the outer walls—that miraculously escaped destruction.

In the very early Indus Valley Culture of the third millennium BCE, there was likely a ritual *hieros gamos*, judging from images on seals recovered by archaeologists. Then, in the second millennium, a Vedic king could decide to celebrate an elaborate horse sacrifice to the gods. Toward its close, the chief royal wife would simulate copulation with the dead "consecrated" stallion the night before its dismemberment: "divine power from the horse . . . entering the queen and thereby entering the king and the people."[57] In the later *Bṛhadāraṇyaka Upaniṣad*, we find the fire sacrifice unabashedly correlated to a woman sexually:

> Her vulva is the sacrificial ground; her pubic hair is the sacred grass; her labia majora are the Soma-press; and her labia minora are the fire blazing at the center. A man who engages in sexual intercourse with this knowledge . . . appropriates to himself the merits of the women with whom he has sex. The women, on the other hand, appropriate to themselves the merits of a man who engages in sexual intercourse with them without this knowledge.[58]

---

[55] Jung, *CW* 14, par. 512.

[56] Jung, *Nietzsche's "Zarathustra,"* 2:800.

[57] Flood, *Hinduism*, 44.

[58] Olivelle, *Early Upaniṣads*, BU 6.4.3.

Notice the exchange of "divine power" between the sacred horse and a woman and the exchange of "merit" between a man and a woman during sexual intercourse.

The ascetic movement that emerged in the sixth century, then, would forever sit in tension with this deeply-rooted "religio-erotic" attitude. In Tantra, we might say this attitude is reasserting itself but was not that anomalous.

Jung acknowledges that sex "is the strongest and most immediate instinct, standing out as *the* instinct above all others" [his italics]—receiving, therefore, a great deal of attention by the many religions, but usually with the aim of curtailing it:

> These organizations or systems are "symbola" . . . which enable man to set up a spiritual counterpole to his primitive instinctual nature, a cultural attitude as opposed to sheer instinctuality. This has been the function of all religions.[59]

And yet:

> I must emphasize that the spiritual principle does not, strictly speaking, conflict with instinct as such, but only with blind instinctuality, which really amounts to an unjustified preponderance of the instinctual nature over the spiritual. The spiritual appears in the psyche also as an instinct, indeed as a real passion, a "consuming fire," as Nietzsche once expressed it.[60]

Missing this point, Christianity fostered an actual split between "sex and religion."

To correct this unnatural polar opposition—Jung believes—Western alchemy developed as a kind of underground "protest." Ostensibly speaking only of chemicals, alchemy considered the colors "red and white" to be symbolic opposites that needed to be combined. Jung writes:

> For a thousand years red was regarded as the masculine and white as the feminine color. The alchemists spoke of the *servus rubeus* (red slave) and the *femina candida* (white woman): their copulation produced the supreme union of opposites.[61]

This was our own culture's more recent attempt to express—even using sexual imagery—what the tantric Buddhists have called "nonduality." The symbolic colors of alchemy were assigned differently, however, since the "red" associated to the masculine sun (rather than female blood) and the "white" associated to the feminine moon (rather than to male semen).

Buddhist revaluations? Western religions still struggle with the split between sex and religion, while late Buddhist Tantra—as their symbols and rituals show—was able to close the gap somewhat.

---

59 Jung, *CW* 8, par. 111.

60 Jung, *CW* 8, par. 108.

61 Jung, *CW* 10, par. 790.

But I think it is an overstatement to claim, as one often reads, that the Anuttarayoga is an "affirmation of the body, the senses, and sexuality" and a "revaluation of the status and role of women."[62]

For one thing, we know from an earlier chapter that women were increasingly absent from the Buddhist religion, the *bhikṣuṇī* ordination lineage dying out by the tenth century in India (and never actually established in Southeast Asia or Tibet).[63] Davidson showed us that the participation of women in Buddhism "precipitously declined" during the tantric period. And should one think that social fact is offset by the inclusion of women in the antinomian initiations, it is not at all clear that they are more than instruments for the male yogin's use. Instructions in the literature, furthermore, are predominantly directed toward a male disciple.

As for affirmation of the body, a passage in the HVT is frequently cited as evidence: "Without bodily form, how should there be bliss?"[64] Eliade writes joyfully:

> In tantrism, the human body acquires an importance it had never before attained in the spiritual history of India. . . . The Upaniṣadic and post-Upaniṣadic pessimism and asceticism are swept away. The body is no longer the source of pain, but the most reliable and effective instrument at man's disposal for "conquering death."[65]

But we will see below that the Anuttarayoga is really interested in a subtle "tantric body" that is only ambiguously related to our physical body—that has always been denigrated by Buddhism. Indeed, we will witness below a divine Fire that destroys the body completely, both in its gross and subtle forms.

Finally, it is difficult to agree that the sexual instinct in this last phase of Buddhism is "revalued." What we have seen is so highly "choreographed" and limited to only the very few—not to mention, kept strictly secret—that one is hard put to feel that a healthy sex life has been lovingly affirmed. As for the occasional suggestion that *tāntrikas* had found a way to indulge their lusts, Wayman writes:

> But, to be practical, it is passing strange that anyone would bother with the Tantra to justify his "degenerate" practice, for who so bent among worldly persons would divert his energies by muttering a *mantra* a hundred thousand times at dawn, noon, sunset, and midnight, with fasting and other inhibitions, to engage in a "degenerate" practice, when, as we know so well, people at large engage in degenerate practices without bothering to mortify themselves at dawn, noon, sunset, and night![66]

I even wonder how these "erotic" rites could be performed by chaste men (if not also women) dedicated for many years to the suppression, even extirpation, of their sexual urges. Would that

---

62 See, for example, Jackson, *Tantric Treasures*, 24; and Tribe, "Mantranaya," 149.

63 Karma Lekshe Tsomo, "Nuns," *EB* 2:607.

64 Senllgrove, HVT, 1:92.

65 Eliade, *Yoga*, 227.

66 Wayman, *Buddhist Tantras*, 6.

instinct be happily available to an initiate who had been wrapping a mantrafied string around his waist every night to prevent even nocturnal emission of semen?

Nevertheless, it is true that the symbolism of "revaluation" is expressed by these tantric practices—the way that the "Evil" side of the Divine is symbolically expressed by "Wrathful" *devatās*, even though Buddhism does not intend that we read it that way. And today we do need new attitudes toward the missing, devalued, unconscious side of our lives—especially toward the Feminine dimension, however defined, that must include the social role of women, the body, and sex as not just procreative but legitimately pleasurable. I think that need explains the overstatements in praise of Tantra and the popularity of books on "Tantric sex"—that have little or nothing to do with India or with Tantra.

Of course, there has not been as much interest in the "revaluation" of feces and in learning how to drink urine and menstrual blood with equanimity. Nor has there been much interest in the shadow side of the psyche that is really difficult to "swallow."

Origins

Let us pause in our exploration to consider the origins of Buddhist Tantra. Earlier, I alluded to very old religious forms practiced in villages or among the hill tribes of India. They would have preserved ways of worship regardless of developments in mainstream urban India. Although difficult to demonstrate, that history seems more likely with regard to the Anuttarayoga—and similar expressions among the Hindus.

Also, it is surprising to find Buddhism becoming so ritually "concrete" at such a late date in its unfolding. As a rule, religions develop from concrete expressions toward more "spiritual" ones—that actually anticipate our modern psychological understanding. For example, child sacrifice in the background of Israelite religion (witness Abraham's willingness to sacrifice his son) developed into the sacrifice of a significant body part (circumcision of a son's genital organ associated with "life"), and then into more inward expressions (Jeremiah's calling for a circumcision of the "heart").

It follows that concrete tantric rites in Buddhism are not the result of a natural evolution within the religion and, instead, the result of having absorbed concrete forms existing intact elsewhere—outside Buddhism. Snellgrove observes:

> That new elements are introduced, the effect of which is far-reaching, there is no denying, but there is no essential break in the development of the doctrine. One might even claim that these new elements far from issuing in a degeneration, brought about a rejuvenation, nourished in the hidden well-springs of Indian religious life.[67]

Thus, Tantra—Hindu or Buddhist—represents a kind of "synthesis," India's religions becoming more culturally complete.

White's work on tantric Hinduism proves useful here. He writes of village India:

---

[67] Snellgrove, HVT, 1:40.

> In ancient times as in the present, village India has had its own local or regional deities that it has worshipped in its own ways and in its own contexts. These deities, which are multiple rather than singular, often form a part of the geographical as well as human landscapes of their various localities: trees, forests, mountains, bodies of water; but also the malevolent and heroic dead, male and female ancestors, and ghosts, ghouls, and rascally imps of every sort. . . . these multiple (and often feminine) deities are, before all else, angry and hungry, and very often angry because hungry. Their cultus consists of feeding them in order that they be pacified.[68]

When pacified, these deities provide benefits like fertile fields, a large family, freedom from disease, and a long life. Since these blessings were understood as the gods' "life Blood," the best way for human beings to express gratitude—and to replenish that Blood for future blessings—was understood to be the bloody sacrifice of humans (and, if possible, the blood of animals as a substitute).

At some point, White demonstrates, this exchange of "vital fluid" in Indian village religion became sexualized whereby goddesses in particular—the well-known Apsarases of water and Yakṣiṇīs of trees, in addition to strange beings called Yoginīs and Ḍākinīs (that we find suddenly in tantric Buddhism)—could be satisfied not by blood but by a yogin's semen. And this would stimulate the deity's own sexual discharge (understood as her life-giving menstrual Blood).

An "erotico-mystical practice" evolved among proto-tantric groups worshipping not only local deities but also the more mainstream, yet heterodox, high god Śiva—and his wife, who was variously named for her śakti ("power, energy"):

> Only through initiation by and continued interaction with the Yoginīs could these male practitioners access this fluid essence and boundless energy of the godhead. It was therefore necessary that male practitioners be "inseminated," or more properly speaking "insanguinated," with the sexual or menstrual discharge of the Yoginīs—rendering the "mouth" of the Yoginī their sole conduit to membership in the clan [*kula*, "family;" hence, the Kula or Kaula tradition of Hinduism] and all its perquisites. Here, the "mouth" of the Yoginī was the vulva, and "drinking female discharge" (*rajapāna*), the prime means to fulfilling these male needs.[69]

These religious practices and their symbolism appear to have been absorbed, nearly intact, by Buddhist Tantra. That would account for the rituals of "sexual intercourse" and the "ingesting" of sexual fluids. It even accounts for the ambiguity concerning the "filth" of the woman—for, on the one hand, it is the disgusting discharge of traditional Buddhism; on the other hand, it is the life-giving essence of the feminine Divine.

---

[68] David Gordon White, *Kiss of the Yoginī: "Tantric Sex" in its South Asian Contexts* (Chicago: Chicago University Press), 2003), 3.

[69] White, *Kiss of the Yoginī*, 11.

Post-initiatory Practice

The practice of a successfully empowered candidate in the Anuttarayoga class of Tantra is not entirely dissimilar from practice in the earlier three classes—Kriyā, Caryā, and Yoga classes. In fact, one must do what the others do in what is now called the A) "Stage of Generation." The multi-step "Vase" initiation belongs to all classes and provides a paradigm for the worship of Buddhist *devatās* using a *maṇḍala* image to attract them, identifying with these supernatural Beings in "deity yoga" to train one's mind to see or experience as does the "Mind" of a Buddha.

But now one may also practice in the higher B) "Stage of Completion" for which the new consecrations provide the most advanced paradigm in Buddhism. Put simply, one knows from the Secret, Wisdom, and Fourth initiations how to "feed" the gods and how to be "nourished" by them in a higher exchange of Vital Fluids. The GST exhorts:

> In a deserted place, the *sādhaka* should always perform the special practice with a twelve-year-old Caṇḍāla girl of noble mind; he should make a four-sided *maṇḍala* there, according to the rite, with excrement and urine and the other sacred substances, meditating on the Vajra *maṇḍala* . . . . he will become like the Buddha.[70]

Wedemeyer concludes, however, that there were not many tantric Buddhists who did this or did so for very long. He writes:

> modern scholarship has consistently and markedly misconstrued the nature of practice in the antinomian traditions, insofar as references to *caryā* ["practice, ritual"] employed as a term of art have been understood instead as referring in the generic to Tantric practice. . . . the practice referred to in these passages (and many others) is by no means *the* practice of initiated Tantric Buddhists, but merely one, very rarified, practice. That is to say, it is perhaps better construed as a proper noun—not practice, but "The Practice."[71]

He is saying that only a relatively few highly advanced *sādhakas* ever engaged in what the GST has just called "the special practice" of transgressive behavior. And they would do so for no more than six months at a time.

Thus, this same Anuttarayoga *tantra* reads: "he will soon become the Buddha, the Lord, the vast Ocean of Wisdom; in six months he will attain all this, there is no doubt."[72] And if "Buddhahood" did not arrive within that time frame? Then the practitioner would return to his monastery to engage in more acceptable exoteric—and esoteric—activities like studying scripture, including the *tantras* and their commentaries.[73]

---

[70] Fremantle, trans, GST, 97.

[71] Wedemeyer, *Making Sense*, 134-135.

[72] Fremantle, trans., GST, 121.

[73] Wedemeyer, *Making Sense*, 177.

Vesna Wallace makes the important point that the "bliss" or "joy" experienced initially during the Wisdom initiation is never repeated afterward for its own sake, even for a "glimpse" of the goal. Instead, it "refines the mind by diminishing conceptualizations and thus makes it fit for the realization of the empty nature of phenomena"—the usual "ultimate" (or penultimate) Buddhist goal.[74]

Group Practice

Apparently, there were also group practices. They were called the *gaṇa-cakra-pūjā*, "worship of the group circle"—that Snellgrove translates loosely as, "tantric feast." This means that a number of Anuttarayoga *sādhakas* would gather for a brief period—what Wedemeyer calls, "a one-night affair"—albeit at regular places and times.[75] Vajragarbha asks the Lord in the HVT:

> "What, O Lord, are these places of meeting?"
> The Lord replied: "They are the *pīṭha* ["seat, abode"] and the *upapīṭha* ["subsidiary seat"].[76]

And the Buddha names twenty-four locations, Jālandhara, Uḍḍiyāna, etc. that are in the main recognizable geographical places in India. They do not include, however, the "four sites of pilgrimage" of exoteric Buddhism marking key moments in the Life of Gautama Buddha—his birth at Lumbinī, his breakthrough at Bodhgayā, etc. So here there is a break with Buddhist tradition and, instead, common ground with pilgrimage sites of Śaivite Hinduism.

As for the times, the Lord continues:

> The day too I will tell you when the *yoginīs* [female practitioners or Female divinities?] meet together, for the purpose of the welfare of all beings in the Yoginī-tantra of Hevajra.
> Vajragarbha said: "Lord, which are those days?"
> The Lord replied: "The fourteenth and the eighth days in the dark fortnight."

Thus, there were meetings at special places every week for ritual sex and the eating of taboo substances with persons of questionable class status. That there is a schedule reminds us that since earliest Buddhism monks and nuns gathered every two weeks to recite the *prātimokṣa* code—that strictly forbade transgressive behavior. Indeed, tantric inversions of non-tantric Buddhism are often exact and—were it not for the evident seriousness of this style of the religion—we would consider it parody.

The closest expression in Christianity would be the "Black Mass" of the late Middle Ages that Bruce Long sees as, "the last gasp of a set of native European practices that had preceded the rise

[74] Cited by Samuel, *Origins*, 331.
[75] Wedemeyer, *Making Sense*, 192.
[76] Snellgrove, HVT, 1:68-71.

of Christianity by centuries."[77] The practices of Tantra, however, are not some last gasp of what had gone before and are, instead, "new blood" for a religion that was having trouble surviving in medieval India.

A Problem of Language

Sign Language

Entrance to a "tantric feast" required the use of a secret code that would identify all parties. This added a layer of complexity to Buddhism's long-standing "problem" with language that: on the one hand, could truthfully teach the Dharma; and, on the other hand, made false substantial "realities" out of mere parts. Tantra accepted what had already been taught about words but introduced a code of hand gestures for the Anuttarayoga group meetings. Not to be confused with *mudrās* (sacred hand gestures accompanying *mantras*), they were called *chomā*. We read the following in the HVT:

> Now we shall expound the chapter on secret signs [*chomā*], by which the yogin and yoginī may be recognized with certainty. Whoever shows one finger, implies: Am I welcome? The showing of two implies he is welcome. . . . If he presents the fourth finger, he should be shown the little finger, [etc.].[78]

In this way, a sacred tantric gathering could effectively exclude the uninitiated and the frauds.

"Twilight" Language

Tantra also introduced a verbal code that is more interesting than this sign language—since it applies not only to communal feasts but also to tantric texts in general. This code is called, *saṃdhā-bhāṣā*, literally meaning "joining language" but often translated as "hidden language." It carries the extended meaning of "twilight language," pointing to those liminal times when day and night "join" at evening and at dawn. This is important to Buddhism since in the "Life," Gautama conquered Māra at dusk and was Enlightened at daybreak. Moreover, the coming together of the pair, "day and night," at twilight alludes to the truth of "nonduality."

The Anuttarayoga claims it is very important:

> He who has been consecrated in Hevajra and does not use this hidden language will lose the sacramental power, of that there is no doubt. From calamities or thieves, demons, fevers, poisons, he will die, even though he be a Buddha, if he does not speak this secret language.[79]

---

[77] J. Bruce Long, "Demons: An Overview," *ER* 4:286.

[78] Snellgrove, HVT, 1:66.

[79] Snellgrove, HVT, 1:100.

One could say something similar about symbolic religious language in general—since it provides access to the Sacred, the loss of which is a spiritual calamity.

Nevertheless, *saṃdha-bhāṣa* is not very symbolic and, instead, another artificial code or mere "sign" like *chomā*. In a long list of equivalents, the HVT informs us, for example:

> *padmabhājana* (lotus-vessel) is *kapāla* (skull)
> *catuḥsama* (a potion of four ingredients) is *gūtha* (dung)
> *kasturikā* (musk) is *mūtra* (urine)
> *sihlaka* (frankincense) is *svayaṃbhu* (blood)
> *karpūra* (camphor) is *śukra* (semen)[80]

My selection makes it clear that the first word in the equation is inoffensive and should be used to "hide" the offensive term that follows. In fact, we find this vocabulary applied in certain passages of scripture (although not consistently since codes vary); it helps us understand the actual transgressive practice intended.

But, then, the equations can be taught in the opposite direction. The HVT continues:

> Likewise, the Buddhas of the Five Families may be referred to by means of hidden speech: Ḍombī for the Vajra-family, Nartī for the Lotus-family, Caṇḍālī for the Gem-family [etc.].

In this passage, the offensive terms come first—i.e., the names of low-class fierce goddesses of the Anuttarayoga pantheon—referring to the Families of deities that belong to all tantric classes.

An explicit denial of transgression appears with a set of presumably offensive commands in "twilight language" that we heard at the beginning of this chapter. The Lord advised:

> You should slay living-beings.
> You should speak lying words.
> You should take what is not given.
> You should frequent others' wives.[81]

But, then, this same Lord goes on to explain that the commands are not at all offensive if one knows what they mean:

> Now to practice singleness of thought is the "taking of life," for the thought is the life. To vow to save all men is interpreted as "lying-speech." That which is "not given" is the bliss of woman, and she is your own Nairātmyā who is the "wife of all others."

---

[80] Snellgrove, HVT, 1:99-100.

[81] Snellgrove, HVT, 1:97. Slightly altered.

The HVT does not call this passage *saṃdhā-bhāṣā*. But the language is coded whereby what offends "hides" what mainstream Mahāyāna has long taught: that a Bodhisattva "lies" when vowing to save all beings (since there are no "beings" to save), that the Perfection of Wisdom is symbolically feminine (yet this "wife" belongs to everyone), etc.[82]

We could even say there is something effectively symbolic about putting Buddhist truths this way. It gives nuance to religious paradox to call it a "lie," as even the *Lotus* suggested. One's feeling is stirred to say that getting in touch with Wisdom is a kind of "adultery"—even suggesting what drives ordinary adultery. But the Buddha's orthodox interpretation of meaning here should not be applied to all tantric practices, some of which are actually transgressive. On the other hand, we should never have expected that a *tāntrika* could have actually gotten away with killing, lying, stealing and adultery—even for six months of the "Practice"—and returned to the monastery unscathed.

The Tantric Body

Channels and "Cakras"

We now approach a very difficult topic in Buddhist Tantra that all but defies understanding from outside—if not also from within the tradition. It explains Strickmann's comment earlier that Tantra is the "ultimate challenge" for the scholar of religion, if not also for the reader's patience. The topic is the "tantric body" or esoteric physiology of the "Stage of Completion"—that overlaps bewilderingly with our normal, exoteric physiology.

The Wisdom initiation may have actually introduced us to this "body" since some ancient commentators claim that the ritual sex between the candidate and the woman was much more difficult than we could tell—reflecting an advanced post-initiatory practice. Isaacson comments: "But it must be said that in the context of what should be an initiatory rite, the entrance of a pupil into the religion, it is highly unnatural that that pupil should be expected to perform so advanced a feat."[83]

Here is the feat, as described by Nāropa, an eleventh-century *mahāsiddha*:

> The coming of the śukra ["semen"] . . . from the lotus with four petals of the uṣṇīṣa to the lotus with sixteen petals of the forehead and its permeation of both, is the [1] *First Joy*.
>
> Thereafter follows the [2] *Perfect Joy*, in the throat and in the heart: the coming of the śukra from the lotus with thirty-two petals of the throat to the lotus with eight petals of the heart and their complete permeation is Perfect Joy.
>
> Thereupon follows the [3] *Joy of Cessation*: the coming of the śukra from the lotus with sixty-four petals of the navel to the lotus with thirty-two petals of the sexual organ and their permeation is the Joy of Cessation. And while the śukra is in the navel it is characterized by various delights such as close embraces, the

[82] See Snellgrove, *Indo-Tibetan Buddhism*, 1:174.

[83] Isaacson, "Tantric Buddhism," 17.

> sudden drawing-in of breath and deep moanings due to thrills of pleasure, etc. However, as the bliss arising when the śukra is in the sexual organ eludes concrete description, the Joy of Cessation, arising at the end of sexual union, is the mere perception of bliss, being characterized by the thought "I am experiencing bliss." But a delight which is gone is not [ultimate] bliss, therefore, the coming of the drop which has the sixteen lunar digits from the lotus of the sexual organ to the lotus with eight petals of the Vajra-Jewel which is hidden therein is the [4] *Simultaneously-arisen Joy*. It is permanent due to the absence of emission of śukra through the force of retention.[84]

This strange passage describes, as Kvaerne informs us, the "downward movement of the Thought-of-Enlightenment [i.e., *bodhicitta* as a code name for semen, also called here a "drop"] from its reservoir in the brain, through the seven cakras or 'lotuses' of the body, to the tip of the penis (the 'Vajra-Jewel')"—which the semen reaches but from which it is not allowed to be ejaculated. That, Nāropa says, is really how the "Four Joys" arise in the third consecration of the Anuttarayoga! More likely, it is how they arise in post-initiatory practice after much training.

First of all, let us note that semen was believed by ancient India to have its source in a man's head. The marrow there (what Kvaerne calls the "brain") was plentiful, full of life, and seemed clearly to be the origin of the life-giving "white" of a man. The Indians were not alone in this view of biology since the Greeks and Romans agreed. Richard Onians explains Greek *psyche* as the "life-principle" or "soul" that survives the death of the body:

> The *psyche* is itself "seed" (*sperma*), or rather is in the "seed," and this "seed" is enclosed in the skull and spine and explicitly identified with the marrow or, as it is once called "generative marrow" and flows thence in the propagation of a new life. It breathes through the genital organ.[85]

The Romans called this same "life stuff," *genius,* since it was "generative." Perhaps we should not be surprised by the similarity of view since all three ancient cultures have a common Indo-European substratum.

Specifically, for India—if not just for tantric India—the semen produced in the head passed down through the body along the spine within a central tube or "channel" called a *nāḍī*. In doing so, it encountered clusters of other *nāḍīs* at specific locations along this central channel. In Nāropa's view, these channel clusters are found at the crown of the head (the *uṣṇīṣa*), the forehead between the eyebrows, the throat, heart, navel, the base of the sex organ, and (in a man) the glans of the penis called here the "gem of the *vajra*."

Since it is from these clusters that numerous other channels radiated outward to other parts of the body, they were called *cakras* or "wheels" with many spokes—or, as in our passage, *padmas*, "lotuses" with many petals, variously numbered. Ancient physiologists claimed that the human body

---

[84] Kvaerne, "Sahaja," 180-181.

[85] Richard Broxton Onians, *The Origins of European Thought* (1951; repr., Salem: Ayer Company, Publishers, 1987), 119.

is served by 72,000 of these *nāḍīs* of which the most important are 120, 32, or just 3. When only three are discussed, they are the central channel and two other channels located to the left and right of the spine. See Figure 16.2 for a Tibetan diagram of five *cakras* created by *nāḍī* clusters along a central channel with two side channels looping to meet periodically.

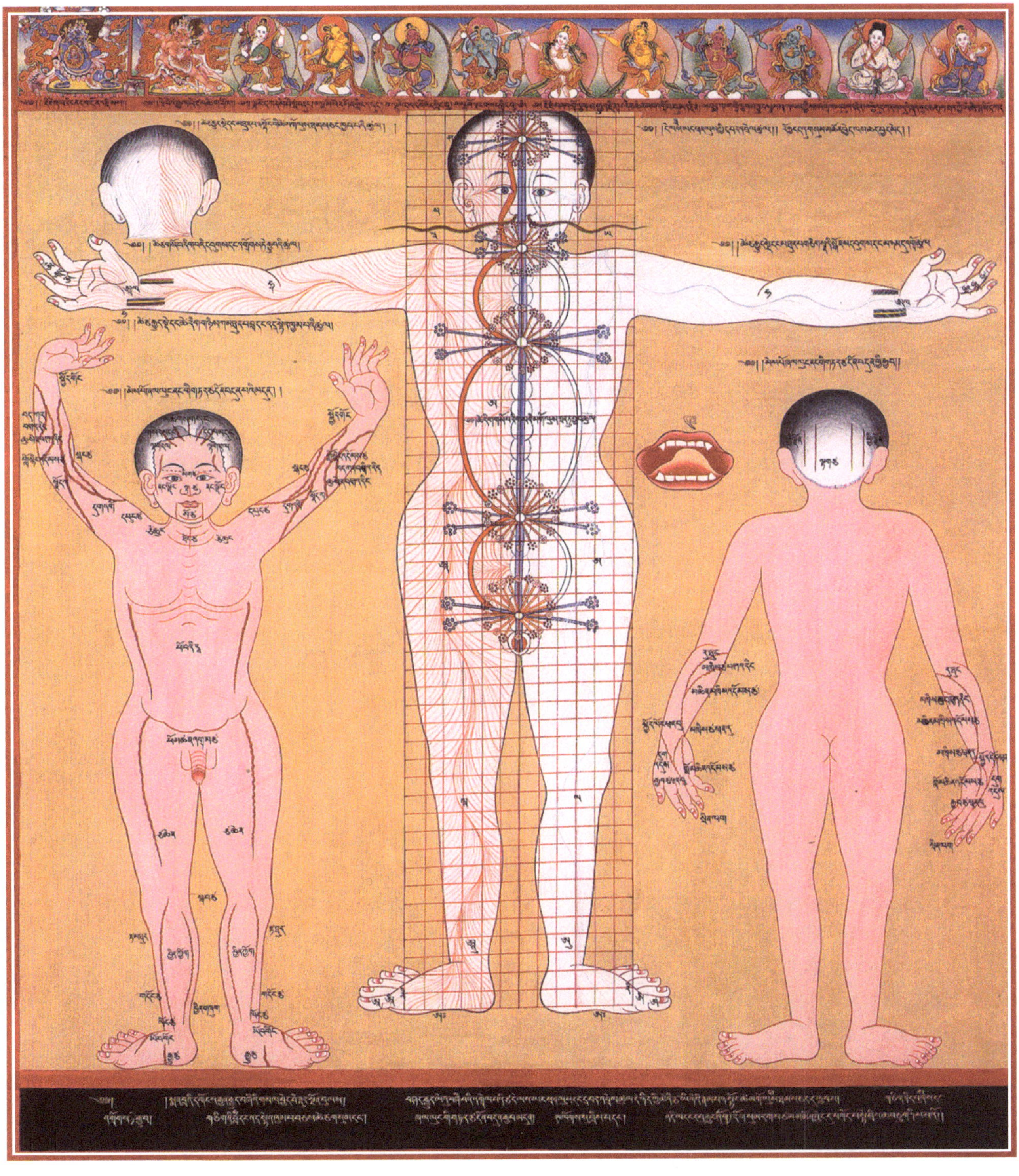

Figure 16.2 Tantric Body

The Body "Maṇḍala"

In tantric Buddhism, this system of channels and *cakras* is sometimes called the "body *maṇḍala*." That is due in part because it is a "complete" system, for which the word *maṇḍala* is often used. In particular, it is because this esoteric body's many features are regularly identified in Tantra with Buddhist deities—a sort of Anuttarayoga version of "self-generation" found first in the lower *tantras*. Hence, the first chapter of the HVT lists 32 *nāḍīs* and names them for thirty-two female *devatās*. They include the goddess Avadhūtī as the central channel, with Lalanā to the left and Rasanā to the right.

The text goes on to identify its four main *cakras*—at the navel, heart, throat, and head—with the Bodies of the Buddha. To fit the system, this required adding to the Three Bodies of mainstream Mahāyāna a fourth Body—the Mahāsukha-kāya ("Great Bliss Body") or Sahaja-kāya ("Innate Body")—at the head. These same "wheels" are identified with the four divine Consorts (Locanā, etc.).

But, then, the scripture goes on to correlate these four *cakras* with the Four Joys, and the Four Noble Truths—informing us that the two side channels are not just goddesses but the celestial sun and the moon, and at the same time the vowels and consonants of Sanskrit. The identifications become so thorough and so unwieldy—crossing categories of reference—that Snellgrove is forced to remark upon their "absence of any rationality."[86] Instead, the point seems to be to find everything in the cosmos, explicitly divine or otherwise, within the structures of the "tantric body"—microcosmically. It allows the great adept Saraha to exclaim: "Here are the sacred places, here the *Pīṭhas* and the *Upa-pīṭhas*—I have not seen a place of pilgrimage and an abode of bliss like my body."[87] By this, he means his esoteric body.

This correlation between macrocosm and microcosm in the "body *maṇḍala*" was already expressed by the external *maṇḍala* of powdered colors or paint. It, too, contained the "whole," emanating from its center to the periphery. David White suggests we take another "god's eye" view of the matter:

> This body, which comprises energy channels (*nāḍīs*) and centers (*cakras*), drops, and winds, is itself a maṇḍala. If it were to be viewed from above, the vertical central channel of the subtle body . . . would appear as the center point of the maṇḍala, with the various *cakras* aligned along that channel appearing as so many concentric circles, wheels, or lotuses radiating outward from that center.[88]

It would be like looking down on the sacred monument of Borobodur, but in miniature human form.

---

[86] Snellgrove, HVT, 1:37.

[87] Eliade, *Yoga*, 228.

[88] White, *Tantra in Practice*, 14.

The Winds

White has just mentioned "winds" (*prāṇa, vāyu*). They are an additional esoteric feature of the tantric body and said to circulate inside the many channels. While it is true that semen could flow through a central channel from the head to the penis, it needed to be propelled by a wind—and ejaculation was "proof" that a wind (or air pressure?) was behind it. There are five kinds of wind in Buddhist Tantra that allow the body to function: *prāṇa* controls breathing and is often called the "vital wind"; *apāna* propels semen, menstrual discharge, urine, and feces (flatulence or "breaking wind" is "proof" that wind is involved); *vyāna* controls blood circulation, the spurting of blood from a wound; *udāna* is behind speaking; and *samāna* has to do with digestion. But this is to mix ostensibly esoteric winds with exoteric bodily functioning, raising the question: Are these channels, *cakras*, and winds actually there or are they only imagined to be there?

Gavin Flood, commenting on the Hindu version of the tantric body, believes that the "texts do not intend to reify the subtle body and its centers" as actually there, "ontologically." And his proof is the "mercurial nature of the accounts"—that number and locate the "wheels" differently, that may refer to ten "winds" and not just five, etc.[89] Thus, he concludes these features are present only during visualization exercises—albeit effectively so—for religious purposes. In fact, we have already observed the Buddhist tantric body with seven *cakras* but also with only five or four.

Yet the earliest Upaniṣads do speak of the ordinary body as having five winds—gathering at the heart when someone sleeps, and from which that "person" travels during dream. It is from the crown of the head that these same winds depart at death. I personally think the authors of these materials were not quite sure of the status of these structures, if they were "there" or not there, and that is why we encounter variety and ambiguity—as we do elsewhere in Buddhism.

Whatever the case, we must wonder if all men were believed to experience the first three Joys "of this world" as semen passed down through the central channel and that it is only the trained yogin who experiences the fourth "Innate Joy," as a foretaste of Nirvāṇa's Bliss. If so, according to Nāropa, that is because the semen is not ejaculated—but held between the sixth and seventh *cakras*. Holding or stabilizing it there provides a more "permanent" foretaste of Nirvāṇa—beyond the painful "impermanence" of Saṃsāra.

Let us add that, sexually, that form of *coitus reservatus* would be no easy feat. We must also wonder if controlling the semen in this way allowed for any vital fluid exchange between the partners, any mixing of the red and the white—carrying the important symbolic meaning of the Red and White as "nondual" Bodhicitta.

Apparently noticing this problem, Vīravajra comments—according to David Gray—that in the Wisdom initiation of the *Cakrasamvara Tantra* (CST) disciples do ejaculate ("make oblations of seminal essence with the ladle of the secret vajra into the fire pit of the lady's vulva") but then reverse that flow in what Gray describes as the "reabsorption of sexual fluids via reverse urethral suction."[90] Now, that would be difficult. The technique, however, allows for a mixing of male and female sexual fluids in the vagina before their "combined" reabsorption. Or, as Hugh Urban

---

[89] Gavin Flood, *The Tantric Body: The Secret Tradition of Hindu Religion* (London: I. B. Tauris, 2006), 161-162.

[90] Gray, CST, 121.

explains, "not only seminal retention but actually the sucking or withdrawal of the female sexual fluids out of the woman's body into the male body (what some call the 'fountain pen technique')."[91]

In a late fifteenth-century Hindu text called the *Haṭha-yoga-pradīpikā*, we read the following instruction:

> By means of a pipe, one should blow air slowly into the passage in the male organ. By practice, the discharged *bindu* ["drop," semen] is drawn out. One can draw back and preserve one's own discharged *bindu*. The Yogī who can protect his *bindu* thus, overcomes death; because death comes by discharging *bindu*, and life is prolonged by its preservation. (3:83-87)[92]

In this passage, we hear the general Indo-European fear of dissipation, of losing one's "vitality" and shortening one's lifespan unnecessarily by loss of semen. Much earlier, the *Bṛhadāranyaka Upaniṣad* had provided a prayer for a man who accidentally ejaculated: "I retrieve this semen . . . May I regain my virility. . . . As he recites this he should take the semen with his thumb and ring finger and rub it between his breasts or brows" (to reabsorb it?).[93] The use of a pipe in this *haṭha* ("forceful") yoga appears to involve the bladder in the attempt at reabsorption.

Jungian thoughts A critic might say, with justification, that we have come too far from Gautama Buddha's teaching. On the other hand, there is rich "withdrawal" symbolism embedded in these concrete ritual acts, however performed. After all, the first Buddhist rite of its kind was renunciation—leaving the home, "withdrawing" from the wife or from the harem (in Gautama's case), and being "reabsorbed" into the monastic group for the sake of one's salvation.

Early Buddhism spoke of the natural "flowing out" of the *āsravas*—those deep-seated defilements—that needed to be withheld; their "reversal" was an early technical term for having attained Nirvāṇa, being *an-āsrava*, We could say that the reversal of seminal emission is a concrete expression of Yogācāra's *parāvṛtti*, that "devolution" of "mind-only" whose externalized *pravṛtti* keeps us bound to the world—and unable to experience what Vasubandhu called "the inconceivable, . . . Bliss."

In any case, we are told that the advanced *tāntrikas* believed that either retaining one's semen at the brink of orgasm or absorbing it after ejaculation was the "most direct method" of generating this same nirvāṇic Bliss.

A subtle "body" We, of course, do not believe that semen originates in the head and flows down a central channel along the spine. Nevertheless, the psychological principle remains that whatever we find in the many religions is a "self-portrait" by the psyche itself from which we can learn about

---

91 Hugh Urban, "The Yoga of Sex: Tantra, Orientalism, and Sex Magic in the Ordo Templi Orientis," in *Hidden Intercourse: Eros and Sexuality in the History of Western Esotericism*, eds. Jeffrey J. Kripal and Wouter J. Hanegraaff (Leiden: Brill, 2008), 408.

92 Geoffrey Samuel and Jay Johnston, eds., *Religion and the Subtle Body in Asia and the West: Between Mind and Body* (London: Routledge, 2013), 137.

93 Olivelle, *Early Upaniṣads*, BU 6.4.5.

ourselves. For one thing, the "tantric body" of Buddhist or Hindu Tantra is a variant of the "subtle body" (*sūkṣma-śarīra*) witnessed throughout the religious history of India. Although that term is not common in Buddhism, it is in Hinduism where it contrasts with the "gross body" (*sthūla-śarīra*), the physical body we all know. And Buddhism has long claimed there are two bodies, one like a "scabbard" that contains within itself another like a "sword."

We interpreted this other body—with which Gautama believed he could fly, walk through walls, walk on water; the body with which Jesus walked on water and was believed to ascend to his heavenly Father—as the psyche itself. The ancients were not fully aware of the psyche's reality, as distinct from the physical, but knew that something like that existed and was very important. The Buddhists even called it a "body made of mind" (*manomaya-kāya*)—but a "body," nonetheless, something real. We are to take that as the psyche's "teaching" us through this self-portrait that it is real, as real as the physical body although different. It is the basis of Jung's own "working hypothesis"—what he calls, the "reality of the psyche."

Tantra makes it especially clear that the psyche is not some vague wispy something about which we can muse and perhaps dismiss. In fact, we ignore this psychological reality to our peril, just as we ignore our physical bodies to our peril, lest we get sick and die. Indeed, the tantric body is highly structured with its "channels" and "wheels" and their more or less precise number and locations. Jung would say that the mercurial variety of their descriptions is due to the epistemological difficulty of saying anything definite about the psyche from within the psyche—forcing us to speak in symbols.

He writes of the *cakras*:

> They symbolize highly complex psychic facts which at the present moment we could not possibly express except in images. The cakras are therefore of great value to us because they represent a real effort to give a symbolic theory of the psyche. The psyche is something so highly complicated, so vast in extent, and so rich in elements unknown to us, and its aspects overlap and interweave with one another in such an amazing degree, that we always turn to symbols in order to try to represent what we know about it.[94]

To anticipate his fuller commentary on Hindu Tantra, Jung interprets the *cakras* as symbols of psychological attitudes or states of mind, even stages in psychological development, of which we may or may not be capable. Thus, Jungian analysts sometimes refer to "cakras" in their books but not technically and, instead, as colorful ways to speak of the psyche.

It is meaningful that Tantra is uncertain about what is there or not there physically—because the physical body and the mind do overlap. It is an undeniable fact that there is some kind of "psycho-somatic" connection that we do not fully understand. After all, it seems entirely right to say—as if there were *cakras*—that we think with our "head," feel in our "heart," and have a "gut" sense about something. There can even be a stirring in the "loins" although sexually satisfied. And we all know that anxiety over some psychological event can be physically distressing. To think otherwise is to perpetuate an unfashionable "Cartesian split" between body and mind—that the symbolism of a

[94] Jung, *Kundalini Yoga*, 61.

tantric body discourages. On the other hand, the modern correction of this split has gone too far with "brain" today not only a synonym—but a substitute—for "mind."

Canalization of libido We can interpret the circulating "winds"—that we know more accurately to be breathing, blood pressure, peristalsis, etc.—as psychological libido or energy. And, experientially, our psychological energies do seem to flow in certain directions or "channels," if not by count in 72,000 ways and in the vicinity of the spine. One of the difficulties of psychotherapy is getting a troubled person's interest or desire already "channeled" in an inappropriate or even a self-destructive direction to flow differently—in the direction of adaptation, authenticity, or life.

Jung frequently refers to libido not as "wind" but as "water"—its natural flow as a "river," even capable of the powerful beauty of a "waterfall." The archetypes, then, are the "riverbeds" along which libido has flowed through the millennia to bring us to this point in our cultural development. These same archetypes reveal, however, that our psychological energy is not meant to flow entirely in a natural way—in the service of biological aims alone—but can and needs to be channeled (Jung prefers to say, "canalized") *contra naturam* in order to create consciousness and culture.

That is made possible, says Jung, by symbols. They are produced by the unconscious itself as "transformers" of libido. He writes in his essay, "On Psychic Energy":

> The transformation of instinctual energy is achieved by its canalization into an *analogue of the object of instinct* [Jung's italics]. Just as a power-station imitates a waterfall and thereby gains possession of its energy, so the psychic mechanism imitates the instinct and is thereby enabled to apply its energy for special purposes.[95]

He goes on, "The psychological mechanism that transforms energy is the symbol." That is why exposing oneself to the symbolism found in profounder expressions of art, music, dance, literature—and religion, including Tantra—is vitally important. It is why a person whose "winds" or "waters" are misguided must pay close attention to dreams and fantasies. They carry symbols that are actually attempting to "transform" or channel his or her interests toward a greater degree of consciousness—to better serve the preservation and development of culture.

Controlling the Winds

The strange *interruptus* of normal sexual intercourse in tantric Buddhism actually interrupts a completely externalized act, even making the sexual partner somewhat superfluous. Indeed, a more advanced post-initiatory procedure—controlling the winds that flow through the channels—is much more internalized, if not entirely so.

Tsunehiko Sugiki writes of ritual coitus:

[95] Jung, *CW* 8, par. 83 and 88.

> Sometime shortly after the eighth century, composers of later Buddhist tantras preserved this practice to a certain extent by internalizing sexual practices. This was an attempt to resolve the contradiction between monastic vows of celibacy and engaging in sexual practices, which occurred as tantric traditions originating outside monasteries were incorporated into monastic Buddhism.[96]

In a close study of progressively more recent texts, Sugiki shows that the older GST materials require sex as "support" for other procedures while the newer SPT treats what could be construed as sexual in a symbolic way. Thus, we begin to see what Tsoṅ-kha-pa meant by saying the Anuttarayoga was reserved for superior candidates who "delight in inner *samādhi* completely."

David White criticizes this gradual shift from what he calls "hard core" to "soft core" Tantra as an unfortunate "censoring" and "sublimation" of the flesh-and-blood "minglings" that "once took place on isolated hilltops on new moon nights."[97] He writes of a "de-feminization" and "masculinization" of both Hindu and Buddhist Tantra. While factually correct, White's complaint stems, I believe, from the modern longing for a better solution to the problem of "sex and religion" in our own culture. In its day, however, Buddhism could not long accommodate concrete religious acts and fulfill its function of "spiritualizing" India, i.e., of demonstrating that there really is a difference between the entirely somatic "scabbard" and the psycho-somatic "sword."

Phase One: Union of "Left and Right"

With internalization of tantric techniques, the Red and the White do not disappear. Instead, their manifestation as gross blood and semen becomes subtler, befitting a "subtle body." We now find them as mysterious red and white "drops" throughout the channels, even coating the walls of the 72,000 *nāḍīs* "like frost."[98] Apparently, they have proliferated in this subtle form from the original drops of physical semen and menstrual blood received from parents at conception. It is useful to know that in ancient embryology the image of the *gandharva* as it arrives in the womb is that of a "rider on a horse"—i.e., "consciousness (*vijñāna*) riding on the wind." It follows that the "red and white," whatever else they signify, are opposite kinds of consciousness (female and male, etc.) associated with the winds that flow throughout the body.

Now it is the yogin's task to gather these winds (along with their drops) and force them into the two main side channels—usually red drops into the left channel (Lalanā) and white drops into the right channel (Rasanā). This is achieved by controlled breathing (*prāṇāyāma*), intense contemplation, and perhaps with the "support" of a sexual rite—although it would be truly difficult for a man to keep an erection, retain semen, and focus on other things at the same time.

Snellgrove describes what is happening:

---

[96] Tsunehiko Sugiki, "Oblation, Non-conception, and Body: Systems of Psychosomatic Fire Oblation in Esoteric Buddhism in Medieval South Asia," in Richard K. Payne and Michael Witzel, eds., *"Homa" Variations: The Study of Ritual Change Across the "Longue Durée"* (Oxford: Oxford University Press, 2016), 172.

[97] White, *Kiss*, 242.

[98] Daniel Cozort, *Highest Yoga Tantra: An Introduction to the Esoteric Buddhism of Tibet* (Ithaca: Snow Lion Publications, 1986), 72.

> Now the breath to which thought is harnessed [like a "horse and rider"] is first made to pass regularly up and down the two outer channels, which thereby enact under strict control the process of *saṃsāra*. The breath becomes quiescent and the two psychic streams thus controlled are held and forced, as other escape is denied them [by "plugging" the orifices with *mantras*], to enter the base of the central channel. At their meeting they arouse the *bodhicitta* which resides there.[99]

It so happens that at their lowest extent all three main channels meet in the HVT at the navel *cakra*—at the "base of the central channel." And the coming together there of the contents of the two side channels, left and right, is a moment of great consequence: since the "opposites" of Red and the White are "uniting" in a subtler and more advanced way than at the initiations.

Indeed, in terms of the body *maṇḍala*, all the pairs of opposites are uniting—female and male, sun and moon, etc. Thus, we read: "Lalanā has the nature of Wisdom and Rasanā consists in the Means, and Avadhūtī is in the middle, free from the notions of subject and object."[100] "Freedom" from conceptual distinctions—including the pair of opposites, "subject and object"—is a mainstream definition of "nondual" Nirvāṇa. And that is why the "Mind of Enlightenment" or Bodhicitta has been "aroused," as Snellgrove puts it. Indeed, the "Practice" could almost cease at this point since so much has been attained—symbolically.

Phase Two: Union of "Below and Above"

"Bodhicitta" can be understood, however, as either the "aspiration" to Enlightenment at the beginning of the Path or its eventual "fulfillment" at the end of it. And the texts merely pause at this meeting of the two side channels, paying attention instead to the central channel with its several *cakras*—and the passage of the wind upward from the bottom to the top of Avadhūtī.

The alignment of "wheels" along this channel from the navel (or genitals) to the head (taken as either the forehead or the crown) proved a rich opportunity to associate this subsequent passage of "consciousness riding on the wind" with the progress of Stages along the Bodhisattva Path toward Buddhahood.

Since the set of four *cakras* were already identified in the body *maṇḍala* with the "Bodies of the Buddha," they could be attained microcosmically in this upward passage: the Nirmāṇa-kāya at the navel, the Dharma-kāya at the heart, the Sambhoga-kāya at the throat, and finally the newly-named Mahāsukha-kāya at the head. This is not quite a spiritual "ladder" since the superior Dharma-kāya comes before its emanated Saṃbhoga-kāya—probably because the "heart" *cakra* develops first in embryology. In any case, it is now the fourth Body at the "head" that matters most.

It seems that the "Four Joys" are experienced again during this ascent of the wind (and its drop of Bodhicitta) through the *cakras*—but in the reverse order from their appearance during the descent of semen. This means that Sahaja-ānanda or "Innate Joy" is now experienced at the head (correlated with what is also called the Sahaja-kāya) and not somewhere near the genitals. This must be the

---

[99] Snellgrove, HVT, 1:36.

[100] Snellgrove, HVT 1:49.

salvific order of the Joys since Tsoṅ-kha-pa informs us, quoting from the SPT, that when the wind reaches that point:

> it passes out from the right nostril and from the orifice of the *ūrṇā-kośa*. Thereupon, it pervades the ten directions like a lightning flash and informs the retinue, the Śrāvakas, the Pratyekabuddhas, and the Bodhisattvas that someone has been made a Buddha. . . .[101]

For Tantra, all this could be accomplished by a *sādhaka* in his subtle body—albeit with much training and doubtless much difficulty—yet here and now, not elsewhere in some far-off Pure Land and not at the end of an impossibly long three incalculable aeons of gathering much merit. One had only to master the gathering of the winds and the esoteric substances they carried.

Surely, this is the *anuttara-yoga,* the "incomparable discipline" for accomplishing Anuttara-samyak-saṃbodhi, the "Incomparable Perfect Complete Enlightenment."

In this second phase of "controlling the winds," the red and white are not left and right but below and above—uniting in "nondual" Bliss at the top of the central channel. It is the same for all other pairs, the sun at the navel ascending to the moon at the head, etc. Even the first word of the *nidāna*, *evaṃ* ("Thus"), is treated in this way: the syllable *e-* is below and completes itself by rising to *–vaṃ* above. The first person singular pronoun *ahaṃ* ("I") is understood as *a-* below rising to meet and unite with *-haṃ* above. Ultimately, this "I" belongs to the macrocosmic Lord Vajrasattva, as he proclaims in the HVT:

> I am the teacher, and I am the doctrine, I am the disciple endowed with good qualities. I am the goal, and I am the trainer. I am the world and worldly things.[102]

Since the goal is to become this "Diamond Being," Snellgrove translates: "The Supreme Self [*ahaṃ*] exists in oneself"—microcosmically.

The "Fire" Within

In a plethora of confusing data, even all that is not the entire Anuttarayoga story. Farrow and Menon translate a very important but cryptic verse from the HVT that we must now try to understand:

> Caṇḍālī blazes up in the navel. She burns the Five Buddhas. She burns Locanā and the others. Ahaṃ is burnt and the Moon flows down.[103]

Two things, at least, are occurring here. First of all, "Caṇḍālī" is the name of a fierce goddess—the same name of the outcaste "ideal" woman who arrived on the scene at the Secret initiation and

---

[101] Lessing and Wayman, *Mkhas grub rje's "Fundamentals,"* 36. Slightly altered.

[102] Snellgrove, HVT, 1:92

[103] Farrow and Menon, HVT, 21. Snellgrove's translation misses an elided Sanskrit "a" and translates incorrectly, "*haṃ*" is burnt."

stayed for the Wisdom one. But the external woman is now completely within. Second, the *homa* ritual of fire sacrifice that we witnessed in an earlier chapter—and that led to a brief comment on the significance of *tapas* or "heat" in religious transformation—is now also internalized. In fact, it is here called *adhyātma-homa*, "internal fire oblation," that Sugiki himself says should be taken as "psycho-somatic" since the sacrifice involves the tantric "subtle body."[104] Indeed, that body—and the gross body, as well—is now being "burned," imaginatively, as an offering to the same Buddhist deities with which that body has been identified in the body *maṇḍala*.

That identification explains the somewhat shocking information in this verse that the "Five Buddhas" along with their Consorts, "Locanā and the others," are being "burned"—as if divine Reality were being destroyed. In a 9th-century commentary, the great adept Kāṇha explains that the body has, indeed, been coded with Buddhist deities: but it is only the "five *skandhas*" that are being burned, along with the "four elements" of the *skandha* of form. And the "Ahaṃ" that is destroyed here is not that of Vajrasattva but the ordinary "ego" (*ahaṃkāra*, "I maker")—as found in the formula for attachment, "I and mine." That sounds orthodox despite the strange irrationality of the procedure. In fact, Kāṇha says that "Caṇḍālī" is herself symbolic of mainstream Mahāyāna teaching:

> The word *caṇḍālī* is composed of *caṇḍā* (the fierce one) which refers to Wisdom (*prajñā*) because Wisdom is fierce when destroying afflictions and distresses and *ālī* which refers to Vajrasattva.[105]

Vajrasattva, the commentary goes on, is "Means." The etymology is contrived but makes the usual orthodox point that Enlightenment results from the union of Wisdom and Means.

In summary, the coming together of the side-channel winds at the *cakra* of the navel is the union of Wisdom and Means that ignites the Fire of transformation; then that symbolism repeats itself with Wisdom at the navel rising to unite with Means at the head—transforming the yogin into a Completely Enlightened Being.

We can now read more of that verse quoted earlier by Tsoṅ-kha-pa from the SPT:

> And that blazing passes from the middle channel and pervades the spaces of the hair pores, crown of the head, and forehead. Having cremated the three "wheels" and the personality aggregates, etc., it passes out from the right nostril and from the orifice of the *ūrṇā-kośa* . . . .[106]

And announces that "someone has been made a Buddha." It would appear that nothing new has occurred by the ignition of an "inner Fire."

Nevertheless, the tone has changed. "Fire," without or within, certainly does not seem very Blissful. The Four Joys are never denied, in either direction, nor does the Mahāsukha-kāya cease

---

[104] Sugiki, "Oblation," 168.

[105] Farrow and Menon, HVT, 21-23.

[106] Lessing and Wayman, *Mkhas grub rje's "Fundamentals,"* 36.

to be a marker for Complete Enlightenment. But the mention of "cremation" is a marker for death, and the passage of the winds at the orifice of the head is where they depart—according to the Upaniṣads—when someone dies. Granted, there follows the symbolism of spiritual "rebirth" in the proclaiming of a new "Buddha," but we are being shown that first one must be destroyed.

I think it is likely that the adopted religious forms of village India are influencing Buddhism at this point. Flood describes female deities of the village as either "hot" or "cool":

> Hot deities are associated with passion, hot diseases such as smallpox which need to be cooled, pollution and lower social layers. Cool deities are associated with detachment, the cooling of passion, purity and higher social levels. The village goddesses, as well as ferocious goddesses such as Kālī, are classified as hot deities in contrast to the cool, mostly male, deities of the Hindu pantheon, such as Viṣṇu and Śiva.[107]

It is even the case that a disease or natural catastrophe inflicted by some "hot" goddess expresses her "grace"—since one has been chosen to participate in her manifestation, even though destructive, giving sacred meaning to one's distress. As we have just seen, the tantric Buddhist goddess "Caṇḍālī" is very hot.

Phase Three: The "Flowing" of the Moon

Finally, we must try to understand the closing phrase in that cryptic verse from the HVT that Farrow and Menon translate as, ". . . and the Moon flows down" (from Sanskrit *sru*, "to flow, drip, emit"). Snellgrove translates, ". . . and the Moon melts." It appears to be a counter-image to the climactic upward "passing out" of the winds from the *cakra* at the head—after Caṇḍāli's "blazing" destroys the the yogin's body. As already noted, his navel *cakra* has been identified with (among many other things) the "red" sun that rises as wind through the central channel to the head *cakra* identified with the "white" moon. That Moon now "flows" or "melts" in yet a third phase of "controlling the winds."

In his commentary on the HVT, Kāṇha suggests that this is no more than additional symbolism for the goal attained: "'Flows' means because of the burning the Stablised Meditative State of the Innate Radiance arises"—i.e., the *samādhi* of the luminous mind arises or "flows" forth.[108] But Kāṇha's fellow *mahāsiddha* Nāropa suggests otherwise. He shifts imagery from "wind" to "water" to describe the ascent and subsequent descent of the winds along with the Four Joys or "delights":

> "Backward motion": like an elephant drinking water, to make the four delights ascend to the head region and to keep them stable. "Saturation": like a farmer

[107] Flood, *Hinduism*, 193.
[108] Farrow and Menon, HVT, 23

> watering his crops carefully to saturate every pore and experience the delight as consummation.[109]

Siddharājñī, a twelfth-century female *tāntrikā*, tells us what that delightful fluid is:

> The deities at the secret place burn;
> The chiefs of the four *cakras* also burn completely.
> The fire, having touched the A at the navel,
> Burns the A and touches the Haṃ at the crown,
> Whereby a stream of elixir drips, filling the four *cakras*,
> Whose deities burn, increasing their great bliss.[110]

She knows of the "burning" of the four *cakras*, the rising of "*a-*" to union with "*-haṃ*" as "Ahaṃ—and knows, too, that afterward the "elixir" of *amṛta* ("deathless") drips down through the practitioner's *cakras* that have been unexpectedly reconstituted by this outpouring of the Elixir of Immortality. Why the deities who are identified with the "wheels" still burn is unclear, but they are filled with the "great bliss" of Sahaja.

In the Wisdom initiation, semen was said to flow down from the head, inducing experiences of Joy—but interrupted to cause an experience of "unworldly" Joy. The GST could understand this as a sacrifice—following the Upaniṣads—with the melted "clarified butter" as semen flowing into the "hearth" of the woman's vagina. But we have left this external analogizing far behind, says the SPT. Sugiki summarizes from this more "interior" *tantra*:

> When heated [by the Fire of Caṇḍālī] the skullbone in the head produces the body fluid, which Abhayākragupta calls "the awakening mind" [Bodhicitta]. . . . the body fluid flows downward through the central channel, *avadhūtī*, passing through the throat *cakra* (i.e., the enjoyment [Saṃbhoga] *cakra*) and the heart *cakra* (i.e., the Dharma *cakra*), which are the mouth of an inner small ritual ladle (i.e., the mouth of the *rasanā* channel) and the mouth of an inner large ritual ladle (i.e., the mouth of the *lalanā* channel), respectively. Finally, the body fluid flows into the creation]Nirmāṇa] *cakra* (i.e., the inner hearth).[111]

Although complicated and still obscure, this summary is helpful. It shows us that after the attainment of the Mind of Enlightenment at the head and the "upward" passing out of the winds into the ten directions of all the other Buddhas of the universe, there follows a "down going"—apparently, out of compassion.

After all, following Gautama's own tantric Enlightenment, Vairocana's Dharmakāya emanated from Akaniṣṭha as a Saṃbhoga-kāya down to Mt. Meru to teach the Celestial Bodhisattvas,

---

[109] Herbert V. Guenther, trans., *The Life and Teaching of Nāropa: Translated from the original Tibetan with a Philosophical Commentary based on the Oral Transmission* (London: Oxford University Press, 1963), 78.

[110] Shaw, *Passionate Enlightenment*, 124.

[111] Sugiki, "Oblation," 184.

then on down to earth as a Nirmāṇakāya to teach us. That religious drama is occurring now—microcosmically—as a "flow" of "liquid Nirvāṇa" through the *cakras* of the yogin's tantric body. It is accompanied by more experiences of Joy.

Jungian commentary The closest Jung came to these practices in Buddhist Tantra was "right-hand" tantric Hinduism—and we must go there now, despite having to detour a bit off topic. He had read John Woodroffe's pioneering work, *The Serpent Power: The Secrets of Tantric and Shaktic Yoga*, soon after its appearance in 1919.[112] And he was struck by the imagery within its short sixteenth-century text of fifty-five verses, the *Ṣaṭ-cakra-nirūpaṇa* ("An Investigation of the Six Cakras"—hereafter, SCN). It was published with a long introduction by Woodroffe and a native commentary.

This author, incidentally, was a British high court judge in Calcutta who had "secretly" taken initiation in Hindu Tantra—the reputation of which, even among Indians at the time, was dubious (hence, Woodroffe's pseudonym, Arthur Avalon).

The images that impressed Jung were those of a *cakra* system which began at the perineum associated with the element "earth" and the god Indra riding his white elephant. The next *cakra* was at the base of the genitals associated with the element "water" and the god Varuṇa, etc. It so happens that Jung had been treating a woman who was suffering terribly but whose symptoms and dreams made no sense to him. After all, what was he to make of her "excitation in the perineal region" and dream of a "white elephant" coming out of her genitals? What to make of her subsequent "extreme hyperaesthesia of the bladder" requiring frequent urination—but for which there was no organic cause? And what of the patient's feeling "that the top of her skull was growing soft, that the fontanelle was opening up, and that a bird with a long sharp beak was coming down to pierce" that opening in the crown of her head? As Jung reports: "To my astonishment I found in this book an explanation of all those things I had not understood in the patient's dreams and symptoms."[113]

Getting his bearings, he was eventually able to help his patient. She had spent her childhood in India (or Java, according to a different account) and, as Jung puts it, "somehow these Eastern ideas got into her unconscious." But they had not been integrated into her adult consciousness in any meaningful way and were, instead, like an "angry goddess" manifesting herself as disease—because "hungry," i.e., not understood, not honored.

Never losing interest in *The Serpent Power*, Jung sponsored a seminar in 1932 to which the German Indologist Wilhelm Hauer was invited to speak. Hauer gave a series of six lectures on the *Ṣaṭcakranirūpaṇa*—of which he had made his own translation from the Sanskrit. His wife helpfully provided enlarged pictures of the text's *cakras* with their distinctive shapes, specific number of petals, colors, associated animals, and sacred letters. In fact, the iconography of this Hindu scripture is visually more complex than that of Indian tantric Buddhism—likely due to its relative lateness, having centuries more time to work out the logic and the look of what it wished to say.

---

[112] Arthur Avalon (Sir John Woodroffe), trans., *The Serpent Power: Being the "Ṣaṭ-cakra-nirūpaṇa" and "Pādukā-pañcaka"* (1919; repr., New York: Dover Publications, 1974).

[113] Jung, *Kundalini Yoga*, 104-106. In this 1932 seminar, the patient is said to be "born in India." In a 1937 lecture, Jung says she was "born in Java," *CW* 16, par. 558.

Jung, then, gave four lectures as a psychological commentary. And Jung's lectures, along with his comments in Hauer's lectures, are available today in *The Psychology of Kundalini Yoga: Notes of the Seminar*. As we learn from its editor, Sonu Shamdasani, no fewer than thirty persons attended Professor Hauer's lectures while upwards of eighty attended Jung's, so that eventually it became difficult to find a seat.[114] Again, it was as if a "goddess" was being "fed" and responding to all the attention.

The "Divine Couple" Hauer no doubt informed his audience of the metaphysics behind the SCN. It had long been known in Hinduism that the name for Ultimate Reality was "Brahman"—or it was "Ātman." But that expresses the Sacred impersonally, almost abstractly. Eventually, Brahman-Ātman became personified as a "trinity" of anthropomorphic high Gods: Viṣṇu, Śiva, and Brahmā (a masculine form of neuter "Brahman"). But, then, Devī (the "Goddess") would eclipse Brahmā and open the door to personifications of the Ultimate as either Male or Female—or as a Divine Couple.

The SCN assumes that Brahman is best imaged as a Divine Couple, specifically the personal deity Śiva ("auspicious") and his divine mate, Śakti ("energy, power")—although her name here is rather impersonal. Elsewhere, this Consort of the Lord is known more personally as Pārvatī or Umā. The two unite in "Male-Female" transcendence beyond the universe, metaphysically. Yet they are responsible at the same time for the Creation of the universe, even ourselves.

Their myth states that periodically Śiva sends out his creative Śakti who unfolds or emanates as the world itself, an expression of radical divine immanence. This means that, if we look about ourselves and have eyes to see, all is sacred. And yet all is not right. Because Śakti, the "Wife" of Śiva, has become separated from her "Husband"—who has remained in transcendence—and wishes to return to her Beloved. She does so, according to the myth, as the devolution of the world's "Energy" (*śakti*) in stages—until, once more, the God and Goddess unite in Sat-Cit-Ānanda, "Being-Consciousness-Bliss," the classic definition of Brahman. All of this takes place over a vast expanse of time, what is called a Great Kalpa, and explains the cycles of the universe.

For the Hindu *tāntrika*, however, the macrocosmic process of evolution and devolution takes place microcosmically within his (or her) "tantric body"—that looks very much like the tantric body of Buddhist Tantra. It, too, is structured as 72,000 *nāḍīs* or "channels" that serve the entire organism by carrying a "vital wind" called *prāṇa*—while three of these channels are most important. The one in the middle of the body (called Suṣumṇā) runs the length of the spine, while the two running parallel on either side (Iḍā to the left and Piṅgalā to the right) loop to meet the central channel at intervals—just as in Buddhism.

The SCN does not pay much attention to these side channels, however, since its focus is on the central channel with its "six *cakras*" or "lotuses." They appear at: (1) the perineum between the anus and genitals, (2) the genitals, (3) the navel, (4) the heart, (5) the throat, and (6) the forehead between the eyebrows—all of which, Woodroffe says, are "seats of Śakti."[115] We notice an overlap with Anuttarayoga Buddhism that features variously seven, five, or four "wheels" along its central *nāḍī*.

[114] Jung, *Kundalini Yoga*, xxxviii.

[115] Avalon, *Serpent Power*, 114.

Where they do not quite overlap is at the SCN's seventh *cakra*. Despite its title, this scripture claims that there is an additional "lotus" at the crown of the head (alternatively, twelve finger-lengths above the crown) with a "thousand" (*sahasrāra*) petals. In India, the number "thousand" is symbolic of Eternity. Thus, the Sahasrāra *cakra* transcends the subtle body system altogether: and it is there that Śiva and Śakti embrace in Eternal Union—before Creation, when the world has not yet evolved.

It is the task and holy privilege of the Hindu *tāntrika* who lives in this world to help the Goddess return to her Lord—i.e., to assist the ascent of Śakti from her lowest manifestation in his tantric body (at the perineum) upwards through the other *cakras* (to the head). He will do so—as does the Buddhist *tāntrika*—by the withdrawal of the senses, mental worship, intense contemplation, breath control, the recitation of *mantras*, but also the performance of *āsanas* or a set of standard postures of the body. These "postures" train the gross body not to interfere with the subtle one, purify the channels and aid the flow of *prāṇa*. Incidentally, these are the same *āsanas* found today at our yoga classes—taken entirely out of context!

Should the practitioner succeed in his efforts, he will not only help Śakti but help himself. For, as Woodroffe informs us, each of the *cakras* reached—and breached or "pierced"—brings with it "long life, freedom from desire and sin, control of the senses, knowledge, power of speech and fame."[116]

Should "complete knowledge of the Sahasrāra" be gained, the practitioner enjoys along with the Goddess herself "the most intense form of physical delight representing on the worldly plane the Supreme Bliss arising from the union of Śiva and Śakti on the 'spiritual' plane." The devotee of the Divine Couple—and especially of "Bhagavatī, who is the Devatā who pervades all beings"—becomes *jīvanmukti*, "Released while living," and will not be reborn.[117]

We learn at the tenth verse of the SCN that Śakti in the yogin's subtle body has the special name of "Kuṇḍalinī;" thus, the practice to assist her is called Kuṇḍalinī yoga.[118] This new name for the Goddess is derived from Sanskrit *kuṇḍala* ("ring, earring, bracelet; coil, coil of a rope"). She is the "Ring-like One." Or she is, says the text, "like the spiral of the conch-shell." But the verse adds that Kuṇḍalinī has a "shining snake-like form"—and it is this association to a "coiled serpent" that has gripped the imagination of both India and the West. Hence, Woodroffe's title, *The Serpent Power*, i.e., "Serpent Śakti." Primarily, this Kuṇḍalinī-Śakti is lovely. The commentary advises:

> Meditate upon the Devī Kuṇḍalinī as your Iṣṭa-devatā ["tutelary deity"] as being ever in the form of a damsel of sixteen in the full bloom of her first youth, with large and beautifully formed breasts, decked with all the varied kinds of jewels, lustrous as the full moon, red in color, with ever restless eyes.[119]

---

[116] Avalon, *Serpent Power*, 17.
[117] Avalon, *Serpent Power*, 445.
[118] Avalon, *Serpent Power*, 346.
[119] Avalon, *Serpent Power*, 349.

This is reminiscent of the young ideal *caṇḍālinī* of the sexo-yogic Anuttarayoga Buddhist initiations. But we know that the lovely Buddhist "woman" became an "inner Fire." Now we are learning that the beautiful "damsel" Hindu Goddess is, at the same time, an "inner Serpent."

In Indian religion, that could allude positively to the coiled Serpent upon which Viṣṇu sleeps at the close of a *kalpa*. But it could, also, allude negatively to the mythic Serpent Vṛtra that Indra had to slay to create cosmos out of chaos. There is ambiguity of tone at this point, just as we felt when Fire was introduced in Buddhist Tantra. Besides, Kuṇḍalinī is "sleeping" in the lowest *cakra* (Jung calls her, "Sleeping Beauty"), and it is one's religious task to "awaken" Her. But if she is also a sleeping coiled Serpent, do we really want to disturb it?

Jung's lectures During one of Hauer's lectures, Jung said that Hindu Tantra is "poison." The participants were surprised; and one wonders if the visiting professor and his wife were a little shocked. He said that he found tantric materials "highly complicated" even when scholars tried to simplify and that it was "so ill defined that one cannot touch it anywhere!" (84) The problem is, as Jung clarified in one of his own lectures, that tantric symbols "have a terribly clinging tendency":

> They catch the unconscious somehow and cling to us. But they are a foreign body in our system—*corpus alienum*—and they inhibit the natural growth and development of our own psychology. It is like a secondary growth or a poison. Therefore one has to make almost heroic attempts to master these things, to do something against those symbols in order to deprive them of their influence. (14)

Those attending already knew that Jung could not accept the metaphysics of Hinduism or Buddhism, any more than he could the metaphysics of Christianity, but he seems particularly wary of the danger of becoming possessed by the archetypal contents of Tantra.

Jung's patient had already proven this point. And Wilhelm Hauer—once a Christian missionary to India and a respected scholar—would do so, as well. The following year, he founded a "new religion" based on pre-Christian German folk elements that he called the *Deutsche Glaubensbewegung* ("German Faith Movement"). Hauer offered it to Hitler and Göbbels as an "Indo-Aryan" alternative to Christianity for the Third Reich. But they were not impressed.[120]

It follows that we should not try too hard to interpret the psychology of Anuttara-yoga or Kuṇḍalinī yoga, lest we become poisoned. Besides, a thorough review of what Jung said at the Zurich seminar is beyond the scope of this book. The principle remains, however, that Tantra is a "self-portrait" drawn by the psyche itself, and there is wisdom in it. Thus, Jung also told his audience:

> tantric yoga is a really invaluable instrument to help us in classification and terminology, and to create concepts of those things. That is why the study of tantric yoga is so fascinating. (97)

---

[120] Wikipedia contributors, "Jacob Wilhelm Hauer," *Wikipedia, The Free Encyclopedia*, https://en.wikipedia.org/w/index.php?title=Jacob_Wilhelm_Hauer&oldid=1034667348.

And, for Jung, its most important lesson is "psychic objectivity." He explains:

> My term for the process which tantric yoga calls the awakening of Kundalini is psychic objectivity. . . . These things happen in the nowhere; they are universal and impersonal—and if you do not understand them as impersonal, you simply get an inflation through your identification with the universal. So the whole process begins with the fact that certain things in the mind are purely impersonal. You are not responsible for their existence. . . . and they are not produced by any intentional purpose. (93)

That last thought expresses Jung's usual criticism of Eastern religions, that they are too "intentional" or willful. The Buddhists and Hindus sit in yogic posture, apply learned techniques, and expect certain results (Western disciples imitate that attitude). Still, they are expecting results from an objective, impersonal process within the psyche—namely, what occurs symbolically once individuation has been constellated.

We have already heard Jung say that the central point in a *maṇḍala* expresses a central point in the psyche—the Self archetype in the collective unconscious. And it is from there that one may feel the irresistible "urge" to "become [in reality] what one is [in potential]." Now that same urge is being felt at the lowest point of the tantric body—at the perineum *cakra* of the SCN (or at the navel *cakra* in Buddhist texts like the HVT):

> And that is Kundalini, something absolutely unrecognizable, which can show, say, as fear, as a neurosis, or apparently also as a vivid interest; but it must be something which is superior to your will. Otherwise you don't go through it. You will turn your back when you meet the first obstacle; as soon as you see the leviathan you will run away. But if that living spark, that urge, that need, gets you by the neck, then you cannot turn back; you have to face the music. (21)

And that is, also, Caṇḍālī.

Kuṇḍalinī and Caṇḍālī are both "beautiful" because, on the one hand, it is a beautiful thing to be called to a life of greater meaning. On the other hand, they are a "Serpent" and a "Fire" that swallow up or burn away one's happy *participation mystique* with family or the group, that upset one's conventional values and plans, one's anodyne self-perception. Elsewhere, Jung calls the activation of the Self archetype—that has been "asleep" in one's unconscious for the first half of one's life—a "moment of deadliest peril!"[121]

The SCN does not say how this activation occurs, except by the devotee's own efforts. The Buddhist materials are actually richer in this regard. We heard from Snellgrove that usually the "winds in the side channels," go up and down in an uncontrolled way. I take that to mean that normally we are barely aware of how our libido is being spent and do not really notice that it flows by way of opposites—except when one side of a pair shows up for which we are unprepared

---

[121] Jung, *CW* 9i, par. 217.

and with which we disagree. But the Buddhist yogin deliberately "forces" those opposite "red and white" winds down to their meeting place at the navel—where they ignite the transforming Fire.

That tells us symbolically that in actual psychological experience there are times when the opposites do not just flow beyond our awareness but meet and clash—and that is what "wakes" us up! Or, better, it "wakes" up the Unconscious—and that wakes us up.

Jung once remarked: the "union of opposites is terribly shocking to us. To the Eastern mind it is too little shocking; they should be shocked a little more."[122] Yet it is this "clash of opposites"—over something that may look to be saṃsāric or merely personal—that instigates the requirement to live more completely, more transpersonally out of the Self. The clash is often experienced as some failure ("*the experience of the self is always a defeat for the ego*" [Jung's italics]).[123] Or it is a "conflict of duties" in which one is wrong and right no matter what one decides: to abort Mother Nature's conception of a child or to bring into the world a child who will always know it was not wanted; to honor one's solemn marriage vow or to divorce someone no more flawed than oneself; to continue to put up with all this pain or commit suicide. If one can endure the "shocking" conflict and not act too quickly, Kuṇḍalinī may actually "awaken," Caṇḍālī may "blaze"—changing one's entire perspective and initiating a new purpose for living.

Jung's analysis of the "cakras" Let me merely summarize Jung's interpretation of the *cakras* in the *Ṣaṭcakranirūpaṇa*, assuming that they are somewhat related to the *cakras* in tantric Buddhism:[124]

1) At the perineum *cakra* (called *mūlādhāra* in the SCN), we are symbolically in the "first half of life" and living as we should—conventionally adapted and contributing to society. It is there, however, that the "gods are sleeping." Yet it is, also, precisely there—"in the most banal place in the world, a railway station, a theater, the family, the professional situation"—that the inactive archetypes may "awaken" out of their unconscious condition. (15)

2) At the genital *cakra* (called *svādhiṣṭhāna*), we are forced by the activated Self to go into the unconscious: "the worldwide idea of the baptism by water with all its dangers of being drowned or devoured by the makara [a mythic "sea monster" depicted in Mrs. Hauer's painting of this tantric "wheel"]." (17)

3) This means trouble: "We think we are living quite consciously and with great intensity. What is the next effect when you become acquainted with the unconscious and take it seriously? . . . Yes, desire, passions, the whole emotional world breaks loose"—and that is *maṇipūra cakra* at the navel (where the sixfold or sevenfold Hindu tantric system begins to overlap with the usual fourfold Buddhist system). (33)

4) At the heart *cakra* (*anāhata*) in both Hinduism and Buddhism, a breakthrough occurs: "You stop yourself in your wild mood and suddenly ask, 'Why am I behaving like this?'" A perspicacious

[122] Jung, *Dream Analysis*, 636.

[123] Jung, *CW* 14, par. 778.

[124] Quotations in this following section are from Jung, *Kundalini Yoga*, 15, 17, 33.

seminar attendee asked, "Is the process you describe the beginning of individuation in psychological terms?" Jung answered, "Yes"—even though individuation supposedly began several *cakras* earlier.

But what had been happening more or less consciously now becomes much more conscious. "So *anāhata* is really the center where psychical things begin, the recognition of values and ideas . . . . the first inkling of the power and substantiality, or the real existence of psychical things." It becomes obvious now that the psyche is as real as the body. Indeed, one might well take this realization as the summit of one's psychological development, enough for one person in a lifetime. (39, 45)

5) But Jung says it is at least possible to go on to *viśuddha cakra* at the throat where "all one's psychical facts have nothing to do with material facts." Here, "You begin to consider the game of the world as your game, the people that appear outside as exponents of your psychical condition . . . . because in *viśuddha* the whole game of the world becomes your subjective experience. The world itself becomes a reflection of the psyche." I am quite certain that Jung lived psychologically at that "location." (49-50)

He certainly did not live at 6) *ajṇā cakra* at the forehead (correlating with the highest *cakra* in Buddhist Tantra) that claims the attainment of "complete consciousness." Jung says this state is "naturally completely beyond our reach." Nor did he even speculate on 7) *sahasrāra cakra*, at or just above the crown, where Śakti returns to unite with Śiva in Perfect Bliss—since that metaphysical claim is "beyond any possible experience." Critics have written that Jung's rather loose relationship to the text throughout his lectures culminated in his just "lopping off" the top two *cakras*—since he was too "pessimistic" about the tantric religious journey.[125]

This, however, was Jung's way of doing "something against those symbols in order to deprive them of their influence"—to avoid being poisoned by Tantra. He did not want to mistake the yogic activity of sitting in meditation and controlling one's imagined "winds"—thereby inducing a set of prescribed experiences, blissful though they may be—for the actual development of one's individual psyche through self-knowledge. That process occurs slowly and unpredictably, in everyday life, where the opposites of "Red and White" actually reside.

Knots

Of course, there are resistances along any religious Path—and Tantra knows that. These are the "knots" (*granthi*) that appear in both Buddhist and Hindu scriptures. Although mentioned in passing, they are not always discussed by scholars; and that is because it is never quite clear what these "knots" are or where they occur. We do know from pictures of the "tantric body" that they are caused by the side channels "looping" toward and away from the central channel.

In the Tibetan Buddhist Figure 16.2, we see "knots" occurring at the several *cakras*—leading some interpreters to equate them with the *cakras* themselves. That seems confirmed by scriptures that

[125] See the criticisms in Georg Feuerstein, *Tantra: The Path of Ecstasy* (Boston: Shambhala, 1998), 83, 266-267.

speak of "piercing" (*bheda*, "breaking open") the wheels along the central channel, as if loosening knots. In the frontispiece of Woodroffe's book, however, these "knotty" looping conjunctions appear between the *cakras*—in fact, in classic Hindu Kuṇḍalinī yoga there are seven *cakras* and only three *granthis*—so they are not the same thing.

Here, then, is a definition of the *granthis* in Buddhist Tantra from a major scholarly dictionary:

> It is said that the right and left channels wrap around the central channel, forming knots at the cakras. Much tantric practice is devoted to techniques for loosening these knots in order to allow the winds or energies that course through the other channels to flow freely and enter into the central channel.[126]

Does this mean the "knots" occurring "at the cakras" of the central channel create those *cakras* by wrapping around it? And is there a problem of the flow of "winds" in the central channel, or in the side channels, or in all "other channels"?

However one locates or defines them, these esoteric "knots" are consistently said to "constrict" the flow of "winds" in some way—i.e., the flow of libido. I take them to be an image of our psychological "complexes" that keep us from functioning at our best; and they are "personal" since caused by the saṃsāric side channels. David White writes that in Hinduism, the *granthis* "knot together spirit and matter."[127] Indeed, personal complexes are the sore spots in our psychologies because we have yet to distinguish objectively what belongs to ourselves and what belongs to the outer person or circumstance.

Thus, an "inferiority complex" constricts one's perception to winning or losing, acceptance or rejection; the "mother complex" confines relationships to women (or to anyone or anything that "nourishes") to how one perceives one's personal mother; the "father complex" makes it difficult to relate naturally to men (or to anyone or any situation) that symbolizes "authority," etc. Pictures of the tantric body show us that unless these constricting "knots" are sorted out there will be no individuation process—or perhaps the pictures are saying that during individuation we will always be dealing, at the same time, with our personal complexes. Let me note that the word "analysis" comes from Greek *lysis*, "to loosen."

"Flow"

Finally, a word about that difficult phrase in the HVT, " . . . and the Moon flows down." The metaphysics of the SCN appears to allude to this flow. We read of the Goddess' activity from "above":

> "Kuṇḍalinī, Thou sprinklest all things with the stream of Nectar [*sudhā*; elsewhere, *amṛta*] which flows from the tips of Thy two feet."[128]

---

[126] *PDB*, "cakra," 162.

[127] White, *Kiss of the Yoginī*, 226.

[128] Avalon, *Serpent Power*, 475.

Then, when Śakti lies "below" at her farthest extent in Creation:

> "She is the receptacle of that continuous stream of ambrosia which flows from the Eternal Bliss."[129]

The goal of Kuṇḍalinī yoga, of course, is to bring this divine Serpent Power or "Energy" back to its Source forever.

Apparently, that is very rare. So Woodroffe comments on the challenge:

> Kuṇḍalī does not at first stay long in Sahasrāra. The length of stay depends on the strength of the Yogi's practice.[130]

Thus, the Goddess "ascends" but, then, "descends" repeatedly during a practitioner's lifetime since either not able to reach upper *cakras* or stay at the highest. This mixed success and failure is gratifying, nevertheless.

Woodroffe, the good high court judge and secret *tāntrika* obliged to write as "Arthur Avalon," reports: "Refreshment, increased power and enjoyment, follows upon each visit to the Well of Life." This would be in Kuṇḍalinī yoga the periodic blissful experience of the "flow" of Amṛta—both upward like an "elephant drinking water," then downward "like a farmer watering his crops," to quote the tantric Buddhist Nāropa.

Jung has already said he did not think it possible to bring "Śakti" permanently home. But he does know of repeated visits to the "Well of Life"—understood as a "thirsty" ego's return to the Source of its libido. Making contact with the unconscious—by paying more attention to one's dreams, by deliberate active imagination, and pondering the world's scriptures to facilitate one's relationship to the depths—encourages the grace of renewed energy and the satisfaction of meaning. In his final great work, *Mysterium Coniunctionis*—exploring the "mysterious conjunction" between psychological opposites in alchemy—Jung writes of a "flowing" in two directions:

> The ever-flowing fountain expresses a continual flow of interest toward the unconscious, a kind of constant attention or "religio," which might also be called devotion.[131]

As a consequence:

> If attention is directed to the unconscious, the unconscious will yield up its contents, and these in turn will fructify the conscious like a fountain of living water.

[129] Avalon, *Serpent Power*, 351.
[130] Avalon, *Serpent Power*, 240-243.
[131] Jung, *CW* 14, par. 193.

It follows that Jung's description of the meeting between the "greater Personality" and the "lesser" one—making one's personal "life flow into that greater life"—is not only a moment of "deadliest peril" but also the harbinger of many occasions of joy.[132]

Mahāsiddhas

Scholars often say that the ideal "Buddhist saint" in Early Buddhism is the Arhat; in mainstream Mahāyāna, it is the Bodhisattva; while in Tantra, it is the Mahāsiddha. The distinctions are a bit misleading. We know that the Arhat ("worthy one") is Enlightened as much as a Buddha and living in Nirvāṇa (either here or in Akaniṣṭha as a "Nonreturner"), awaiting complete Parinirvāṇa at death. The Bodhisattva ("a being intent upon Enlightenment"), however, is not fully Enlightened. Still, that saint is considered by the Mahāyāna to be far in advance of the Arhat even if still human—but especially so if a Celestial Bodhisattva residing in a Pure Land at the feet of a Celestial Buddha. Then, there is the Mahāsiddha (the "great accomplished one" or "great adept"). This person appears to be a human being residing here (at least in the hagiographies and in Buddhist art). And he or she is not just a Bodhisattva but perhaps fully Enlightened and already a Buddha "in this lifetime"—but that is not entirely clear.

Most of the *mahāsiddhas* are said to have existed historically between the seventh and twelfth centuries when Buddhist Tantra was presumably "popular" in India. Nevertheless, they are an elusive category of Buddhist saint if, indeed, they are even Buddhist! Roger Jackson writes: "We don't know exactly who they were, what religious allegiance they claimed, where or when—or even if—they lived, or how many of the works attributed to them really are theirs."[133] Still, they have names, and we have heard some of them—Nāropa, Kāṇha, Saraha, the tantric Nāgārjuna. There is a famous list of eighty-four *mahāsiddhas* compiled in the twelfth century by Abhayadatta in his *Caturaśītisiddhapravṛtti* ("Lives of the Eighty-four Siddhas").[134] This list, incidentally, includes only four female "great adepts." But they are all accomplished in the Anuttarayoga.

It is misleading, therefore, to say that the "tantric saint" is a Mahāsiddha when that distinction belongs only to the fourth class of *tantras*—and there are three other classes with their own highly accomplished masters. Adding to the confusion, the name of any one Anuttarayoga Mahāsiddha may appear in several forms, but modern works tend to use the spelling as found in the late Sanskrit dialect of Apabhraṃśa. Let us look at some of them.

Lūyipa

The first in Abhyadatta's list is Lūyipa—meaning literally, says Donald Lopez, "Mr. Fish Guts."[135] He got the name from his peculiar practice that led to the transmundane *siddhi* of Mahāmudrā ("Great Seal")—the Enlightened Truth that puts its "seal" on all ordinary phenomena. Born into

---

[132] Jung, *CW* 9i, par. 217.

[133] Jackson, *Tantric Treasures*, 5.

[134] See "Caturaṣītisiddhapravṛtti," *PDB*, 170-171.

[135] Donald S. Lopez, Jr., *Seeing the Sacred in Samsara: An Illustrated Guide to the Eighty-Four Mahāsiddhas* (Boulder: Shambhala, 2019), 45.

royalty, he refused his father's wishes to become king, renounced, wandered as a mendicant—all of this in the pattern of Siddhārtha Gautama—until initiated into the *Cakrasaṃvara Tantra*. We are told:

> One day he visited a tavern. The tavern keeper was in fact a ḍākinī who saw that he had achieved great realization but that he still had some remaining obstacles to overcome, so she filled his bowl with rotten food. When he threw it away in disgust, she told him that he had yet to abandon the concepts of good and bad.

We recall that Gautama, also, had trouble passing the "food test" as a novice ascetic but quickly overcame his disgust. Here, Lūyipa deliberately cultivates his aversion in order to overcome it by sitting on the banks of the Ganges River for twelve years—eating the fish guts left by fishermen cleaning their catch.

It is an instance of a *tāntrika* overcoming the "conceptual distinction" between the opposites of good food and bad food and, ultimately, between good and evil. It is also a specific instance of the tantric "path of passion" whereby one uses the offensive act or feeling to overcome it. It is essentially "homeopathic"—as we saw in the sexual practices intended to overcome the pleasure (if not just the compulsive pleasure) of sexual desires. In any case, one deliberately engages rather than avoids what is "wrong" for a higher end.

Something similar occurs in psychological work when one suspects a projection "out there"—and it is disturbing one's life. One can starve the projection and see if that helps. Or one can engage it, go into what is almost certainly a charged situation to determine if there really is a "snake" distorting a "rope" and what kind of "snake" it is. After all, projections are manifestations of our own psyches; and individuation (if not just common decency) requires that we gather and correct our errors of perception.

Jung writes of this in a more introverted way as the temptations of an "inner voice" that brings "evil before us in a very tempting and convincing way in order to make us succumb." I quoted the following passage earlier when Gautama "succumbed" in part to Māra at the Bodhi Tree:

> If we succumb completely, then the contents expressed by the inner voice act as so many devils, and a catastrophe ensures. But if we can succumb only in part, and if by self-assertion the ego can save itself from being completely swallowed, then it can assimilate the voice, and we realize that the evil was, after all, only a semblance of evil, but in reality a bringer of healing and illumination.[136]

Or we discover it really was evil, and that we have escaped by the "grace of God."

Obviously, homeopathic psychology is dangerous and open to abuse (like a Chögyam Trungpa claiming, "I'm a highly advanced tantric master beyond moral categories;" or a wayward Jungian claiming, "I'm just integrating my shadow"). The HVT, however, knows this procedure is dangerous:

---

[136] Jung, *CW* 17, par. 319.

"With the very poison, a little of which would kill any other being, a man who understands poison would dispel another poison."[137]

Thus, the safeguard is "understanding"—bringing as much consciousness as possible to a dubious situation. Dreams are unbiased informants, and the reaction of others in one's environment can be a clue to what is happening within one's own psychology. Sitting daily in honest examination of one's shadow is essential for integrating shadow contents. It used to be called, "eating crow"—the modern equivalent of sitting by the Ganges "eating fish guts."

Nāropa

We have heard this name already several times. He, too, was born a prince, even with the "Thirty-two Marks" of a Great Person. So his father exclaimed with pride, "He will be like Prince Siddhārtha!"[138] True to type, Nāropa eventually married a sixteen-year-old girl (the age of puberty significant in tantric ritual). But eight years later, he became disgusted with life in the home and wished to "go forth" into homelessness. He did not leave secretly in the night, however, but explained to his parents: "Women are full of guile, and Vimalā, of course, has countless faults. I cannot live with her any longer." The wife dutifully agreed to the charge, and a divorce was arranged. Proving himself an excellent *bhikṣu* and then a scholar, Nāropa became abbot of the great monastic complex at Nālandā in Magadha.

One day, while studying his books outdoors, "a terrifying shadow fell on them," as Herbert Guenther translates from a Tibetan source:

> Looking round he saw behind him an old woman with thirty-seven ugly features [all of which are listed]. . . .She said to Nāropa, "What are you looking into?" "I study the books on grammar, epistemology, spiritual precepts, and logic," he replied. "Do you understand them?" "Yes." "Do you understand the words or the sense?" "The words." The old woman was delighted, rocked with laughter, and began to dance waving her stick in the air.[139]

We recognize the dance of a Ḍākinī, that ambivalent deity in the tantric Buddhist pantheon able to confound a great abbot. It might be noted that the subjects in which Nāropa was expert included not only the *sūtras* but also the *tantras*—presumably the "lower" tantric classes. Before disappearing as the "sky-walker" she really was, the ugly, old woman advised the crestfallen scholar to seek out her brother, Tilopa, already a "great adept," who could teach him the "sense" or meaning of Buddhist words.

This criticism of scholarship for its own sake is a repeated motif in the hagiographies of the *mahāsiddhas*. It is a motif in the history of religions when religious experience is missing—as it was for the famous Muslim professor al-Ghazālī whose tongue would swell when he tried to lecture

---

[137] Snellgrove, HVT, 1:93.

[138] Guenther, *Nāropa*, 9.

[139] Guenther, *Nāropa*, 24.

on things he did not really know; as with Luther who, despite having earned a doctorate in biblical theology, had problems with his gut and felt miserable. Here, Nāropa felt obliged to renounce his own academic post, and with great difficulty found Tilopa—as his life story tends to recover the *duḥkha* that Gautama himself experienced.

Indeed, Tilopa was famously cruel to his new disciple who he would initiate into the *Guhyasamāja Tantra*. For example, he instructed, "Get a girl"—after which there was much practice in "stimulating one's sexual power" and " absorbing the partner's equivalent, so producing a constant feeling of bliss and nothingness."[140] This we would expect. But Tilopa showed up and unexpectedly scolded: "Nāropa, how is it that you who have renounced the world according to the teaching of the Buddha, as a Bhikṣu are living with a girl? This is not a proper thing, punish yourself." Dutifully, if perhaps confused, the disciple smashed his penis with a rock. And his *guru* asked sadistically, "Nāropa, is something wrong with you?"

After twelve ordeals of this kind—as if enduring the twelve labors of Hercules—the ill-treated disciple finally heard these precious words: "Nāropa, you are a worthy vessel." And upon his death, this new worthy *mahāsiddha* attained the Dharma-kāya of a Buddha.

Our translator, Herbert Guenther, who is a Buddhist, surprisingly cites Jung and offers his own "Jungian" interpretation of the "ugly, old woman." He writes of Nāropa:

> All that he had neglected and failed to develop was symbolically revealed to him as the vision of an old and ugly woman. She is old because all that the female symbol stands for, the emotionally and passionately moving, is older than the cold rationality of the intellect . . . . And she is ugly, because that which she stands for has not been allowed to become alive or only in an undeveloped and distorted manner. Lastly she is a deity because all that is not incorporated in the conscious mental make-up of the individual and appears other-than and more-than himself is, traditionally, spoken of as the divine.[141]

There is nothing seriously wrong with this interpretation and worth pondering. But it is a bit "flatter" than what Jung would say since there is no mention of the unconscious at "depth" nor is there any hesitation about "incorporating" unconscious contents. The unconscious shadow can be incorporated in part (although one always has a shadow); at best, however, one can only learn to "relate" to the archetypal psyche.

Saraha

The name "Saraha" means, "he who has shot the arrow"—reminding us, once more, of Siddhārtha ("he who has achieved his aim"). This *mahāsiddha*, however, was not born into royalty but into the highest class of the *brāhmaṇas*. He and his brothers were well educated and could recite all the Vedas; but this youngest one renounced and ordained as a Buddhist monk. Becoming

[140] Guenther, *Nāropa*, 78.

[141] Guenther, *Nāropa*, ii-iii.

a renowned scholar in "countless subjects," he also found himself "face-to-face" with the Celestial Bodhisattva Sukhanātha—the kind of visionary experience described in mainstream Mahāyāna.

This divine Being instructed Saraha to go into the marketplace and look for the "arrowsmith woman." He did so. And she said—as Guenther translates from the Tibetan:

> My dear young man, the Buddha's meaning can be known through symbols (*brda*) and actions, not through words and books.[142]

Then, holding up an arrow to see if its shaft was perfectly straight, the low-caste yet skilled and mysteriously wise artisan advised: "shoot the arrow of nonduality into the heart of duality." Understanding immediately not only these "words" but their "meaning," Saraha responded: "You are not an ordinary arrowsmith woman, you are a teacher of symbols"—a point we have been making about religious language for several chapters.

Together they went off to the cremation grounds to "practice"—and not just the art of making arrows. Indeed, their behavior was so unseemly that the *brāhmaṇas* of Saraha's class were appalled at the "shameful practices" by one of their own. To which the *mahāsiddha* responded with his many famous "songs" (*dohās*) in the local dialect of Apabraṃśa. In them, Saraha derides his self-righteous accusers; in fact, he derides the religious pretensions of everyone!

Orthodox Hindus:

> Bah! Brahmins—
> they don't know what's what:
> in vain they incant
> their four Vedas.

Heterodox Śaivas:

> These "saints"
> smear their bodies with ashes
> and wear their matted locks
> piled on their heads.
> . . . .
> he grants consecration—
> for a fee.

The "sky-clad" Jains:

> If going naked means release,
> then the dog and the jackal
> must have it.

---

[142] Herbert Guenther, *Ecstatic Spontaneity: Saraha's "Three Cycles of Dohā*" (Berkeley: Asian Humanities Press, 1993), 5.

And even his fellow Buddhists:

> Self-proclaimed
> novices, monks and elders,
> these dress-up
> friars and ascetics!
> Some sit writing comments
> on the sūtras . . . .
> Others run around
> in the Great Way,
> where scripture turns to sophistry
> and word play.
> Some contemplate
> the maṇḍala circle,
> others describe the Fourth [Joy]
> as the real.

The problem is:

> You may give up the innate [i.e., the here and now]
> and fancy nirvāṇa,
> but not an ounce of the ultimate
> will you gain.

These lines, cleverly translated by Roger Jackson, are as refreshing as the irreverent tales of Zen Buddhist masters.[143] They scoff at our seriousness and bring us "face-to-face" with the shadow side of being religious.

[143] Jackson, *Tantric Treasures*, 53-59.

Figure 16.3 Saraha

Jungian thoughts Mahāsiddhas like Saraha, however, are hardly models for us today—and not just because of "tantric sex" in the charnel ground. In Figure 16.3, we see this great adept depicted on a seventeenth century Tibetan *thaṅ ka* that must preserve something of the Indian tradition. He holds his eponymous arrow and gazes intently at his target of discursive thought (and pretension). But he looks rather like a Hindu Śaiva with his top-knot, hairy face, and headdress of skulls. Yes, he is Enlightened as much as a Buddhist could be in his day and, therefore, honored by the artist with a reddish nimbus and a stylized Lotus seat like that of a Buddha. And, true, he is much more worldly in his posture and dress than the traditional images of the Buddha that we have seen—therefore, more "in the world" although wisely unattached and "not of it."

Saraha, however, is still too strange in his appearance to be even a "symbol" (Tib., *brda*) of psychological wholeness. The other *mahāsiddhas* around him on the painting—all gazing intently in the same direction—are even stranger; one looks dangerous, another rides a tiger. In fact, many on the list of the "Eighty-four Mahāsiddhas" whom we did not select were born into the lowest social strata and were engaged in the most polluted occupations. Many, also, were as celebrated for their mundane *siddhis*—that could magically heal or harm—as they were for their supramundane "attainment."

It follows that we are not observing a "Buddhist image of human perfection"—as one author suggests—and not an image of what Jung called psychological "completion." Instead, Saraha symbolizes an aspect of individuation: namely, "not belonging to the group," being the maverick away from the herd, and incurring the herd's disapproval—for not following it and for implicitly criticizing the herd by stepping away.

In *Psychological Types*, Jung defined "individuation" as: "the development of the psychological individual as a being distinct from the general, collective psychology."[144] It is the opposite of *participation mystique*, a psychological "belonging" that amounts to identification with the group—and that includes the group's approval. Thus, Christianity began by Jesus' refusal to agree with family: "For I have come to set a man against his father, a daughter against her mother, a daughter-in-law against her mother-in-law. A man's enemies will be those of his own household." (Matthew 10:35-36) And Buddhism began by Gautama's forsaking his family's expectations, much of it conventionally honorable. Both of these "individuals," then, became founders of new religious "groups" that were, shall we say, only better versions of *participation mystique*—so there would always be protests against what was founded.

There is, however, a problem with "not belonging." And it is that we always do belong, and must for our survival. Buddhists discovered that particular "pair of opposites" by having to rely on the larger community in order to live as monks in a "monastery" (from the Greek, *monos*, "alone"). There is even something wrong with trying to be alone. Jung wrote about that surprisingly early, in 1916:

> Individuation cuts one off from personal conformity and hence from collectivity. That is the guilt which the individuant leaves behind him for the world, that is the guilt he must endeavor to redeem. He must offer a ransom in place of himself, that is, he must bring forth values which are an equivalent substitute for his absence in the collective personal sphere. Without this production of values, final individuation is immoral and—more than that—suicidal.[145]

This is a strong statement written when Jung was discovering the difficult consequences of going his own way personally and professionally. It was also written before he had yet to "pay his debt" to society for "stepping away" psychologically. He would do so over the decades by treating as many

[144] Jung, *CW* 6, par. 757.
[145] Jung, *CW* 18, par. 1095.

patients as he could, by lecturing and arranging seminars, and by writing the many works that we now have to "treat" ourselves.

Let us observe that the *mahāsiddhas* did not just renounce a second time but, to the extent they were literate, wrote hundreds of commentaries and new religious texts. Saraha sang "songs" to his critics that were the "equivalent substitute for his absence" from mainstream society, even mainstream religion. This is perhaps another way to understand that mysterious phrase—"the Moon flows down." After the "ascent" to a higher consciousness than that of one's group, there must follow a "down-going" into that same community with new values and ideas that "refresh" one's fellow human beings either in the present or reserved for the future—in some individual way required by the Self.

Decline of Buddhism in India

Approximately seventeen centuries after the rise of Buddhism—after the extraordinarily rich development we have explored and despite its great influence—the religion died out in its homeland. It is such a remarkable historical fact that early scholars of Buddhism can be excused for assuming that it must have been the religion's late phase—i.e., Tantra, with its "disgusting" practices—that led to its demise. We know now, however, that the controversial practices were only a small slice of tantric Buddhism reserved for the few. Thus, we must look elsewhere, to powerful events in cultural history. Peter Harvey gives us the dates:

> From 750 CE, the mostly Buddhist Pāla dynasty ruled in the northeast, patronizing Buddhism and supporting five monastic universities, the major one being the internationally renowned Nālandā. In the eleventh century, Pāla rule weakened, and it was followed in 1118 by the Hindu Sen dynasty. From 986 CE, the Muslim Turks started raiding north-west India from Afghanistan, plundering western India early in the eleventh century. . . . By 1192, the Turks established rule over north India from Delhi. The north-eastern stronghold of Buddhism then fell, with the destruction of Nālandā university in 1198.[146]

—and the burning of hundreds of thousands of manuscripts in the library. There are reports that the Turks thought Nālandā's monastic structures were a fort or could be used as a fort for armed resistance. And Buddhism suffered a severe blow.

It is also true that official patronage of the religion had already been uncertain for centuries and that Buddhist lay support—essential for the daily functioning of the monasteries—had dwindled. Harvey remarks: "Mahāyāna writers were quite critical of Hinduism, but the surface similarities of Hindu and Mahāyāna devotional cults and Tantrism may have led the laity to perceive the two religions as quite similar." Hinduism, too, had been borrowing from Buddhism in a general "dilution of the distinctiveness" of the two. In that sense, Buddhism did not actually "die out" but was absorbed by India's cultural tendency to "include" rather than "exclude"—like branches on an

[146] Harvey, *Introduction to Buddhism*, 194.

ever-burgeoning Sacred Tree. Indeed, the Buddha was declared the ninth *avatāra* of Viṣṇu, a Hindu solution that survived the Buddhist myth that it was Vajrapāṇi who conquered Viṣṇu.

Dissolution of the Relics

In earlier chapters, we learned that the sixth-century Gautama Buddha did not expect his religion to last. For one thing, "all is impermanent" in Saṃsāra. For another, there was that troublesome decision to ordain women as Buddhist nuns that he believed would shorten the religion's duration. Finally, the dynamics of Buddhist cosmology made it impossible to expect—after a periodic dissolution of the world in a cosmic cycle—that anything would survive below the "heavens of Brahmā." Different Buddhist traditions, however, imagined what that apocalyptic End would be like; and they tended to agree that the "dissolution of the relics" would be the final event.

Let us recall that the historical Buddha was said to disappear in Complete Nirvāṇa (*parinirvāṇa*) at death. Yet he somehow "remained" Present to our world in his relics (not to mention in his sacred teachings, in *stūpas* and statues, and in visions). Buddhists realized that these remaining precious objects, too, would have to disappear in an apocalypse—and called it the "*parinirvāṇa* of the relics."

Buddhaghosa describes this in a rich religious fantasy:

> Then, the relics, not receiving honor and veneration in various places, will, by the power of the resolve of the Buddhas, go to those places where they will receive honor and veneration. Over time, however, the honor and veneration in such places will cease . . . . [The Buddha's relics will] gather at the great Bodhi Tree [in Bodhgayā]. Not a single relic, even so small as a mustard seed, will be lost en route. All the relics at the great Bodhi Tree throne will come together in a heap like a single mass of gold, emitting six-colored rays of light. They will illuminate ten thousand world systems. Taking on the form of the Buddha, they will display the glory of the Buddha's body seated crosslegged on the throne of Awakening. . . . Then, from the relic-body, a fire will leap up. It will reach up as high as Brahmā's heaven, and burn as long as there are relics, even the size of mustard seeds. When the relics are consumed, the fire will go out, and that body will become non-existent.[147]

Of course, after a very long period of time, the Savior Maitreya will arrive from Tuṣita to teach what all the Buddhas always teach.

I think it is possible to consider a book such as this one as a "gathering of relics" of a great Indian religion that is still alive for very many people but which—from the Jungian point of view—cannot survive the cultural "apocalypse" in which we now find ourselves. The Western religions of Judaism and Christianity have already died or have become essentially secular—merely social (even political) congregations and, at their best, forms of social work. Islam's violent fundamentalism is

[147] Strong, *Relics of the Buddha*, 224.

evidence of a last desperate stand against modernity. Psychologically, these religions no longer function to keep us in touch with the deepest reaches of our creative selves. The Eastern religions of Hinduism and Buddhism may try to take their place but will, I believe, prove incapable of doing so.

Part of the problem is that, despite all they do have to offer, none of the great religions has an adequate understanding of evil—to which we have become increasingly exposed. The horrors of World Wars I and II may escape our consciousness as we "shoot for the moon" with technology—but our unconscious has not forgotten and casts a pall over all our successes. Buddhism itself is too "Light" while the tantric Buddhism of this final chapter is too "Blissful." Too often we hear from India's religions that we have only to transcend "dualism"—including the moral opposites of good and evil—to fulfill the human task. Has anyone ever done so? Those who make the claim are usually found not only to be unsuccessful but secretly evil.

Here is Jung's position on this troublesome subject:

> No one stands beyond good and evil, otherwise he would be out of this world. Life is a continual balancing of opposites, like every other energic process. The abolition of opposites would be equivalent to death. Nietzsche escaped the collision of opposites by going into the madhouse. The yogi attains the state of *nirdvandva* (freedom from opposites) in the rigid lotus position of non-conscious, non-acting *samadhi*. But the ordinary man stands between the opposites and knows that he can never abolish them. There is no good without evil, and no evil without good. The one conditions the other, but does not become the other or abolish the other.[148]

Rather than say more, I direct the reader to Jung's reflections in "Answer to Job" where the problem of Evil requires a new understanding of the "image of God."[149] And to understand what that means, one might consult Edward Edinger's work, *The New God-Image,* that I have already cited.

It remains true, however, that any new solution our culture finds in the future will have to be "deeply rooted in the best spiritual tradition." That will necessarily include the spiritual tradition of Buddhism, the "most psychological" of all the world's religions.

---

[148] Jung, *CW* 18, par. 1417.

[149] Jung, *CW* 11, pars. 553-758.

BIBLIOGRAPHY

Allchin, F. R., with contribution from George Erdosy, et al. *The Archaeology of Early Historic South Asia: The Emergence of Cities and States*. Cambridge: Cambridge University Press, 1995.

Amore, Roy. "Comparative Study of Buddha's Pre-enlightenment Dreams: Implications for Religion." In *The Notion of "Religion" in Comparative Research*, edited by Ugo Bianchi, 541-546. Selected Proceedings of the Sixteenth Congress of the International Association for the History of Religions. Rome, 1990.

Anacker, Stefan trans. *Seven Works of Vasubandhu: The Buddhist Psychological Doctor*. Revised, Delhi: Motilal Banarsidass Publishers, 2005.

Apuleius, *The Golden Ass*. Translated by Jack Lindsay. Bloomington: Indiana University Press, 1960.

Arberry, Arthur J., trans. *The Koran Interpreted*. New York: The Macmillan Company, 1955.

Armstrong, Karen. *Buddha*. New York: Penguin Books, 2001.

Asher, Frederick M., ed. *Art of India: Prehistory to the Present*. N.p.: Encyclopedia Britannica, 2003.

———. *Bodh Gaya*. New Delhi: Oxford University Press, 2008.

Aśvaghoṣa. *Buddhacarita: Acts of the Buddha*. Translated by E. H. Johnston. 1936. Reprint, Delhi: Motilal Banarsidass, 1972.

Augustine. *The Confessions of St. Augustine*. Translated by John K. Ryan. Garden City: Image Books, 1960.

Avalon, Arthur (Sir John Woodroffe), trans. *The Serpent Power: Being the "Ṣat-cakra-nirūpaṇa" and "Pādukā-pañcaka."* 1919. Reprint, New York: Dover Publications, 1974.

Barzun, Jacques. *From Dawn to Decadence: 500 Years of Western Cultural Life*. New York: Harper Collins, 2000.

Basham, A. L. "Ājīvikas." In *Encyclopedia of Religion*, vol. 1, 163-165.

———. *The Wonder That was India*. New York: Grove Press, 1954.

Batchelor, Stephen. *Buddhism Without Beliefs: A Contemporary Guide to Awakening*. New York: Penguin Group, Riverhead Books, 1997.

Bays, Gwendolyn, trans. *The Voice of the Buddha: The Beauty of Compassion*. 2 vols. Berkeley: Dharma Publishing, 1983.

Benn, James A. "The *Lotus Sūtra* and Self-Immolation." In *Readings of the "Lotus Sūtra,"* edited by Stephen F. Teiser and Jacqueline I. Stone, 107-131. New York: Columbia University Press, 2009.

Bettelheim, Bruno. *Freud and Man's Soul*. New York: Vintage Books, 1982.

Blackstone, Kate. "Damming the Dhamma: Problems with Bhikkhuṇīs in the Pali Vinaya." *Journal of Buddhist Ethics* 6 (1999): 292-312.

Blum, Mark L., trans. Vol. 1, *The Nirvana Sutra (Mahāparinirvāṇa-sūtra.* Berkeley: Bukkyo Dendo Kyokai America, 2013.

Bodhi, Bhikkhu, trans. Revision of Bhikkhu Ñāṇamoli, trans., *The Middle Length Discourses of the Buddha: A Translation of the Majjhima Nikāya*. Boston: Wisdom Publications, 1995.

———. *The Noble Eightfold Path: The Way to the End of Suffering*. Kandy: Buddhist Publication Society, revised 2005. http://www.accesstoinsight.org/lib/authors/bodhi/waytoend.html.

———. "Nourishing the Roots: Essays on Buddhist Ethics." *Access to Insight (BCBS Edition)*, 30 November 2013. http://www.accesstoinsight.org/lib/authors/bodhi/wheel259.html.

———, trans. *The Numerical Discourses of the Buddha: A Translation of the Aṅguttara Nikāya.* Boston: Wisdom Publications, 2012.

———, trans. *The Connected Discourses of the Buddha: A Translation of the Saṃyutta Nikāya.* Boston: Wisdom Publications, 2000).

Boisvert, Mathieu. "Skandha (Aggregate)." In *Encyclopedia of Buddhism*, vol. 2, 779.

Bolle, Kees W. *Religion Among People: Essays on Religions and Politics*. Eugene: Cascade Books, 2017.

Bronkhorst, Johannes. *Buddhist Teaching in India*. Boston: Wisdom Publications, 2009.

Brown, Raymond E., trans. *The Gospel According to John*. 2 vols. The Anchor Bible. Garden City: Doubleday and Company, 1970.

Buddharakkhita, Acharya, trans. *The Dhammapada: The Buddha's Path of Wisdom,* "Malavagga: Impurity." *Access to Insight (BCBS Edition)*, 30 November 2018. http://www.accesstoinsight.org/tipitaka/kn/dhp/dhp.18.budd.html.

Burnouf, Eugène. *Introduction to the History of Indian Buddhism*. Translated by Katia Buffetrille and Donald S. Lopez, Jr. Chicago: University of Chicago Press, 2010.

Cartlidge, David R. and David L. Dunga, trans. *Documents for the Study of the Gospels.* Philadelphia: Fortress Press, 1980.

Campbell, Joseph. *The Mythic Image*. Princeton: Princeton University Press, 1974.

Cleary, Thomas. *The Secret of the Golden Flower: The Classic Chinese Book of Life*. San Francisco: Harper Collins Publishers, 1991.

Clooney, Francis X. with Hugh Nicholson. "Vedānta Deśika's *Īśvarapariccheda* ("Definition of the Lord") and the Hindu Argument about Ultimate Reality." In Neville, *Ultimate Realities*, 95-123.

Cole, Alan. *Text as Father: Paternal Seductions in Early Mahāyāna Buddhist Literature.* Berkeley: University of California Press, 2005.

Collins, Steven. "Indian Ideas of Mind." In *The Oxford Companion to the Mind*, edited by Richard L. Gregory, 357-361. Oxford: Oxford University Press, 1987.

———. *Selfless Persons: Imagery and Thought in Theravāda Buddhism.* Cambridge: Cambridge University Press, 1982.

Conze, Edward. *Buddhist Studies, 1934-1972: Thirty Years of Buddhist Studies and Further Buddhist Studies.* San Francisco: Wheelwright Press, n.d.

———, trans. *Buddhist Wisdom Books: Containing "The Diamond Sutra" and the "Heart Sutra."* New York: Harper and Row, 1958.

———, trans. *The Perfection of Wisdom in Eight Thousand Lines and its Verse Summary.* Bolinas: Four Seasons Foundation, 1973.

———, trans. *The Short Prajñāpāramitā Texts.* London: Luzac and Company, 1973.

Cowell, E. B. and W. H. D. Rouse, trans. *The Jātaka: Stories of the Buddha's Former Births.* 6 vols. Cambridge: Cambridge University Press, 1895-1907.

Cozort, Daniel. *Highest Yoga Tantra: An Introduction to the Esoteric Buddhism of Tibet.* Ithaca: Snow Lion Publications, 1986.

Dalai Lama. "The Buddhist Concept of Mind." In *Mind Science: An East-West Dialogue*, edited by Daniel Goleman and Robert A. F. Thurman, 11-18. Boston: Wisdom Publications, 1991.

———. *Deity Yoga: in Action and Performance Tantra.* Translated by Jeffrey Hopkins. Ithaca: Snow Lion, 1981.

———. *How to Practice: The Way to a Meaningful Life.* Translated by Jeffrey Hopkins. New York: Simon and Schuster, 2002.

Dallapiccola, A. L. "Stūpa." In *Encyclopedia of Buddhism*, vol. 2, 803-808.

Dalton, Jacob P. "Ḍākinī." In *Encyclopedia of Buddhism*, vol. 1, 192.

Dasgupta, Surendranath. *A History of Indian Philosophy.* Vol. 1. 1922. Reprint, Cambridge: Cambridge University Press, 1969.

Davidson, Ronald M. "The Bodhisattva Vajrapāṇi's Subjugation of Śiva." In *Religions of India in Practice*, edited by Donald S. Lopez, Jr., 547-555. Princeton: Princeton University Press, 1995.

———. *Indian Esoteric Buddhism: A Social History of the Tantric Movement.* New York: Columbia University Press, 2002.

Dayal, Har. *The Bodhisattva Doctrine in Buddhist Sanskrit Literature.* 1932. Reprint, Delhi: Motilal Banarsidass, 1970.

DeCaroli, Robert. *Haunting the Buddha: Indian Popular Religions and the Formation of Buddhism.* Oxford: Oxford University Press, 2004.

———. *Image Problems: The Origin and Development of the Buddha's Image in Early South Asia.* Seattle: University of Washington Press, 2015.

Dhammika, Bhante Shravasti. "Missions and Missionaries." In "Guide to Buddhism A to Z." http://www.buddhisma2z.com.

Duckworth, Douglas. "Buddha-Nature and the Logic of Pantheism." In *The Buddhist World*, edited by John Powers, 235-247. London: Routledge, 2016.

Eckel, Malcolm David with John J. Thatamanil. "Cooking the Last Fruit of Nihilism: Buddhist Approaches to Ultimate Reality." In Neville, *Ultimate Realities*, 125-150.

Edinger, Edward F. *The Aion Lectures: Exploring the Self in C. G. Jung's "Aion."* Toronto: Inner City Books, 1996.

———. *Anatomy of the Psyche: Alchemical Symbolism in Psychotherapy.* LaSalle: Open Court, 1983.

———. *The Christian Archetype: A Jungian Commentary on the Life of Christ.* Toronto: Inner City Books, 1987.

———. *The Creation of Consciousness: Jung's Myth for Modern Man.* Toronto: Inner City Books, 1984.

———. *Ego and Archetype: Individuation and the Religious Function of the Psyche*. 1972. Boston: Shambhala, 1992.

———. *Ego and Self: The Old Testament Prophets*. Edited by J. Gary Sparks. Toronto: Inner City Books, 2000.

———. "Ralph Waldo Emerson: Naturalist of the Soul." In Elder and Cordic, *An American Jungian: In Honor of Edward F. Edinger*, 136-157.

———. *Melville's "Moby-Dick": An American Nekyia*. Toronto: Inner City Books, 1995.

———. *The Mysterium Lectures: A Journey through C. G.Jung's "Mysterium Coniunctionis."* Toronto: Inner City Books, 1995.

———. *The New God-Image: A Study of Jung's Key Letters Concerning the Evolution of the Western God-Image*. Edited by Dianne D. Cordic and Charles Yates. Wilmette: Chiron Publications, 1996.

———. *The Psyche in Antiquity*. Book 1. *Early Greek Philosophy*. Edited by Deborah A. Wesley. Toronto: Inner City Books, 1999.

———. *The Sacred Psyche: A Psychological Approach to the Psalms*. Edited by Joan Dexter Blackmer. Toronto: Inner City Books, 2004.

———. *Transformation of Libido: A Seminar on C. G. Jung's "Symbols of Transformation."* Edited by Dianne D. Cordic. Los Angeles: C. G. Jung Bookstore, 1994.

Elder, George R. *The Body: An Encyclopedia of Archetypal Symbolism*. The Archive for Research in Archetypal Symbolism. Vol. 2. Boston: Shambhala, 1996.

———, ed. *Buddhist Insight: Essays by Alex Wayman*. Delhi: Motilal Banarsidass, 1984.

———. "Crossroads." In *Encyclopedia of Religion*, vol. 4, 166.

———. "Dependent Origination in Buddhist Tantra." In *Researches in Indian and Buddhist Philosophy: Essays in Honour of Professor Alex Wayman.* edited by Ram Karan Sharma, 143-161. Delhi: Motilal Banarsidass Publishers, 1993.

———. "Problems of Language in Buddhist Tantra." *History of Religions* 40, no. 3 (February, 1976): 231-250.

———. "Psychological Observations on the Life of Gautama Buddha." In *The Couch and the Tree: Dialogues in Psychoanalysis and Buddhism*, edited by Anthony Molino, 145-160. New York: North Point Press, 1998.

———, trans. *The Saṃpuṭa Tantra: Edition and Translation, Chapters 1-4*. PhD diss., Columbia University, 1978. Unpublished.

———. *The Snake and the Rope: A Jungian View of Hinduism*. Indianapolis: Dog Ear Publishing, 2012.

——— and Dianne D. Cordic, eds. *An American Jungian: In Honor of Edward F. Edinger*. Toronto: Inner City Books, 2009.

Eliade, Mircea. "Yoga." In *Encyclopedia of Religion*, vol. 15, 519-523.

———. *Yoga: Immortality and Freedom*. Princeton: Princeton University Press, 1969.

Eliot, T. S. "The Waste Land." In *The Norton Anthology of English Literature*. Vol. 2, 1781-1797. Revised, New York: W. W. Norton and Company, 1968.

Emerson, Ralph Waldo. "Self-Reliance" In *The Selected Writings of Ralph Waldo Emerson*, edited by Brooks Atkinson, 145-169. New York: Modern Library, 1940.

Encyclopedia of Buddhism. Edited by Robert E. Buswell. 2 vols. New York: Macmillan Reference USA, Thomson/Gale, 2004.

Encyclopedia of Religion. Edited by Mircea Eliade. 16 vols. New York: Macmillan Publishing Company, 1987.

Epstein, Mark. *Thoughts Without a Thinker: Psychotherapy from a Buddhist Perspective*. Cambridge: Basic Books, 1995.

Evans-Wentz, W. Y., ed. *The Tibetan Book of the Dead: Or the After-Death Experiences on the "Bardo" Plane, according to Lāma Kazi Dawa-Samdup's English Rendering*. 1927. London: Oxford University Press, 1960.

Farrow, G. W. and I. Menon, trans. *The Concealed Essence of the Hevajra Tantra: With the Commentary "Yogaratnamālā."* Delhi: Motilal Banarsidass Publishers, 1992.

Faure, Bernard. *Chan Insights and Oversights: An Epistemological Critique of the Chan Tradition*. Princeton: Princeton University Press, 1993.

———. *The Red Thread: Buddhist Approaches to Sexuality*. Princeton: Princeton University Press, 1998.

Feuerstein, Georg. *Tantra: The Path of Ecstasy*. Boston: Shambhala, 1998.

Flood, Gavin. *An Introduction to Hinduism*. Cambridge: Cambridge University Press, 1996.

———. *The Tantric Body: The Secret Tradition of Hindu Religion*. London: I. B. Tauris, 2006.

Foucher, A. *The Life of the Buddha: According to the Ancient Texts and Monuments of India*. Translated by Simone Brangier Boas. 1949. Reprint, New Delhi: Munshiram Monoharlal Publishers, 2003.

Francis, H. T. and E. J. Thomas, eds. *Jātaka Tales*. Bombay: Jaico Publishing House, 1957.

Fremantle, Francesca, trans. *A Critical Study of the Guhysamāja Tantra*. PhD diss., School of Oriental and African Studies, University of London, 1971. Scribd.com/doc/29906080.

Fussman, Gérard. "Histoire du monde indien: Lecture du texte sanskrit du *Vimalakīrtinirdeśa*," *Cours et travaux du Collège de France*. Résumés 2007-2008. Annuaire 108è année, 643-648. Paris: Collège de France.

Garfield, Jay L. trans. *The Fundamental Wisdom of the Middle Way: Nāgārjuna's Mūlamadhyamakakārikā*. New York: Oxford University Press, 1995.

George, Christopher, trans. *The Caṇḍamhāroṣaṇa Tantra: A Critical Edition and English Translation, Chapters 1-8*. New Haven: American Oriental Society, 1974.

Gethin, Rupert. "Cosmology." In *Encyclopedia of Buddhism*, vol. 1, 183-187.

———. "Cosmology and Meditation: From the Aggañña-Sutta to the Mahāyāna." *History of Religions* 36, no. 3 (February, 1997): 183-217.

——. *The Foundations of Buddhism*. Oxford: Oxford University Press, 1998.

Giebel, Rolf W., trans. *Two Esoteric Sutras: The Adamantine Pinnacle Sutra [and] the Susiddhikara Sutra*. Berkeley: Numata Center for Buddhist Translation and Research, 2001.

Gier, Nick. "The Virtues of Asian Humanism." Keynote Address at the 40th Annual Meeting of the Institute of Oriental Philosophy, Soka University, Japan (n.d.). www.class.uidaho.edu/ngier/307/budhumanism.

Gimello, Robert M. "Apophatic and kataphatic discourse in Mahāyāna: A Chinese view." *Philosophy East and West* 26, no. 2 (April, 1976): 117-136.

———. "Bodhi (Awakening)." In *Encyclopedia of Buddhism*, vol. 1, 50-53.

———. "Mysticism and Meditation." In *Mysticism and Philosophical Analysis*, edited by Steven T. Katz, 170-199. London: Sheldon Press, 1978.

Ginzberg, Louis. *The Legends of the Jews.* 7 vols. Philadelphia: Jewish Publication Society of America, 1909.

Goldstein, Joseph and Jack Kornfield. *Seeking the Heart of Wisdom: The Path of Insight Meditation.* Boston: Shambhala Publications, 1987.

Goleman, Daniel and Robert A. F. Thurman, eds. *Mind Science: An East-West Dialogue.* Boston: Wisdom Publications, 1991.

Gombrich, Richard R. "Buddhist Cultic Life in Southeast Asia." In *Encyclopedia of Religion*, vol. 15, 463-467.

———. "The Consecration of a Buddhist Image." *The Journal of Asian Studies* 26, no. 1 (November, 1966): 23-36.

———. *How Buddhism Began*. London: Routledge, 2006.

———. *What the Buddha Thought*. Sheffield: Equinox, 2009.

Gómez, Luis O. "Bodhicitta (Thought of Awakening)." In *Encyclopedia of Buddhism*, vol. 1, 54-56.

———, trans. *The Land of Bliss: The Paradise of the Buddha of Measureless Light.* Honolulu: University of Hawai'i Press, 1996.

———. "Meditation." In *Encyclopedia of Buddhism*, vol. 2, 520-530.

———. "Oriental Wisdom and the Cure of Souls: Jung and the Indian East." In Lopez, *Curators of the Buddha,* 197-250.

———. "Two Tantric Meditations: Visualizing the Deity." In Lopez, *Buddhism in Practice*, 318-327.

Gray, David B., trans. *The "Cakrasamvara Tantra": The Discourse of Śrī Heruka.* New York: American Institute of Buddhist Studies at Columbia University, 2007.

———. "Tantra and the Tantric Traditions of Hinduism and Buddhism." In *Oxford Research Encyclopedia of Religion.* April, 2016. https://doi.org/10.1093/acrefore/9780199340378.013.59.

Gregory, Peter N. "Is Critical Buddhism Really Critical?" In Hubbard and Swanson, eds., *Pruning the Bodhi Tree,* 286-297.

Grosnick, William H., trans. *The Tathāgatagarbha Sūtra*. In Lopez, *Buddhism in Practice*, 92-106.

Guenther, Herbert. *Ecstatic Spontaneity: Saraha's "Three Cycles of Dohā."* Berkeley: Asian Humanities Press, 1993.

———, trans. *The Life and Teaching of Nāropa: Translated from the original Tibetan with a Philosophical Commentary based on the Oral Transmission*. London: Oxford University Press, 1963.

Gummer, Natalie D. "Women." In *Encyclopedia of Buddhism,* vol. 2, 893-902.

Gunasekara, Victor A. "Humanism and Buddhism." University of Queensland, Australia. http://www.uq.net.au/slsoc/manussa/humbud.htm.

Hamilton, Edith. *Mythology: Timeless Tales of Gods and Heroes*. New York: New American Library, 1942.

Hamlin, Edward. "Magical *Upāya* in the *Vimalakīrtinirdeśa-sūtra*." *The Journal of the International Association of Buddhist Studies* 11, no. 1 (1988): 89-122.

Hannah, Barbara. *Jung: His Life and Work*. New York: G. P. Putnam's Sons, 1976.

Harding, M. Esther. *The Way of All Women*. New York: Harper and Row, 1933.

Harrison, Paul M. "Buddhānusmṛti in the *Pratyutpannabuddhasaṃmukkhāvasthita-samādhi-sūtra.*" In *Buddhism: Critical Concepts in Religious Studies*, vol. 3, edited by Paul Williams, 84-107. London: Routledge, 2005.

———. "Canon." *In Encyclopedia of Buddhism*, vol. 1, 111-115.

Harvey, Peter. "Portrayals of Ultimate Reality and of Holy and Divine Beings." In *Buddhism*, edited by Peter Harvey, 95-124. London: Continuum, 2001.

———. *An Introduction to Buddhism*. 2nd ed. Cambridge: Cambridge University Press, 2013.

Hawkes, Jason, and Akira Shimada, eds. *Buddhist Stupas in South Asia: Recent Archaeological,Art-Historical, and Historical Perspectives*. Oxford: Oxford University Press, 2008.

Henderson, Joseph L. *Shadow and Self: Selected Papers in Analytical Psychology.* Wilmette: Chiron Publications, 1990.

Heesterman, Jan C. "Vedism and Brahmanism." In *Encyclopedia of Religion*, vol. 15, 217-242.

Hick, John. In the Foreword to Padmasiri de Silva, *An Introduction to Buddhist Psychology.* Lanham, Md.: Rowman and Littlefield Publishers, 2000.

Hodge, Stephen, trans. *The Mahā-Vairocana-Abhisaṃbodhi Tantra: With Buddhaguhya's Commentary*. London: Routledge, 2015.

Holt, John Clifford. *The Buddhist Viṣṇu*. Delhi: Motilal Banarsidass Publishers, 2008.

Hopkins, Gerard Manley."Carrion Comfort." In *Gerard Manley Hopkins: A Selection of his Poems and Prose*, no. 42. Harmondsworth, Middlesex: Penguin Books, 1953.

Hopkins, Jeffrey. "Jung's Warnings Against Inflation." *Chung-Hwa Buddhist Journal* 21 (2008): 159-174.

———, trans. *Tantra in Tibet: The Great Exposition of Secret Mantra by Tsong-ka-pa*. London: George Allen and Unwin, 1977.

Hopkins, Thomas J. *The Hindu Religious Tradition*. Encino: Dickenson Publishing Company, 1971.

——— and Alf Hiltebeitel. "Indus Valley Religion." In *Encyclopedia of Religion,* vol. 7, 215-223.

Hubbard, Jamie and Paul L. Swanson, eds. *Pruning the Bodhi Tree: The Storm Over Critical Buddhism*. Honolulu: University of Hawaii Press, 1997.

Hume, David. *A Treatise of Human Nature.* 1739. Reprint, New York: Penguin Books, 1985.

Huntington, Susan L. *The Art of Ancient India*. New York: Weatherhill, 1985.

——— and John C. Huntington. "Leaves from the Bodhi Tree: The Art of Pāla India (8th-12th Centuries) and Its International Legacy." *Orientations* 20, no. 10 (October, 1989): 26-46.

Hurvitz, Leon. *Scripture of the Lotus Blossom of the Fine Dharma*. New York: Columbia University Press, 1976.

Hutton, Kathryn. "Lions." In *Encyclopedia of Religion,* vol. 8, 556-558.

Isaacson, Harunaga. "Tantric Buddhism in India (from c. A.D. 800 to c. A.D. 1200)." Revision of a lecture originally given in 1997. http://www.buddhismuskunde.uni-hamburg.de/pdf.

Jackson, Roger, trans. *Tantric Treasures: Three Collections of Mystical Verse from Buddhist India.* Oxford: Oxford University Press, 2004.

James, William. "Psychology: Briefer Course." In *William James: Writings 1878-1899.* Reprint, New York: Library of America, 1992.

Jacobi, Jolande. *The Psychology of C. G. Jung.* New Haven: Yale University Press, 1942.

Jayawickrama, N. A. trans. *The Story of Gotama Buddha: The Nidāna-kathā of the Jātakaṭṭhakathā.* 1951. Revised, Oxford: The Pali Text Society, 1990.

Jones, J. J., trans. *The Mahāvastu.* 1895. Vol. 2. London: Luzac and Company, 1952.

Jung, C. G. *Analytical Psychology: Notes of the Seminar Given in 1925.* Princeton: Princeton University Press, 1989.

———. "Approaching the Unconscious." In *Man and his Symbols,* edited by Carl G. Jung, 18-103. New York: Doubleday, 1964.

———. *Children's Dreams: Notes from the Seminar Given in 1936-1940.* Edited by Lorenz Jung and Maria Meyer-Grass. Princeton: Princeton University Press, 2008.

———. *The Collected Works of C. G. Jung.* Edited by William McGuire, et al. 20 vols. Princeton: Princeton University Press, 1953-1979.

———. *Dream Analysis: Notes of the Seminar Given in 1928-1930.* Edited by William McGuire. Princeton: Princeton University Press, 1984.

———. "The Houston Films." In *C. G. Jung Speaking: Interviews and Encounters.* Edited by William McGuire and R. F. C. Hull. Princeton: Princeton University Press, 1977.

———. *Letters.* Edited by Gerhard Adler and Aniela Jaffe. 2 vols. Princeton: Princeton University Press, 1975.

———. *Memories, Dreams, Reflections.* Edited by Aniela Jaffe. New York: Vintage Books, 1961.

———. *Nietzsche's "Zarathustra": Notes of the Seminar Given in 1934-1939.* Edited by James L. Jarrett. 2 vols. Princeton: Princeton University Press, 1988.

———. *The Psychology of Kundalini Yoga: Notes of the Seminar Given in 1932.* Edited by Sonu Shamdasani. Princeton: Princeton University Press, 1996.

———. *Visions: Notes of the Seminar Given in 1930-1934.* Edited by Claire Douglas. 2 vols. Princeton: Princeton University Press, 1997.

Kabat-Zinn, Jon. *Full Catastrophe Living: Using the Wisdom of Your Body and Mind to Face Stress, Pain and Illness.* New York: Bantam Books, 1999.

Kalupahana, David L., trans. *Nāgārjuna: The Philosophy of the Middle Way.* Albany: State University of New York Press, 1986.

Kearney, Patrick. "Still Crazy After All these Years: Why Meditation Isn't Psychotherapy." http://www.buddhanet.net/crazy.htm.

Kinnard, Jacob N. *Imaging Wisdom: Seeing and Knowing in the Art of Indian Buddhism.* Delhi: Motilal Banarsidass Publishers, 1999.

King, Sallie B. "The Doctrine of Buddha-Nature Is Impeccably Buddhist." In Hubbard and Swanson, eds, *Pruning the Bodhi Tree,* 174-192.

King, Winston. *Buddhism and Christianity*. Philadelphia: The Westminster Press, 1952.

Kloetzli, W. Randolph. "Cosmology: Buddhist Cosmology." In *Encyclopedia of Religion*, vol. 4, 113-119.

Kornfield, Jack. *The Wise Heart.* New York: Random House Publishing, 2008.

Kvaerne, Per. "On the Concept of Sahaja in Indian Buddhist Tantric Literature." *Temenos* 11 (1975): 88-135.

Lamotte, Étienne. *History of Indian Buddhism.* 1958. Translated by Sara Webb-Boin.

Louvain-la-Neuve: Institut Orientaliste, 1988.

Landesman, Susan S. "Goddess Tārā: Silence and Secrecy on the Path to Enlightenment." *Journal of Feminist Studies in Religion* 24, no. 1 (Spring, 2008): 44-59.

Lessing, Ferdinand D. and Alex Wayman, trans. *Mkhas grub rje's "Fundamentals of the Buddhist Tantras."* Mouton: The Hague, 1968.

Lindahl, Jared R. and Willoughby B. Britton. "'I Have This Feeling of Not Really Being Here': Buddhist Meditation and Changes in Sense of Self," *Journal of Consciousness Studies* 26, no. 7-8 (2019): 157-183.

Liu, Ming-Wood. "The Problem of the *Icchantika* in the Mahāyāna *Mahāparinirvāṇa Sūtra*." *The Journal of the International Association of Buddhist Studies* 7, no.1 (1984): 57-82.

Long, J. Bruce. "Demons: An Overview." In *Encyclopedia of Religion,* vol. 4, 282-288.

———. "Reincarnation." In *Encyclopedia of Religion,* vol. 12, 265-269.

Lopez, Donald S., Jr. "Authority and Orality in the Mahāyāna." *Numen: International Review for the History of Religions* 42, no.1 (January 1995): 21-47.

———. *Buddhism and Science: A Guide for the Perplexed.* Chicago: University of Chicago Press, 2008.

———, ed. *Buddhism in Practice*. Princeton: Princeton University Press, 1995.

———, ed. *Curators of the Buddha: The Study of Buddhism Under Colonialism.* Chicago: Chicago University Press, 1995.

———. *The "Lotus Sūtra": A Biography*. Princeton: Princeton University Press, 2016.

———. *Prisoners of Shangri-La*. Chicago: University of Chicago Press, 1998.

———. *Seeing the Sacred in Samsara: An Illustrated Guide to the Eighty-Four Mahāsiddhas.* Boulder: Shambhala, 2019.

———. *The Story of Buddhism: A Concise Guide to its History and Teachings*. San Francisco: Harper Collins Publishers, 2001.

——— and Jacqueline I. Stone. *Two Buddhas: Seated Side by Side*. Princeton: Princeton University Press, 2019.

Luczanits, Christian. "On the Earliest Mandalas in a Buddhist Context." In *Mahayana Buddhism: History and Culture*, edited by Darrol Bryant and Susan Bryant, 111-136. New Delhi: Tibet House, 2008.

Lusthaus, Dan. *Buddhist Phenomenology: A Philosophical Investigation of Yogācāra Buddhism and the "Ch'eng Wei-shih lun."* London: Routledge-Curzon, 2002.

———. "Yogācāra School." In *Encyclopedia of Buddhism,* vol. 2, 914-921.

Mabbett, I. W. "The Symbolism of Mount Meru." *History of Religions* 23, no.1 (August, 1983): 64-83.

Macdonell, Arthur Anthony. *A Vedic Reader for Students*. Oxford: Oxford University Press, 1917.

Mahony, William K. "Karman: Hindu and Jain Concepts." In *Encyclopedia of Religion*, vol. 8, 261-266.

———. "Soul: Indian Concepts." In *Encyclopedia of Religion,* vol. 13, 438-443.

Marshall, John. *A Guide to Sanchi*. Calcutta: Superintendent Government Printing, 1918.

Masefield, Peter. *Divine Revelation in Pali Buddhism*. Boston: George Allen & Unwin, 1986.

Matilal, Bimal Krishna. "Cārvāka." In *Encyclopedia of Religion,* vol. 3, 105-106.

Matsumo Shirō. "The Doctrine of *Tathāgata-garbha* Is Not Buddhist." In Hubbard and Swanson, *Pruning the Bodhi Tree*, 165-173.

Maugh, Thomas H., II. "Migration of monsoons created, then killed Harappan civilization." *Los Angeles Times*, May 30, 2012. http://www.latimes.com/news/science/sciencenow.

McBride, Richard D., II, "Mantra." In *Encyclopedia of Buddhism,* vol. 2, 512.

McMahan, David L. *The Making of Buddhist Modernism*. Oxford: Oxford University Press, 2008.

Midal, Fabrice. *Recalling Chögyam Trungpa*. Boston: Shambhala, 2005.

Moacanin, Radmila. *Jung's Psychology and Tibetan Buddhism: Western and Eastern Paths to the Heart*. London: Wisdom Publications, 1986.

Monier-Williams, Monier. *A Sanskrit-English Dictionary*. 1899. Reprint, Oxford: Oxford University Press, 1970.

Moon, Beverly. "Archetypes." In *Encyclopedia of Religion*, vol. 1, 379-382.

Morse, Anne Nishimura. "Ritual Objects." In *Encyclopedia of Buddhism,* vol 2, 726-729.

Mun, Ajaan Bhuridatta. "A Heart Released." Translated by Thanissaro Bhikkhu (1995), section 10. *Access to Insight (BCBS Edition)*, 30 November 2013. http://www.accesstoinsight.org/lib/thai/mun/released.html.

Ñāṇamoli, Bhikkhu, trans. *The Life of the Buddha: According to the Pali Canon*. Onalaska: Pariyatti Publishing, 1972.

———, trans. *The Path of Purification (Visuddhimagga) of Bhadantācariya Buddhaghosa*. 2 vols. Berkeley: Shambhala, 1976.

Narr, Karl J. "Paleolithic Religion." In *Encyclopedia of Religon,* vol. 11, 149-159.

Nattier, Jan. *A Few Good Men: The Bodhisattva Path according to The Inquiry of Ugra*. Honolulu: University of Hawai'i Press, 2003.

———. "The Realm of Akṣobhya: A Missing Piece in the History of Pure Land Buddhism." *Journal of the International Association of Buddhist Studies* 23, no. 1 (2000): 71-102.

Neumann, Erich. "The Moon and Matriarchal Consciousness." In *The Fear of the Feminine*, translated by Boris Matthews, et al., 64-118. Princeton: Princeton University Press, 1994.

Neville, Robert Cummings, ed. *Ultimate Realties*. Albany: State University of New York Press, 2001.

Nyanatiloka Mahathera. "Fundamentals of Buddhism: Four Lectures." *Access to Insight (BCBS Edition)*, 1 December 2013. http://www.accesstoinsight.org/lib/authors/nyanatiloka/wheel394.html.

Nyanaponika Thera. *The Heart of Buddhist Meditation*. New York: Samuel Weiser, 1962.

Obeyesekere, Gananath. *The Awakened Ones*. New York: Columbia University Press, 2012.

———. *Imagining Karma: Ethical Transformation in Amerindian, Buddhist, and Greek Rebirth.* Berkeley: University of California, 2002.

O'Flaherty, Wendy Doniger. *Śiva: The Erotic Ascetic*. Oxford: Oxford University Press, 1973.

Olivelle, Patrick. *The Early Upaniṣads: Annotated Text and Translation*. Oxford: Oxford University Press, 1998.

Onians, Richard Broxton. *The Origins of European Thought*. 1951. Reprint, Salem: Ayer Company, Publishers, 1987.

Otto, Rudolf. *The Idea of the Holy: An Inquiry into the non-rational factor in the idea of the divine and its relation to the rational*. Translated by John W. Harvey. 1923. New York: Oxford University Press, 1958.

Pagels, Elaine. *The Gnostic Gospels*. New York: Vintage Books, 1979.

Payne, Richard K. "Burning with the Fire of Shingon." *Lion's Roar: Buddhist Wisdom For Our Time*. https://www.lionsroar.com/burning-with-the-fire-of-shingon.

Powers, John. *A Bull of a Man*. Cambridge: Harvard University Press, 2009.

———. *Introduction to Tibetan Buddhism*. Revised, Boston: Snow Lion, 2007.

———. *Wisdom of Buddha: "The Saṃdhinirmocana Sūtra."* Berkeley: Dharma Publishing, 1995.

Prebish, Charles. "Councils: Buddhist Councils." In *Encyclopedia of Religion,* vol. 4, 119-124.

Princeton Dictionary of Buddhism. Edited by Robert E. Buswell, Jr. and Donald S. Lopez, Jr. Princeton: Princeton University Press, 2014.

Pruden, Leo M., trans. English translation of Louis de la Vallée Poussin's French translation (1931), *Abhidharmakośabhāṣyam of Vasubandhu*. 4 vols. Berkeley: Asian Humanities Press, 1991.

Radhakrishnan, Sarvepalli, trans. *The Principal Upaniṣads*. London: George Allen and Unwin, 1953.

——— and Charles A. Moore, eds. *A Sourcebook in Indian Philosophy*. Princeton: Princeton University Press, 1957.

Radice, Betty, trans. *The Letters of Abelard and Heloise*. London: Penguin Books, 1974.

Rahula, Walpola. *What the Buddha Taught*. New York: Grove Press, 1959.

Ray, Reginald A. *Buddhist Saints in India*. Oxford: Oxford University Press, 1994.

Reynolds, John Myrdhin, trans. *Self-Liberation Through Seeing with Naked Awareness* Barrytown: Station Hill Press, 1989.

Rhys Davids, C. A. F. "Buddhism and the Negative." *Journal of the Pali Text Society* 8 (1924-1927): 237-250.

Rhys Davids, T. W. *Buddhism: Its History and Literature*. 1896. Reprint, New York: Cosimo Classics, 2005.

———. *The Hibbert Lectures, 1881: Lectures on the Origin and Growth of Religion as Illustrated by Some Points in the History of Indian Buddhism*. Reprint, Leopold Classic Library, n.d.

———, trans. *The Questions of King Milinda*, 2 vols. 1894. Reprint, New York: Dover Publications, 1963.

——— and William Stede. *The Pali Text Society's Pali-English Dictionary*. 1921-1925. Reprint, London: Routledge and Kegan Paul, 1972.

Roberts, Peter Alan, with Tulku Yeshi, trans. *The Basket's Display: Kāraṇḍavyūha*. Published by 84000, Translating the Words of the Buddha (2013), xii. http://www.84000.co.

Robinson, Richard, Willard L. Johnson, and Thanissaro Bhikkhu. *Buddhist Religions: A Historical Introduction*. 5th edition. Belmont: Thomson/Wadsworth, 2005.

Roebuck, Valerie J., trans. *The Upaniṣads*. New Delhi: Penguin Books India, 2000.

Rowland, Benjamin. *The Art and Architecture of India*. New York: Penguin Books, 1977.

Rudolph, Kurt. "Mystery Religions." In *Encyclopedia of Religion,* vol. 10, 230-239.

Samuel, Geoffrey. *The Origins of Yoga and Tantra: Indic Religions to the Thirteenth Century*. Cambridge: Cambridge University Press, 2008.

——— and Jay Johnston, eds. *Religion and the Subtle Body in Asia and the West: Between Mind and Body*. London: Routledge, 2013.

Śāntideva. *Entering the Path of Enlightenment*. Translated by Marion L. Matics. London: The Macmillan Company, 1970.

Sargeant, Winthrop, trans. *The Bhagavad Gītā*. Edited and revised by Christopher Chapple. Albany: State University of New York Press, 1994.

Schopen, Gregory. "Diamond Sūtra." In *Encyclopedia of Buddhism*, vol. 1, 227-228.

———. "Mahāyāna." In *Encyclopedia of Buddhism*, vol. 2, 492-499.

Sengupta, Sulagna. *Jung in India*. New Orleans: Spring Journal Books, 2013.

Sharf, Robert. "Mindfulness and Mindlessness in Early Chan." *Philosophy East and West* 64, no. 4 (October, 2014): 933-964.

———. "Is Mindfulness Buddhist? (And Why It Matters)." *Transcultural Psychiatry* 52, no. 4 (2015): 470-484.

———. "On the Buddha-nature of Insentient Things." Unfinished essay. University of Michigan. http://www.buddhism.org/kr/koan/Robert_Sharf-e.htm.

———. "Visualization and Mandala in Shingon Buddhism." In *Living Images: Japanese Buddhist Icons in Context*, edited by Robert H. Sharf and Elizabeth Horton Sharf, 151-197. Redwood City: Stanford University Press, 2002.

———. "The Zen of Japanese Nationalism." In Lopez, *Curators of the Buddha,* 107-160.

Shaw, Miranda. *Buddhist Goddesses of India.* Princeton: Princeton University Press, 2006.

———. *Passionate Enlightenment*. Princeton: Princeton University Press, 1994.

Silk, Jonathan A. "Taking the *Vimalakīrtinirdeśa* Seriously." *Annual Report of The International Research Institute for Advanced Buddhology at Soka University for the Academic Year 2013*, vol. 17 (2014): 157-188.

Sinha, Jadunath. *Indian Psychology*. 2 vols. Calcutta: Sinha Publishing House, 1958.

Skorupski, Tadeusz. "The Buddha's Stūpa and Image: The Icons of his Immanence and Transcendence." *Rocznik Orientalistyczny* 65, no. 1 (2012): 180-194.

Smith, Huston. *The Religions of Man*. New York: Mentor Books, 1958.

Snellgrove, D. L., trans. *The Hevajra Tantra*. 2 vols. London: Oxford University Press, 1959.
———. *Indo-Tibetan Buddhism: Indian Buddhists and Their Tibetan Successors*. 2 vols. Boston: Shambhala, 1987.
Snodgrass, Adrian. *The Symbolism of the Stupa*. Delhi: Motilal Banarsidass, 1992.
Stone, Jacqueline. "Some Reflections on Critical Buddhism." *Japanese Journal of Religious Studies* 26, nos. 1-2 (1999): 159-188.
Strong, John S. *The Buddha: A Short Biography*. Oxford: Oneworld Publications, 2001.
———, ed. *The Experience of Buddhism*. Belmont: Thomson/Wadsworth, 2008.
———. *Relics of the Buddha*. Delhi: Motilal Banarsidass Publishers, 2004.
Stryk, Lucien, ed. *World of the Buddha*. New York: Doubleday and Company, 1969.
Sugiki, Tsunehiko. "Oblation, Non-conception, and Body: Systems of Psychosomatic Fire Oblation in Esoteric Buddhism in Medieval South Asia." In *"Homa" Variations: The Study of Ritual Change Across the "Longue Durée,"* edited by Richard K. Payne and Michael Witzel, 167-213. Oxford: Oxford University Press, 2016.
Sutherland, Joan. *Vimalakirti and the Awakened Heart: A Commentary on "The Sutra that Vimalakirti Speaks."* Santa Fe: Following Wind Press, 2016.
Suzuki, Daisetz Teitaro, trans. *The Lankavatara Sutra*. London: Routledge and Kegan Paul, 1932.
———. *Studies in the Lankavatara Sutra*. London: Routledge and Kegan Paul, 1930.
Swearer, Donald K. "Consecration." In *Encyclopedia of Buddhism,* vol. 1, 178-181.
———. "Hypostasizing the Buddha: Buddha Image Consecration in Northern Thailand." *History of Religions* 34, no. 3 (1995): 263-280.
Taylor, Charles H. and Patricia Finley. *Images of the Journey in Dante's "Divine Comedy."* New Haven: Yale University Press, 1997.
Teiser, Stephen F. "Ghost Festival." In *Encyclopedia of Buddhism,* vol. 1, 307-309.
——— and Jacqueline I. Stone. "Interpreting the *Lotus Sūtra*." In *Readings of the "Lotus Sūtra,"* edited by Stephen F. Teiser and Jacqueline I. Stone, 1-61. New York: Columbia University Press, 2009.
Ṭhānissaro Bhikkhu. "Affirming the Truths of the Heart: The Buddhist Teachings of Samvega and Pasada" (1997). *Access to Insight (BCBS Edition)*, 8 March 2011. https://www.accesstoinsight.org/lib/authors/thanisssaro/affirming.html.
———, trans. "Bhikkhunī Pāṭimokkha." *Access to Insight (BCBS Edition)*, 17 December 2013. http://www.accesstoinsight.org/tipitaka/vin/sv/bhikkhuni-pati.html.
———, trans. *Buddhist Monastic Code I*. 3rd ed. Valley Center: Metta Forest Monastery, 2013. http://www.accesstoinsight.org/lib/authors/thanissaro/bmc1.pdf.
———, trans. "Nanda Sutta." *Khuddaka Nikāya*, Udāna 3.2. *Access to Insight (BCBS Edition)*, 30 August 2012. http://www.accesstoinsight.org/tipitaka/kn/ud/ud.3.02/than.html.
———, trans."Tittha Sutta: Sectarians (3)." *Khuddaka Nikāya*, Udāna 6.6. *Access to Insight (BCBS Edition)*, 3.September 2012. http://www.accesstoinsight.org/tipitaka/kn/ud/ud.6.06.than.html.
———. "The Roots of Buddhist Romanticism." In *Purity of Heart*. dhammatalks.org/books/PurityofHeart/Section0009.html.

Thapar, Romila. *A History of India*. Baltimore: Penguin Books, 1966.

Thomas, Edward J. *The Life of Buddha: As Legend and History*. London: Routledge and Kegan Paul, 1927.

Thurman, Robert A. F. "The Buddhist Messiahs: The Magnificent Deeds of the Bodhisattvas." In *The Christ and the Bodhisattva,* edited by Donald S. Lopez, Jr. and Steven C. Rockefeller, 65-98. Albany: State University of New York Press, 1987.

———. *The Holy Teaching of Vimalakīrti: A Mahāyāna Scripture*. University Park: Pennsylvania State University Press, 1976.

———. *Inner Revolution: Life, Liberty, and the Pursuit of Real Happiness*. New York: Riverhead Books, 1998.

———. "The Teaching of Vimalakīrti." In *Approaches to the Asian Classics*, edited by William Theodore de Bary and Irene Bloom, 232-240. New York: Columbia University Press, 1990.

———. "We can be Buddhas." TEDSalon 2006. https://www.ted.com/talks/robert_thurman_we_can_be_buddhas/transcript?language=en.

Tola, Fernando and Carmen Dragonetti, trans. "Nāgārjuna's Catustava." *Journal of Indian Philosophy* 13 (1985): 1-54.

Tribe, Anthony. "Mantranaya/vajrayāna—tantric Buddhism in India." In Williams, *Buddhist Thought,* 143-184.

Tsomo, Karma Lekshe. "Nuns." In *Encyclopedia of Buddhism*, vol. 2, 606-611.

Urban, Hugh. "The Yoga of Sex: Tantra, Orientalism, and Sex Magic in the Ordo Templi Orientis." In *Hidden Intercourse: Eros and Sexuality in the History of Western Esotericism*, edited by Jeffrey J. Kripal and Wouter J. Hanegraaff, 401-443. Leiden: Brill, 2008.

Victoria, Brian Daizen. "A Buddhological Critique of 'Soldier-Zen' in Wartime Japan." In *Buddhist Warfare*, edited by Michael K. Jerryson and Mark Juergensmeyer, 105-130. Oxford: Oxford University Press, 2010.

von Franz, Marie-Louise. *The Problem of the Puer Aeternus*. Toronto: Inner City Books, 2000.

———. *A Psychological Interpretation of "The Golden Ass" of Apuleius.* Rev. ed. Irving: Spring Publications, 1980.

Waldron, William S. *The Buddhist Unconscious: The Ālaya-vijñāna in the Context of Indian Buddhist Thought*. London: Routledge-Curzon, 2003.

Wallace, Vesna A. "The Six-Phased Yoga of the *Abbreviated Wheel of Time Tantra* (*Laghukālacakratantra*) according to Vajrapāṇi." In *Yoga in Practice*, edited by David Gordon White, 204-222. Princeton: Princeton University Press, 2012.

Wallis, Glenn. *Mediating the Power of the Buddhas: Ritual in the "Mañjuṣrīmūlakalpa."* Albany: State University of New York Press, 2002.

Walshe, Maurice, trans. *The Long Discourses of the Buddha: A Translation of the Dīgha Nikāya*. Boston: Wisdom Publications, 1987.

Warder, A. K. *Indian Buddhism*. Delhi: Motilal Banarsidass Publishers, 1970.

Warren, Henry Clarke, trans. *Buddhism in Translations*. 1896. Reprint, New York: Atheneum, 1970.

Wasson, R. Gordon. "The Last Meal of the Buddha." *Journal of the American Oriental Society* 102, no. 4 (October-December, 1982): 591-603.

Watson, Burton, trans. *Chuang Tzu: Basic Writings*. New York: Columbia University Press, 1964.
———, trans. *The Lotus Sutra*. New York: Columbia University Press, 1993.
———, trans. *The Vimalakirti Sutra*. New York: Columbia University Press, 1997.
Watt, Jeff. "Himalayan Art Resources." https://www.himalayanart.org.
Watt, W. Montgomery, trans. *The Faith and Practice of Al-Ghazālī*. London: George Allen and Unwin, 1953.
Wayman, Alex. "Buddhism." In *Historia Religionum*, edited by C. J. Bleeker and G. Widengren, 372-464. Vol. 2. Leiden: E. J. Brill, 1971.
———. *Buddhist Insight*. Edited by George R. Elder. Delhi: Motilal Banarsidass, 1984.
———. *Buddhist Tantras*. New York: Samuel Weiser, 1973.
———. "Contributions Regarding the Thirty-two Characteristics of the Great Person." *Sino-Indian Studies: Liebenthal Festschrift*, (1957): 249-255.
———. "Esoteric Buddhism." In *Encyclopedia of Religion,* vol. 2, 472-482.
———. "Reflections on the Theory of Barabuḍur as a *Maṇḍala*." In *Barabudur: History and Significance of a Buddhist Monument*, edited by Luis O. Gómez and Hiram W. Woodward, 139-172. Berkeley: University of California, 1981.
———. "The Ritual in Tantric Buddhism of the Disciple's Entrance into the Mandala." *Studia Missionalia* 33 (1984): 41-57.
———. *Untying the Knots in Buddhism: Selected Essays*. Delhi: Motilal Banarsidass Publishers, 1997.
———. "Vijñāna." In *Encyclopedia of Religion*, vol. 15:260-264.
———. "Yogācāra and the Buddhist Logicians." *The Journal of the International Association of Buddhist Studies* 2, no. 1 (1979): 65-78.
——— and R. Tajima. *The Enlightenment of Vairocana*. Delhi: Motilal Banarsidass, 1992.
——— and Hideko Wayman, trans. *The Lion's Roar of Queen Śrīmālā: A Buddhist Scripture on the Tathāgatagarbha Theory*. New York: Columbia University Press, 1974.
Wedemeyer, Christian K. *Making Sense of Tantric Buddhism*. New York: Columbia University Press, 2013.
Weinberger, Steven Neal. "The Significance of Yoga Tantra and the *Compendium of Principles* (*Tattvasaṃgraha Tantra*) within Tantric Buddhism in India and Tibet." PhD diss., University of Virginia, 2003. http://www.libra2.lib.virginia.edu/public.
White, David Gordon. *Kiss of the Yoginī: "Tantric Sex" in its South Asian Contexts*. Chicago: Chicago University Press, 2003.
———, ed. *Tantra in Practice*. Princeton: Princeton University Press, 2000.
Wijesekera, O. H. de A. "The Freudian Unconscious and Bhavaṅga." *The Journal of the International Association of Buddhist Studies* 1, no. 2 (1979): 63-66.
Wikipedia, The Free Encyclopedia. "Jacob Wilhelm Hauer." https://en.wikipedia.org/w/index.php?title=Jacob_Wilhelm_Hauer&oldid=1034667348.
———. "Offering (Buddhism)." https://en.wikipedia.org/w/index.php?title=Offering_(Buddhism)&oldid=1031893319.
Williams, Paul. *Mahāyāna Buddhism*. London: Routledge, 1989.

———, with Anthony Tribe and Alexander Wynne. *Buddhist Thought: A Complete Introduction to the Indian Tradition*. 2nd ed. London: Routledge, 2012.

Wynne, Alexander. *Buddhism: An Introduction*. London: I. B. Tauris, 2015.

Young, Serinity. *Dreaming in the Lotus: Buddhist Dream Narrative, Imagery, and Practice.* Boston: Wisdom Publications, 1999.

Yü, Chü-fang. *Kuan-yin: The Chinese Transformation of Avalokiteśvara*. New York: Columbia University Press, 2001.

Zimmer, Heinrich. *The Art of Indian Asia*. 2 vols. Princeton: Princeton University Press, 1960.

———. *Myths and Symbols in Indian Art and Civilization*. Edited by Joseph Campbell. New York: Harper Books, 1946.

———. *Philosophies of India*. Edited by Joseph Campbell. Princeton: Princeton University Press, 1951.

Zimmermann, Michael, trans. *A Buddha Within: The Tathāgatagarbhasūtra*. Tokyo: International Research Institute for Advanced Buddhology, Soka University, 2002

INDEX

Milton Keynes UK
Ingram Content Group UK Ltd.
UKHW052208091023
430265UK00002B/31

9781958889206